DIVINE OMNISCIENCE AND OMNIPOTENCE IN MEDIEVAL PHILOSOPHY

SYNTHESE HISTORICAL LIBRARY

TEXTS AND STUDIES IN THE HISTORY OF LOGIC AND PHILOSOPHY

VOLUME 25

DIVINE OMNISCIENCE AND OMNIPOTENCE IN MEDIEVAL PHILOSOPHY

Islamic, Jewish and Christian Perspectives

Edited by

TAMAR RUDAVSKY

Dept. of Philosophy, The Ohio State University, Columbus

D. REIDEL PUBLISHING COMPANY

A MEMBER OF THE KLUWER ACADEMIC PUBLISHERS GROUP

DORDRECHT / BOSTON / LANCASTER

Library of Congress Cataloging in Publication Data
Main entry under title:

CIP

Divine omniscience and omnipotence in medieval philosophy.

(Synthese historical library ; v. 25)
"Papers presented at a conference held at the Ohio State University on March 3 and 4, 1982" – P.
Bibliography: p.
Includes index.
1. God–Omniscience–History of doctrines–Middle Ages, 600–1500–Congresses. 2. God–Omnipotence–History of doctrines–Middle Ages, 600–1500–Congresses. I. Rudavsky, Tamar, 1951– . II. Series.
BT131.D58 1984 291.2'11 84–8312
ISBN 90–277–1750–8

Published by D. Reidel Publishing Company,
P.O. Box 17, 3300 AA Dordrecht, Holland.

Sold and distributed in the U.S.A. and Canada
by Kluwer Academic Publishers,
190 Old Derby Street, Hingham, MA 02043, U.S.A.

In all other countries, sold and distributed
by Kluwer Academic Publishers Group,
P.O. Box 322, 3300 AH Dordrecht, Holland.

Printed in The Netherlands

TABLE OF CONTENTS

PART FOUR
CHRISTIAN PERSPECTIVES

EDITORIAL PREFACE

The chapters of this book originated as papers presented at a conference held at The Ohio State University on March 3 and 4, 1982, entitled 'Divine Omniscience, Omnipotence and Future Contingents in Medieval Islamic, Jewish and Christian Thought.' All the papers have been revised on their way to becoming chapters in this volume. Chapters 4, 6, and 8 were originally presented as comments; they have been amplified and have been placed immediately after the chapters to which they relate. None of the chapters have been published elsewhere.

The book is divided into an introduction and three specific parts dealing with Islamic, Jewish and Christian writers, respectively. Within each of those three parts the chapters are arranged in historical order.

Chapters 1 and 2 introduce the issues of divine omniscience, omnipotence and future contingents. In chapter 1, Calvin Normore introduces the logical and epistemological complexities involved in medieval discussions of divine omniscience and omnipotence. In particular, he concentrates on two sets of problems prominent in medieval texts: the necessity of the past, and the contingency of the future. The first issue, the question of whether God can change the past, is discussed further in chapters 3, 4, 10, 11 and 13. The second issue is the problem of God's knowledge, which is also discussed in chapters 5, 6, 7, 8, 9 and 12.

Chapter 2 raises the issue of the nature of contingency. Taking Boethius's commentaries on Aristotle's *De Interpretatione*, chapter 9, as the basis for his discussion, Norman Kretzmann argues that Boethius explains all contingency in terms of free choice. The nature of chance is presented as a particularly important issue, one which is taken up in subsequent chapters as well.

Chapters 3–6 are devoted to the Islamic setting of omniscience and omnipotence. In chapters 3 and 4, the doctrine of divine omnipotence is developed in light of an-Naẓẓām, a ninth century Mu'tazilite. The Mu'tazilites were an offshoot of the Islamic Kalam; these Kalam theologians were noted, among other things, for their doctrines of human freedom and the denial of attributes separate from God's essence. In chapter 3, Josef Van Ess presents the details of an-Naẓẓām's position, emphasizing in particular his assertion that God is

T. Rudavsky (ed.), Divine Omniscience and Omnipotence in Medieval Philosophy, vii–ix.

unable to do evil. In chapter 4, Richard Frank amplifies upon this last point, asking how the Arabic term "qadara" (= is able to) is used in such questions as "is God able to do evil?" According to Frank, an-Naẓẓām must consider the status of the objects of an agent's ability to act. Developing an ontology of such objects based on the Baṣrian masters, Frank then applies this analysis to an-Naẓẓām's doctrine.

Chapters 5 and 6 are devoted to divine omniscience in Alfarabi, Avicenna, and Averroes. In chapter 5, Michael Marmura is concerned to explain how God is said to know the indeterminate future. Alfarabi's solution is stated in his commentary to Aristotle's *De Interpretatione* 9. Distinguishing between something's being necessary in relation to others and being possible in itself, Alfarabi maintains that God's foreknowledge does not remove the possibility of an object or event viewed in this latter way. Avicenna, however, introduces causation into his discussion. Unlike Alfarabi, Avicenna must explain how in an emanative scheme in which will and intellect are closely aligned, God's foreknowledge has no causative force. Marmura analyzes Avicenna's attempt to claim that God knows particulars "in a universal way"; according to his analysis, God knows temporal particulars in a timeless way. The theological dimensions of divine omniscience are developed in chapter 6, wherein Barry Kogan examines Averroes' discussion of divine omniscience both in the *Dāmima* and in the *Tahāfut al-Tahāfut*.

Chapters 7–10 are devoted to the formulations of Jewish philosophers. The Binding of Isaac is a paradigmatic Bible story within Jewish thought and functions as a prooftext for subsequent discussions of divine omniscience. In chapters 7 and 8, Jewish commentaries upon this story are analyzed. Seymour Feldman shows in chapter 7 how a number of noted Jewish philosophers, including Saadya Gaon, Maimonides, Gersonides, Crescas and Isaac Arama, used the Binding of Isaac to support their theories of divine omniscience. Gersonides, for example, argued that God did not know the outcome of the event before it happened, whereas Crescas used it to develop his doctrine of the eternity of God's knowledge. In chapter 8, Jeremy Cohen amplifies this discussion further, noting the importance of rabbinic sources, in particular *Genesis Rabbah*, in understanding these philosophical discussions.

Chapter 9 is devoted to Maimonides' discussion of providence, divine omniscience and omnipotence. Distinguishing between the esoteric and exoteric reading of Maimonides, Alfred Ivry contends that the esoteric position is Maimonides' true view. This is seen most clearly in Maimonides' discussion of divine providence and possibility. In chapter 10, I discuss the implications of Gersonides' theory of divine omniscience with respect to prophecy. In particular, I note the difficulties Gersonides has in reconciling a theory of prophecy with an indeterminist scheme according to which God has no foreknowledge of future contingents.

Chapters 11–13 present Christian philosophical positions. In chapters 11 and 13 the problem of divine omnipotence is developed. In Chapter 11, Ivan Boh surveys the development of the notion of omnipotence in the early *Sentence* literature. Boh raises a number of issues which were discussed by these writers, such as, whether God can sin, whether God can make more things than he does make, and whether God can do everything he wills to do. In chapter 13, William Courtenay traces the distinction between the absolute and ordained powers of God. Noting the origin of the distinction hinted in Peter Damian, Courtenay follows it through the high and later middle ages, with special reference to William of Ockham's use of the distinction. Courtenay discusses a number of philosophical difficulties encountered by those who wished to distinguish these two ways of speaking about God's power.

In chapter 12, John Wippel analyzes the views of Thomas Aquinas and Henry of Ghent with respect to divine omniscience. Wippel emphasizes a number of features in Thomas' discussion, including his distinction between necessity and contingency, the importance of his doctrine of analogical predication, and the causal aspect of God's knowledge. This last point becomes of paramount importance for Henry of Ghent, who emphasizes the primacy of will in God's knowledge of particulars.

The editor and contributors to this volume are grateful to a number of sources for sponsoring the original conference. These include: the National Endowment for the Humanities, The Ohio State University College of Humanities, The Ohio State University Philosophy Department, and The Ohio State University Melton Center for Jewish Studies. In addition, I am grateful to a number of persons, including Mark Lambeth, David Yacobucci, and John Martin for their many hours spent working on the footnotes and bibliography; Kimberly Holle and Mary Lee Raines for typing the manuscript; and especially Ivan Boh, whose help in co-sponsoring the original conference was indispensable.

PART ONE

INTRODUCTORY

CHAPTER 1

DIVINE OMNISCIENCE, OMNIPOTENCE AND FUTURE CONTINGENTS: AN OVERVIEW

Calvin G. Normore

1. INTRODUCTION

We can generate a family of problems of future contingents by working variations on a single simple theme. Suppose that some claims about the future are, in some sense, contingent. Suppose that some claims about the past are in that same sense necessary. We now propose various principles which purport to show that every claim of the first kind is entailed by a claim of the second kind. If entailment preserves necessity then every claim of the first kind is necessary after all.

In this paper I will consider three principles and their associated claims that (some) sentences about the past are necessary. The first is the very general principle that necessarily if it was the case that it will be the case that p then it will be the case that p. Associated with this principle is the claim that if it was the case that p then necessarily it was the case that p. This principle and claim together make up a version of the doctrine sometimes called logical fatalism.

A second principle, less sweeping, is that necessarily if it is (or was) known that it will be the case that p then it will be the case that p. The less sweeping claim associated with it is that if it is (was) known that q then necessarily it is (was) known that q. (This has as a special case that if it is (was) known that it will be the case that p then necessarily it is (was) known that it will be the case that p.) This principle and associated claim raise problems for doctrines which admit foreknowledge of contingent events.

The third principle, narrower yet, is that necessarily if it is prophesied that p then it will be the case that p. And its associated claim is that if it is (was) prophesied that p then necessarily it is (was) prophesied that p.

These principles and claims form a hierarchy. One can reject some while accepting subsequent ones, but one cannot, so far as I can see, reject later ones and accept earlier ones. The principles and claims also generate a hierarchy of problems each of which is harder than the ones before. These are not the only problems about future contingents but they are, I think,

T. Rudavsky (ed.), Divine Omniscience and Omnipotence in Medieval Philosophy, 3–22.

central ones and the ones which pose some of the clearest challenges to a philosophical theory of God's relation to time.

Crucial to this procedure for generating problems of future contingents and central to the claims made, is the intuition that the past is in some way not contingent. This intuition seems to be and to have been widespread. Aristotle apparently had it, and, of the commentators on the Master Argument of Diodorus Cronus whose views have come down to us, only Cleanthes seems to have questioned the necessity of the past.[1] Yet despite the popularity of the intuition it is far from clear what grounds it. Is it just a reflection of a belief that causal chains run from past to future? Is it grounded in our relative ignorance of the future? Is it perhaps a brute intuition? There are a number of problems which may help focus our views about this issue and may also help us see how medieval theology in the various religious traditions would reshape Greek views on our subject. One is a problem of petitionary prayer, another is a problem of predestination.

2. CONTINGENCY OF THE PAST

Does it make sense to pray for an outcome which has already either definitely come to pass or definitely not? If a friend has had to choose between the lady and the tiger and you know *that* he has chosen but not *what* he has chosen does it make sense to *pray* that he has chosen the lady? It seems that under certain assumptions the answer is yes. Perhaps God, to whom all of time is (tenselessly) present, takes your prayer into account in guiding your friend's choice. If such be so you are as well-advised to pray after the event as before it. But suppose that just as you are about to begin prayer you learn that your friend has chosen the tiger. Does it *now* make sense to pray that he have chosen the lady? It seems not. You know now that your prayer will not achieve the desired effect and it seems pointless and perhaps impious to ask God to do what you know won't be done. Finally suppose that you learn that your friend has chosen the lady. Does it now make sense to pray that he make just this choice? For all you know God acted on your prayer in guiding his choice. Perhaps it is because God tenselessly saw you praying that your friend is safe. Perhaps were you not to pray he would have made the other choice! On the other hand you know what choice has already been made. You now have good reason to believe *that* you will pray but it is hard to see *why* you should. If God's guidance was based on foreseeing your prayer and you don't pray, then God is mistaken. Whether God is mistaken or not your friend is safe.

This form of the puzzle about prayer is related to a puzzle about predestination. Suppose God predestines on the basis of foreseen merits. Suppose that predestination is a certain indelible character of soul given (or not) at birth. Imagine someone who reaches the age of consent and is considering whether to choose a life of vice or a life of virtue. He might reason that, if he chooses a life of vice, God, being infallible, will have (fore)seen it and not predestined him whereas if he chooses virtue God will certainly have (fore)seen that and have predestined him. Since he wants to have been predestined he will choose virtue. On the other hand he might reason that either the mark of predestination is there or it's not. If it is there, nothing he does now will rub it out; if it is not there, nothing he does now will put it there. So virtue won't help in the search for predestination and he might as well choose the low road of vice.

This puzzle is a theological version of a special case of Newcomb's Problem. In the 'classical' version of Newcomb's Problem you are led before a predictor of whom you believe that the probability that he will correctly predict your choice is very high (say 99%). You are offered a choice between two alternatives, the first of which is the contents of box A and the second the contents of box A together with those of box B. You know box B contains $1000 and you are told (and believe) that box A contains a million dollars if and only if the predictor predicts you will choose the first alternative (box A) alone; otherwise A is empty. You are told (and believe) that the predictor has already made his prediction and already acted on it. You are now to choose.[2]

Contemporary wisdom about Newcomb's Problem has it that what is crucial is whether or not your *choice causally* affects the contents of box A. If it does not, then you should take the second alternative, gaining the thousand dollars in box B as well as the contents of A. But if what A contains depends causally on your choice then you may well be better off with the first alternative. Whether the content of A depends causally on your choice itself depends on whether the predictor's prediction depends on your choice (rather than merely on, for example, knowledge of your character, circumstances, and past choices). Within the ranks of those whose view this is there is a division between those who take causal dependence as primitive for purposes of their account and those who claim that what is central is counterfactual dependence. On this second view you should not choose the first alternative if the probability of "If I were to choose the first alternative there would be a million dollars in box A" is no higher than that of "If I were to choose the second alternative there would be a million dollars in box A."

In the puzzle about predestination described above we have the special case of a predictor (God) who never makes mistakes. If it is merely a matter of contingent fact that God never makes mistakes, the counterfactual decision theorist is not likely to be impressed (God is just *very* lucky and one doesn't, rationally, count on luck). But what if, as I think the tradition has it, God not only never does make mistakes but never would. What if I choose the second alternative, God predicts that I so choose, and were I to have chosen the first alternative God would have predicted *that*? Here I think intuitions conflict especially sharply.

I have tried to describe the cases above so that one might think that your friend's safety or your predestination does indeed counterfactually depend upon your future action. Still I want to claim the fact that you are already predestined and the fact that your friend is already safe strip these dependencies of much of their motivating force. You need not fear damnation and you needn't work to avoid it – though you will. I think that what supports my claim and makes it plausible is the intuition that the past is fixed or necessary in a way the future is not, even if there are "backtracking" counterfactual connections between the past and the future. In short I am claiming that though our intuitions about the fixity of the past may get some of their force from facts about deliberation, they also spring at least in part from a picture of actuality which has it that the present and the past are *actual* in a way the future is not.[3]

When we focus as agents on the counterfactual connections between the past and the future, our intuitions lead us one way – towards prayer or virtue in the cases constructed. When we instead focus as knowers on the fact that the outcome is already there, is actual, our intuitions lead us a different way.

3. DIVINE OMNIPOTENCE AND THE NECESSITY OF THE PAST

Once we consider constructing a theory which applies to God as well as to finite agents and knowers, this conflict of intuitions becomes especially acute. God's deliberative activity is often thought to be one act which cannot be dated; if this is so, the past is as open to his causal activity as the future.[4] On the other hand God is present to all of time and knows in one act, so what is future is as available to God as what is past and both would seem to have the fixity or necessity which characterizes the actual.[5]

Within Latin Christendom these considerations pull different writers in different directions. Some early writers, Peter Damian, for example, held that God can make the past otherwise than it is, but the majority opinion to the time of Duns Scotus seems to be that, even for God, what has been or is, necessarily has been or is.[6] Scotus's device of dividing an instant of time into distinct instants of nature and his attendant view that the will has a simultaneous capacity for opposites changed all that. We can get an understanding of the problem he was concerned with and of the radical nature of his solution by considering one of his examples.[7]

Suppose an angel who exists only for a single instant *i*. (Since angels are substances such is possible if instants are possible.) Suppose that at that instant the angel wills freely. If one is an incompatibilist one will hold that if the angel wills freely to do *x* it must have been or be possible for the angel to have willed not-*x*. But when is it possible? Not before or after *i* because then the angel doesn't exist and so has no capacities. Therefore at *i*. So while the angel wills *x* it is still possible for it to be willing not-*x*. So much for the tag "*Omne quod est quando est necesse est esse*", and so much for the necessity of the present.

Suppose that one grants the will a simultaneous capacity for opposites. Then one has admitted that there are cases in which the conjunction of *p* and *possibly not-p* is true where *p* is as pure a present-tensed assertoric sentence as one might like. But if there is no contradiction in asserting *p* and possibly not-*p*, then God's having verified *p* does not falsify *possibly not-p*; so, since God can do anything which can be done, God has the power to verify *not-p*. Hence unless we put some restrictions on *p*, Adam's having existed isn't necessary because God has the power to make it the case that Adam never existed.

This argument gains additional plausibility from the usual story about God's relationship to time. This story strongly suggests that everything is to God much as the present is to us.[8] If God has a simultaneous power for opposites, it seems it should extend to everything that is presently in his power; that is, to everything. But then everything, or at least everything outside God, is contingent and so the past is. Thomas Bradwardine draws this conclusion, so do, for example, Gregory of Rimini and Peter of Aliaco.[9]

The Bradwardinian attack on the necessity of the past seems closely connected with a continuing debate in the fourteenth century over the scope of divine power. Everyone agreed that God was omnipotent and everyone agreed that anything distinct from God is dependent on him, but there was widespread disagreement about just what these claims covered. During the early middle ages the concept of power was itself a fundamental one and claims that something was possible were explicated in terms of it and the related concepts of potentiality and act. Thus Roger Bacon and

Burleigh are merely mouthing commonplaces when they say that possible being is being in its causes. The concepts of potentiality and power are so closely related within an Aristotelian framework to that of time that it is unclear what, if any, sense could be made within that framework of a power following temporally upon its exercise. Even when the model was extended to include God, the link between the actualization of a power and the order of time was usually maintained, though there were some – like Damian – who demurred.

Duns Scotus changed this. He attacked the connection between power and possibility by emphasizing the notion of "logical possibility" (his term) as the absence of a *repugnantia terminorum* (a semantic inconsistency) and by claiming that rational wills possessed a power for opposites which survived being actualized. In making this second claim he was forced to present a revised theory of *Obligations* and in doing this he gave content to his conception of logical possibility. For Scotus, it seems, a sentence was possible just in case it could be maintained without contradiction in the type of Obligatio known as *positio*. Christopher Martin has shown that in revising the rules for this type of Obligatio Scotus dropped the rule which ensured that if a non-modal present tensed sentence p was conceded and $\Diamond \sim p$ was also conceded then one could not also concede "It is now the case that $\sim p$." where 'now' picks out the time of the Obligatio. In doing this he widened the range of divine power to include the power to make the present other than it is. Scotus did claim that God cannot (now) make the past different from the way it in fact is, but Ockham attacked him for this, claiming that maintaining the necessity of the past while rejecting the necessity of the present is an inconsistent position. Their successors seem to have agreed, for those, like Gregory of Rimini and Bradwardine, who accept Scotus's extension of divine power to the power to make the present different go on to claim that God also has the power to make the past different.[10]

Admitting that the past *is* contingent on God's will in the same sense that the future is, undercuts *logical* fatalism and abandons the absolute necessity of the past but leaves open the possibility that the past is necessary in some sense. Suppose Scotus is right and our present actions, like our future ones, remain in our power, still *our* past may be now outside *our* power. Perhaps that is just what it is for some action of ours to be past *for us*. To those who think that the necessity of the past and present are rooted in a special relation to actuality, this relative distinction will seem far too weak, but, despite attempts, by Ockham for example, to argue otherwise, it is not clearly inconsistent.

The force of Scotus's example of the will which exists only for an instant depends on the context in which the argument is embedded. As it stands, it can be taken as reason to abandon incompatibilist accounts of the will, or as an argument against instants or even as an argument which shows that the present is more like the future than like the past. I will use it as a peg on which to hang short discussions of each of these issues.

4. DIVINE OMNISCIENCE: THE INCOMPATIBILIST POSITION

First, about compatibilism – that is the view that my freely doing A at *t* doesn't entail that it is possible for me to refrain from A at *t*. I have come to think that compatibilism of one sort or another is the dominant position within the traditions of all three religions dealt with in this book. I suspect that the deepest reason for this is that without some sort of compatibilism one ends up positing something, even if it is only an act (of will), which is not made by God. But whatever the deep reasons for its emergence, compatibilism is made very attractive in the Latin West because of the view entrenched in Christian theology by Augustine in his struggle with the Pelagians that God from all eternity has predestined some to salvation. On one interpretation (the "Ockhamist" line) he does this on the basis of foreseen merits, but on the more usual view there is some sort of "premotion" – some causal influence exerted by God – which does not undermine freedom of will but which nevertheless guarantees final repentance. There has been much debate about just what sort of premotion could meet these conditions but, whatever it is, those who believe in it are compatibilists.[11]

Incompatibilists faced with Scotus's argument can claim that Scotus's case is impossible simply because there are no instants. This view, that time is a structure of intervals rather than of atomic moments no matter how numerous, can also be developed into a story of *how* all of time can be present to God. There are at least three remarkably similar medieval tellings of this story – by Jean Buridan, John Wycliff and Luis de Molina. The key to the story is the view that how much time counts as present varies from context to context and that there are some contexts in which all of time is taken as present: for example when we say "We are in term", we take the term as present and when we say "The world is eternal", we take all of time as present. This view, which Wycliff calls the 'ampliation' of time, has a certain plausibility but it also raises problems; for if the duration of the present is conventional or context dependent, so is the distinction between past and future, and this seems to conflict with our intuitions about the difference between them.[12]

Suppose the incompatibilist (hereafter 'we') abandons the present to the future. Can we hold on to the claim that there is an objective difference between the past and the future which justifies our treating the past as necessary in some way in which the future is not? Well, here is an argument to the contrary.[13]

Suppose *a* is a variable ranging over the sentences of some language and *s* is a particular apparently future contingent sentence, say "The antichrist will come".

Let 'P' be read "It was the case that . . . ."
'F' be read "It will be the case that . . . ."
'N' be read "It is now the case that . . . ."
'L' be read "It is necessarily the case that . . . ."
'T' be read "It is true that . . . ."
'–' be read "It is not the case that "
'&' be read "and"
'*v*' be read "or"
'→' be read "If . . . then . . . ."

Then what follows is a proof that the seven plausible principles which begin the argument are inconsistent.

$Pa \to LPa$	Principle 1	Necessity of past
$Fa \to PNFa$	Principle 2	Immutability of Truth
$L(a \to b) \to (La \to Lb)$	Principle 3	
$L(PNFa \to Fa)$	Principle 4	
$Ta \vee T{-}a$	Principle 5	Bivalence
$Ta \to a$	Principle 6	
$-LFs\ \&\ -L{-}Fs$	Principle 7	Contingency of future

$TFs \vee T{-}Fs$	Principle 5, Reiteration	
	TFs	
	$TFs \to Fs$	Prin. 6
	TFs	Duplication
	Fs	Modus Ponens
	$Fs \to PNFs$	Prin. 2
	$PNFs$	Modus Ponens
	$PNFs \to LPNFs$	Prin. 1
	$LPNFs$	Modus Ponens

$L(PNFs \rightarrow Fs) \rightarrow (LPNFs \rightarrow LFs)$	Prin. 3
$L(PNFs \rightarrow Fs)$	Prin. 4
$LPNFs \rightarrow LFs$	Modus Ponens
$LPNFs$	Duplication
LFs	Modus Ponens
$LFs \; v \; L{-}Fs$	Disjunction Intro.

$T{-}Fs$

exactly as above with $-Fs$ replacing Fs and $-Fa \rightarrow PN-Fa$ replacing 2

$LFs \; v \; L{-}Fs$

$LFs \; v \; L{-}Fs$	Disjunction Elimination
$-(-LFs \; \& \; -L{-}Fs)$	A tautologous transformation of the last line
$-LFs \; \& \; -L{-}Fs$	Prin. 7

Faced with this argument one has at least seven possible responses, but there are, I think, just two that someone who wants to maintain both incompatibilism and an objective difference between past and future is likely to make. Such a person can abandon bivalence and with it the argument form

$$\frac{x \vdash A, -x \vdash A}{\vdash A}$$

(that is that if A follows from x and also follows from not-x then A is a logical truth) or that person can restrict the scope of claims that the past is in some sense necessary (that is the scope of principle 1) by excluding certain classes of sentence.

5. OMNISCIENCE, BIVALENCE AND TRUTH CONDITIONS

Both of these strategies have long histories, but both can also be illustrated nicely with fourteenth century Christian examples. Petrus Aureoli advocated and worked out some of the consequences of restricting bivalence; his younger contemporary William Ockham subjected Aureoli's proposal to a careful and devastating scrutiny and then in propria persona took the other tack.[14]

To see what Aureoli is about, we must first distinguish between the principle of bivalence and the law of excluded middle. The law of excluded middle is the claim that every sentence of the form $p \vee - p$ is valid or necessarily true. The principle of bivalence is the claim that of any pair of contradictories p, $-p$, exactly one is true. Within many logical systems it is difficult to distinguish these but there is a picture due to Aureoli and Ockham, and van Fraassen and Thomason, within which it is natural to distinguish them.[15]

Suppose we picture possible histories of the world as left-to-right lines on the page and times as vertical lines. Then if the past is necessary, the histories which are still possible – those which contain the here and now – will share a past and then diverge. On this view there is one possible past but many possible futures. Our picture might look as in Figure 1.

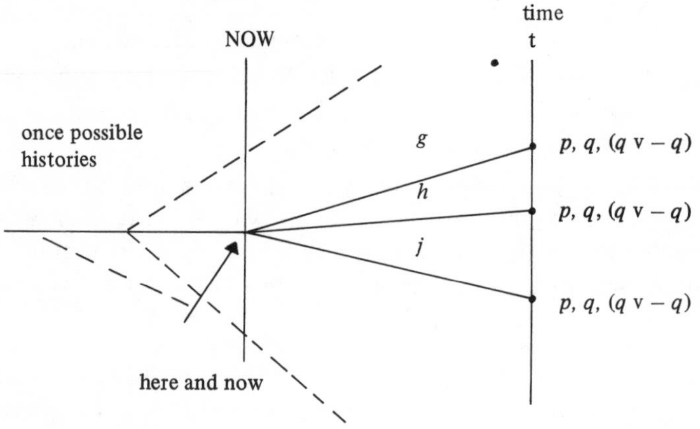

Fig. 1

Let us say that a sentence is true here and now if the history of the world up to now determines its truth.

Then in our illustration, p is true at time t because it is true in every possible future at t. On the other hand q is not true at time t because it is not true in futures g or j at t. Again because not-q is not true in h at time t, it is not simply true at t. So neither q nor not-q is yet true at t. (Neither is false either if we preserve the rule that a sentence is false only if its negation is true). Nevertheless $(q \vee - q)$ is true in every history at t (it is true in h because q is and in g and j because $- q$ is). Thus here bivalence fails while excluded middle does not.

Aureoli's claim is that although excluded middle holds, bivalence should be abandoned. But, like all of the medieval Islamic and Christian writers whom I know to have abandoned bivalence in dealing with the problem of future contingents, he only admits to abandoning it for singular claims.[16]

There is an obvious theological cost to giving up bivalence: it becomes mysterious *how* God knows the contingent future. How after all could God know what isn't true. Moreover, if God knows exactly everything that is true, then it seems that taking Aureoli's way out entails that God's knowledge changes. Aureoli himself seems to have responded to this difficulty by claiming that since God's knowledge is not discursive or propositional, God can know what isn't true – and does.

At first hearing this doctrine sounds absurd. It seems part of the semantics of 'knows' that if x knows that p then 'p' is true. But one might argue that 'x knows that p' does not entail "p' is true' but only entails 'p'. If there is to be a difference marked by this distinction we will have to give up one half of Tarski's convention T – we will have to deny that 'p' entails "p' is true' – but there are independent reasons from the theory of semantic paradoxes for doing this. If we do restrict convention T then we can claim that God's knowledge extends beyond what is true and that God knows whatever is true and whatever will be true. This position may be coherent but it does require a new theory of truth and a new theory of the future tense. It is thus a hard saying.

Does the other alternative fare better? Well, first what is it? As Ockham explains his own view, he proposes to restrict the "necessity" which attaches to the past to sentences which are *really* and not merely "verbally" about the past. His criterion seems at first ad hoc (a sentence is really about the past only if it is *not* entailed by an "atomic" sentence about the future), but it can, I think, be made at least plausible.

First notice that it is generally true that if a premiss of a valid argument is contingent so is its conclusion. Hence if some sentences about the future are contingent, so must be any sentences they entail. Second we can provide for a suitably formal language a purely grammatical test to determine the time a sentence is about. Roughly an atomic sentence is about its time of utterance, a complex sentence (one whose main operator is one-place) is about the times of evaluation of its atomic components and a molecular sentence is about the times of evaluation of its immediate constituents. Thus, where a and b are atomic,

(1) $\mathrm{PF}a\&b$

is about the present (because b is) and is also about the future of every past (because PF*a* is true just in case F*a* is true at some past time and that is so just in case *a* is true at some time future relative to some past time). But unless time has a first moment, this means that PF*a* is about every time and so (1) is. Now we say a sentence is *really* and entirely about the past only if it is not *also* really about the future.

The next and perhaps the crucial element in Ockham's view is the claim that "is true" doesn't express a real property of a sentence over and above what the sentence itself expresses. In short, he embraces a disappearance theory of truth.[17]

With this machinery Ockham can solve the "logical" problem of future contingents while maintaining his incompatibilism and his "temporalist" view that there is an objective difference between past and future. The key to his solution is abandoning the claim that the present (or past) tense in '*x* is (was) true' or '*x* is (was) the case' expresses the present (or past) possession of a property by *x*. But truth or being the case are not the only properties of a sentence which generate problems. And one might wonder whether Ockham's approach could be extended to predicates like 'being known by God' or 'being prophesied'. Can one work out an incompatibilist and temporalist account of divine foreknowledge and of prophecy?

Ockham himself extends his account of how a sentence about the future can be contingent and true to an account of how such a sentence can be contingent and foreknown by the simple device of a "disappearance" theory of divine knowledge. If I understand him aright, "being known by God" no more expresses a property of a sentence distinct from what the sentence says than "being true" does. Whatever its apparent promise, this approach has one serious defect – it makes extremely obscure what it is for God to know something and how God knows something. Ockham himself freely confesses that this is a mystery to him.[18]

In the wake of the stir created by some examples of Edmund Gettier's, 20th century epistemologists have all but abandoned the view that knowledge is nothing more than justified true belief and have sought the grail of a fourth condition – a requirement of total evidence or a requirement that the belief be casually connected with what it is about. Now even if we grant that for God to know *p* is not for God to be in a "psychological" state different from the way God would be if he didn't know *p* – and there is certainly strong pressure in Islam and Christianity at least to grant that – there is still the question of what makes God's knowledge *knowledge* – the question of how God's intellect is connected to the world.

The majority opinion within all of the religious traditions we are considering seems to be that God knows what will happen because he makes whatever happens happen and so knows the history of the world by knowing his own intentions; but this view seems ultimately acceptable only if compatibilism is. A second view, scorned in Islam but advocated in 14th century Europe, is that God's knowledge of the contingent future is at least counterfactually dependent on the causes of that contingent future. This view, advocated by Campsall and Holkot, for example, has two problem.[19] First, it seems to undermine divine impassibility and self sufficiency. Second, it makes it seem that if we want to say that God knows now whether Jerry Brown will die in grace, we must admit that Jerry Brown's death can now produce (affect) God's knowledge and thus that it already *is*.

6. MIDDLE KNOWLEDGE

Although it was not worked out to solve just this problem but rather the closely related problem of how God knew which creation containing free beings would best suit his plans, the most ingenious attempt I know to slip between the horns of the dilemma posed by supposing God's knowledge to be causally related to the world is the doctrine of the scientia media worked out near the end of the 16th century by Luis de Molina and Francisco Suarez. Call two subjunctive counterfactual conditionals conditional contradictories if they have the same antecedent and contradictory consequents. De Molina claims that the principle of conditional excluded middle holds – that exactly one of any pair of conditional contradictories is true – and that God knows which. From this knowledge and his knowledge of his own intentions at creation God can deduce the history of the world. But even if we grant de Molina conditional excluded middle (and Suarez has an ingenious argument for it), there remains the question of how God knows the conditionals. At this point de Molina and Suarez, like Leibniz after them, lapse into obscurity – de Molina speaking of God's supercomprehension and Suarez of a primitive habitus in a person which grounds the conditional.[20] Here is my attempt to make sense of such talk.

Imagine that God's mind contains a perfect model of each possible thing – a complete divine idea of a particular or, if you like, an individual concept. Imagine that God simulates possible histories by thinking about how the being which is A would behave under circumstances C – i.e. he simulates C and 'sees' how A behaves. Now *if* there is a way in which A *would* behave in C, a perfect model should reflect it, so if conditional excluded middle is valid such a model is possible and God knows the history of the world by knowing that model, i.e. by knowing his own intellect and his creative intentions.

But would the belief 'state' which God would be in on the basis of such a model be a state of knowledge? Would it not rather bear to knowledge much the same relation which veridical hallucination bears to perception? Here we have a particularly striking form of another problem of divine omniscience. How can God be transcendent on the one hand and, on the other, know what transpires in the world? It seems to me that anyone who claims that a *transcendent* God knows contingent facts will have to admit significant disanalogies between divine and human knowledge. It also seems to me that supposing God's knowledge of the world to be like veridical hallucination locates these disanalogies in the right place. First it goes some way toward accounting for the intuitive (as contrasted with discursive) character of divine knowledge; God knows contingent facts intuitively because he 'sees' rather than infers that they obtain. Second by admitting counterfactual connections (however mysterious) between divine belief and its mundane objects, such an account preserves at least some of the intuition that God *knows* and is infallible. Third by making these connections indirect it suggests a way one might also admit divine impossibility. Moreover almost any mediaeval writer would have considered that the counterfactual connections suggested weaker than true (Aristotelian) causal connections.[21]

7. DIVINE OMNISCIENCE AND PROPHECY

Even if we can make sense of divine omniscience without causal interaction between God and the world, there remains the problem of seeing how prophecy of contingent truths about the future is possible. This is a new problem because although the truth of contingent sentences about the future and even God's knowledge of this truth can be more or less plausibly denied to be 'real', features of the present p's being revealed by God cannot.

The point can be made in another way. Since the falsehood of p entails the falsehood of "God reveals that p", the truth of the latter *depends* upon that of p. A procedure like Ockham's for determining when a sentence is about then entails that if p is about the future, "God reveals that p", though present-tense in wording, is nevertheless really about the future.

If we consider only revelations from prophets, this account is fairly plausible. A putative prophet is a true prophet only if his prophecies come true. It might be supposed that the question of whether someone is a true or a false prophet (and, therefore, of whether or not his prophecies constitute divine revelation) is just not settled until his prophecies have come true or false. This is not to say that it was not *true* at the very time of his prophecies that Elijah, for example, was a genuine prophet. It *was* true, just as it is now true (let us suppose) that Antichrist will sin. It was just not *necessary*. It was both contingent and dependent upon future vindication of his prophecies.

But if God can prophesy directly, then this approach cannot be applied everywhere. For suppose God prophesies about a contingent act. Suppose for example that, God yesterday wrote in the clouds '*p*', namely that you will freely give alms on the day which is tomorrow. This inscribing in the clouds is a concrete datable event so "God wrote *p*" is a proposition entirely about the past, and, if true, necessarily true. But how can this inscription by an all-knowing and truthful God be necessary if *p* is contingent. How can we break the chain

1. Necessarily (God wrote that *p*)
   – because "God wrote that *p*" is about the past.
2. Necessarily (if God wrote that *p* then *p*.)
   – because God cannot lie.
3. Necessarily *p*.
   from 1 & 2 by Modus Ponens.

At this point it might be well to survey the available options.[22] If it is necessary that what is revealed is true, it cannot be the case for any future contingent proposition *p* that it is necessary that God revealed that *p*. There are, of course, a number of different accounts one might give of the contingency of revelations of future contingents. We cannot just extend Ockham's account of the contingency of God's foreknowledge, because that grants that true claims about concrete past events are necessary while denying that being known by God is such an event. But a more straightforward account of the contingency of past revelations might proceed by maintaining that whatever God did, concrete event or not, it is now contingent that he did it. This approach leads directly to a denial of the necessity of the past. If it is (now) contingent that God did what he did then it is (now) contingent that what he did is done.

Once we exempt God's productions from the necessity of the past it is not easy to stop the slide towards exempting the acts of creatures and thus undermining even a 'relative' distinction of past and future. Some prophecies are about the free acts of created agents and some of those prophecies seem to be or to be caused by divine productions. For example, according to Christian theology Christ is God and so Christ's prophecy to Peter that Peter would deny him before the cock crowed is a divine production. Yet this prophecy was contingent after it was uttered because it remained in *Peter's* power to deny Christ or not. Had Peter exercised his power and not denied Christ, then either Christ would have spoken a falsehood or Christ would never have had uttered the prophecy in the first place. Even if it is only God who could actually bring it about after the fact that Christ never said those words, we are forced to admit either that it was in Peter's power to make Christ utter a falsehood or that what Christ did was counterfactually dependent on what Peter was going to do. Both are a bit startling.

If we're not going to deny that it is necessary that God acted as he did, we must deny that God's action necessarily constituted a revelation of a future contingent. One way of doing so is to maintain that the very *meaning* of the words of the revelation is contingent and dependent upon the future. Thus it is contingent that God revealed any particular proposition. This account is discussed briefly by Gregory of Rimini and at length by Peter of Aliaco. Its plausibility derives from the conventionality of language. It is after all contingent that a certain sentence has the truth conditions it does (those words might have been used differently). It is even contingent that just those sounds or marks express anything at all. Hence one might suppose that even if it is not contingent that God made the sounds or marks or their mental equivalents, it is dependent on our future practices, and thus contingent, that those expressions mean what they do. Aliaco argues that this view would force us to suppose that almost any past-tensed sentence might be contingent. For suppose I act on the basis of a revelation so that, had the proposition p not been revealed to me, I would not have done as I did. Then, Aliaco argues, if it is contingent that p is revealed to me it is contingent that I did what I did. But if we start down that path, the necessity of the past will quickly disappear.

Only one alternative remains if the word of God is necessarily true, and that is a radical one. We may deny that God ever *does* reveal future contingent propositions. This is in fact the line Ockham takes in his *Tractatus De Praedestinatione*, where he asserts that all prophecies may be construed as conditionals. Since on his view conditionals are, if true, necessarily true, this would resolve the problem by confining revelation to necessary truths. Although endorsed in the Jewish tradition, this suggestion is not very appealing. Since most prophecies are stated categorically, the view requires that these be fitted with a suppressed antecedent.[23] But it is not easy to imagine how to provide such antecedents in general without trivializing the prophecy. Ockham's own example, Jonah's prophecy that God would destroy Ninevah, can be plausibly construed as the consequent of a conditional with the suppressed antecedent "Unless you citizens of Ninevah repent" just because we can plausibly regard it as a case in which God reveals his *own* intention through Jonah. No antecedent of this sort seems suitable for Christ's prophecy that Peter would thrice deny him. The prophecy is after all made to Peter and would hardly warrant mention if it were a covert way of saying "Unless you choose not to, you will thrice deny me". In fact we can present Ockham with a dilemma here. Peter's denial of Christ is apparently something Peter does freely. Any true conditional whose consequent has "Peter will freely deny Christ" must have as antecedent a proposition which entails that Peter *chooses* to deny Christ. But such a conditional can hardly be a revelation; Peter can easily figure out for himself that he will deny Christ if he chooses to. So either the conditional is false, or it has a strong antecedent and is trivial.

The only alternative remaining if we are to permit divine prophecies about contingent acts of creatures is to deny

Necessarily (If God says that p then p).

This too seems fraught with theological difficulties. If it is possible that God can claim that p even though not-p is the case, it must either be that God can be mistaken or that God can deceive. The first alternative seems to impugn divine perfection in a straightforward way and the second at least raises puzzles about divine goodness.

I am inclined to think that, despite the apparent difficulties, it is in this last possibility – the possibility that God can deceive – that the most fruitful approach to the problem of contingent prophecy lies. But this takes us at once to the heart of a problem central to theodicy in all the religions treated in this book and takes us also into a thicket of problems about how to reconcile the reasonable believer's recognition that God could deceive and his certainty that God never will. Here we are poised on the edge of another discussion – one which I am glad to leave to another occasion.[24]

NOTES

[1] There is a vast secondary literature on the scanty primary literature on discussions of the necessity of the past in antiquity. For an introduction to and discussion of both, see R. Sorabji's *Necessity, Cause, and Blame*, Cornell University Press, Ithaca, N.Y. 1980.

[2] Newcomb's Problem was first introduced into the philosophical literature by Robert Nozick in 'Newcomb's Problem and Two Principles of Choice,' in *Essays in Honor of*

Carl G. Hempel, N. Rescher *et al.* (eds.), D. Reidel, Dordrecht, 1970, and has given rise to an extensive literature. The conventional wisdom about it was formed largely by A. Gibbard and W. Harper in 'Counterfactuals and Two Kinds of Expected Utility,' *Foundations and Applications of Decision Theory*, Vol. I, Hooker *et al.* (eds.), D. Reidel, Dordrecht, 1978. That Newcomb's problem is closely connected to fundamental problems of decision theory was demonstrated by D. K. Lewis in 'Prisoner's Dilemma Is a Newcomb Problem,' *Philosophy and Public Affairs* 8 (1979), 235–240. I have benefitted in thinking about this subject from an unpublished paper by Professor A. Falk, 'New Wrinkles on Old Fatalisms' (xerox 1982).

[3] One might wonder whether the claim that the past is fixed or necessary is consistent with the claim that there are "backtracking" connections between it and the future. For example, one might reason thus: Even if I am predestined and so have an indelible mark on my soul it is still possible for me to choose a life of vice. But (1) if I were to choose a life of vice God would know it – so it is possible that God know it. But (2) if God were to know I would choose a life of vice he would have not marked my soul – so it is possible that God has not marked my soul. But my soul is already marked and hence necessarily already marked. Therefore, my soul is necessarily already marked and possibly not already marked. And that is absurd. This reasoning seems valid but one must be careful. Subjunctive reasoning is not in general transitive. As we shall see later perhaps the most plausible account of what would happen if I were to choose a life of vice (supposing my soul is already marked) is that God would have made a mistake.

[4] The idea that all of God's activity is a single act which is outside of time creates interesting disanalogies to human action. For example a human being who saved someone's life and then years later broke both that person's arms would ordinarily be thought to have performed *two* separate acts – one good, one bad. But if God did this it would be one act – that of saving-a-life-while-armbreaking. If this act is a good one, then, one may claim, God has done nothing bad.

[5] One way of attempting to ground the intuition that the present and past are fixed or necessary in a way the future is not is to claim that the future is merely possible while the past and present are actual and that the actual, being "outside its causes'" doesn't, when actual, depend on anything for its existence and so can't have its existence prevented (though of course it may depend on something for its continued existence). I think this approach has promise though I will not attempt to defend it here.

[6] Damian's view is not that God can change the past, e.g. make it that today Adam existed and tomorrow he did not, but that God can now make the past otherwise, e.g. make it that Adam never existed. The clearest discussion of this I know is in unpublished work by Paul Oppenheimer.

[7] This example appears in Scotus, (*Opus Oxon*) I Sent. d. 39 in L. Wadding (ed.), *Opera Omnia* Vatican Scotistic Commission, vol. 5, part II, p. 1301. I discuss this question further in 'Instants of Time and Instants of Nature,' (unpublished manuscript).

[8] It is not easy to see how God can be present to all of time as agent or as knower. Relativity theory would seem to provide a model because there are analogies which can be drawn between the way in which all of history is present to God and the way in which all of *its* history is present for a photon. The problem with such models is that if one thinks of the past and/or present as real or actual in a way the future is not, such models force one to think of actuality or reality as perspective-relative. For the best-articulaed model of the sort mentioned see E. Stump and N. Kretzmann, 'Eternity,'

The Journal of Philosophy 78 (1981), 429–58. For criticisms of such views see John Duns Scotus, *Lectura* I Sent. d. 39, q. 1–5. (*Lectura in Librum Primum Sententiarum* in John Duns Scotus, *Opera Omnia*, vol. XVII, Civitas Vaticana ed. by C. Balić *et al.*, 1966.)

9 This conclusion is the burden of much of Thomas Bradwardine's *Summa de causa dei contra Pelagium et de virtute causarum ad suos Mertonenses libri tres*, Lyon 1618 (reprinted, Minerva 1964). For examples see Bk. I ch. 14 or Bk. III ch. 14. For Gregory of Rimini's views see I *Sent.* ch. 35; for Peter of Aliaco's discussion see *Quaestiones super libros Sententiarum cum quibusdam in fine adiunctis*, Strasburg 1490 (reprinted, Minerva 1968).

10 I discuss this further in 'The Limits of God's Power: Some Fourteenth Century Discussions,' *Paideia*, forthcoming.

11 This claim may be too strong. For example, while it is hard to see how the 'physical' premotion advocated by sixteenth century Thomists is consistent with incompatibilism, it is not clear to me that the 'moral' premotion advocated by sixteenth century Scotists is not. An interesting discussion of Scotus's view is contained in D. Langston, *When Willing Becomes Knowing: The Voluntarist Analysis of God's Omniscience* (unpublished manuscript).

12 Buridan discusses this view of time in his *Johannes Buridanus: Sophismata* ch. 7, T. K. Scott (ed.), Stuttgard-Bad Connstatt, 1977, and his *Quaestiones super octo libros Physicorum Aristotelis*, Paris 1509, Bk. IV. De Molina takes it up in his *De Scientia Dei*, F. Stegmüller (ed.), in *Geschichte der Molinismus*, Bd. I, *BGPM* **32** (1935), 202ff.

13 This argument owes a lot to A. N. Prior's discussion in *Past, Present and Future*, Oxford University Press, Oxford 1967, ch. VII. J. Etchemendy and P. Oppenheimer have pointed out to me that the 'now' operator makes some of the premisses of the argument stronger than they seem. Remember that 'now' doesn't mean "at the actual world-state" but merely "at this *time*".

14 Some of this history (and some more) is presented in my chapter 'Future Contingents' in the *Cambridge History of Later Medieval Philosophy*, N. Kretzmann *et al.* (eds.), Cambridge University Press, Cambridge 1982, pp. 358–381.

15 The tense logical ideas employed here were presented by R. Thomason in 'Indeterminist Time and Truth-Value Gaps,' *Theoria* **36** (1970), 264–281. The underlying logical technique – that of supervaluations – is due to Bas C. van Fraassen.

16 The historical inspiration for the view that the only exceptions to bivalence are found among singular sentences is Aristotle's discussion in *De Interpretations* ch. 9, but the philosophical motivation is less clear. Holding that some singular sentences are neither true nor false but that every particular or universal sentence is bivalent forces one to give up the usual entailment relations between singular sentences and others – relations which are summarized for 14th century logicians in the rules of descent which are part of the theory of personal supposition. Fourteenth century logicians are aware of this consequence of the view but, to my knowledge, never attempt to motivate it. It is perhaps the feature which most clearly separates Aureoli's picture and the one Ockham ascribes to Aristotle from Thomason's "supervaluational" approach.

17 Professor Anil Gupta has pointed out to me that Ockham's position may not entail that "is true" can be eliminated from every context and so may not be a full disappearance theory. Ockham's discussion of these issues can be found passim in his *Tractatus de praedestinatione et de praescientia dei et de futuris contingentibus*, P. Boehner

(ed.), Franciscan Institute, St. Bonaventure, N.Y. 1945.

[18] Cf. Ockham *op. cit.* Assumption 6.

[19] A particularly striking statement of this view can be found in the 'Notabilia' of Richard of Campsall. Cf. E. A. Synan, 'Sixteen Sayings by Richard of Campsall on Contingency and Foreknowledge' *Medieval Studies* **24** (1962), 250–262.

[20] For more on this see R. M. Adams, 'Middle Knowledge and the Problem of Evil,' *American Philosophical Quarterly* **14** (1977), 109–117, and the article referred to in note 12.

[21] The counterfactual connections suggested seem to give what medieval theorists called *sine qua non* causality, which seems very close to the concept D. K. Lewis analyzes. For *sine qua non* causality see W. J. Courtenay, 'The King and the Leaden Coin: the Economic Background of 'Sine qua non' Causality' *Traditio* **28** (1972), 185–210, and M. M. Adams, 'Was Ockham a Humean about Efficient Causality,' read to the New Jersey Philosophical Association, April 1980. For D. K. Lewis' analysis cf. 'Causation,' *Journal of Philosophy* **70** (1973), 556–567.

[22] Professor A. Edidin and I do this a bit more fully in 'Ockham on Prophecy,' *International Journal for the Philosophy of Religion* **13** (1982), 179–189. What follows is largely borrowed from that article.

[23] This is the view of among others, Levi ben Gerson (Gersonides); see Professor T. Rudavsky's paper in this volume.

[24] But not with out a Parthian shot. Gilson and others have claimed that fourteenth century 'nominalism' paved a road to scepticism. I suggest that if there is any truth in this it is not so much because of the problems about intuitive cognition or causal principles on which the debate has focussed as because of the claim that God can deceive taken together with the view that one cannot be certain of what can be otherwise. Whether the view that one cannot be certain of what can be otherwise is true is a question still much debated by those interested in the foundations of Bayesian epistemology and its relations.

CHAPTER 2

NOS IPSI PRINCIPIA SUMUS: BOETHIUS AND THE BASIS OF CONTINGENCY

Norman Kretzmann

1. INTRODUCTION

Boethius's two commentaries on Aristotle's *De interpretatione* contain an account of the metaphysical foundations of contingency in their discussions of Chapter 9.[1] For the countless medieval discussions of future contingents only *De interpretatione* 9 itself is of greater historical importance than Boethius's discussions of it. In this chapter, however, my concern is with the content of Boethius's theory of contingency and not with its historical sources or influences. In order to give his theory the kind of consideration I think it deserves, I need to extract it from the other material in the commentaries and expound it in its own right; I also want to examine some of its consequences. Because those tasks are the only ones I can undertake in this paper, I am not now concerned with what the later medievals thought about Boethius or with what Boethius thought about Aristotle or with what Aristotle thought about contingency, but only (or as nearly as possible only) with what Boethius thought about contingency in his two commentaries on *De interpretatione*.[2]

2. LOGICAL DETERMINISM

Boethius's theory of contingency is developed in opposition to determinism, and the determinism that is the first (though not the main) object of his attention is logical determinism – the view that every future event or state of affairs is inevitable simply in virtue of the fact that every proposition[3] (including every proposition about the future) either is true or is false.[4] Here is one of Boethius's many presentations of logical determinism:

> If that is the way it is as regards all affirmations and negations – that the one is definitely false, the other definitely true – then whatever the true one says is going to come about, it is *necessary* that it come about; [and] whatever [it says] will not come about, it is *necessary* that it not come about.[5]

The affirmations and negations he is particularly talking about are the

T. Rudavsky (ed.), Divine Omniscience and Omnipotence in Medieval Philosophy, 23–50.

affirmative and negative members of a contradictory pair of singular future-tense temporally definite propositions,[6] such as 'The vernal equinox in 1995 will occur on March 20 at 5:32 p.m. EST', 'The vernal equinox in 1995 will not occur on March 20 at 5:32 p.m. EST'. Saying that the first of these is now "definitely true" and the second "definitely false" means, as Boethius uses those expressions, that there is a present state of affairs which in virtue of certain laws of nature makes the occurrence of the vernal equinox at that time not contingent but naturally necessary, inevitable, and so theoretically predictable with certainty. And, as Boethius says, "If that is the way it is as regards *all* affirmations and negations" – including such propositions as 'I will write more than 500 words on [tomorrow's date]', 'I will not write more than 500 words on [tomorrow's date]' – then the future is entirely determined in that way on the basis of what appear to be nothing more than elementary, unimpeachable observations regarding truth and falsity. For surely either it is true that I will write more than 500 words tomorrow or it is false that I will write more than 500 words tomorrow.

Boethius rejects logical determinism on the basis of a distinction between indefinitely true and definitely true future-tense propositions. A definitely true proposition is one the truth of which is unalterably determined by a present state of affairs. Thus every true proposition about the past or the present is definitely true, and so are some propositions about the future – such as one or the other of the vernal equinox propositions introduced above. But, Boethius claims, there are contradictory pairs of propositions about the future such that their truth and falsity are determined by no present state of affairs but only (eventually) by the future states of affairs they are about. Even though one of the pair of propositions about my writing tomorrow will turn out to have been true and the other to have been false, there is no present fact which determines their truth-values. The status of the truth-value of a proposition depends on the metaphysical status of the thing, event, or state of affairs the proposition is about; the time of the vernal equinox in 1995 is not contingent but determined, and my writing more than 500 words tomorrow is not determined (or definite) but contingent (or indefinite).

> The contingents are whichever ones . . . are equally disposed to being or to not being. And just as they themselves have indefinite being and not being, so also affirmations and negations regarding them have indefinite truth and falsity; for one is always true [and] another always false, but which of them is true or which false is not yet known [even to nature[7]] as regards contingents. For just as regarding those that must be it is definite that they be and regarding those that cannot be it is definite that they not be, so also regarding those that both can be and can not be it is definite neither that they be nor

that they not be. But truth and falsity is acquired on the basis of the being of the thing (or event or state of affairs[8]) [the proposition is about] and on the basis of the not being of that thing; for it that which is said *is*, it is true, [and] if that which is said *is not*, it is false. Therefore just as being and not being itself is variable as regards those that are contingent and future (although it is necessary that they be or not be), so also truth and falsity is indeed uncertain as regards affirmations and negations presenting these contingents; for in accordance with the nature of these propositions it is unknown which is true and which is false. All the same, it is necessary that one be true [and] another false.[9]

In order to sustain the distinction between definite and indefinite truth on the basis of which he rejects logical determinism, Boethius must say much more about contingent events and states of affairs than about the propositions that are contingent because of them. And so although he begins by confronting logical determinism, his principal concern is with natural determinism, the view that *all* truth and falsity of propositions about the future is *definite*, determined in present facts.

3. NATURAL DETERMINISM AND NATURAL NECESSITY

Boethius himself believes that some singular propositions about the future are definitely true; people do occasionally make *well-founded* true predictions, something they are able to do only when the outcomes they predict really are inevitable, when the things, events, or states of affairs they predict really are subject to natural necessity:

... it is necessary, [if] anyone has made a true prediction about some thing, that the thing which he declared beforehand come about. Nevertheless, the necessity of things does not depend on the truth of prediction; rather, the truth of prophesying depends on the necessity of things. For the fact that something true has been predicted is not the reason why it is necessary; instead, something could be truly predicted regarding that thing because it necessarily was going to be. ... Those things that are going to be, it is necessary that they be because they have a certain necessity in their own nature. If someone stumbles upon that necessity, what he predicts is true. ... For it is not because of the saying or the denying that there is necessity in things; it is rather that truth or falsity is found in foretelling in virtue of the necessity belonging to things.[10]

Natural determinism holds good just in case absolutely all things, events, or states of affairs "have a certain necessity in their own nature". Boethius denies natural determinism but, as we have already seen, he accepts natural necessity. So the contingency Boethius defends will have to coexist with that necessity, at which we will have to look more closely.

I find the concept of natural necessity explicitly or implicitly in several different kinds of contexts in Boethius. There is, for instance, the necessity associating things of certain natural kinds with their essential natural characteristics (*propria nata*): fire is necessarily hot, snow necessarily cold, man necessarily mortal.[11] Again, there is the necessity of laws of nature: heavy bodies necessarily tend to fall and light bodies necessarily tend to rise; water is necessarily susceptible to warming and cooling.[12] But the natural necessity that is especially pertinent to the subject matter of this paper is the causal necessity of particular natural events. (Because in these commentaries Boethius is so sparing in his references to causation, I will more often refer to this necessary causal connection simply as necessitation.) Boethius's clearest examples of this necessitation are of two sorts, astronomical and medical. For example,

> . . . that the sun is now in Sagittarius and that after a few days it will move into Aquarius . . . is necessary.[13]
>
> . . . if a physician observes a fatal symptom in his patient's face, so that it cannot be otherwise than that he is dying, although it is unknown to us because of our inexperience in the art [of medicine], it must not for that reason be judged that the sick man's being about to die is undetermined (*utrumlibet*) and of a contingent nature. Rather, the only things that should be thought to be undoubtedly so are those that are unknown to us in virtue of the fact that by their own nature they cannot be known in respect of what sort of outcome they have . . .[14]

Those particular things, events, or states of affairs the outcomes of which *can* be known "by their own nature" are subject to one significant further division as Boethius views them: those that occur in the heavens, where *everything* is naturally necessitated, and those that occur below the sphere of the moon, when we live, the only region where contingency has a chance.[15] Because natural determinism does hold above the sphere of the moon, the necessity of the sun's progress through the zodiac does not provide as relevant a contrast with contingency as does the natural necessity of the patient's dying of the fatal disease; and so I will be concentrating on sublunary necessitation, which shares its realm with such natural contingency as there may be.

Boethius's treatment of the case of the fatal symptom is further evidence that he believes that at least some aspects of the future are present in the things, events, or states of affairs that necessitate them. As he says,

> . . . *in nature* this was *beforehand*, but the outcome of the thing itself made it clear *to us*. Accordingly, if all things whatever that will come about *are*, and those that are going to be could have been predicted, then it is necessary that *all* things that are said are either definitely true or definitely false, since *their outcome is definite as regards present time*.[16]

In the case of the fatal symptom the future event that is present in the state of affairs which necessitates it is revealed to at least one observer – the physician – but the actual presence of such necessitation in nature is of course independent of any such foreknowledge, as Boethius clearly recognizes. For, as he says of generally similar cases, "even if the nature of the truth has not been made manifest in them, still, nothing prevents there being a fixed constancy of necessity in nature".[17] If there are genuinely contingent things, events, or states of affairs, they must be so "as a result of their own nature, not relative to our ignorance and knowledge".[18] We should not be deluded into thinking that contingency can be preserved on the basis of mere epistemic indeterminacy or simply "because we do not know how to listen in on the future"; if contingency can be preserved at all in the midst of natural necessitation, that will be only "because the same thing (or event or state of affairs) can both be and not be".[19]

We will be considering natural necessitation further, but it is already clear that Boethius believes that some future events are necessitated in that their inevitable occurrence can theoretically be predicted with certainty on the basis of present states of affairs (whether or not anyone is actually in a position to make such predictions), and that only actual exceptions to such necessitation and not mere limitations on knowledge will constitute an acceptable basis for contingency.

4. NATURALLY NECESSARY AND CONTINGENT FUTURE SINGULAR PROPOSITIONS

We have also seen that Boethius believes there are genuinely contingent propositions, propositions that are neither definitely true nor definitely false and that require real contingency for their interpretation.[20] All such propositions are about the future and so are typically in the future tense. But the ordinary future tense appears to present us with definite truth or definite falsity, partly because '*x* will be A' is analogous to '*x* was A' and '*x* is A', which do present definite truth or definite falsity, and partly because the future tense must also serve for propositions that are about the future but are not contingent. Boethius recognizes this potentially misleading feature of his language (and ours) and suggests a way of marking the distinction by means of a form of speech which he probably thinks of as reserved for technical discourse:

> . . . anyone who says of one of the things that come about contingently that it *will be* says something false in that he says that that which perhaps comes about, contingently,

is going to be. Even if the thing he predicts should occur, he still has said something false; for it is not the coming about that is false, but the manner of predicting it. For he ought to have said 'Tomorrow a sea battle *contingently* will come about' – that is to say, if it does come about, it comes about in such a way that it could fail to come about. Whoever speaks in that way says what is true, for he has predicted the outcome contingently. But whoever begins 'Tomorrow there *will be* a sea battle' says it as if it were necessary.[21]

So Boethius recognizes both naturally necessary and contingent singular propositions about the future, and he is concerned that our ordinary forms of speech should not blur the distinction. But how are we supposed to decide whether a given singular proposition about the future is naturally necessary or contingent? On one level the answer is perfectly obvious: "If the things (or events or states of affairs) come and go contingently, the proposition that puts them forward is designated contingent".[22] The effect of that correct but unhelpful criterion is to shift our attention from logic and linguistics to metaphysics: in a world that is otherwise naturally necessitated, which *are* the things, events, or states of affairs that come and go contingently, and how do they get away with it?

In extracting and extrapolating Boethius's theory of contingency from his answers to those questions I will not be presenting a Boethian refutation of natural determinism. In these commentaries he is not concerned with proving that there really is contingency; he takes its reality for granted. What he says about Aristotle on this score may fairly be said about Boethius himself: "he thinks that these (viz., chance, possibility, and free choice) are so established in reality that there is no need for any demonstration regarding them; instead, any theory that tries to overturn either the possible, or chance, or that which is up to us is judged to be impossible".[23] Boethius's aim is not to establish but to explain natural contingency. But in pursuing *that* aim he does differ from Aristotle in *De interpretatione* 9, where, as Boethius observes, "he does not now *explain* what chance is, or what is possible, or what is up to us".[24]

5. THE THREE MODES OF THE CONTINGENT

The trio of possibility, free choice, and chance, encountered more than once in those passages and more than twenty times in the two commentaries,[25] is obviously a very important component of Boethius's theory. But what are the relationships of those three to contingency and to one another, and what, exactly, does Boethius mean by each of them?

As a first approximation regarding the relationship between contingency and the trio we might be inclined to suppose that Boethius's claim is that contingency simply occurs in three different forms, as possibility, as free choice, and as chance. He does sometimes express the relationship in just that way – for example, "Now according to the Aristotelian doctrine, that is contingent which chance brings, or which comes from anyone's free choice and his own will, or which in virtue of a readiness of nature it is possible to bring into both parts – viz., that it happen and that it not happen"[26] – and when he does so he takes possibility, free choice, and chance to be "the three modes of the contingent."[27] The frequent repetition of the simple list of those three modes is to be explained by the fact that, besides being the concepts at the heart of Boethius's theory, possibility, free choice, and chance are the seemingly undeniable features of our ordinary experience that must be rejected as mere appearance if natural determinism is true. For, as Boethius points out, "it is impossible on that view that anything be contingent. For it will come about that all things whatever that are or happen happen of necessity and nothing by *chance*; *and* that of nothing is it *possible* that it be and *possible* that it not be; *moreover*, nothing would be left to the governance of *free choice* . . ."[28] For, as he says in another place, "Those are properly contingents . . . which are neither in nature nor in necessity, but either in *chance*, or in *free choice*, or in the *possibility* of nature".[29]

The often repeated, almost formulaic list of the three modes is designed to keep Boethius's reader from forgetting what must be given up if natural determinism is accepted. But because it also presents the three concepts that have the most important parts to play in Boethius's theory, the familiar list of them is misleading in its suggestion that he thinks of possibility, free choice, and chance as being on a par with one another, as independent, alternative modes in which contingency enters into reality. Most of us would be inclined to say offhand, even without the backing of a particular theory about them, that they are *not* independent of one another. Boethius would agree: his theory is primarily an explanation of contingency in terms of the interdependence of the three modes.

6. POSSIBILITY

To begin with, two of the modes, free choice and chance, would ordinarily be thought to presuppose open natural possibility – the kind of possibility invoked by Boethius in such phrases as "possible that it be and possible that it not be". His treatment of possibility as one of the modes shows that he has such a concept of its nature and of its relationship to the other two modes. Perhaps his recognition of the essential openness of the sort of possibility on which contingency is based is indicated even terminologically, for he seems to have a preference for associating '*utrumlibet*' with this mode in particular:[30]

And this possibility of coming about or not coming about we call *utrumlibet*; for as regards things of this sort, it turns out in either of two ways (*utrumlibet*).

And a little later he says:

Accordingly, this sort of capacity for coming about or not coming about is called *utrumlibet*, because as regards these things it is granted that they come about in either of two ways (*utrumlibet*) . . .[31]

In at least one passage he actually uses '*utrumlibet*' in place of 'possibility' in the familiar list:

For chance and that which is *utrumlibet* is abolished, and free will is also taken away, if all things whatever that will happen are of necessity going to be.[32]

Boethius is careful to distinguish in this way the sort of possibility required as part of the basis of contingency because he recognizes that although naturally necessary events must be possible also, the explanation of their occurrence does not typically require the open, *utrumlibet* possibility that underlies contingent events:

For in one way it is said to be possible when I am seated that I walk, in another way that the sun is now in Sagittarius and that after a few days it will move into Aquarius; for the latter is possible in such a way that it is also necessary.[33]
. . . although what is necessary is possible, there is another, *extrinsic* nature of possibility, which is detached both from the impossible and from necessity.[34]

All natural necessity presupposes not merely logical but real possibility, and real possibility is usually conceived of by Boethius in terms of potentiality; nevertheless, he seems not to consider all necessitated events or states of affairs as actualized potentialities. For among the heavenly bodies "there is nothing at all in potentiality, but everything in actuality. For example, with respect to the sun light is never in potentiality; indeed, there is no darkness with respect to it, or rest with respect to the heavens as a whole".[35] Presumably, then, the possibility presupposed by the necessity of the sun's being in Aquarius a few days from now is not a potentiality; it is a merely *intrinsic* real possibility of the sort presupposed by the natural necessity of that state of affairs.[36]

I think that in Boethius's view the occurrence of any necessitated event *on earth* does count as the actualization of a potentiality, but in some such cases the potentiality that gets actualized existed in the absence of a real alternative, and so perhaps such cases also should be said to present *intrinsic* real possibility. For example, Jones's having turned grey by age sixty and Smith's retaining his original hair color at that age are both necessitated outcomes, given that the two men have managed to live for sixty years. Jones's originally black hair had the potentiality for greyness at age sixty but no potentiality for remaining black; Smith's originally black hair had no potentiality for greyness by age sixty. But because men differ individually in this way as regards the gene for retention of hair color, we have to say of men's hair color *generally* that it does have real alternative potentialities or, as Boethius would put it, an affinity for contraries.[37] And on the basis of experience of this sort of outcome, *necessitated* one way or the other *in individuals*, Boethius can say *generally* of men as old as Jones and Smith what would be ludicrously false of Jones or Smith individually, that "it does indeed happen more often that he turns grey, but that he not turn grey is not ruled out".[38] The appearance of contingency can sometimes be merely a statistical phenomenon.

The open possibility that is part of the basis of real contingency must, then, be an affinity for contraries on the part of *individual* things or states of affairs: "This wood, for example, can be cut up; but it nevertheless has an affinity for contraries, for it can be not cut up";[39] again, "that this reed be broken is indeed possible, but also that it not be broken; and this they [the Peripatetics, among whom Boethius is including himself] trace back . . . to the nature of the thing itself".[40] This wood's being cut up or this reed's being broken is an individual state of affairs "which in virtue of a readiness of nature it is possible to bring into both parts – viz., that it happen and that it not happen".[41] And this natural affinity for contraries, this open possibility traced back to the nature of the thing itself, this readiness of nature, has its place in Boethius's picture of the world in virtue of his concept of matter:

> . . . some things, indeed, are in potentiality, others in actuality. [This] water, for example, is indeed hot in potentiality,[42] for it can be made hot, but it is cold in actuality, for it *is* cold. Now this 'in actuality' and 'in potentiality' comes from matter. For since matter is susceptible to contrariety and has within itself an affinity for both [parts] of a contrariety, if it is considered in itself it has nothing of those [contraries] to which it is susceptible in itself. Indeed, in itself it is nothing in actuality but everything in potentiality. . . . Therefore what is in potentiality in things (or events or states of affairs) comes from matter.[43]

So part of the required basis of contingency, individuated *utrumlibet* possibility, is a feature of reality in virtue of being a feature of matter, part of the basis of physical reality itself.

7. ACTUALIZING AGENCY

It is clear, however, that this one of the three modes does not by itself introduce contingency into the world. There are two reasons for its insufficiency, one general and one specific. In the first place, the real potentiality that stems from matter cannot *introduce anything*; it is completely and essentially passive. The actualization of any such potentiality requires *agency*, which cannot be attributed to matter itself. In the second place, there are actualizations of potentialities that do not count as contingent, even in cases characterized by an affinity for opposites. When Krakatoa exploded in 1883, that actualization of the volcano's potentiality for eruption was a naturally necessitated, not a contingent event. Even though no one was good enough at vulcanology to be certain before August 26, 1883, that Krakatoa would erupt on that day, it was, as Boethius would say, certain to nature; for its eruption then was part of the natural scheme of things, nature's plan. Here is his description of nature as the necessitated actualizing agency in such cases:

> And so things are disposed on the basis of matter in such a way that everything would be in potentiality, but nothing in actuality, [which is effected] under the direction of nature, which distributes individual changes in matter itself in keeping with a plan and puts individual properties of qualities in individual parts of matter. In this way nature itself ordains some things (or events or states of affairs) as necessary in such a way that as long as the thing would exist its property would remain in it, as heat in fire; for as long as there is fire, it is necessary that fire be hot. But on other things nature has imposed qualities such that the things can lack them. And the former, necessary quality informs the substance of each and every thing, for that quality of it is conjoined with matter itself by nature. But the other, latter qualities are extra: they can be admitted and also not admitted. . . . Therefore it is on the basis of nature and on the basis of matter itself that there comes to be possibility in things (or events or states of affairs).[44]

It may be permissible in Boethius's view to speak of fire's potentiality for heat, but since such a potentiality has no real alternative, it is of no further interest to us in investigating the basis of contingency. Water's potentiality for warmth, on the other hand, has a real alternative, and so the affinity for contraries in a given sample of water fully qualifies as an instance of the sort of possibility contingency is founded on. The question whether a given sample of water's having become warm on a given occasion is a contingent event then involves subsidiary questions, the most obvious of which is the question of which agency actualized that potentiality; for it is another necessary condition of contingency that the actualizing of the individual potentiality involve agency that is not itself necessitated.

As might have been expected, free choice and chance, the other two modes, are the sources to which Boethius looks for such unnecessitated actualizing agency, expressly recognizing that there could be neither free choice nor chance without possibility of the sort we have been considering:

> It is on the basis of possibility also that chance sometimes surprises [us] in reality ... Even the essence of free choice comes out of that possibility, however; for it were not *possible* for anything to happen but all things necessarily were or necessarily were not, free choice would not remain.[45]

8. FREE CHOICE

Free choice can play its essential role among the three modes of contingency because Boethius conceives of it along thoroughly indeterminist lines. In contrasting his Peripatetic conception with that of the compatibilist Stoics he says "that which is up to us is free choice, which is devoid of all necessity, freeborn, and with power of its own over those things of which we are in any way the masters, either to do them or not to do them".[46] And so "some things (or events or states of affairs) flow from the source of free choice and from the spring of our actions",[47] and at least those will have the requisite unnecessitated actualizing agency. The proposition "'Tomorrow Socrates is going to be disputing in the Palaestra' is contingent", Boethius explains, just "because it comes from free choice".[48] And it is free choice on which the occurrence or non-occurrence of tomorrow's sea battle depends: "both the one and the other could come about. But this is so because the outcome of the things (or events or states of affairs) is *not* dependent on certain older causes, as if somehow there were a sort of chain of necessity: but these [the occurrence or the non-occurrence] are based instead on our choice and free will, in which there is no necessity".[49]

And as for the source of those free choices of ours that are themselves this source of contingency, Boethius the incompatibilist of course maintains that it cannot be traced to anything outside ourselves: "what happens as a result of us and our judgment finds its source in nothing external".[50] We ourselves are the sources: *nos ipsi principia sumus*.[51]

Boethius's indeterminist libertarianism, then, is not founded on the notion of acts of volition as uncaused events, but is (or at any rate closely resembles) the sort of indeterminist libertarianism that relies on the concept of agent causation.[52] And, as we shall see, *nos ipsi principia sumus* is the first principle of more than his theory of free choice. For it turns out that if God is left out of account (as he is almost everywhere in these two discussions of *De interpretatione* 9[53]), the *only* unnecessitated actualizing agency is in us; and so we ourselves are the sources of *all* contingency. The least that is required in support of that claim is some explanation of Boethius's view of us as the ultimate sources of our freely chosen actions, and some consideration of the role of chance in the basis of contingency.

We ourselves are the ultimate sources of our free choices because reason, our essence, is the ultimate source of judgment, and judging rather than wanting is the essence of free choice:

> . . . we do not say that the free choice of the will is whatever anyone might *want*; [it is] rather whatever anyone might *decide* on the basis of judgment and examination. . . . if wanting or not wanting something should rightly acquire the designation of free choice, it would belong not only to men but also to the other animals. . . . Free choice is rather what those very words disclose: a *judgment* of the will that is free for us. For as often as certain images come together in the mind and stir the will, reason weighs them carefully and judges regarding them, and then when it has carefully weighed in choice and considered in judgment, it does what seems better to it. And for *that* reason we disdain some things that are sweet and that give the appearance of usefulness; other things that are bitter we bravely endure even though we do not *want* them. To that extent free choice corresponds *not* to the *will*, but to the *judgment* of the will; and it is based not on the imagination, but on the careful weighing of that same imagination. And it is for *that* reason that of certain actions we ourselves are the sources, not the attendants; for to use reason is to use judgment . . . [and] we are distinguished by reason alone.[54]

Free choice identified as rational decision is free choice essentially connected with deliberation, reason's progress toward judgment. And since human beings are rational by nature, and since free choice is the means by which we serve as sources of at least some of the contingency in nature, it may be seen that even though it is we ourselves who are the ultimate sources of that contingency, it is part of nature's plan that we should be so. Boethius's argument along that line is his closest approximation in these commentaries to a proof of indeterminism:

> Everything that is by nature is not in vain, but deliberating is something that human beings have naturally; but if necessity alone will have mastery over things, deliberation

is for no reason. But deliberation is not in vain, since it is by nature; therefore there cannot be necessity as regards all things.[55]

9. CHANCE

Some evidence that the account I have been developing of Boethius's theory is accurate so far can be found in the fact that he several times claims that absolutely everything that happens is to be explained by reference to one or another of just three actualizing agencies: natural necessitation, free choice, or chance: "chance, will, and necessity is in charge of everything".[56] But the fact that in every one of the eight or more versions of that claim Boethius explicitly mentions *chance* along with natural necessity and free choice certainly looks threatening to my promise that we ourselves would turn out to be the source of *all* contingency; and some versions of the claim may make my reductionist attitude toward the role of chance in Boethius's theory look plainly wrongheaded – for instance:

> The Peripatetics, whose leader is Aristotle, affirm with the weightiest authority as well as the clearest reasoning chance, *and* the choice of free judgment, *and* necessity in things that happen and that are done.[57]

And he says this just after having embraced them as "our own Peripatetics". Again,

> . . . it must be asserted that as regards things (or events or states of affairs) some can be by chance, some are effected by the will, and some are constrained by necessity; and a line of reasoning that undermines *any* of these is to be judged impossible.[58]

Obviously our next question must be 'What is chance?'.

The short Boethian answer to that question is that chance is any unintended outcome of an action arising from free choice:

> For when people do something by free choice, chance, *arising from the same causes*, [sometimes] intervenes on behalf of some other thing (or event or state of affairs). For example, if someone digging a trench in order to plant a vine should find a treasure, the digging of the trench did indeed arise from free choice, [but] chance alone contributed the finding of the treasure – a chance *which nevertheless has that cause which the will contributed*; for if he had not dug the trench, the treasure would not have been found.[59] . . . as often as something is done and what comes about is not that on account of which the thing that was being done was begun, that which comes about is to be thought to have come about by chance. Thus there is indeed no chance without some action . . . .[60]

Those two passages present the heart of the Boethian account of chance.

Before considering the rest of it, I want to look more closely at what we have so far.

It is already clear that Boethian chance is not an independent source of real randomness in nature; it is not a third kind of agency, alongside free choice and natural necessitation (or nature). Boethius knew an account of chance that did elevate it to such an independent status – the Epicurean theory of natural indeterminacy, based on the random swerving of the atoms – and he rejected it out of hand.[61] In fact, for Boethius 'chance' is simply a designation for one sort of outcome of free choice operating on real potentiality. If I strike a match, intending to light some candles, then insofar as I succeed in lighting them the event is correctly described as an instance of free choice; and if I inadvertently drop the match and burn the tablecloth, that event is chance.

10. THE RELATIONSHIPS OF THE THREE MODES

Perhaps we already have enough information on which to base a preliminary sketch of the relationships of the three modes of contingency with one another and with nature (or natural necessitation): *free choice* depends on *possibility* for its genuine alternatives; *possibility* depends on agency, either *free choice* or *nature*, for its actualization; *chance* depends on certain combinations of *free choice* and *nature*. The only unnecessitated actualizing agency in that picture is free choice. We ourselves are the sources, the *only* sources, of contingency.[62] And so in order to appreciate the status of chance as a mode for contingency, we need to look more closely at the operation of free choice in conjunction with natural necessitation.

11. FREE CHOICE AND NATURAL NECESSITATION

We ourselves alone are the sources of our *decisions*, but those sources flow into the main stream of necessitated nature as soon as our decisions are put into action. The event that is my decision to touch my right ear has me as its only source, but the immediately subsequent event that is my intentionally touching my right ear as a consequence of having decided to do so has nature as a tributary source; I cannot put my decision into action unless my physical apparatus continues to operate in accordance with the laws of nature. In such ordinary, humdrum cases our decisions are so easily put into action that we can easily overlook nature's contribution to the outcome, as Boethius does when he remarks that "just as having breakfast or reading and other such things stem from our will, so too do their outcomes often depend on our will".[63] But we realize that we are not omnipotent when our decisions are blocked at their source, as in Boethius's example of the Roman who foolishly decides to rule over the Persians even though he evidently has no prospects of doing any such thing: "the choice of his will is indeed up to him, but a sterner necessity holds back the outcome and prohibits it from being brought to completion".[64] And such cases of thwarted decisions are only the most flagrant reminders of the general truth that in *every* case our decisions, once sent into the flow of events either naturally necessitated or springing from the free choices of others, begin to acquire directions and to carry debris in a way that is to some extent out of our control, as Boethius recognizes:

> . . . the *will* of our actions is indeed up to us, for our will is in a way the mistress of our actions and of the whole plan of life; but their *outcome* is not also in our power in the same way.[65]

Of course our discovery that we are not omnipotent leads us to keep our intentions *vaguer* than those appropriate to omnipotence, but even so what flows from our decisions is often noticeably more or less unlike what we intended. And for all that we have seen of Boethian chance so far, 'chance' appears to be Boethius's general designation for *all* instances of a type very familiar to us, in which an action has (or associated actions have) an outcome different from the outcome consciously and rationally intended by the agent (or agents) whose free decision initiated the stream of events leading to that outcome.[66] Before considering anything else Boethius may have to say about chance in these commentaries, I want to summarize and to some extent extrapolate from as much as we now have of his theory of contingency.

12. A BOETHIAN THEORY OF CONTINGENCY

An event (or state of affairs or thing) is necessitated if and only if it is present in its causes for some time prior to its occurrence and is therefore inevitable (or theoretically predictable with certainty) for some time prior to its occurrence. A necessitated event that is present in its causes and so theoretically predictable for *all* time prior to its occurrence I will describe as necessitated *simpliciter*. An event is necessitated *simpliciter* only if it is brought about by necessitated agency (nature) alone. A necessitated event that is present in its causes and so theoretically predictable for *only some* time prior to its occurrence I will describe as necessitated *ut nunc*: as of now, or as of some given time.[67]

An event is contingent if and only if it is brought about not by nature alone but either (C1) by free agency alone or (C2) by free agency and nature together in such a way that the actual outcome either (C2a) is or (C2b) is not the one consciously and rationally intended by the agent(s) whose free choice is a contributory cause of the event. No event satisfying condition (C1) is inevitable at any time prior to its occurrence, and the only events satisfying (C1) are the decisions of free agents. Events satisfying (C2a) are instances of free choice; events satisfying (C2b) are instances of chance.

Obviously no contingent events are necessitated *simpliciter*, but since conditions (C2a) and (C2b) involve nature as well as free agency, it is reasonable to expect that all contingent events other than free decisions themselves will involve necessitation *ut nunc* in some way and to some extent. A few examples will help to illuminate the distinction between the two types of necessitation and to illustrate the involvement of necessitation in contingency.

Events necessitated *simpliciter* are all and only those that were inevitable no later than the time of the Big Bang – that is, all and only those events that could have been infallibly predicted then by someone knowing all there is to know about the potentialities of matter and the laws of nature. I assume that among such events (or states of affairs or things) are the origin and most of the natural history of the solar system and of this planet in particular, including, for instance, the migrations of the continents, the eruption of volcanoes, and the occurrence of earthquakes. So the 1883 eruption of Krakatoa is a paradigm of an event necessitated *simpliciter*.

On the other hand, the destruction of Hiroshima in the bombing of 1945 is a paradigmatic instance of free choice; President Truman made a free decision, and its outcome was what he had intended: Hiroshima was destroyed by a single bomb. Of course, a great many free decisions along the chain of command intervened between the decision of the President and the decision of the bombardier, and so until the bombardier carried out his own free decision by pushing the button, the occurrence of the outcome was not necessitated in any way. Since our paradigm of free choice is Truman's destruction of Hiroshima and not merely his issuing the order that led eventually (and contingently) to the bombing, the necessitation *ut nunc* in this instance of free choice is necessitation as of the instant when the button was pushed and the laws of nature took over. But in every instance of free choice involving overt action the laws of nature take over sooner or later, and the fact that they do so in no way compromises the status of the event as an instance of free choice. The destruction of Hiroshima was indeed present in its causes and thus inevitable, but no sooner than the instant at which the bombardier made his unnecessitated, evitable decision.

13. THE RANGE OF BOETHIAN CHANCE

Paradigms of Boethian chance are as easy to find as those I have introduced for necessitated events and free choice. Rather than introducing another paradigm, I want to consider an example of a sort that is to be classified as chance, but perhaps not obviously: the destruction of Lisbon in the earthquake of 1755. The earthquake then and there was necessitated *simpliciter*, but the destruction of a city by that event was contingent. The event (broadly conceived of) would not be known as the *Lisbon* earthquake if it had not been for the fact that one free decision after another caused a city to rise at that location before 1755. The historical event was contingent, and the geological event that was one of its contributory causes was necessitated *simpliciter*. The contingent historical event was indeed inevitable, but for a shorter time than might be supposed: obviously not in the period between the Big Bang and the time of the first settlement along the banks of the Tagus, but not even after the city had been built there, because its inhabitants could have decided to move away and succeeded in doing so. Considered as the *Lisbon* earthquake, the event was inevitable only within a temporal interval so short that laws of nature made it physically impossible for the inhabitants to leave before the occurrence of the geological event, even if they had decided to do so. The Lisbon earthquake was present in *both* its free and its naturally necessitated causes only in the last minutes before the geological event occurred. And on Boethius's theory (as I read it) the fact that none of the countless human decisions that contributed to the occurrence of the Lisbon earthquake was guided by the intention that that city be destroyed by an earthquake requires that contingent historical event to be classified as chance.

If my reading of Boethius's account of chance is accurate, obviously an enormous number of events on earth that might otherwise seem necessitated will turn out on his view of them to be contingent events – more specifically, chance events. Indeed, the prevalence of Boethian chance on this interpretation of his theory is so vast that it is hard to establish a firm outer limit for contingency; since July 1969 not even the sphere of the moon will do. And on earth an apparently ever-increasing range of what used to be locked up as natural history, apparently necessitated *simpliciter*, is set free; even such previously untouchable features as earth's climate are now to some degree contingent in virtue of being the cumulative unintended outcomes of streams of events of which we ourselves are essential tributary sources.[68]

I think the theory of contingency I have been attributing to Boethius is immeasurably more promising as an account of the basis of contingency than those that associate chance not with free choice but with randomness in nature. The fundamental insight in Boethius's theory as I see it is his recognition that we ourselves are the sources of all real contingency, and given that starting point it is only natural that for all events there should be just three classifications such as he adopts. But Boethius himself may not have sorted events into those classifications in the way I have been sorting them, because he may not always have been aware of all the implications of his own theory. I see no reason for thinking that his own view of free choice differs from the one I have been presenting, but I see two different sorts of reasons for thinking that he may have described as necessary many events I think his theory should designate as chance. The first of those reasons appears in this passage:

> One must not fail to know, however, that these are not contingents in the same way [as the paradigms he has just been discussing]: the ones that say 'Socrates will die' and 'Socrates will not die', and the ones that say 'Socrates will die tomorrow' and 'Socrates will not die tomorrow'. For the former ones are not contingent at all but are necessary, since Socrates of necessity will die. But the latter, which define the time, are not received into the number of the contingents either, for this reason: Socrates's dying tomorrow is indeed uncertain to us, but it is not uncertain to nature . . .[69]

So Boethius takes both these pairs of propositions to be presenting necessary rather than contingent states of affairs, and his reason for offering both pairs is, no doubt, that the necessary truth in the first pair is known to us while the necessary truth in the second pair is known only to nature. It seems to me, however, that by his own lights Boethius should have described both pairs as contingent. Beginning with the second pair, we can suppose that Socrates has a fatal disease such that, *other things being equal*, his death on [tomorrow's date] is inevitable. The hypothesis of the fatal disease helps Boethius's position, but not enough, as can be seen by the evident need for the *ceteris paribus* clause; for, after all, Socrates may kill himself or be killed accidentally or deliberately before he dies of the disease. And the effect of the *ceteris paribus* clause is to cancel the description of Socrates's death tomorrow as inevitable – i.e., to contradict Boethius's claim that "it is *not* uncertain to nature". But suppose that in fact neither free choice nor chance does intervene before Socrates dies of his disease tomorrow. In that case we might first ask about the nature of his disease. It could be cirrhosis of the liver, the unintended outcome of many freely chosen drinks of wine, or another disease brought on by diet or lifestyle. In that case Socrates's death tomorrow, although necessitated *ut nunc* (*ceteris paribus*), ought to count as Boethian chance. But suppose, finally, that the fatal disease Socrates dies of is a genetic defect in him. In that case, too, his dying of it ought to be classified as Boethian chance, although the free decision which constitutes a contributory cause in this case is not his but that of his parents (or at least of his father). The sexual intercourse that resulted in the conception of Socrates resulted from free decision, whether or not it was intended to produce a child. And whatever his parents' intentions may have been on that occasion, they did not intend to produce that particular individual, much less to produce him with a genetic defect that would (*ceteris paribus*) kill him on [tomorrow's date].

That discussion of Boethius's second pair of propositions shows us what is to be said about the first pair. Even though the mortality of human beings generally may be described as a naturally necessary state of affairs, the event that is the death of this particular human being is not a necessary but a contingent event – necessitated *ut nunc* from the instant of his conception, but chance nevertheless, in just the way the existence of this particular human being is not necessary but chance.

That the author of a theory should miss some of its implications is not surprising, particularly when his main concern is not with propounding his own theory but with expounding another author's text. Nor is it hard to see why Boethius should have been led to say what he says about these examples. Still, what he says here blurs the insights of his own theory.

My second reason for thinking that Boethius and I may differ about the range of Boethian chance is quite different, stemming not from what I take to be an oversight on his part but from what may have been his deliberate effort to restrict the scope of chance. I say "may have been" because I know of only one passage in his discussions of *De interpretatione* 9 where he expresses himself in this way, and what concerns me in that passage could be no more than an accident of style.

Boethius offers just two paradigms of chance – the well-known buried-treasure example we have already seen, and the case of a man's meeting his friend when he leaves his house with no intention of seeing him that day.[70] There is a feature common to those examples that I think ought to be considered inessential to Boethian chance,[71] but in the following passage Boethius may be indicating that he takes it seriously.

Therefore for the man who is doing something, and yet doing something else, a different thing has taken its place. This, therefore, is said to come about by chance: whatever comes about as a result of some action [but] not on account of the thing that was begun, whose place will have been taken by something [else] for the agent.[72]

The expressions that concern me in this passage are 'for the man who is doing something' and 'for the agent'. Since the 'for' reflects only the fact that the corresponding Latin expressions are in the dative case, they ought not to be read as 'for the benefit of . . .' (although in both paradigms the unintended outcome does happen to benefit the agent). But because those Latin expressions are nominalizations of the present participle of the verb meaning 'to do', they do seem to suggest a restriction of Boethian chance to cases like those of the paradigms in that the agent himself is surprised by the unintended outcome's occurring *while* the agent is doing what he intended to do. Such a drastic restriction is destructive of the orderly arrangement of what I take to be Boethius's theory. If, for instance, the farmer had not struck a pot of gold but had instead unknowingly cracked the dome of rock above a pool of oil which made its *ut nunc* necessitated appearance on the surface only the next day, the farmer's uncovering oil would not count as chance. And so I would reject this reading of that passage at once if it were not for the fact that I can imagine a Boethian motive for such a restriction. For it seems possible that his preoccupation with logical determinism as he encountered it in *De interpretatione* 9 might have led him to try to restrict chance to theoretically unpredictable outcomes, effectively reducing to zero the length of time during which a future-tense proposition regarding such an outcome could be said to be definitely true. If 'for the agent' does mean *while* the agent is doing what he intended to do, then chance is restricted to *immediate* unintended outcomes of intentional actions. Until the farmer thrust down his spade with just the right amount of force at just the point where the treasure lay buried, it was not known even to nature that he would find it; until the man and his friend do actually meet, no one could have predicted with certainty that their paths would cross.

Whether or not such a risky reading of a single passage reflects Boethius's own definitive, restrictive view of chance,[73] I think Boethian chance should be broader than that. The fundamental insight of his theory is that all the contingency in the world stems from free choice, and a theory of contingency with that starting point needs a category as broad as Boethian chance is in my view of it if it is not to surrender to necessity a great deal of the vast territory marked out as contingent solely in virtue of having us among its sources.[74]

NOTES

[1] The Latin texts of the commentaries are published in Migne's *Patrologia Latina*, Vol. 64, cols. 329–342 and 487–518; and in the critical edition by C. Meiser, *Boetii Commentarii in Librum Aristotelis Π ΕΡΙ ΕΡΜΗΝΙΑ Σ*, Leipzig: Teubner, 1877–1880 (2 vols.), Vol. I, pp. 103–126, and Vol. II, pp. 185–250. All my references to and quotations from Boethius's commentaries in the notes will be taken from Meiser's edition. For the definitive edition of Boethius's translation of Aristotle see L. Minio-Paluello (ed.), *Aristoteles Latinus II 1–2: De Interpretatione vel Periermenias*, Desclée de Brouwer, Bruges 1965.

[2] See also Boethius, *Consolation of Philosophy* in *Boethius. The Theological Tractates and the Consolation of Philosophy*, H. F. Stewart and E. K. Rand (eds), Harvard University Press, Cambridge Mass 1968, Bk V, esp. Prose 1 and 2; and *In Ciceronis Topica* in *Ciceronis Opera*, J. C. Orelli and G. Baiterus (eds), Zurich 1833, Bk V, chs. 15.60–17.64. I owe the latter reference to Eleonore Stump.

[3] Boethius and later medieval philosophers use '*propositio*' in a way that is closer to 'sentence' than to 'proposition' in contemporary philosophical usage; my use of 'proposition' in this paper mirrors Boethius's use of '*propositio*'.

[4] There is, of course, much more to be said about logical determinism than need be said here. For a very good discussion of logical determinism in *De interpretatione* 9 and in recent literature on it, see Gail Fine, 'Truth and Necessity in *De interpretatione* 9' (forthcoming). See also my 'Boethius and the (Indefinite) Truth About Tomorrow's Sea Battle' (forthcoming), a companion-piece to this essay.

[5] "hoc si est in omnibus adfirmationibus atque negationibus, ut una definite falsa sit, altera vera definite, quidquid vera dicit eventurum necesse est evenire, quidquid non eventurum non evenire necesse est." I, 109.9–13.

[6] Although Boethius's examples always involve indexicals rather than temporally definite expressions, it is clear that he takes them to be temporally definite. See the passage quoted on p. 40 above (and in n. 69), where he expressly says of propositions involving 'tomorrow' that they "*define* the time".

[7] Without the insertion of this phrase it might appear that Boethius associates the contingency of propositions with mere epistemic indeterminacy. As we shall see – e.g., on p. 27 above – he expressly denies such an association. The appropriateness of the wording of the inserted phrase will become clear in the light of further passages quoted from Boethius in this paper.

[8] The Latin word '*res*' means not only thing, but also event or state of affairs. I will sometimes append those other meanings in parentheses after 'thing' in my translations, as here.

[9] "contingentia autem sunt (ut supra iam diximus) quaecumque vel ad esse vel ad non esse aequaliter sese habent, et sicut ipsa indefinitum habent esse et non esse, ita quoque de his adfirmationes < et negationes > indefinitam habent veritatem vel falsitatem, cum una semper vera sit, semper altera falsa, sed quae vera quaeve falsa sit, nondum in contingentibus notum est. nam sicut quae sunt necessaria esse, in his esse definitum est, quae autem sunt inpossibilia esse, in his non esse definitum est, ita quae et possunt esse et possunt non esse, in his neque esse neque non esse est definitum, sed veritas et falsitas ex eo quod est esse rei et ex eo quod est non esse rei sumitur. nam si sit quod dicitur, verum est, si non sit quod dicitur, falsum est. igitur in contingentibus et futuris sicut

ipsum esse et non esse instabile est, esse tamen aut non esse necesse est, ita quoque in adfirmationibus <et negationibus > contingentia ipsa prodentibus veritas quidem vel falsitas in incerto est (quae enim vera sit, quae falsa secundum ipsarum propositionum naturam ignoratur), necesse est tamen unam veram esse, alteram falsam." II, 200.11–201.2. For an interpretation of Boethius's theory of indefinite truth and falsity, see my forthcoming paper cited in n.4 above.

[10] "licet necesse sit, quisquis de re aliqua vera praedixerit, rem quam ante praenuntiaverit evenire, non tamen idcirco rerum necessitas ex praedictionis veritate pendet, sed divinandi veritas ex rerum potius necessitate perpenditur. non enim idcirco esse necesse est, quoniam verum aliquid praedictum est, sed quoniam necessario erat futurum, idcirco de ea re potuit aliquid vere praedici. quod si ita est, eveniendi rei vel non eveniendi non est causa is qui praedicit futuram esse vel negat. non enim adfirmationem et negationem esse necesse est, sed idcirco ea esse necesse est quae futura sunt, quoniam in natura propria quandam habent necessitatem, in quam si quis incurrerit, verum est quod praedicit. . . . non enim propter dicentem vel negantem in rebus necessitas est, sed propter rerum necessitatem veritas in praenuntiatione vel falsitas invenitur." II, 228.3–16; 20–23.

[11] Fire: II, 187.29–188.2; 236.8–15; 237.12–13; 239.3–8; 243.13–16; snow: 236.5–8; man: I, 122.14–15; II, 187.27–29.

[12] Bodies, II, 195.15–17; water: 238.14–21.

[13] ". . . solem nunc esse in sagittario et post paucos dies in aquarium transgredi . . . necesse sit." II, 234.4–6. For the complete passage, see p. 30 above and n. 33 below. See also I, 105.25–26; II, 200.1–9; 241.3–7; 244.22–245.3. As Carol Kaske pointed out to me, Capricorn occurs between Sagittarius and Aquarius. Either Boethius's knowledge of the zodiac is sketchy, as mine is, or he intends '*post paucos dies*' to be interpreted very generously.

[14] "nec si letale signum in aegrotantis facie medicina deprehendit, ut aliud esse non possit nisi ille moriatur, nobis autem ignotum sit propter artis inperitiam, idcirco illum aegrum esse moriturum utrumlibet et contingentis naturae esse iudicandum est, sed illa sola tanta sine dubio esse putanda sunt, quaecumque idcirco nobis ignota sunt, quod per propriam naturam qualem habeant eventum sciri non possunt . . ." II, 193.10–18.

[15] See his approving remarks regarding Alexander's view on this point, II, 219.29–220.8; see also II, 244.25–245.3.

[16] "hoc enim in natura fuit antea, sed nobis hoc rei ipsius patefecit eventus. quare si omnia quaecumque evenerunt sunt et ea quae sunt futura esse praedici potuerunt, necesse est omnia quae dicuntur aut definite vera esse aut definite falsa, quoniam definitum eorum eventus secundum praesens tempus est." II, 210.2–8.

[17] "nam etiam si in his non sit manifesta veritatis natura, nil tamen prohibet fixam esse necessitatis in natura constantiam. . ." II, 187.9–11.

[18] "et hoc per suam naturam, non ad nostram ignorantiam atque notitiam." II, 208.17–18. See also II, 193.6–8; 245.24–28.

[19] "hoc autem non quod audientes de futuro nesciamus, sed quod eadem res et esse possit et non esse." II, 245.19–21. See also II, 187.20–24; 192.5–9; 193.6–21; 194.17–195.2; 245.10–12.

[20] There are passages that read as if he takes every singular future-tense proposition to be contingent – e.g., I, 106.5–8; 107.22; 108.24–25; II, 189.23–190.1 – but the many passages in which he expressly recognizes non-contingent, naturally necessary

propositions of that form show that these must simply be imprecisely expressed.
[21] "ergo qui dicit, quoniam erit aliquid eorum quae contingenter eveniunt, in eo quod futurum esse dicit id quod contingenter evenit fortasse mentitur; vel si contigerit res illa quam praedicit, ille tamen mentitus est; non enim eventus falsus est, sed modus praedictionis, namque ita oportuit dicere: cras bellum navale contingenter eveniet, hoc est dicere: ita evenit, si evenerit, ut potuerit non evenire. qui ita dicit verum dicit, eventum enim contingenter praedixit. qui autem ita infit: cras bellum erit navale, quasi necesse sit, ita pronuntiat." II, 212.8–18. For a further discussion of the significance of this passage in Boethius's response to logical determinism, see my forthcoming paper cited in n. 4 above.
[22] "sin vero res contingenter venientes atque abeuntes, quae illas prodit contingens propositio nuncupatur." II, 188.25–27.
[23] "haec enim ita constituta in rebus putat, ut non de his ulla opus sit demonstratione, sed inpossibilis ratio iudicetur, quaecumque vel possibile vel casum vel id quod in nobis est conatur evertere." II, 219.5–9.
[24] "non exponat nunc, quid sit casus quidve possibile quidve in nobis..." II, 218. 27–28.
[25] I, 110.24–27; 111.21–22; II, 190.1–6; 192.27–193.1; 203.2–13; 203.17–20; 204.6–7; 204.11; 204.19–21; 207.17–18; 209.2–4; 211.20–26; 217.14–15; 218.25–219.9; 220.17–19; 229.16–18; 240.4–5; 240.6–7; 240.21–22.
[26] "contingens autem secundum Aristotelicam sententiam est, quodcumque aut casum fert aut ex libero cuiuslibet arbitrio et propria voluntate venit aut facilitate naturae in utramque partem redire possibile est, ut fiat scilicet et non fiat." II, 190.1–6.
[27] "tres supra modos proposuimus contingentis..." II, 190.12–13.
[28] "inpossibile quiddam ex hac positione continget. eveniet namque omnia quaecumque sunt vel fiunt ex necessitate fieri et nihil a casu nihilque esse possibile quod sit et non esse possibile. nihil etiam in liberi arbitrii moderamine relinqueretur..." I, 110.23–27.
[29] "sed illae sunt proprie contingentes, quae neque in natura sunt neque in necessitate, sed aut in casu aut in libero arbitrio aut in possibilitate naturae..." II, 203.2–5.
[30] Sometimes Boethius associates the entire division into three modes with *utrumlibet* rather than with contingency – e.g., II, 192.27–193.4; 204.17–22; 211.17–21; 240.6–7. '*Utrumlibet*' is the word Boethius uses in his translation of *De interpretatione* 9 for Aristotle's "*hopoter' etuchen*" (e.g., at 18b6, 7, 8–9); William of Moerbeke uses '*quodcumque contingit*' in his thirteenth-century translation (see Minio-Paluello, 1965 [n. 1 above], p. 47). When Boethius uses '*utrumlibet*' broadly, as his word for whatever is contingent, he seems careful to associate that usage with Aristotle particularly, even claiming at one point that Aristotle explained "what the nature of the contingent is when he explained what is *utrumlibet*" ("Exponit enim quae sit contingentis natura, cum quid sit utrumlibet exposuit." I, 112.22–23). It is only proper for Boethius the conscientious commentator to speak of *utrumlibet* rather than of contingency when expounding Aristotle directly; after all, Boethius found no place in his translation of Chapter 9 at which to use the Latin words '*contingentia*' or '*contingens*'. But it strikes me as peculiar that he should present Aristotle as dividing *utrumlibet* into possibility, free choice, and chance. Aristotle does not mention free choice explicitly in the chapter at all, and at 18b5–6 and 15–16 he speaks of *utrumlibet* and chance in ways that suggest he was *not* thinking of chance as a mode of *utrumlibet*. My reason for pointing out that Boethius has a broad use for '*utrumlibet*' which he associates with Aristotle

is that I think he uses '*utrumlibet*' more narrowly in his own theory of contingency, as the next three quoted passages will show.

[31] "et hanc eveniendi vel non eveniendi possibilitatem utrumlibet vocamus. in huiusmodi enim rebus utrumlibet contingit, . . . quare haec huiusmodi eveniendi et non eveniendi potentia utrumlibet vocatur, quod in his utrumlibet . . . evenire conceditur." I, 106. 13–15; 20–23.

[32] "Casus namque et id quod est utrumlibet exstinguitur, libera etiam voluntas adimitur, si omnia quaecumque fient ex necessitate futura sunt." I, 112.9–11. In this passage, however, he is echoing Aristotle at 18b5–6, which he translates as "Nihil igitur neque est neque fit nec a casu nec utrumlibet . . .". The explicit inclusion of free will is his own contribution.

[33] "aliter enim dicitur possibile me esse ambulare cum sedeam, aliter solem nunc esse in sagittario et post paucos dies in aquarium transgredi. ita enim possibile est ut etiam necesse sit." II, 234.3–6.

[34] "sed quamquam quod necessarium est possibile sit, est tamen alia quaedam extrinsecus possibilitatis natura, quae et ab inpossibili et a necessitate seiuncta sit." II, 236. 1–4.

[35] "alioquin divinis corporibus nihil omnino est potestate, sed omne actu: ut soli numquam est lumen potestate, cui quidem nulla obscuritas, vel toto caelo nulla quies." II, 238.22–25.

[36] This use of 'intrinsic' is merely a terminological suggestion on my part, based on Boethius's use of "*quaedam extrinsecus possibilitatis natura*" (n. 34 above). I have not seen Boethius using the parallel adverb '*intrinsecus*' in this connection.

[37] See the discussion at II, 236.5–238.1.

[38] "fit quidem frequentius ut canescat, non tamen interclusum est, ut non canescat." II, 188.12–14. This is Boethius's paradigm of Aristotle's for-the-most-part contingencies. Leaving aside Aristotle's understanding of such cases, Boethius's presentation of them suggests that he may have been uncertain of their status. From my own point of view he puts the case best at I, 121.5–6: "turning grey [happens] in more sixty-year-old men than not turning grey" (*canescere in pluribus sexagenariis quam non canescere*). But he is also capable of putting it in this misleading way: "whoever would say that a man turns grey in old age and claim that this is of necessity would say what is false, for he can also not turn grey" (*quicumque dixerit hominem in senecta canescere et hoc ex necessitate esse protulerit mentietur, potest enim et non canescere*); II, 248.20–22. See also II, 192.19–21; 240.17–21.

[39] "lignum hoc potest quidem secari, sed nihil tamen minus habet ad contraria cognationem, potest enim non secari . . ." II, 236.22–24. Boethius discusses Aristotle's similar example of the cloak at II, 237.21–238.1 and at II, 190.24–191.2, where it serves as the paradigm of *utrumlibet* possibility.

[40] "ut hunc calamum frangi quidem possible est, <sed> etiam non frangi, et hoc non ad nostram possibilitatem referunt, sed ad ipsius rei naturam." II. 197.20–23.

[41] "facilitate naturae in utramque partem redire possibile est, ut fiat scilicet et non fiat." II, 190.4–6. See also II, 233.26–234.1: "possibile esse dicitur quod in utramque partem facile naturae suae ratione vertatur, ut et cum non sit possibile sit esse nec cum sit ut non sit res ulla prohibeat."

[42] Reading '*potestate*' for '*possibilitate*'.

[43] "alia quidem potestate sunt, alia actu: ut aqua calida quidem est possibilitate, potest

enim fieri calida, frigida vero actu est, est enim frigida. hoc autem actu et potestate ex materia venit. nam cum sit materia contrarietatis susceptrix et ipsa in se utriusque contrarietatis habeat cognationem, si ipsa per se cogitetur, nihil eorum habet quae in se suscipit et ipsa quidem nihil actu est, omnia tamen potestate. . . . ergo quod potestate est in rebus ex materia venit." II, 238.6–13; 21–22. Boethius's recognition of permanently unactualized real potentialities seems clear in his discussions of the examples of the wood, the reed, and the cloak; and it may be brought out even more clearly in some of his examples of free choice as at II, 207.20–23; 235.22–26.

[44] "ita sese ergo habent ex materia, ut omnia ipsa essent potestate, nihil autem actu, arbitratu naturae, quae in ipsa materia singulos pro ratione distribuit motus et singulas qualitatum proprietates singulis materiae partibus ponit, ut alias quidem natura ipsa necessarias ordinarit, ita ut quamdiu res illa esset eius in ipsa proprietas permaneret, ut igni calorem. nam quamdiu ignis est, tamdiu ignem calidum esse necesse est. aliis vero tales qualitates adposuit, quibus carere possint. et illa quidem necessaria qualitas informat uniuscuiusque substantiam. illa enim eius qualitas cum ipsa materia ex natura coniuncta est. istae vero aliae qualitates extra sunt, quae et admitti possunt et non admitti. . . . ex natura igitur et ex materia ista in rebus possibilitas venit." II, 239.14–15; 20–24.

[45] "[possibilitas] qua in re casus quoque aliquando subrepit . . . ex hac autem possibilitate etiam illa liberi arbitrii ratio venit. si enim non esset fieri aliquid possibile, sed omnia aut ex necessitate essent aut ex necessitate non essent, liberum arbitrium non maneret." II, 239.14–15; 20–24.

[46] "illud enim in nobis est liberum arbitrium, quod sit omni necessitate vacuum et ingenuum et suae potestatis, quorundamque nos domini quodammodo sumus vel faciendi vel non faciendi." II, 218.8–12.

[47] "videmus enim quasdam res ex principio liberi arbitrii et ex nostrorum actuum fonte descendere . . ." II, 230.4–6.

[48] "*cras Socrates disputaturus est in palaestra* contingens est, quod hoc ex libero venit arbitrio." II, 203.11–13.

[49] "et illud enim et illud poterit evenire. hoc autem idcirco est quoniam non est ex antiquioribus quibusdam causis pendens rerum eventus, ut quaedam quodammodo necessitatis catena sit, sed potius haec ex nostro arbitrio et libera voluntate sunt, in quibus est nulla necessitas." II, 246.14–19.

[50] "id quod fit ex nobis et ex nostro iudicio principium sumat nullo extrinsecus . . ." II, 195.8–9.

[51] "atque ideo quarundam actionum nos ipsi principia, non sequaces sumus." II, 196.24–25. For the context, see pp. 17–18 and n. 54 below. Some version of this principle is found also at I, 120.2–6; 19–21; 121.9–10; II, 230.4–6; 231.5–8; 232.11–13; 233.19–20.

[52] For an excellent, well-known contemporary statement of the theory of agent causation, see R. M. Chisholm, 'Freedom and Action,' in *Freedom and Determinism*, K. Lehrer (ed.), Random House, New York 1966, pp. 11–44.

[53] I have found references to God or gods at only five places, all in the second commentary, but I have not made a point of looking for them. All those references are casual, none of them intrinsic to the theory of contingency Boethius is developing. There are also about ten references to fate or providence, but they too have no part to play in the theory.

[54] "nos autem liberum voluntatis arbitrium non id dicimus quod quisque voluerit, sed quod quisque iudicio et examinatione collegerit. . . . si velle aliquid vel nolle hoc recte liberi arbitrii vocabulo teneretur, non solum hoc esset hominum, sed ceterorum quoque animalium . . . sed est liberum arbitrium, quod ipsa quoque vocabula produnt, liberum nobis de voluntate iudicium. quotienscumque enim imaginationes quaedam concurrunt animo et voluntatem irritant, eas ratio perpendit et de his iudicat, et quod ei melius videtur, cum arbitrio perpenderit et iudicatione collegerit, facit. atque ideo quaedam dulcia et speciem utilitatis monstrantia spernimus, quaedam amara licet nolentes tamen fortiter sustinemus: adeo non in voluntate, sed in iudicatione voluntatis liberum constat arbitrium et non in imaginatione, sed in ipsius imaginationis perpensione consistit. atque ideo quarundam actionum nos ipsi principia, non sequaces sumus. hoc est enim uti ratione uti iudicatione . . . sola ratione disiungimur." II, 196.4–6; 9–11; 13–26; 27–28.

[55] "omne quod natura est non frustra est; consiliari autem homines naturaliter habeat; quod si necessitas in rebus sola dominabitur, sine causa est consiliatio; sed consiliatio non frustra est, natura enim est; non igitur potest in rebus cuncta necessitas." II, 220. 10–15. On deliberation and the principle *nos ipsi principia sumus* see also I, 120.2–6; 19–21.

[56] "omnium rerum et casus et voluntas et necessitas dominatur . . ." II, 224.17–18. See also II, 197.5–10; 223.12–22; 230.20–26; 239.14–20. The similar passage at II, 240.2–5 strikes me as confused because it treats *possibility* as on a par with necessity, chance, and free choice.

[57] "Peripatetici enim, quorum Aristoteles princeps est, et casum et liberi arbitrium iudicii et necessitatem in rebus quae fiunt quaeque aguntur cum gravissima auctoritate tum apertissima ratione confirmant." II, 193.26–194.2.

[58] "ponendum in rebus est casu quaedam posse et voluntate effici et necessitate constringi et ratio, quae utrumvis horum subruit, inpossibilis iudicanda est." II, 226.22–25.

[59] "pro alia namque re aliquid ex libero arbitrio facientibus ex isdem veniens causis casus interstrepit. ut [cum] scrobem deponens quis, ut infodiat vitem, si thesaurum inveniat, scrobem quidem deponere ex libero venit arbitrio, invenire thesaurum solus atulit casus, eam tamen causam habens casus, quam voluntas attulit. nisi enim foderet scrobem, thesaurus non esset inventus." II, 224.2–9. See also II, 194.8–13. (Cf. *The Consolation of Philosophy* V, 1)

[60] "quotiens aliquid agitur et non id evenit, propter quod res illa coepta est quae agebatur, id quod evenit ex casu evenisse putandum est, ut casus quidem non sine aliqua actione sit . . ." II, 194.3–6.

[61] II, 239.24–25.

[62] I have not yet tried to find this theory of the basis of contingency in later medieval philosophers, but I can offer this passage from Ockham as an interesting preliminary sample: "nothing of which the Philosopher speaks here [*De int.* 9, 19a39–19b4] is fortuitously (*utrumlibet*) contingent except what is in the power of someone acting freely or what depends on such an agent. Therefore in pure natural things – i.e., in animate things only the sensitive soul, and in [all] inanimate things – there is no contingency, nor any chance or fortune, unless they depend in some way on a free agent. In all the other things of which the Philosopher speaks here, however, there is inevitability and necessity." The passage is from Ockham's commentary on *De interpretatione* as translated (in part) in Appendix II of M. M. Adams and N. Kretzmann, *William*

Ockham: Predestination, God's Foreknowledge, and Future Contingents, Appleton –Century-Crofts, New York 1969; second, revised edition published in 1983 by William Hackett Publishing Company of Indianapolis), p. 106.

63 "prandere enim vel legere et alia huiusmodi sicut ex nostra voluntate sunt, ita quoque eorum saepe ex nostra voluntate pendet eventus." II, 224.11–13.

64 "quod si nunc imperare Persis velit Romanus, arbitrium quidem voluntatis in ipso est, sed hunc eventum durior necessitas retinet et ad perfectionem vetat adduci." II, 224.13–16.

65 "et actuum quidem nostrorum voluntas in nobis est. nostra enim voluntas domina quodammodo est nostrorum actuum et totius vitae rationis, sed non eodem modo eventus quoque in nostra est potestate." II, 223.22–224.1.

66 The modifiers 'consciously and rationally' have no counterparts in Boethius's discussion. I have introduced them as perhaps overly economical means of turning aside troublesome examples of a sort presented to me by Newton Garver, Carl Ginet, Christopher Hughes, and Allen Wood. In my view the most troublesome of these is Allen Wood's example of the gambler who intends to roll a seven on the dice and does so. Must that event be classified as free choice by Boethian criteria? I am inclined to say that although the gambler *wants* to roll a seven, it is only out of ignorance that he or we can say that he *intends* to do so. But modifying 'intends' with 'rationally' seems a more cautious and no less effective antidote.

67 I am grateful to Eleonore Stump for suggesting this way of drawing the distinction. The *ut nunc/simpliciter* terminology is familiar in connection with the classification of inferences in the theory of consequences, on which see E. Stump, 'Topics: Their Development and Absorption into Consequences' and I. Boh, 'Consequences', Chapters 14 and 15 respectively in *The Cambridge History of Later Medieval Philosophy*, N. Kretzmann *et al.* (eds.), Cambridge University Press, Cambridge 1982.

68 Richard Sorabji drew on his own thorough study of the Aristotelian background of the issues addressed in this paper in order to provide me with extensive, learned comments designed to show, among other things, that if my account of Boethius's theory of contingency is correct, then Boethius is going considerably beyond the Peripatetic tradition according to which we are the source not of all *contingency* but merely of all *chance*, chance being a carefully defined and very restricted subdivision of the contingent. I am very grateful to Professor Sorabji, I think that he is right about that implication of my account, and of course I think my account is correct. I have not, however, seen any evidence that Boethius was *aware* that he had made such a radical (and in my view promising) departure from the tradition.

69 "non autem oportet ignorare non esse similiter contingentes has quae dicunt *Socrates morietur* et *Socrates non morietur* et illas quae dicunt *Socrates cras morietur, Socrates cras non morietur*. illae enim superiores omnino contingentes non sunt, sed sunt necessariae (morietur enim Socrates ex necessitate), hae vero quae tempus definiunt nec ipsae in numerum contingentium recipiuntur, idcirco quod nobis quidem cras moriturum esse Socratem incertum est, naturae autem incertum non est . . ." II, 202.21–203.1.

70 II, 203.5–7; 190.14–19; 191.12–18, 192.9–12; cf. I, 120.28–29.

71 Actually there are three such features: the one that concerns me, the one I dismiss in a parenthesis near the top of p. 42 above, and the fact that in both these examples the chance occurrence is a consequence of the interaction of *two* free choices. I pay no attention to the third because I assume that even Boethius would have accepted it as a

case of chance if the vine-planting farmer had struck a vein of gold rather than a treasure someone else had deliberately buried.

72 "ergo agenti aliquid homini, aliud tamen agenti res diversa successit. hoc igitur ex casu evenire dicitur, quodcumque per quamlibet actionem evenit non propter eam rem coeptam, quae aliquid agenti successerit." II, 194.13–17.

73 It should be compared especially with *The Consolation of Philosophy* V, 1, where some of these difficulties do not appear (although others take their place).

74 I am grateful to Newton Garver, Carl Ginet, Christopher Hughes, and Allen Wood for thought-provoking questions about Boethian chance, and to Terry Irwin for an illuminating discussion of II, 194.13–17. I am grateful also to Gail Fine, Carl Ginet, and Robert Stalnaker for helpful comments on an earlier draft, and especially to Eleonore Stump, who pointed out several shortcomings for which she generously suggested remedies.

PART TWO

ISLAMIC PERSPECTIVES

CHAPTER 3

WRONGDOING AND DIVINE OMNIPOTENCE IN THE THEOLOGY OF ABŪ ISḤĀQ AN-NAẒẒĀM

Josef van Ess

1. INTRODUCTION: THE FRAGMENTARY NATURE OF MU'TAZILĪ WRITINGS

The history of Islamic theology during the second and third centuries of the Muslim era (8.–9. century AD) is primarily a history of the Mu'tazila. The name of Abū Isḥāq an-Naẓẓām (died ca. 221/836) can then not go unmentioned; he was one of the principal thinkers of this intellectual movement. This does not mean that in all we hear about him he represents the accepted opinion of his school. On the contrary: the information we get is concerned in large part with his "deviations", that is, those idiosyncrasies characteristic of him and him alone. There are two explanations for the character of this information.

The early Mu'tazilīs were individual thinkers who liked to experiment – not only with divergent ideas but also with contrasting vocabularies and with new systematical structures; never again has Islam known such an openness for original, though sometimes untenable positions. Second – or rather first, for this is the point where we start – we have to take into consideration the character of our sources. They are mostly of a doxographical or polemic nature; they stress certain points and forget about others or take them for granted. They want to show where a certain theologian differed from his colleagues or where he went wrong, but they do not necessarily lead us to the nerve of his system. They shed light on the eccentric fringe, but they give us almost no texts which deal with the center of his thought or which let him speak for himself. And in any case, what we have are only fragments; we are usually not told how they fit together. We may reconstruct systematic coherence, but we must be aware of the fact that our reconstructions are hypothetical. We cannot even be sure that there was any "system" at all – in the sense that a certain *mutakallim* always and necessarily proceeded from an overall concept and not just reacted against isolated attacks by making isolated statements which perhaps roughly corresponded to his basic axioms but were not planned in advance. We are dealing, after all, with

T. Rudavsky (ed.), Divine Omniscience and Omnipotence in Medieval Philosophy, 53–67.

dialectical theologians for whom being proven right was at least as important as the objective truth.

With no one among these early thinkers are we in a better position than with an-Naẓẓām. We have a lot of material in which we not only get statements but also reasons. But even here we lack any coherent account; an-Naẓẓām's reasons are hidden in a jungle of argument and counterargument, evasive justifications and willful distortions presented in dialectical debates which were summarized and as a result frequently distorted again. We have thus to invest a lot of philology and exegesis before we can come to any conclusions. A work like this is not the place to expound these philological or exegetical preliminaries; I must restrict myself to the conclusions. Unfortunately, philology and exegesis are sometimes the main thing; the conclusions then look rather normal and are not exciting at all. What we are able to reconstruct is, even under the relatively favorable circumstances described, only a bare skeleton. And the time for broad comparisons has not yet come.

2. THE LIMITS OF DIVINE OMNIPOTENCE ACCORDING TO AN-NAẒẒĀM

an-Naẓẓām is known by the doxographers as the Mu'tazilī theologian who believed that God not only does not do evil but is also not able to do it.[1] A similar position had already been held by Origen in his *Contra Celsum*: "We say that God *is unable* to do evil; otherwise He would be able not to be God. For if God *does* anything evil He is not God."[2] Origen's argument gets its rhetorical persuasiveness from the fact that the last sentence is a quotation from Euripides.[3] This also explains why he moves so easily from denying God's capacity of performing evil to denying his actually doing so.

The Mu'tazilīs, on the contrary, soon clearly stressed the difference between these two positions. Certainly, said an-Naẓẓām's colleague and contemporary al-Murdār, God will never *do* evil because this would contradict the perfection of his nature, but this does not mean that he does not always remain *able* to do it; otherwise we would unduly curtail his omnipotence. Since God's capacity is without limits, it also encompasses evil. We must avoid only one thing, namely envisaging, just for the pleasure of intellectual experimentation, the possibility that he might ever really act this way. This would be as indelicate as if we were to speculate about the possibility of fornication on the part of a person like the first caliph Abū Bakr who, as the closest confidant of the Prophet, commands our common respect.[4] We are dealing with a problem of taste rather than of principle; in principle,

God remains "powerful over everything", as says the Koran in so many places. This was the attitude of the majority. The Baṣrian theologians of the fourth and fifth century A.H. (10.–11. century AD), who became so important for the final scholastic formulation of Mu'tazilī doctrine, only denied, as had done al-Murdār, God's actual volition, not his capacity.[5] In the long run, an-Naẓẓām's doctrine did not have much of a chance.

As usual, the structure of his reasoning is known to us in its rough outline, but not in its original form and coherence. We have to rely upon the remarks of certain opponents summarized by a critic of the Mu'tazila about one generation after an-Naẓẓām's death, a man by the name of Ibn ar-Rēwandī[6], and upon the defense of his ideas by the Mu'tazilī doxographer al-Khayyāṭ who is usually well informed.[7] From these testimonies we are able to infer the following argumentation[8]: God performs, says an-Naẓẓām, his actions merely for their own sake, that is, for their internal value. This, however, is thinkable only with respect to equitable and good actions; it would be absurd with regard to unjust and evil ones. For we may do justice for the sake of its being good, but we never do injustice for the sake of its being bad. If somebody performs injustice he does so for two other reasons: he either follows (1) a personal need (*ḥāja*) insofar as he tries to reap profit or to avert personal harm, or (2) he does not know what he is doing or what kind of heavy, possibly eternal punishment is awaiting him. This cannot be said of God: he does not have any need, nor is he, of course, ignorant of what he is doing.

What is characteristic about this theory is that it centers around God's activity, not his essence. In Islamic theology, God is not ψύσει ἀγαθός; this idea is only found in philosophical works influenced by Neoplatonic thought, like the *Liber de Causis* (which was called in Arabic *Kitāb al-Īḍāḥ fī l-khayr al-maḥḍ, Liber de expositione bonitatis purae*). For the Mu'tazilīs, as well as for all other Muslim theologians, God was not "good" but merely *muḥsin* "doing what is good". God's relation towards injustice was normally discussed together with the question whether he is able to "lie," to make a false statement; accordingly it was put, right from the beginning, into the context of his acting and dealing with his creation – or, to use a distinction invented by the Mu'tazilites themselves, into the realm of his "predicates of action" (*ṣifāt al-fi'l*) instead of his "predicates of essence" (*ṣifāt adh-dhāt*). an-Naẓẓām believed that there are actions that are ethically good or bad in themselves[9], and he seems to have thought that those which are bad in themselves form a separate class (*jins*) which cannot be the object of God's choice, neither his choice to perform them nor even his choice not to perform them.[10] God only performs the good, and he chooses it for its own sake.

But, asked an-Naẓẓām's opponents, is this really true? First, does it ever happen that somebody performs justice for its own sake? Yes, answered an-Naẓẓām. Even man, who as a matter of fact always thinks about his profit or harm, is nevertheless aware of the fact that justice is good in itself and lets himself be instigated by this insight. God, however, is beyond all deficiencies and does not calculate any profit at all. Second, continued his opponents, is it not true that if God knows what he is doing and if he does not perform justice for an immediate profit, he should have performed it from eternity onward? For his knowledge is eternal, and justice has been equally good for its own sake from eternity onward; only immediate profit would have bound it to a specific moment. Yet it must be bound to specific moments, for justice realizes itself, as we saw, in action, and action is only possible if there is an object. The object of God's justice, however, namely man and the world he is living in, did not exist from eternity onward. Thus, God cannot perform justice for its own sake alone. an-Naẓẓām pointed out, in reply, that God uses his justice in free decision, and free decision implies free choice of the moment. It seems that he explained this by focussing upon the difference mentioned above between predicates of action and predicates of essence:[11] knowledge is an essential predicate of God and as such an eternal attribute, whereas justice, as a predicate of action, is not eternal and therefore is only realized when God wants to realize it. But then it is realized for the sake of justice itself.

In concentrating upon justice instead of injustice, neither argument seems to address the point with which we started. For what was regarded as decisive in an-Naẓẓām's doctrine were the conclusions he drew concerning God's relationship towards injustice, and in this respect those Baṣrian theologians who later on believed that God *is* able to do injustice but will never do it tended to use the same argument he had used: "it is established that God *knows* that evil is evil and that He has no *need* of it. And anyone in this condition does not choose evil at all."[12] Similarly, an-Naẓẓām's observation that God's knowledge of an event does not imply its immediate realization was not at all characteristic to his approach alone; rather, it had been almost a commonplace of Mu'tazilī theology from the very first. We get the impression that, in the beginning, the discussion turned around an-Naẓẓām's theory as a whole and that, as far as injustice was concerned, an-Naẓẓām, while successfully refuting his opponents, did not yet see that his argumentation was valid for their position as well as his own. He seems to have been the first to develop the way of reasoning we mentioned, and in spite of the opposition he encountered right from the beginning, his basic assumption was in the long run accepted by his adherents and opponents alike. To put it in somewhat simpler terms, this assumption is that just as there are two possible reasons for wrongdoing, namely egotism or ignorance, there are also two possible reasons for well-doing, namely egotism or knowledge, and if action results from knowledge, then well-doing comes about for its own sake. The conflict between the majority of the Mu'tazila who only denied God's volition of evil, and an-Naẓẓām who denied his capacity for evil as well can obviously not only be explained from this side.

3. OPPOSITION TO AN-NAẒẒĀM'S THEORY

There was, as a matter of fact, another dimension to this discussion. Up to now, we proceeded from the assumption that the opposition against an-Naẓẓām arose within the Mu'tazila itself. There are good reasons for that, but this is not exactly the way our source describes the situation. There, his opponents remain unidentified, and what is more interesting: from time to time non-Mu'tazilī adversaries turn up, people who did not even belong to the Muslim community at all. The Dayṣānīya,[13] for example, were a group of dualists who took their name, although apparently not all their doctrine, from Bardesanes, the famous Christian gnostic who had died at Edessa six centuries before, in 222 A.D.; whereas the Manicheans[14] started from a similar dualist approach and varied from the Dayṣānīya, as far as the relationship between good and evil was concerned, only in certain minor, though characteristic details. Both denominations had gained some influence in Iraq after Zoroastrian predominance had collapsed with the arrival of Islam, and both had obviously become partners and dangerous competitors to the Muslim intellectuals who conversed with them in the newly founded capital of Baghdad (and had perhaps already done so in older centers of learning like Basra). We know that an-Naẓẓām attacked them, but he also learned a lot from their world-view and their way of combining theology, i.e., dualist theology, with physics and cosmology. However, the arguments raised against his theory of divine justice which we mentioned before do not seem to have been formulated by them; for one of these proofs (the last one mentioned) presupposed that justice is not eternal insofar as it only comes into existence with its object, namely man, and this is a Mu'tazilī rather than a dualist axiom. The pieces on the dialectical chessboard were obviously distributed in a slightly more complex way. It is true that those who formulated the arguments against an-Naẓẓām were members of his own school, i.e., Mu'tazilites[15], but in order to lend greater strength to their refutation they maliciously pointed out the parallels between his system and that of those dualists he had tried to refute himself. They were certainly right insofar as he could not have developed his ideas without taking the dualist approach into account.

This can be best demonstrated in the case of the Manicheans, for an-Naẓẓām tried to refute them with a proof very similar to the one he had used in order to support his own system. The Manicheans assumed that Light and Darkness, the two eternal principles of Good and Evil, are first separated and then mix with each other; the result of this mixture is the sublunar world. But, asked an-Naẓẓām, why do they mix? If they are separated by their own nature they can never mix except by losing their nature. If they mix by a decision of their own, how can we be sure that Light does not decide *against* the Good, or Darkness *against* the Evil?[16] Now, admittedly, God as conceived by an-Naẓẓām also chooses the good and justice out of his own free decision. So, asked an-Naẓẓām's Muslim opponents, why should it not be possible that Allah, too, is able to choose evil, for the same reason an-Naẓẓām had used against the Manicheans?

This is where an-Naẓẓām introduced, as a distinction, an idea with which we are already familiar:

> I notice that wrongdoing only proceeds either from somebody who is instigated to do it by a defect (*āfa*) or a need, or from somebody who does not know it (to be wrongdoing). Ignorance and need, however, point to the fact that he to whom these (features) are attributed is contingent; God is exalted far above that. What assures me that God does not do anything evil is the fact that these things which point to the contingency of him to whom they are attributed cannot be predicated of God. The Manicheans, on the contrary, are not able to argue as I do, for they claim that Light obtains profit and averts harm, that it is liable to defects and overwhelmed by Darkness to such an extent that it becomes ignorant of everything. Since this is the case they are not able to prove that evil and wrongdoing cannot proceed from it. This, if they claim (at all) that Light possesses capacity of decision . . .[17]

The conclusive difference between Light in Manicheism and God in Islam has thus to be seen in the fact that God does the good for the sake of itself whereas Light does it in order to avert a nuisance, namely to be overwhelmed by Darkness. And whoever does not do the good for its own sake is able to decide on the side of evil. Thus, only God, i.e., God as conceived by an-Naẓẓām, cannot do evil; Light can – in spite of what the Manicheans used to say. an-Naẓẓām tries to outdo the Manicheans; this explains the rigor of his own position.

The Dayṣānīya had to be treated differently. They assumed that Light touches Darkness right from the beginning; there is no initial separation.[18]

Nevertheless, they agreed with Manicheism that the struggle between the two elements, "mixture" in their terminology, starts later, in time. But, says an-Naẓẓām, this eternal contact with Darkness is a defect which, according to their mythology, can only be mended by "mixture". Mixture certainly is a long and painful process, but it is an intermediary stage which as such is inevitable, and it would be wise to start it as early as possible. So why does Light postpone its attack? The Dayṣānīs pretend that Light is wise; wisdom is one of its eternal attributes. But then it should have put this attribute into action from eternity onward.[19] The argument fails to appreciate the mythological character of Dayṣānī thought, but logically it is quite valid; it is a good example of Islamic rationalism. an-Naẓẓām's Muslim opponents, however, for whom the Dayṣānīs had probably already ceased to be a living reality, quelled their admiration and rather drew attention to a dangerous parallel between the heretics and their victor. Inasmuch as the time-lag between Light's wisdom and its decision to mix with Darkness is like the time-lag between God's knowledge and his decision to apply justice, why then did an-Naẓẓām not draw the same consequence for his own system?[20] We do not known an-Naẓẓām's answer, but we may be sure that he found one, probably on the line of what his defender al-Khayyāṭ said: God possesses free will whereas the two elements of the Dayṣānīya are forces of nature. Or: God may well be as determined in his eternal knowledge as Light is in its eternal wisdom, but justice is a predicate of Divine action, and God is free to act whenever he wants.[21] The Dualists did not have such a distinction. an-Naẓẓām's Muslim opponents may then have felt that he simply failed to take the last step: if God is free to act, why should he not be free to do evil? What still seemed stringent and logically necessary in the refutation of the Manicheans here appeared, in the refutation of the Dayṣānīs, as a final residue of dualist determinism. If God cannot do evil, says a later – and malevolent – heresiographer with respect to an-Naẓẓām's position, he acts like a force of nature.[22]

Once one had arrived at this point it was easy to saddle an-Naẓẓām with further absurdities. If God cannot but do justice, why should he be praised for it?[23] And if he cannot do evil, whatever he does should be good for those who are affected by his actions; so he is obliged to grant the inhabitants of Paradise eternal bliss instead of making them die in the end, for bliss is better for them than death. The fact that Paradise lasts eternally, beyond the mere retribution for works of obedience on earth, would thus not be a token of Divine favor and grace, but a "must" grounded in God's nature.[24] The argument was not as bizarre and farfetched as it looks. It alludes to the doctrine of an early Muslim theologian, Jahm b. Ṣafwān who had pretended that Paradise and Hell, like creation altogether, are a mere interlude in God's eternal existence; in the end he will again be the Only and the One he was in the beginning.[25] Compared with this position, an-Naẓẓām not only seemed to say that this *will* not be the case as all Muslim theologians used to hold against Jahm, but also that it *cannot* be the case.

Both objections show the difference of perspective between an-Naẓẓām and his opponents. The opposition started from God's nature and then stated a certain limitation of his omnipotence – a subjective perspective, as it were. an-Naẓẓām concentrated on the object, the character of justice and wrongdoing: God should be praised because he performs justice for its own sake and *thus* cannot but do it.[26] Eternal bliss gets its binding force because it has been predicted by God in his revelation and *then*, as a published decision of God, cannot but happen.[27] It is true that an-Naẓẓām believed this world to be the best of all worlds; "nothing is more optimal (*aṣlaḥ*) than the favor (*luṭf*) wrought by God". But it nevertheless remains a favor, it is not a mechanical "must". And there are innumerable favors of equal value which God could also have wrought; he could not have done anything less optimal, but he retains an infinite choice. He cannot choose anything evil, but when choosing something good he has innumerable options all of which are equally optimal. He is not like fire which can perform only one thing, namely heating, because it is "natured" (*maṭbūʿ*) like that.[28]

The comparison with fire was old. "God is not involuntarily good the way fire is warming", Clement of Alexandria had said, "He does not do good out of necessity but out of free choice . . . ."[29] And, pursued an-Naẓẓām, if he always chooses the best for his creatures it is because he cannot be "stingy"[30], and if he always performs justice for its own sake it is because he is perfect, exempt from any shortcoming or "defect" (*āfa*).[31] This catchword, "defect", may lead us further in our analysis. We remember having heard it mentioned already: a "defect" was discovered by an-Naẓẓām in the principle of Light advocated by the dualists, for Light is overwhelmed by Darkness.[32] As far as an-Naẓẓām's own system is concerned, however, the "defective" agent κατ ἐξοχήν was man who is responsible for most of the wrongdoing which cannot be performed by God. With this we come to the logical complement of what has been treated up to now, namely to an-Naẓẓām's anthropology.

4. FREE CHOICE AND 'DEFECT' (ĀFA) IN MAN AND GOD

The "defect" in man is his body. The body oppresses the soul and confines it like a prison[33]; in his essence, man is to be identified with his soul, but the activities of the soul are always affected (hampered, or modified, or conditioned) by the body. This looks like an idea taken over from Platonism, but the impression quickly changes when we hear that the soul is a material principle, a "subtle body", a kind of *pneuma* permeating all limbs. And there are more of these "bodies": colors, e.g., smells, noises, things which materially penetrate man from outside and other ones which are already part of him, such as his qualities. I have described this concept somewhere else[34], and I do not want to go into detail here. Suffice it to say that the key-notion in this system is the idea of mixture, an idea which we encountered already when talking about the dualists and which was, as a matter of fact, developed in their milieu although it was ultimately derived, as it seems, from the Stoic concept of *κρᾶσις δι ὅλου*.

The example which best illustrates this mixture of different material elements in man is sense perception. We hear a sound because it arrives at the ear as a material body and then mixes with the soul which itself is also a material body. Before penetrating the soul the sound was not an isolated, unmixed entity either, for then it was mixed with the air which it had affected when being produced by some event of nature or by a speaker.[35] The soul is what is common to all sense perceptions; as such it forms the *sensus communis*[36]. But only the body differentiates between all perceptions; the "defect" explains their individual character. If we ask why the eye sees but does not hear, we cannot but answer that it allows colors to enter while keeping sounds out; its impediment or "defect" reacts like glass which can be permeated by colors and not by sounds. In the same way, the sense of hearing is mixed with, and thus obstructed by, a kind of darkness which gives free way to sounds but not to colors.[37] Functioning is an interplay of different elements or ingredients of a "mixture"; this explains both its existence as well as its limitations.

If left alone the soul would function by itself. But for the same reason it would not be free in the real sense of the word; the soul, so it seems, reacts, as a material body, always in the same way.

> The soul (*rūḥ*) dwells in this (definite) body insofar as this (body) is a defect for it and instigates it to make a choice (*bāʿit lahū ʿalā l-ikhtiyār*). If (the soul) were without it it would act by secondary causality (*tawallud*, i.e., by mechanically influencing other agents) and by necessity.[38]

Capability of action (*istiṭāʿa*) is not, as other Muʿtazilīs said, an independent and separate ingredient of man's nature; according to an-Naẓẓām it is given with man's essence itself, i.e., with his soul.[39] But "man cannot, by himself, be capable to do what he normally does (*min sha'nihī an yaf'alahū*) as long as there does not arise a defect in him. (This) defect is (identical with) the incapability of acting (*'ajz*); it is different from man (himself)."[40] Like sense perception, free will is thus a result of limitation; capability is in need of incapability in order to present a choice. And since incapability derives from the body, it is not identical with man, who is soul.

We would be glad to hear more about this strange theory. We recognize that it shares certain axioms common to all Mu'tazilī thinking. Free will is interpreted as free choice; liberty always develops with respect to alternatives in that man either does something or omits it. But an-Naẓẓām speaks not about omission (*tark*) but about incapability which mixes with capability; the discussion is transferred into the realm of physics instead of jurisprudence. How does the "mixture" of soul and body, of capability and incapability, produce a choice? Another passage suggests that "incapability" was perhaps not so much a separate ingredient but only an abbreviated expression for all those "bodies" which form, together with the corporeal soul, the phenomenological appearance of man: colors, tastes, smells, etc. All of them are "defects" to the soul, and "the souls are mixed with these defects so that trial and appropriate test ensue in this world."[41] Trial and test, this means the choice between good and evil for which man gets his retribution in the hereafter. Without "colors, tastes, smells, etc." the soul would thus not only act according to its nature, but obviously also do only the good. Or, as an-Naẓẓām used to put it: one and the same class (*jins*) cannot produce two different kinds of action.[42] Fire always burns, and snow always cools; similarly the soul which is a "class" by itself and always remains so[43] cannot produce more than one kind of action, namely the good. If man performs, as we know by experience, good and evil alike it is because of the unity of his person, not because of his soul.[44]

The difficulties of such a construction could not be overlooked. What about the hereafter, for instance? Trial and test are over then, man no longer has and needs a choice, and we should assume that the soul is given a chance to leave its "prison". On the other hand, the Muslim concept of Paradise is rather corporeal, and it is not easy to see how man should be able to eat and drink in Paradise if his soul is not further "mixed" with the body, with smells and tastes, etc. As a matter of fact, this is flatly admitted by al-Khayyāṭ when he tries to defend an-Naẓẓām; he seems to acknowledge that Ibn ar-Rēwandī was right when he said that, according to an-Naẓẓām, only some of the "defects" are taken away in the hereafter whereas other ones have to remain in order to keep man functioning.[45] He only adds – if I understand him correctly – that these "defects" are no longer defects.[46] Man remains man even in Paradise, a human and somehow defective being; only God is perfect.[47]

This brings us to a second problem – and back to our main topic: How does all this fit with an-Naẓẓām's concept of God's justice? Man is free because of his "defects", and only because of his defects; God, on the contrary, is free by being exalted above all defects. Did an-Naẓẓām want to say that choice and freedom of decision have to be understood differently in both cases, man's freedom meaning freedom for sin and evil, God's freedom meaning decision for good and justice? Or did he simply not have a "system" and discovered God's freedom only when he wanted to escape the parallels with the dualist concept put to light by his opponents? We do not know; we are working with fragments. But we can attain a certain probability. an-Naẓẓām pretended, says al-Khayyāṭ,

> that injustice and lie only proceed from a defective body. If somebody attributes to God the capability of performing them he describes him as a defective body. For if somebody is capable of something it is not self-contradictory that this (also) proceeds from him; and if these two, (i.e., injustice and lie) were to proceed from him this would prove that he is a defective body.[48]

This statement seems to speak in favor of our first interpretation. Actions which are bad in themselves form a class of their own and can only be realized in connection with a "defect". God does not have this "defect", so he does not realize them. This does not mean, as we saw, that he does not have a choice; it merely means that his choice moves in the realm of the good.

The model we tried to reconstruct reminds us, to a certain extent, of a distinction worked out by the Byzantine theologian Maximus Confessor (580–662): man's "personal will" (θέλημα γνωμικόν) is a sign of his imperfection. His "natural will" (θέλημα φυσικόν) always tends towards the good; the perfect nature has no need of choice, for it *knows* naturally what is good. When we follow our "personal will", however, we limit our true freedom.[49] We do not hear much about an-Naẓẓām's ideas about human will. But we know that, again in contrast to the Baṣrian school, he denied God a separate will.[50] And al-Ka'bī who here, as on other points,[51] agreed with him much more closely than did the Baṣrians, then added the comparison we are waiting for: human will functions in connection with man's ignorance or imperfect knowledge with respect to whether his intentions can and will be realized; God, on the contrary, is omniscient and can do without a separate will. Will is realization in his case.[52]

5. CONCLUSION: AN-NAẒẒĀM'S LEGACY IN ISLAMIC THOUGHT

In all this euphoria of reconstruction some scepticism remains. We would have expected an-Naẓẓām's opponents to point out the discrepancies we discovered between his anthropology and his concept of God. But there is no trace of anything like that. Criticism was apparently mainly directed against what an-Naẓẓām said about God; his anthropology was silently forgotten. This is perhaps characteristic for Islam: the main concern was God's omnipotence, even for the Mu'tazilīs. an-Naẓẓām's idea that God cannot do evil was accepted by a few of his disciplies, by 'Alī al-Uswārī and al-Jāḥiẓ,[53] but it remained the great exception. The later Baṣrian masters did not take it over, as we saw,[54] and the great Abū l-Hudhayl, an-Naẓẓām's predecessor and uncle on whom they relied and who had paved the way for so many concepts discussed again by his nephew, had not believed in it either. Like them, he had said that God can do evil though he will never do it.

It is true that Abūl-Hudhayl had still used a formulation which shows that, in intention, he was not so far away from an-Naẓẓām: it is "absurd", he had said, self-contradictory (*muḥāl*) that God ever does evil.[55] But even this word gave the later Baṣrian theologians some misgivings and was therefore omitted. Origen was much too Greek for Islam, as Richard Frank has remarked.[56] Mu'tazilī theology was never more Greek than in an-Naẓẓām, and even there it looks quite peculiar, at least completely un-Aristotelian. Islamic theology is interested in man, not in nature – in the relation between human free will and God's omnipotence, not in future events and their determination by God's foreknowledge. It is not metaphysics or logic which gives us the key but jurisprudence and grammar – or, as in the case of an-Naẓẓām (which again is somewhat exceptional), physics. We have to adjust our perspective, but perhaps this is not bad for a change.

NOTES

1 See Abû l-Ḥasan 'Alî b. Ismâ'îl Ash'arî, *Maqâlât al-Islâmiyyîn*, H. Ritter (ed.), Istanbul 1929–33, p. 555. 1 f; 'Abd al-Jabbâr b. Aḥmad, *al-Mughnî fî abwâb at-tawḥîd wal-'adl*, vol. VI, part 1: *at-Ta'dîl wat-tadjwîr*, Ahmad Fu'âd al-Ahwânî (ed.), Cairo 1962, p. 127, 4 f; many later and derivative reports (e.g., Abû Muḥammad 'Alî Ibn Ḥazm, *al-Fiṣal fî l-milal wal-ahwâ' wan-niḥal*, vol. IV, Cairo 1317 H, p. 193, 13 ff; Djuwaynî, *Ash-Shâmil fî uṣûl ad-dîn*, 'Alî Sâmî an-Nashshâr (ed.), Alexandria 1969, p. 372, 4 f: Abū Ya'lâ Ibn al-Farrâ', *al-Mu'tamad fî uṣûl ad-dîn*, W. Z. Haddad (ed.),

Institut de Lettres orientales de Beyrouth, Beirut 1974, p. 140, 4 f; Ibn Abî d-Dam, in Khalîl b. Aybak Ṣafadî, *al-Wâfî bil-wafayât*, vol. VI, H. Ritter *et al.* (eds.), Leipzig/ Wiesbaden 1931 ff., pp. 15, 18 f).

[2] See Origenes, *Contra Celsum* V 23: *ψαμεν δὲ ὅτι οὐ δύναται αἰσχρὰ ὁ θεός ἐπεὶ ἐσται ὁ θεὸς δυνάμενος μὴ εἶναι θεός. εἰ γὰρ αἰσχρόν τι δρᾶ θεὸς οὐκ ἔστι θεός*; quoted by R. M. Frank in 'The Divine Attributes According to the Teaching of Abû l-Hudhayl al-'Allâf,' in *Le Muséon* 82 (1969), p. 488 n. 122 and by G. Hourani in 'Islamic and non-Islamic Origins of Mu'tazilite Ethical Rationalism,' *Int'l Journal of Middle East Studies* 7 (1976) p. 85, with a slightly different translation.

[3] See Euripides, *Bellerophon*, frag. 292, v. 7, in *Fragmenta Tragicorum Graecorum*, A. Nauck (ed.), Leipzig 1889: *εἰ θεοί τι δρῶσιν αισχρόν οὐκ εἰσὶν θεοί.*

[4] See Ash'arî, *Maqâlât*, p. 555, 9 ff.; 'Abd ar-Raḥîm b. Muḥammad Khayyâṭ, *al-Intiṣâr*, A. N. Nader (ed. and transl.), Beirut 1957, p. 53, 15 ff.

[5] See below p. 56 and n. 12.

[6] For him see *Encyclopedia of Islam*, 2nd ed., vol. III, p. 305 f., art. 'Ibn al-Rāwandī' (by G. Vajda), and my article 'Ibn ar-Rēwandī, or the Making of an Image' in: *Al-Abhath* 27, Beirut 1978–79, pp. 5–26.

[7] For him see *Encyclopedia of Islam*, 2nd ed., Vol. IV, pp. 1162–64, art. 'al-Khayyāṭ'.

[8] What follows is largely an interpretation and a rearrangement of Khayyâṭ, *Intiṣâr*, p. 38, 2 ff. Cf. also the short proof quoted in *Muġnî* VI$_1$, p. 127, 7 f.

[9] Besides other ones which are ethically good or bad simply by virtue of God's command or prohibition. They do not concern us here since they are only relevant for man. Cf. Ash'arî, *Maqâlât*, p. 356, 6 ff.

[10] I owe the ideas in this paragraph to some of the comments made by R. M. Frank during the symposium, which I reproduce almost verbally, though in a rearranged and shortened form. Especially the interpretation given in the last sentence is entirely his own. It is based on an analysis of the position held by the later Baṣrian Mu'tazilites which I cannot repeat here. For contrasting it with an-Naẓẓâm's approach, Frank draws on two statements about Abû l-Qâsim al-Ka'bî (died 319/931) who made some of an-Naẓẓâm's axioms his own and whom I have adduced as a possible witness for an-Naẓẓâm's later thinking (cf. p. 63). The passages are found in Abû Rashîd Sa'îd b. Muhammad an-Naysâbûrî, *al-Masâ'il fî l-khilâf bayna l-Baṣriyyîn wal-Baghdadiyyîn*, M. Ziyâda and R. as-Sayyid (eds.), Institut de Lettres orientales de Beyrouth, Beirut 1979, p. 354, 22 f and p. 210, 18 ff.

[11] This is, at least, what seems to be implied in Khayyâṭ's remark in *Intiṣâr*, p. 39, 1 ff.

[12] See *Muġnî* VI$_1$, p. 177, 3 ff.; translated by G. Hourani, *Islamic Rationalism: The Ethics of 'Abd al-Jabbâr*, Clarendon Press, Oxford 1971, p. 101.

[13] See *Intiṣâr*, p. 38, 11.

[14] *Ibid.*, p. 39, 6 ff.

[15] Either Ibn ar-Rêwandî or the "opponents" to which he refers.

[16] Cf. *Intiṣâr*, p. 39, 6 ff.; for a detailed exposition of a Manichean doctrine in a Muslim source, cf. *Muġnî* V, p. 10, 3 ff. (after an-Naubakhtī), translated in G. Monnot, *Penseurs Musulmans et Religions Iraniennes*, J. Vrin, Paris 1974, p. 152 f.

[17] *Intiṣâr*, p. 39, 13 ff.

[18] *Ibid.*, p. 38, 11 f.; *Muġnî* V, p. 17, 3 ff. and Monnot, p. 166.

[19] *Intiṣâr*, p. 38, 21 ff.; this is at least how Khayyâṭ explains an-Naẓẓâm's argumentation.

[20] *Ibid.*, p. 38, 9 ff.: "If the Eternal knows from eternity onward that justice is good and that whatever He does happens because of His knowing it to be good, and if this according to you does not necessarily postulate the thesis that He has been practicing (it) from eternity onward, then what is the difference between you and the Dayṣânîya . . .?" I understand *mâ* in *mâ fa'alahû* as a relative pronoun. It might be easier to interpret it as a negation, as Nader does in his translation; but then the preceding *li-'ilmihî* has to be given a concessive meaning for which the *li-* does not seem to be appropriate.

[21] See *Intiṣâr*, p. 39, 1 ff.

[22] *Maṭbû' 'alâ l-fi'l*; cf. 'Abd al-Qāhir b. Ṭâhir Baghdâdî, *al-Farq bayna l-firaq*, M. Badr (ed.), Cairo 1910, p. 117, 2 ff and M. Muḥyī d-Dîn 'Abd al-Hamîd (ed.), Cairo n.d., p. 134, 14 ff.

[23] See *Intiṣâr*, p. 42, 6 ff. >Baghdâdî, *Farq*, p. 117, 5 ff. and p. 134, 17 ff.

[24] *Intiṣâr*, p. 22, 1 ff.

[25] For Jahm b. Ṣafwân cf. *Encyclopedia of Islam*, 2nd ed., vol. II, p. 338 and R. M. Frank, 'The Neoplatonism of Ǧahm ibn Ṣafwân' in: *Le Muséon* 78 (1965), 395–424. For his doctrine on Paradise and Hell cf. Ash'arî, *Maqâlât*, p. 148, 11–149, 3.

[26] *Intiṣâr*, p. 43, 2 ff. and before.

[27] *Ibid.*, p. 22, 6 ff.

[28] Cf. Ash'arî, *Maqâlât*, p. 576, 5 ff.; also *Intiṣâr*, p. 25, *apu*, ff.

[29] Cf. Clement of Alexandria, *Stromateis* VII 42. 4 and 6: *οὔτε γὰρ ὁ θεὸς ἄκων ἀγαθὸς ὃν τρόπον τὸ πῦρ θερμαντικόν . . . οὔκουν ὁ θεὸς ἀνάγκῃ ἀγαθοποιεῖ, κατὰ προαίρεσιν δε εὐποιεῖ.* I owe this reference to R. M. Frank.

[30] Cf. *Maqâlât*, p. 576, 10.

[31] Cf. *Intiṣâr*, p. 42, *pu*. f. and 28, 4 ff.

[32] See above p. 58.

[33] Cf. *Maqâlât*, p. 331, 10 f.

[34] Cf. J. van Ess, *Theology and Science: The Case of Abû Isḥâq an-Naẓẓâm*. Ann Arbor 1978 (The Second Annual United Arab Emirates Lecture in Islamic Studies); French version, in *REI* 46, (1978), p. 191 ff.; *Encyclopedia of Islam* ²V 384 f., article 'Kumūn'.

[35] J. van Ess, *op cit.*, p. 14.

[36] 'Abd Allâh b. Muḥammad Nâshi', *al-Kitâb al-ausaṭ*, edited by J. van Ess in *Frühe Mu'tazilitische Hâresiographie*. J. van Ess (ed.), F. Steiner, Wiesbaden, 1971, pp. 113, 13 ff.

[37] See *Maqâlât*, p. 342, 3 ff. (after a report by al-Jāḥiẓ); for the reference to an-Naẓẓâm, cf. *Ibid.*, p. 343, 3 ff.

[38] See *Maqâlât*, p. 334, 2 ff.; rûḥ and *nafs* are identical for an-Naẓẓâm.

[39] *Ibid.*, p. 229, 3 f. and p. 334, 1; also p. 478, 12.

[40] *Ibid.*, p. 229, 5 ff. The editor proposes to read *qad yajûzu* or *innamâ yajûzu* instead of *lâ yajûzu*; but this is not necessary and would not give a better sense.

[41] See *Intiṣâr*, p. 34, 14 ff.

[42] *Ibid.*, p. 30, ult. ff.; also Baghdâdî, *Farq*, p. 119, 15 ff. and p. 136, 16 ff.

[43] *Ibid.*, p. 34, 12 f.

[44] This is what seems to be implied in the remark, *Ibid.*, p. 30, apu. ff.

[45] *Ibid.*, p. 34, 10 ff. and 17 ff.

[46] *Ibid.*, p. 34, 16 f.

[47] With regard to animals which, as an-Naẓẓām thought, are also granted Paradise if they perform the good (i.e., if they have done useful things) he held that they enter it

only with their souls, "free from all defects," and that they will be given other "forms" as God likes (cf. 'Amr b. Baḥr Jâḥiẓ, *al-Ḥayawân* III, 'Abd as-Salām Muḥammad Hārūn (ed.), p. 395, 1 ff.) But they are treated under a different perspective: an-Naẓẓām does not primarily want to ensure their capability of enjoying the pleasures of Paradise, but tries to escape the consequence that Paradise is full of dangerous and voracious beasts.

48 See *Intiṣâr*, p. 28, 4 ff.

49 See V. Lossky, *The Mystical Theology of the Eastern Church*, J. Clarke, London 1957, p. 125.

50 Cf. W. Madelung, *Der Imam al-Qâsim ibn Ibrâhîm und die Glaubenslehre der Zaiditen* de Gruyter, Berlin 1965, p. 165 f.

51 See above, n. 10.

52 See Muhammad b. 'Abd al-Karîm, Shahrastānī, *Nihâyat al-iqdâm fî 'ilm al-kalâm*, A. Guillaume (ed.), Oxford 1931, p. 240, 2 ff. However, Ka'bî believed that God can do wrong, at least in a merely theoretical sense. It would not be against reason, but all the proofs on which reason bases itself would have to be changed to their opposites, i.e., God would have to change the order of the universe (cf. Ash'arî, *Maqâlât*, p. 557, 12 ff.).

53 See *Maqâlât*, p. 555, 1 f.

54 Even Ka'bî did not join him here (cf. n. 52).

55 See R. M. Frank in: *Le Muséon* 82 (1969), p. 487. an-Naẓẓâm used the same expression (cf. above, p. 55), Ka'bî restricted it (cf. n. 52).

56 *Maqâlât*, p. 488.

CHAPTER 4

CAN GOD DO WHAT IS WRONG?

Richard Frank

1. INTRODUCTION: ACTIONS AND THE POSSIBILITY OF ACTING IN MU'TAZILITE THOUGHT

I shall restrict my remarks here to the question of whether or not God can do injustice or act wrongfully by drawing out the basic differences between the apparent position of an-Naẓẓâm and that of the fully developed teaching of the Baṣrian school of the Mu'tazila, for which we have more adequate resources.[1]

According to 'Abd al-Jabbâr, an-Naẓẓâm's position is that "to describe God as being able to wrong someone or to make a false statement . . . involves a contradiction".[2] That is to say, an-Naẓẓâm holds that to assert that God is able to do injustice is to assert that he is other than he is: *fî d̲âlika qalbu d̲âtihî.*[3] This, of course, is exactly what Origen says in the passage cited by Professor van Ess. The thesis is explicitly denied, however, by the leading authorities of the Baṣrian school in the classical period.[4] It is worth noting that the formulation of the question, sc., 'Is God able to do injustice and/or to make a false statement?' (*'a-yaqdiru llâhu 'alà ẓ-ẓulmi wal-kad̲ib*) is important in that to do injustice (to wrong another by doing him harm which is not outweighed by subsequent benefit) and to deceive are actions which, in the Mu'tazilite teaching, are always and as such ethically wrong. The question seems to have been a standard topos from the earliest period.

The expression 'God can do injustice' is ambiguous in English, just as is *δύναται ἀδικεῖν* in Greek, given the unavoidable ambivalence of *δύνασθαι* once Aristotle had done tinkering with the word. As is plain, this phrase is not necessarily the same as 'it is concretely possible that God choose to do injustice'. The latter both an-Naẓẓâm and the Baṣrians will deny. What we must do then is see how they understand and analyze the terms of the question. The Arabic expressions employed here, *'qadara, yaqdiru, qâdirun 'alà* . . .' are best rendered by 'is able to . . .', for even though they still carry connotations of sheer possibility, the primary sense is one of capability, efficient power, and productive competence.

An act (*fi'l*) is conceived by the Mu'tazila as an entity and to act (*fa'l*)

T. Rudavsky (ed.), Divine Omniscience and Omnipotence in Medieval Philosophy, 69–79.

is to cause an act to come to be; occurrences are the coming to be of the existence of entities (*wuqû'u wuǧûdi 'ašyâ'a*). For all the Mu'tazila, 'is able to . . .' (*qâdirun 'alá . . .*) is said of an agent with respect to possible actions: entities the concrete possibility of whose coming to exist is constituted by the ability of the agent to do them. 'Is able to . . .' is not said with respect to an event which some one undergoes, which occurs in or through him by force ("by necessity": *muḍṭarran, ḍarûratan* = *ἠναγκασμένον, ἀνάγκῃ βεβιασμένον, βίᾳ*), i.e., without his being able intentionally or voluntarily to originate or to prevent its occurrence.[5] What an agent is able to do, then, is something which is such that he is able either to do it or not to do it intentionally. The (potential) object of an agent's ability to act (*al-maqdûru lahû*) is the possible object of his choice (*iḫtiyâr*) to do or not to do.

According to the report of al-Khayyâṭ, an-Naẓẓâm's position is this:

> God has done no act save that he is able (a) to do it or (b) to omit doing it or (c) to do something else instead of it. . . . The distinction between what acts by its nature and by necessity, according to Ibrâhîm (an-Naẓẓâm), and that which he says is true of God is that what acts by its nature is able neither to do what it does nor to omit doing it and neither chooses nor elects to do it rather than something else, nor among its acts can there come to be save one kind [of action], like fire . . .[6]

The problem, then, is how one conceives the objects of an agent's ability to act: what attributes, properties, or descriptions are directly and necessarily implied as belonging to an entity when we say of it that it is *maqdûr* (the object of an agent's ability to act) and what properties and attributes belong to it necessarily in consequence of what he does insofar as he is able to do it. It will be best to look at the Baṣrian analysis first, since their teaching is available in our sources in its full detail. Having this as the basis of comparison we shall be able to get a clearer notion of the likely historical significance and structure of the fragmentary data which are available concerning the teaching of an-Naẓẓâm.

2. THE BAṢRIAN ANALYSIS OF HUMAN AND DIVINE AGENCY

Generally speaking, according to the doctrine of the Baṣrian masters, the agent's ability to act posits or has as its objects not individuals but classes (*ajnâs*) of entities: *al-qâdiru 'innamâ yaqdiru 'alà 'îjâdi 1-jins*.[7] Considered simply in respect to his ability to act, an agent can, insofar as he is able to act, cause the existence of an indefinite number of individuals of a given class (any posited instance or its like) or of the contrary of the class.[8] That is, he is able to cause the existence of an act x or of not-x, not-x being such that its existence precludes the possibility of the simultaneous existence of x in the same locus or substrate (*maḥall*). In God's case the classes of the objects of his ability to act are unrestricted. In the case of human agents the classes are limited to several basic acts – some physical and some mental – and secondarily to those few classes of events whose being can be causally produced (*tawallada*) as the effects (*musabbabât*) of these basic acts. In God's case, again, the infinities of objects of his ability to act are posited individually as he knows each of them as such eternally. For the human agent, on the other hand, the individual entity or action is posited and becomes concretely an object of his choice and his ability to act insofar as it is presented in cognition as a prospective action; that is, as presented to him as an object of a motivation to a prospective action or forebearance. (Motivation – *ad-dawâ'î* – is understood as a state of belief that a given action or forebearance is or may be desirable or ethically good.) The prospective act being thus posited, the agent may act intentionally: he may voluntarily realize or not realize the object of his ability to act.[9] Motivation posits an action as worthy of being done – as advantageous to the agent or to another – in a given way and for a given reason (with a given end – *ġaraḍ* – in view). The choice or volition or intention (the terms are equivalent in this context) is made on the basis of the same motivation but is a separate act, distinct from the one which is its object.

Any given action is an object of the agent's ability to act in and by virtue of its being a member of a class of entities whose existence he is able to initiate. The only predicates valid of a possible action (*maqdûrun ma'dûm*) insofar as it is an object of the agent's ability to act, i.e., which are true of it as an individual whose being is posited by the present actuality of the agent's ability to act, are those which describe it as a member of the basic class or kind (*jins*) to which it belongs or which assign it to one or another of the broader classes of things which we distinguish. That the agent is able to act implies that he can cause the existence of the object of his ability to act. When he performs the act it has as a consequence of what he does insofar as he is able to act (insofar as he is *qâdirun 'alayhî*) only those properties which belong to it inevitably as an existent instance of the class of entities of which it is a member: *ṣifâtu jinsihî*. All other attributes which the particular action may prove to have when performed and which are dependent upon the intentional performance of the agent belong to it not by virtue of its being the kind of thing it is (*li-jinsihî*) but because of the mode or manner of its occurrence (*li-wajhi wuqû'ihî*). They depend for their actuality, therefore, on states of the agent other than his being able to act; these states consist in his cognition and in the prescriptive intention (*al-'irâdah, al-qaṣd*) he formed at the moment of his doing the act.[10] Because the being of the agent is qualified, over and above his being able to act, by these other states of belief and intention, he performs the act in a certain way. By virtue of its occurrence in this way and not in another it has characteristics over and above those which belong to it as a member of the class of entities which it instantiates. (Most ethical characteristics are grounded in the mode of the act's occurrence.) An action is defined as an entity whose existence depends upon (originates from) an agent insofar as he was able to cause it to occur.[11] Since an action belongs, strictly speaking, to one and only one essential class (*jins*) which is defined by its essential attributes, acts which occur voluntarily or which occur in a particular way (*wajh*) do not as such constitute a class. To put it another way, the agent who is able to cause the existence of a given kind of materially structured event may, by virtue of his intention and volition, cause it to occur under any one of a number of descriptions; his ability to act, however, is not and cannot, by definition, be restricted to causing the occurrence of the act under one but not another description.[12]

A simple example of how the Baṣrians construe this will be sufficient to illustrate the matter. An agent (whether God or a human being) is able to speak, i.e., to cause the existence of sounds and specifically sounds which by convention are symbolically significant and so constitute sentences (*kalâm*). Included, then, among the objects of the agent's ability to act is the subclass of sentences of which 'John is sitting in a chair in this room' is an example. The materially structured act depends for its existence on the agent's ability to act. The significance of the sentence – that it is not mere noise but a sentence which has the particular meaning it has – depends, however, not upon the agent's ability to act but on his intent (*qaṣd*) in uttering it: the prescriptive intention he formed at the moment he initiated the utterance.[13] As I have spoken the sentence here it is like a sentence in a grammar book: it is a sentence because I intended a subject and a predicate, but it is not really a statement, since the nouns have no reference. The reference of the nouns, and in the Arab analysis of the verb, depends also upon my intention (as does its being a statement, when it is a statement, and not a question). Accordingly, the material truth or falsity of the sentence, if it is a statement and not a question, depends upon this intention.[14]

If I am in error (*jâhil*) regarding the facts, my intention was to inform and the statement is simply false: I have uttered a false statement. If I know the facts but intend an erroneous reference, it is a lie; my act was to utter a false statement with the intention of deceiving. What depends as such and strictly speaking upon my ability to act is, according to the Baṣrian analysis, simply the existence of the sounds; the correct sequence depends upon my knowing which ones to put in front of which. That they constitute a statement (*ḫabar*) and not a question (*istiḫbâr*) depends upon the intention whose object was the purpose of the utterance and which I formed at the moment I began to speak. Given the reference of the nouns, determined by this same intention, the statement's being simply false or a lie is correlated not to my ability to act but to my belief (*i'tiqâd*), i.e., to my knowing (*'ilm*) or being in error (*jahl*) concerning the facts with regard to the beings to which I referred. If it is simply false, the act is ethically bad (*qabîḥ*), as is the erroneous judgment on which it is based; if it is a lie, then the intention (which is a distinct act) is ethically bad. The sentence, however, belongs to one and only one class of entities and is materially the same whether it is true or false.[15]

When then the Baṣrian Mu'tazila insist that God is able to make a false statement, they mean no more than to say that the class of all possible sounds and so all possible structured sequences of syllables (*ḥurûfun manẓûmah*) are objects of his ability to act. That he is able to cause them to occur constitutes the absolute possibility (*ṣiḥḥah*) that he cause any given sequence of sounds to occur and therefore, in principle, that he cause them to occur under any description: "One who is able to do something is able to cause it to exist both in a mode that is ethically good and in a mode that is ethically bad."[16] The concrete possibility (*jawâz*) of the occurrence of a false statement as an action of God's is, however, another matter. That God is able to do something entails the absolute possibility (*ṣiḥḥah*) of its occurrence, but does not entail the concrete possibility (*jawâz*) of his actually doing it in a particular manner.[17]

According to the Baṣrians an agent makes a false statement voluntarily either (a) because he is in error concerning the facts or (b) because he is in error concerning the ethical value (*ḥukm*) of making false statements, thinking it to be good, either generally or under some, including the present, circumstances or (c) because he expects to achieve some benefit or to avoid some harm by doing so, such that the ethical wrongness of the action is outweighed in his judgment by the desirability of doing it. God, however, knows all that can be known and his being is complete in its perfection (*ġanî* = *αὐτάρκης*, *ἀπροσδεής*) in such a way that it is impossible for him to gain benefit or to suffer harm. Since making a false statement cannot, therefore, be desirable to God, the occurrence of a false statement on his part is concretely impossible (*lâ yajûzu*).[18]

3. AN-NAẒẒĀM'S THEORY OF AGENCY COMPARED TO THE BAṢRIAN ANALYSIS

We have very little information concerning an-Naẓẓâm's analysis of *'qadara, yaqdiru'* and not much more concerning his analysis of the predicates of actions. It would seem from the reports of al-Khayyāṭ that he used 'action' (*al-fi'l*) and 'to act' (*al-fa'l*) in a somewhat broader sense, perhaps, than do the Baṣrians – roughly as an equivalent of ἐνέργεια as found in the Patristic literature – and also that he employed *'jins'* (kind, class) in a broader sense than is common in the formal usage of the Baṣrians. Thus, according to an-Naẓẓâm, fire has only one kind (*jins*) of action, viz., heating, and humans have only one kind of action (*jinsun wâḥid*), which includes movements, cognitive judgments (*'ulûm*) and volitions (*'irâdât*).[19]

Concerning his treatment of the ethical predicates 'good' and 'bad', al-Aš'ari reports that an-Naẓẓâm said:

> Every act of disobedience which it is possible (*kâna yajûzu*) that God command is bad by virtue of [His] prohibition against doing it and every act of disobedience which it is not possible (*lâ yajûzu*) that God permit is bad in itself (*qabîḥatun li-nafsihâ*) .... Thus also, whatever it is possible (*jâza*) that God command is good by virtue of [His] command and whatever it is possible only that He command is good in itself (*ḥasanun li-nafsihî*).[20]

It is clear that an-Naẓẓâm distinguishes between acts that are ethically bad or good in themselves and those which are only contingently so. Since, then, as is further evident, he holds that it is not possible that God command men to do what is bad intrinsically (e.g., to make false statements or to act unjustly) or that he fail to command those good acts that are ethically obligatory (*wâjib*) as such and in themselves, an-Naẓẓâm can distinguish two kinds of acts: those whose being good or bad is contingently dependent on God's revelation and those which, though commanded in revelation or forbidden in it, are good (obligatory) or bad as such in terms of what God cannot fail to command or not command.[21] The difficulty is that lacking any information concerning an-Naẓẓâm's ontological analysis of the various kinds of predicates which are said of actions and of 'good' and 'bad' in particular, we cannot know for certain exactly what he understands by "in itself" (*li-nafsihî*) when he says that some actions are good and some bad in themselves.[22]

Now, if we take it that an-Naẓẓâm's position regarding actions which are ethically good or bad in themselves is analogous to that of al-Ka'bî, we can explain the sense of "bad in itself" in a way that will allow us to understand the sense of the thesis that God is unable to do injustice or to make a false statement. There are significant parallels between the doctrine of an-Naẓẓâm and that of al-Ka'bî and the Baghdad school of the Mu'tazila on several matters and thus, although the hypothesis must remain unconfirmed, the analogy is not wholly implausible.

Abû Rašîd an-Naysabûrî cites al-Ka'bî as holding that it is not possible (*kâna lâ yajûzu*) that any accident which exists and is ethically bad exist and be ethically good.[23] In another place he reports that al-Ka'bî held that

It is not possible (*kâna lâ yajûzu*) that a movement which occurs as ethically bad occur as ethically good and further in [al-Ka'bî's] view movements which are ethically bad are not similar to those which are ethically good. Thus he held concerning any two actions one of which is good and the other bad that they are necessarily different.[23]

Here in abû Rašîd's paraphrase, since we are dealing with the Baṣrian context, there is no ambiguity concerning the sense of the position attributed to al-Ka'bî: 'good' and 'bad' describe actions essentially and in their inalienable properties. If, then, we take this to be the position of an-Naẓẓâm concerning those actions which are always bad or always good and so are bad or good in themselves, we can see clearly enough what is implied by 'in themselves'. His position will be this. In the case of actions that are always ethically bad – making false statements, for example – the ethical attribute is an objectively real property or characteristic of the entity which is the act. Furthermore he held that the ethical attributes of such actions belong to them essentially or "in themselves" and are, therefore, such as to define what are properly speaking classes (*ajnâs*) of actions which are intrinsically bad or good. This stands in clear contrast to the teaching of the Baṣrian school, according to which there is no class (*jins*) of voluntary or intentional actions, and a fortiori there can be no class of actions defined by an ethical characteristic. For an-Naẓẓâm, then, acts that are intrinsically bad, e.g., unjust acts (*ẓulm* = ἀδικία or false statements (*kaḏib* = ψεῦδος) will belong to a class of ethically wrongful actions. A true sentence will differ essentially from one which is materially identical but false.

Concerning our original topic, then, an-Naẓẓâm will hold a position something like this: an agent chooses to do what is ethically wrong only because (a) he is in some way deficient (*ḏû ḥâjah* = *ḏû 'âfah*) (i.e., he has a need to achieve some benefit or to avoid some harm) or (b) because he does not know the consequence (*'âqibah*) of his act.[24] Only that class of actions, therefore, which is defined by the attribute of its being good (*al-ḥusn*) can be desirable for God and only such actions, accordingly, can be possible objects of his choice to do or not to do. Motivation is the condition of the possibility of choosing, and motivation here has been excluded. The attribute of being good, in brief, is the defining characteristic of the class of actions which, posited in God's knowledge, are capable of motivaing (*ḥadâ, ba'aṯa*) him to perform them. Since, then, one predicates 'is able to ...' of an agent only with respect to those actions which he can choose to do or not to do, actions which are ethically bad in themselves are excluded as such from those which are (potential) objects of God's ability to act, "because one who is able to do something is such that the occurrence through his agency (*minhû* = πρὸς αὐτοῦ) is not impossible".[25] 'God is able to make a false statement' is thus a selfcontradictory statement (*mustaḥîl, muḥâl*). 'Abd al-Jabbâr says that an-Naẓẓâm's position entails that God cannot do those (good) actions which he knows from eternity he will not do.[26] This contention would seem, however, to be essentially polemical, since an-Naẓẓâm quite explicity holds that God acts by choice and not by his nature.[27]

NOTES

[1] Since I am concerned here only with the basic structure and coherence of their respective positions there is no need to enter into the detail of the various arguments and to cite redundant texts in which essentially the same reasoning appears repeatedly, recast in one or another form according to the exigencies of different polemical contexts.

[2] 'Abd al-Jabbâr, *al-Muġnî fî abwâb al-tawḥîd wal-'adl*, Ministry of Culture, Cairo 1959–65, 6/1, p. 127, 4 f.

[3] *Ibid.*, p. 140, 7.

[4] Origen and the Patristic writers will base this on God's being good (ἀγαθός) by His nature. Note that 'good' is not predicated of God in the Arabic of the *kalâm*. That is, the English term 'good' renders either '*ḥasan*' or '*ḫayr*' and in the lexicon of the *kalâm* neither of these terms can be used to describe God. The former is employed to describe an object in an aesthetic sense (as beautiful) or to describe an action in an ethical sense (as morally good or right), while the latter is used to describe an object, event, state of affairs, or action as in some respect good (or best) for someone, i.e., as beneficial or advantageous to or for. ('*Ḫayr*', indeed, is not a technical term in the *kalâm*.) '*Muḥsin*' (= does what is *ḥasan*) is predicated of God, but the term is derived from the ethical description of an act and is considered to be referential to the act under that description, wherefore it is said of God as an agent and not in himself. 'Just' ('*adl*), however, is said of God essentially according to the Mu'tazila: he is such in his essential being that all his actions are just and good; he transcends (*tanazzaha*) imperfection and error and so will not choose to do what is wrong or unjust. We may note, finally, that '*ḫayr*' is the term used to render the Greek ἀγαθόν in the neoplatonic literature (e.g., in the *Liber de Causis*), but, as is the case with much of the translation vocabulary, the usage is not properly consonant with the native semantics of the Arabic word.

[5] "By necessity" (or "by force") – *ḍarûratan*, etc. – is used also in an ethical or juridical sense to describe an action which is performed intentionally but unwillingly (under

constraint); this usage, however, does not belong to the formal lexicon of the *kalâm*.

6 al-Khayyâṭ, *K. al-Intiṣâr*, A. Nader (ed.), Beyrouth 1957, p. 26, 2–6.

7 Cf. *al-Muġnî*, 6/1, p. 129, 5ff.

8 *Ibid.*, 13, p. 206, 5ff.

9 The Baṣrians (we have no information regarding an-Naẓẓâm) do recognize the occurrence of involuntary actions on the part of human agents, i.e., events which originate in the agent through his ability to act but do so without his awareness or intention; these are, however, such that in principle he is able to do them or to omit them voluntarily. Rational motivation is the basis and the condition of choosing (*al-Muġnî*, 6/1, p. 99, 3f. and an-Naẓẓâm cited in al-Ash'arî, *Maqâlât al-Islâmiyyîn*. H. Ritter (ed.), Istanbul 1929–30, p. 334, 2–4.) Where there is action but no possibility of choice the action of the subject (i.e., the event which takes place in or through the subject) is caused by antecedent events (*tawallada*) and/or occurs necessarily, by its nature (*ibid.*).

10 Cf. *al-Muġnî* 9, p. 66, 2f.; and 13, p. 201, 10f.

11 *Ibid.*, 6/1, p. 5 and 8, p. 91f.

12 The occurrences of actions of a given class in various ways are spoken of as "varieties" or "sorts" (*ḍurûb*) of the class (e.g., *al-Muġnî* 11, p. 496, 19 and abû Rashîd al-Naysabûrî, *K. al-Masâ'il fî l-ḫilâf bayna l-Baṣriyyîn wal-Baġdâdiyyîn*, M. Ziyâdeh and R. al-Sayyid (eds.), Ma'had al-'Inmâ' al-'Arabî, Beyrouth 1979, p. 369, 23f. and cp. the text translated in no. 21 below); these varieties or sorts, however, are not conceived as constituting formally distinct sub-classes. cf. *al Muġnî* 6/1, p. 130, 16ff.

13 For a more detailed discussion of the Baṣrian analysis of this see my *Beings and their Attributes: The Teaching of the Baṣrian School of the Mu'tazila in the Classical Period*, State University of N.Y. Press, Albany, N.Y. 1978, pp. 127ff.

14 *al-Muġnî* 7, p. 65, 9f.

15 *Ibid.*, 12, p. 215, 2 and 7, p. 65, 9f.

16 *Ibid.*, 11, p. 168, 13.

17 *Ibid.*, 6/1, p. 140

18 Thus, 'Abd al-Jabbâr asserts against abû l-Hudhayl (*al-Muġnî* 6/1, p. 128, 7f.; cf. *Maqâlât*, pp. 200, 12–15 and 556, 7f.) that it is not absolutely impossible (i.e., logically contradictory) that God do something which is unjust. He allows, therefore, the formal correctness of the proposition 'If God did an unjust act, then this [act] would indicate (*dalla 'alà*) that He is in error ....' It is valid, however, only as *i'tibâr*, i.e., when one denies the consequent (that there exist an entity such as would require us to infer that God is in error) and thereby the antecedent. 'Abd al-Jabbâr insists, further, that since one cannot grant the (concrete) possibility (*jawâz*) of the truth of the antecedent, no predicate in the conclusion can be either true or false of its subject; see the lengthy discussion of this and other subjunctive conditionals dealing with God's action and his foreknowledge in *al-Muġnî* 6/1 pp. 127–156; rules for conditionals are given *ibid.*, pp. 151–154 and in 4, pp. 292–294; see also the citation of al-Jubbâ'î concerning subjunctive conditionals in *Maqâlât*, pp. 204f. = 560f. Al-Jubbâ'î's example of the invalid form of the subjunctive conditional (sc., that in which the antecedent is possible and the consequent impossible) is worth citing here since it involves the problem of God's foreknowledge and shows quite clearly that the Baṣrian mu'tazila at the end of the 3rd/9th century had a thorough grasp of the problem and its basic elements. He says that the proposition 'If a person of whom God knows and has stated [i.e., has revealed to us]

that he will not believe came to believe,then it would be the case that God's knowing and His statement would be . . .' must be self-contradictory (*mustaḥîl*). That is, the proposition (*al-kalâm*) is self-contradictory since the antecedent is possible in principle (it is true of any unbeliever that he is able to believe, wherefore the existence of his belief – *'îmânuhû* – is possible: *maqdûr*) while the consequent is altogether impossible under any interpretation, for "if (1) one says that [God's] statement 'he will believe' will come to be prior to the event since (a) the previous statement will come not to have been [verified] by his not believing and since (b) God will come not to have known eternally [that he would not believe], then the proposition is impossible, since (a) it is impossible that it come to be the case that what in fact has been come not to have been and since (b) it is impossible that God come not to have known eternally what He knows eternally. If (2) one says that the statement that he would not believe and the knowledge that he would not believe will be true and valid even though the thing of which it was known and of which it was said that it would not come to be came to be, then the proposition is impossible. If (3) one says that the true statement will change into a false statement and the knowing into error, then the proposition is impossible." *Maqâlât*, p. 204, 12ff; p. 561, 5ff.

[19] 'Abd al-Qâhir al-Baġdâdî, *al-Farq bayn al-firaq*, M. 'Abd al-Hamîd (ed.), Cairo n.d., p. 138, 1f; al-Shahrastânî, *K. al-Milal wan-niḥal*, M. Badrân (ed.), Cairo 1375/1955, p. 79, 7ff. These are all considered to be voluntary movements (*at-taḥar-ruku bil-'irâdah*: al-Baġdâdî, p. 137, 2). With this compare the thesis that voluntary movement (προαιρετική κίνησις) is characteristic of man and other animals (τὰ ἔμψυχα) in Methodius, *de Autexusio* 13, 1. The following is worth pointing out in the present context:

(1) Methodius (loc. cit.) plainly takes morally wrongful actions (τὰ κακά) as a γένος and so is able to speak of murder and adultery as two of its εἴδη. That he speaks of them formally in terms of classes (of a genus with its species) is analogous to what appears from the reports to be the teaching of an-Naẓẓâm and al-Ka'bî.

(2) Where, however, Methodius speaks of the εἴδη of a γένος, the Baṣrian Mu'tazila and an-Naẓẓâm speak only of *'ajnâs*. How an-Naẓẓâm conceived, grouped and divided *'ajnâs* is not certain, given the paucity of the indications given in our sources. The Baṣrians employ the term primarily to speak of the lowest, essential classes of beings, though they do commonly use it also for more extensive classes. 'Abd al-Jabbâr, for example, speaks of "the class of visible entities" (*jinsu l-mar'iyyât: al-Muġnî* 4, 132, 7f.), which includes colors, whose basic classes (*'ajnâs*) are black, white, green, etc., but remarks that "to describe the visible as visible does not imply its assignment to one or another class" (*lâ yûjibu tajnîsan*) (*ibid.*, lines 4ff.). When one considers the use of the terms here as compared with that of Methodius it is worth noting that the *mutakallimûn* of the classical period were basically nominalists and so have no place for εἴδη; i.e., the system has no place for forms, for single essences shared or participated in by many individuals or as the intentional presence of such essences to the mind.

[20] *Maqâlât*, p. 356, 6ff.; cp. *al-Milal*, p. 77, 10ff. and for the analogous distinction in the teaching of the Baṣrian school, cf. the passage of *al-Muġnî* translated in the following note. In would seem clear from the consistent usage of the texts in their citations and reports of an-Naẓẓâm and al-Ka'bî that they did not distinguish between '*ṣaḥḥa, yaṣiḥḥu, ṣiḥḥah*' and '*jâza, yajûzu, jawâz*' as did the Baṣrians.

[21] Contrast the statement of 'Abd al-Jabbâr (*al-Muġni* 6/1, p. 58, 6ff.): "Our general

position is this: acts that are bad are of two sorts, (1) thóse which are bad intrinsically and not by virtue of a relationship to something else, e.g., an unjust act's being unjust, a false statement's being false, to will a wrongful act, to command a wrongful act..., and (2) those which are bad by virtue of that to which they are conducive, which is the case with those acts which are revealed by God to be bad (*al-qabâ'iḥu š-šar'iyyah*), wich are bad only in that they are conducive to one's doing something which is rationally bad (*qabîḥun 'aqlî*) ..."

Concerning the distinction made here between what is rationally bad (i.e., known to be bad by autonomous reason) and what is bad since God prohibits it, and the reduction of the latter to the former, see my 'Reason and Revealed Law,' in *Recherces d'Islamologie, Recueil d'articles offert à Georges C. Anawati et Louis Gardet* (Bibliothèque philosophique de Louvain, 26), S. van Riet (ed.), Institut supérieur de philosophie, Louvain-la-Neuve 1978, pp. 124ff.

22 The expression "essential attribute" (*ṣifatun dâtiyyah*) in a-Šahrastânî, *loc. cit.* is equally ambivalent in this context and is most likely no more than a paraphrase of the '*li-nafsihî*' found in al-Ash'arî.

23 *al-Masâ'il,* § 138, p. 354, 22f.

24 *al-Intiṣâr*, p. 38, 24.

25 *al-Intiṣâr*, p. 28, 6: *li'anna l-qâdira 'alà šay'in ġayru muḥâlin wuqû'uhû minhû.*

26 *al-Muġnî* 6/1, p. 141, 7f.

27 'Abd al-Jabbâr appears to recognise this, for in the context of a general apology for the Mu'tazila as a whole he mitigates the statements he makes concerning an-Naẓẓâm's teaching in the *Muġnî* where he is arguing for the correctness ofthe doctrine of his own school. Thus, against the accusation that an-Naẓẓâm held that God does not act by choice but by the necessity of his nature, he says, "This is not so, since he (an-Naẓẓâm) holds that there is no ethically bad action of which one can give a concrete example (*yušâru 'ilayhî*) save that God is able to do acts which are similar to it (*'amṯâluhû*) and which are ethically good, wherefore it is possible (*yaṣiḥḥu*) that He choose one good action over another" (*Faḍl al-I'tizâl*, p. 348, 12–14; cp. *al-Intiṣâr*, p. 39, 1–4).

CHAPTER 5

DIVINE OMNISCIENCE AND FUTURE CONTINGENTS IN ALFARABI AND AVICENNA

Michael E. Marmura

1. INTRODUCTION

If God has knowledge of all future happenings, are not then all human acts predetermined? This, in essence, is the question which Alfarabi (al-Fārābī) (d. 950) poses and discusses in his major commentary on Aristotle's *De Interpretatione*, at the end of his detailed exegesis of the problematic chapter ix of this work.[1] He discusses it, that is, in terms of his understanding of Aristotle's position on the truth-status of declarative statements about future contingents. He does not, as we shall see, bring into his discussion the question of divine causality.

Avicenna (Ibn Sīnā) (d. 1037) also discusses the truth-status of statements about future events in his own *De Interpretatione* of the *Logic of the Healing* (*al-Shifā'*).[2] Unlike Alfarabi, however, he does not introduce the question of divine foreknowledge in its relation to human action in this logical context. Nor does he introduce it in any precise fashion in his metaphysical writings,[3] although some of the main issues raised by it are very much there. We meet them, for example, in his discussions of providence, evil and the fate of the human soul in the hereafter. On the other hand, in related discussions of the nature of divine knowledge, Avicenna makes explicit statements about God's foreknowledge of individual events.[4] The immediate concern of these statements, however, is not theodicy, but the demonstration that such knowledge implies neither change nor a multiplicity of concepts in the divine essence. Nonetheless, these statements do evoke the question posed by Alfarabi. For, according to Avicenna's emanative cosmogony, the world proceeds from God as a consequence of his knowledge. Divine knowledge, in this philosophy, is causative knowledge. Moreover, Avicenna's doctrine of divine causative knowledge embodies his theory that God knows particulars "in a universal way" (*'alā naḥwin kulliyy*).

It is this theory of God's knowledge of particulars that prompts one to ask whether or not it entails the determinism of all human acts. For the expression, "particulars" (*al-juz'iyyāt*), in Avicenna refers not only to things

T. Rudavsky (ed.), Divine Omniscience and Omnipotence in Medieval Philosophy, 81–94.

or entities, but also to events (including those enacted by men) – past, present and future. God, then, according to this theory has foreknowledge of all particular human acts, but "in a universal way." Does such a theory entail determinism? Clearly the question has to be raised and discussed in terms of what is meant by knowing the particular in a universal way. For, as we shall indicate, historically there have been two main interpretations of Avicenna's meaning.

In what follows, we will begin with Alfarabi's formulation and discussion of the question of divine foreknowledge as it relates to determinism in his commentary on *De Interpretatione*. We will then address ourselves to this question as it is evoked by Avicenna's doctrine of causative knowledge, more specifically, by his theory that God knows particulars in a universal way, in each of the two ways this theory has been understood.

2. NECESSITY AND CONTINGENCY IN ALFARABI

A detailed review of Alfarabi's comprehensive exegesis of *De Interpretatione* is beyond our scope here. As we have intimated, our primary concern is with his discussion of divine foreknowledge in the light of his understanding of Aristotle on the truth-status of statements about future contingents. It is to the essentials of this understanding, as we perceive them, that we will now turn.

Alfarabi, in effect, reads Aristotle as upholding the applicability of the law of excluded middle to statements about future contingent events. Accordingly, a statement about such a future event is necessarily either true or false, but, at the present, is neither true determinately nor false determinately (*'alā al-taḥṣīl*). Alfarabi's Arabic expression *'alā al-taḥṣīl*, translates more literally as "by way of realization," "by way of obtainment," or an equivalent of this, the idea conveyed being that of something completed and settled. It also carries with it the idea that the truth or falsity of a statement is something that is realized or accomplished objectively, independently of our knowledge. He thus writes: "The meaning of 'determinateness' (*al-taḥṣīl*) is for one of the two opposite [propositions] to be true in itself (*fī nafsihi*), even if we do not know its truth, the other false, even if we do not know its falsity."[5]

Statements that can be either true or false determinately include properly quantified universal statements and those about particular events in the past and the present. They also include a class of statements about the future, namely, those about non-contingent (causally determined) future events such as eclipses and the like.[6] Statements that are not true or false determinately include indefinite statements ("man is just," for example) and those with which we are concerned, statements about future contingents.

Now, if we read Alfarabi aright, all statements about causally determined events (past, present and future) are true or false determinately, but not every statement that is true or false determinately is about such causally determined events. On the other hand, all determinately true or false statements are "necessary" in one or another sense of this term. Here we encounter perhaps the most tantalizing aspect of Alfarabi's comments. For although he introduces clarifications in the use of this term, some of the ambiguities original with Aristotle persist. Thus – and this is more evident in the sections prior to the discussion of divine foreknowledge – the distinction between the causal, the logical and what one might call the existential use of this term is blurred. Of the various meanings of "necessary" implicit in his comments or explicity discussed by him, two should be singled out as the most relevant for the discussion of divine foreknowledge.

The first is the use of the term to characterize the truth or falsity of statements affirming or denying particular events past and present. These statements are necessary because such events themselves are "necessary". Alfarabi follows Aristotle and seems to hold that such events are necessary because they are "irrevocable" or "temporally necessary", to borrow expressions used in recent comments on Aristotle's meaning. He also seems to relate the necessity of these events to Aristotle's idea that whatever exists, cannot while it exists, not exist. As a consequence of regarding past and present events in this way, Alfarabi in his comments directly relating to Aristotle's texts tends to use the term "contingent" to mean "future contingent", only. But, as we shall see, once he introduces the question of divine foreknowledge, he argues that a thing can be necessary, not in itself, but in terms of some other circumstance, remaining in itself possible. He does not state explicitly that some past and present events, namely those due either to human deliberation or to chance, that are "necessary" in the sense of being "irrevocable", remain in themselves contingent. But the logic of his position seems to lead to this.

The second use of the term "necessary" refers to the relation between a true or false statement and the state-of-affairs with which it corresponds or or does not correspond. A background for this usage is *Categories*, 12, 14b, 11–24, where Aristotle speaks of the relation between a fact and a true statement declaring it.[7] The fact is in a sense the cause of the true statement and "naturally" prior, but the inferential relation between fact and true statement is reciprocal. Thus for Alfarabi, a true statement "necessarily" implies the fact it declares. In discussing God's knowledge of future contingents, as we shall see, he tends to regard this necessity in purely logical terms, saying little about the causative nature of such knowledge.

3. ALFARABI'S DISCUSSION OF DIVINE FOREKNOWLEDGE AND DETERMINISM

With these two uses of the term, "necessary", in mind, we will turn to Alfarabi's remarks introducing the question of divine foreknowledge. As we have noted earlier, future events for him are not all contingent, but include necessary events such as eclipses and the like. From the point of view of human knowledge, he argues, future contingent events are by their very nature unknowable and for this reason they are unknown to us. Future necessary events, on the other hand, are not unknowable by their very nature and when unknowable to us this is simply due to our deficiency. What happens then to this distinction when viewed from the standpoint of divine omniscience? It is in this context that Alfarabi poses the problem of divine foreknowledge and determinism. His formulation of the difficulty bears quotation in full:

If this then is the case, someone may ask about God's knwledge of one of the two opposites in things contingent – does He know it? If it is the case [that He does], then what would be the state of the truth of one of those opposites with Him, exalted be His praise? Would its truth with Him, in terms of His knowledge of it, be determinate or not? If it does not indicate determinateness with Him, then it would fall in [the category of] the non-determinate with Him as it is with us. Hence God would not know regarding future possible things which of the two opposites, the affirmative or the negative, will be realized. These would thus be unknown to God. God then would not know things before their existence. [But] this is repugnant and unacceptable. All the religions have brought forth the opposite of this. It appears that to believe this would be extremely harmful for people.

If this, then [cannot be] the case, and God, [on the contrary], knows the truth of one of the two opposites determinately, then the indeterminateness in it is not intrinsic to the very nature of the thing and the reason for our ignorance of it is not due to the nature of the thing but to a deficiency in our own nature. This being the case, the truth of one of the two opposites is then in itself determinate even if we do not know this. It would thus be on a par with what is indeterminate for us with respect to [future] necessary [things] unknown to us.

But if we accept this, then the doubt Aristotle mentioned confronts us again. This is that whatever is known as a truth that it will be, cannot not be. Hence the existence of what will exist in the future when the prior statement regarding it is true becomes necessary. All things then revert to becoming necessary in themselves, becoming possible only in terms of our knowledge. Hence will, deliberation and all the things Aristotle mentioned cease. It then becomes necessary in all religions that in his doing of anything man has basically no choice. Thus what comes to him by way of punishment in this world and the next is not due to something of his doing that has come about through his will and choice. Thus God, who rewards and punishes, would not then be just in His action. But these things also are all repugnant and reprehensible according to all the religions and very very harmful for people to believe.[8]

Alfarabi begins his attempt at resolving the problem by reporting a general answer which some have offered. God, according to this answer, "knows every existent as it exists . . . the necessary as necessary, the possible as possible . . . the opposites of the necessary in accordance with what they are and the opposites of the possible in accordance with what they are".[9] Not only is such an answer too general, Alfarabi remarks, but in the final analysis it simply concedes that "God does not know the possible before its coming into existence".[10]

The real answer, he insists, is in the distinction between what is necessary in the sense of being a consequence of something else and what is necessary in itself. A thing can be the necessary consequence of another thing while remaining in itself possible. Thus a future event may be necessary in the sense of being the necessary consequent of a preceding true statement, but this does not mean that it becomes necessary in itself, that in itself it does not remain contingent. Thus, he argues, if we have true knowledge that a certain individual, Zayd, will travel tomorrow, it follows necessarily that he will travel.[11] But this does not mean that his traveling is in itself necessary, that it does not come about through Zayd's will and that he does not have the ability or capacity (*al-quadra*) to stay at home. Thus, something may well be necessary in one respect, possible in another. For, Alfarabi goes on to explain, Plato held the view that although something may exist eternally, its non-existence may remain possible, and something may never exist, while its existence remains possible. Thus in one respect the existence or non-existence of something is necessary, in another possible. He continues:

Thus whoever holds the view that something pre-eternal did not exist and continues not to exist but that it is possible for it to exist, or that something exists pre-eternally and continues to exist but that it is possible for it not to exist, must necessarily admit that God, exalted be He, knows with certainty that Zayd will travel and [that accordingly] Zayd will travel, without this removing from Zayd the ability not to travel, even though this travelling will necessarily take place tomorrow.

Reward and punishment do not occur in terms of what is foretold to the effect that Zayd will or will not perform his act, but in terms of his ability of doing or not doing it. If, then, God's knowledge regarding him that he will perform the act is prior, this divine knowledge that he will perform the act does not remove his ability of not doing it. It does follow necessarily, however, that he would do what God knew he would do and that Zayd will not refrain from doing it. This necessity, however, consists in Zayd's act being a necessary consequence of God's knowledge, not that Zayd's act is in itself necessary in addition to what has rendered it a necessary consequence.[12]

This, then, is Alfarabi's solution. Foreknowledge does not remove contingency. In the case of human acts, it removes neither will nor the ability to act differently from what was foreknown. Moreover, men are judged, rewarded and punished, not in terms of the foreknowledge of their acts, but in terms of their choices and abilities to act in alternative ways. The fact that events must correspond with the foreknowledge of their happening, does not mean that such events cease to be contingent. God's foreknowledge hence does not deprive man of his freedom of choice and is not contrary to his justice.

We note in this answer that there is no mention of the relation of divine causality to divine knowledge. It is as though in this discussion God for Alfarabi is only a spectator, only a knower of events past, present and future. It is the omission of explicit references to God's causality that lends his argument its measure of persuasiveness. But in traditional natural theologies the problem has arisen because God not only has foreknowledge of all future happenings, but because he is also the omnipotent creator of all things. He has detailed knowledge of all future events and creates a world that accords with this knowledge. It is here (given the way – whether appropriate or not – the problem has traditionally been formulated) that the difficulty is encountered in reconciling the concepts of divine omnipotence and omniscience with the concepts of man's freedom of the will and of divine justice.

And the difficulty can become compounded when we take into account the emanative doctrine of creation Alfarabi expounds in some of his writings. For his expositions lend themselves to the interpretation that God's knowledge is causative, that the world proceeds as the consequence of his knowledge. But there is not sufficient explicit detail to ascertain Alfarabi's exact position on this point. For this reason it is perhaps best to pursue the ramifications of the question of divine omniscience and future contingents in a derivative emanative system where the doctrine of the causative nature of divine knowledge is explicity stated and developed. This is the system of Avicenna.

4. AVICENNA'S EMANATIVE SCHEME AND DIVINE CAUSATION

Avicenna's doctrine of divine causative knowledge expresses itself in his triadic emanative scheme. Although this scheme is relatively familiar to historians of philosophy, a summary of its essentials is necessary in the attempt to locate the question of God's knowledge of future events within Avicenna's metaphysical thought. The scheme rests on his division of existence into the necessary in itself and the possible in itself. Every existent other than God is in itself only possible, its existence deriving from an external cause. This is its essential proximate efficient cause that coexists with it and necessitates it. Thus, although each existent other than God is in itself only possible, it is rendered necessary by its cause. The world is thus a system of coexisting necessitating causes and necessitated effects, the primary cause necessitating the entire system being God, the existent necessary in himself.

God, who is one and simple, undergoes an eternal act of self-knowledge. This act necessitates directly the existence of one being only, a pure intelligence. Implicit here is the principle that from the one only one proceeds. Plurality proceeds from this intelligence, not directly from God. For plurality is implicit in the very fact that this intelligence is (a) a necessitated existent and (b) an existent that in itself is only possible. The intelligence, in its turn, undergoes an eternal act of knowing. It knows eternally the three circumstances of existence it encounters: God's existence as necessary in itself; its own existence as necessitated by an external cause; and its own existence as in itself only possible. Since from the one only one proceeds, these three acts of cognition necessitate the emanation of three things only, another intelligence, a soul and a body – the outermost sphere of the heavens. A similar cognitive activity is undertaken by the second intelligence, resulting in the emanation from it of a third intelligence, another soul and another body, the sphere of the fixed stars. Such a cognitive activity is repeated by successive intelligence, giving rise to successive triads, each consisting of an intelligence, a soul and a body. These triads include as their bodily components the planetary spheres as well as the spheres of the sun and of the moon. The last of the celestial intelligences is the Active Intellect, from which the world of generation and corruption emanates.

In this scheme, the individual in each celestial triad represents a species that is different from the species of the corresponding individual in the successive triads.[13] Thus in each of these triads each existent represents the only member of its species. Thus, for example, there is the species moon and only one individual member of this species, the one moon of Avicenna's astronomy. The situation becomes different in the world of generation and corruption. For although in this terrestrial world the triads in a sense continue as triads of kinds of existence – since existents in such a world can be classified as either bodies, souls or intellects (that is, rational human souls) – the triad of individuals breaks down. Species divide into subspecies and the subspecies into numerous individual members. This point is basic to our understanding of Avicenna's doctrine of divine knowledge, as we shall shortly see.

Equally important for understanding this doctrine is the function of each member in the celestial triad and its relation to the other.[14] The celestial intelligence is both an efficient and a final cause. It is the efficient cause productive of the triad immediately succeeding it, but within its own triad, acts as the final cause. It is the object of desire of the soul in the triad and it is this soul's desire for the intelligence that causes the circular movement of the sphere. The movement of the sphere in turn is a causal factor in the production of movement and change, of individual events, in the terrestrial world. The intelligence in the triad is akin to God in that it is pure mind whose knowledge is conceptual. Like God it knows particulars only "in a universal way". The celestial soul, on the other hand, is akin to the practical rational soul in man. It cogitates in terms of the particulars it apprehends directly in a manner analogous to sense perception. Moreover, inasmuch as it is efficacious, whether directly or indirectly, in the production of terrestrial events, it has knowledge of individual future happenings.

5. THE NATURE OF DIVINE OMNISCIENCE AND DETERMINISM

God's knowledge of particulars as we have indicated is qualified as being "in a universal way". This qualification has several overlapping meanings that are not always explicity differentiated in Avicenna's texts. Thus, for example, sometimes it refers primarily to the nature of God's knowledge as such, sometimes to the manner of his knowing, sometimes to the object of this knowing.[15] One meaning, however, which is quite explicit in Avicenna and on which his interpreters all agree, refers to the nature of this knowledge as being (a) intellectual or conceptual, not sensory, and (b) eternal, in the sense of being outside time and changeless. Thus, to use Avicenna's oft repeated example, God knows eternally the occurrence of a particular eclipse, its extent and duration; his knowledge, however, remains the same, implying no change in the knower, before, during and after the event.

This concept of God's eternal changeless knowledge of a transient event raises some of philosophy's perennial problems. How does this knowledge which is outside time relate to its temporal object? Or, to express another facet of this question: In what way is this eternal, timeless knowledge prior to such a transient event? Can we speak of this priority as temporal? If not, in what sense can we speak of God as having knowledge of a "future" event? Avicenna does not discuss this point in any detail, his main argument being that if God's knowledge before, during and after an event is different this would mean change in his essence. God's knowledge is eternal and changeless and the events we designate from our standpoint as past, present and future, are all present to him in an eternal, timeless, now. Inherent in this doctrine of divine knowledge is an abstract concept of time that seems very much at variance with the way we normally feel and speak about the passage of events. Here we have in embryo some of the issues currently debated about the nature and language of time.

Another question raised by this concept of divine knowledge is quite basic to Avicenna's emanative scheme. If God's knowledge is essentially self-knowledge, how then does God know others, including particulars known by him "in a universal way?" On this he has something very specific to say. He writes:

> As for the manner of this, it is because when [God] conceives His essence and conceives that He is the principle of every existent, He conceives the principles of the existents [that proceed] from Him and what is generated by them. There is no existent which is not in some way necessitated because of Him – this we have shown. The collisions of these causes result in the existence of particular things. The first knows the causes and their corresponding [effects]. He thus necessarily knows what these lead to, the time [intervals] between them and their recurrences. For it is not possible that He knows [the former principles] and not the latter.[16]

Hence God's self-knowledge includes knowledge of himself as the cause of all other existents, and his knowledge of himself as cause entails knowledge of all the effects of his causality. God thus knows particulars, whether events or entities, as effects of his causality. It is here that we encounter divergence in interpreting this theory. God, according to Avicenna, knows particulars individually, thought in a universal way; does this then mean that he knows all particulars? More specifically, does God in his eternal changeless knowledge know each and every particular in both the celestial and the terrestrial realms?

Some interpreters of this theory have answered in the affirmative.[17] God knows eternally by a conceptual knowledge each and every particular in the celestial and the terrestrial realms. To be sure, these interpreters argue in effect, since God is pure intellect, the object of his knowledge is the universal. This, however, does not prevent God from also knowing intellectually the particular as a particular. For the particulars have attributes or qualities that are universal and hence known to God. Particulars in the world of generation and corruption share common universal qualities. This sharing, however, is never uniform. Each and every particular differs from another in that it possesses different combinations of the common universal qualities. In other words, it is by virtue of the different combinations of these universal qualities that a particular becomes specified and identified for a celestial intelligence that otherwise has no access to knowing it through sensory perception. It is thus that God's eternal conceptual knowledge, whose object by definition is the universal, also knows each and every particular in both the celestial and the terrestrial realms.

If God, then, knows each and every particular in the terrestrial world, he knows each and every individual of the human species and each and every human act. Given this interpretation of Avicenna, it is difficult to see how it can escape the consequence of utter determinism. There is, to begin with, the necessity that all individual terrestrial events, including the individual events enacted by individual men, correspond with divine foreknowledge. Alfarabi's argument that this need not remove human deliberation and free choice is not convincing in this context. For God, in this interpretation of Avicenna, is not a mere spectator. Each and every event is ultimately the consequence of his causality. The terrestrial event is the last effect of a chain of necessitated causes and effects proceeding from God. By knowing himself as cause, he knows all the effects that follow necessarily from his causality. (The object of knowledge is not the cause of divine knowledge. The relation is the reverse: God knows and the existent comes into being as the necessary consequence of this knowledge.)

There is, however, compelling textual evidence indicating that this interpretation does not correspond with what Avicenna actually holds. In his discussions of definition, he makes it quite plain that universal qualities alone can never specify or identify a corruptible individual.[18] In the terrestrial world such identification must ultimately rest on direct sensory perception. God, being pure mind, has thus no knowledge of the terrestrial particular – whether entity or event – as a particular, knowing only its universal qualities. He knows, that is, the kinds of terrestrial particulars and the kinds of terrestrial events, but not each and every particular entity or particular event.

In the celestial world, the circumstances are different. As we have indicated, in each celestial triad, each existent represents the only member of its species. God, as the cause of these sequences of triads, knows this fact. He knows, for example, the universal qualities belonging to the species, sun, and the knows that this species has only one member. It is in this sense that he knows the individual sun, and every other celestial entity. Avicenna also tells us that events attributed to such entities are also known to God individually. "Particular things", he writes, "can be conceived just as universals are conceived when these particulars are necessitated by their causes and are related to a principle where the species is confined to its one individual instance. An example of this is an individual eclipse".[19] This kind of intellectual apprehension of the particular, whether entity or event, is not possible in the terrestrial world for the very reason that the particular in this world is not the only member of its species.

Hence in this interpretation of Avicenna's theory, God does not know each and every particular in the world of generation and corruption. He thus does not know individual men nor individual human acts. It would thus seem that the problem of divine foreknowledge of human acts and determinism does not arise. This, however, in Avicenna's system is not the case. To begin with, there are celestial beings that have foreknowledge of mundane particulars. These are the celestial souls that also act as efficient causes in the production of terrestrial happenings. This point, it should be added, is quite fundamental to Avicenna's theory of prophecy. For it is the reception by the prophet of such knowledge from these souls that enables him to foretell future events.[20] Secondly, the entire chain of existence descending from God is the necessary consequence of divine knowledge. If, in the world of generation and corruption, this knowledge stops at the universal, without penetrating to the particular, this is hardly a guarantee that these particulars, including human acts, are not causally determined, or, rather, "predetermined" since they are ultimately the consequences of God's eternal knowledge.

6. THEOLOGICAL IMPLICATIONS OF AVICENNA'S NECESSITARIANISM

One main difficulty posed by Avicenna's philosophy is reconciling some of his statements that seem to affirm man's freedom of the will with his necessitarian metaphysics.[21] His discussion of providence, evil and the hereafter, on the other hand, seems to be quite consistent with this necessitarianism.[22] A full discussion of this is beyond our scope here, but a reference to the opening statement on the question of fate and evil in the *Isharat* is illustrative. After asking quite pointedly why it is that if there is fate or destiny (*al-qadar*) there is punishment, he answers:

Punishment for the soul for its transgression is similar illness for the body for its gluttony. [Punishment] is one of the consequences led to by past circumstances whose occurrence and the occurrence of what succeeds them are inevitable.[23]

The soul's punishment in the hereafter (eternal unfulfilled yearning for the body, on the one hand, and for the celestial intelligences, on the other)[24] is a natural consequence of its not having actualized its rational potentialities. Its transgressions that impeded this actualization have as their automatic consequence, so to speak, the soul's suffering in the hereafter. Punishment is not meted out by "an external principle for it" (*mabda' lahu min al-khārij*),[25] from a vengeful God.[26] Not that the literal understanding of the scriptures on reward and punishment in the hereafter is not useful and necessary for the well-being of the non-philosophic masses.[27] But properly understood, God does not mete out punishment, the latter being a natural consequence of the soul's history. In this way, as it seems, Avicenna strives to safeguard the concept of divine justice. But this in reality evades the issue. For he leaves unanswered the question of why it is that some souls are destined to sin, some not to sin, some to suffer eternal misery, some to enjoy eternal bliss.

NOTES

1 Al-Fārābī (Alfarabi), *Alfarabi's Commentary on Aristotle's περι ἑρμηνειας (De Interpretatione)*, W. Kutsch and S. Marrow (eds.), Imprimerie Catholique, Beirut 1960, pp. 81–101. This text will be abbreviated, *Commentary*, in the notes. For a modern interpretation of *De Interpretatione* ix with a specific reference to Alfarabi's exegesis, see N. Rescher, 'An Interpretation of Aristotle's Doctrine of Future Contingency and Excluded Middle,' *Studies in the History of Arabic Logic*, University of Pittsburgh Press, Pittsburgh 1963, pp. 43–54.

2 Ibn Sīnā (Avicenna), *Al-Shifā, (Healing): al-Mantiq (Logic) III; al'ibāra (De Interpretatione)*, M. Khudayri (ed.), revised by I. Madkour, National Press, Cairo 1970, pp. 70–75. This text will be referred to in the notes as *'Ibāra*.

3 In his writings on theodicy, Avicenna's most explicit statement regarding divine knowledge occurs in his *Risāla Fī Sirr al-Qadar*. See G. F. Hourani, "Ibn Sīnā's 'Essay on the Secret of Destiny,' " *Bulletin of the School of Oriental and African Studies* 29, part 1, (1966), pp. 25–48. The statement occurs on p. 28 of the Arabic text, p. 31 of Hourani's translation, which is as follows: "The first premise is that you should know that in the world as a whole and in its parts, both upper and earthly, there is nothing which forms an exception to the facts that God is the cause of its being and origination and that God has knowledge of it, controls it, and wills its existence; it is all subject to His control, determination, knowledge and will". This work will be abbreviated as "Secret of Destiny" in the notes.

4 Ibn Sīnā (Avicenna), *Al-Shifâ (Healing); al-Ilâhiyyât (Metaphysics)*, edition supervised by I. Madkour, National Press, Cairo 1960, pp. 358–62; *al-Ishârât wa al-Tanbîhât*, S. Dunya (ed.), Parts II & IV (Metaphysics and Mysticism), Cairo 1958,

pp. 712–728. These works will be abbreviated *Ilâhiyyât* and *Ishārāt, respectively.*
5 *Commentary*, p. 81, lines 12–13.
6 *Ibid.*, p. 83, lines 1–2
7 For a discussion of the relation between a true statement and the state of affairs it refers to in Aristotle, see D. Frede, *Aristoteles und die 'Seeschlacht'*, Vandenhoeck and Ruprecht, Göttingen 1970, pp. 19–23.
8 *Commentary*, p. 97, line 27 and p. 98, line 19.
9 *Commentary*, p. 98, lines 21–24.
10 *Ibid.*, p. 98, lines 25–27.
11 *Ibid.*, p. 99, lines 1–8. The text translates as follows: "But the correct answer is to say that the necessary consequence of one thing from another does not mean that the former is necessary in itself. This is because from the truth of the affirmative statement the existence of the thing follows necessarily. From this it does not follow that the existence of the thing is in itself necessary. Its being a consequence of the truth of the statement, however, is necessary. But it does not follow that when something is a necessary consequence of another it is then in itself necessary, as for example, the conclusions that in themselves are possible that follow necessarily from the premises that yield them, without these necessary conclusions being in themselves necessary. For their possibility is not removed by the necessity of their consequence from the premises".
12 *Ibid.*, p. 100, lines 5–13.
13 *Ilâhiyyât*, p. 409, lines 4–9. The earth, taken as a unit, not the individual happenings within it, is also the only member of its species.
14 *Ibid.*, p. 387, lines 4–8; p. 436, lines 14–15; p. 437, lines 10–11; *Ishârât*, p. 863ff.
15 For a detailed discussion of this, see my article, 'Some Aspects of Avicenna's Theory of God's Knowledge of Particulars,' *JAOS* **82**, 3 (1962), pp. 299–312. This work will be referred to as, 'Some Aspects'.
16 *Ilâhiyyât*, p. 359, line 15 and p. 360, line 2.
17 'Some Aspects', p. 299, n. 5.
18 *Ilâhiyyât*, pp. 245–47; Ibn Sînâ (Avicenna), *Al-Shifâ' (Healing); Mantiq (Logic) I; al-Madkhal (Isagoge)*, edition supervised by I. Madkour, National Press, Cairo 1952, p. 70, lines 9–20.
19 *Ishārāt*, p. 717.
20 Ibn Sînâ (Avicenna), *Aḥwâl al-Nafs*, F. Awhani (ed.), National Press, Cairo 1952, pp. 114–121; see also note 14 above.
21 For example, in his brief discussion of the truth-status of statements about future events (where his position seems to be akin to that of Alfarabi), he argues that if the truth or falsity of statements about the future are assignable before the occurrence of all such events then the absurdities mentioned by Aristotle would follow, namely, that there will be no coincidental events and for men no freedom of choice. *'Ibâra*, pp. 72–73.
22 See Hourani's discussion, 'Secret of Destiny', p. 36ff.
23 *Ishârât*, p. 742.
24 The human rational soul in its earthly existence requires the bodily faculties of sensation, imagination and memory which it needs for cogitation in terms of particular images. This cogitative activity prepares it for the reception of the intelligibles from the Active Intelligence and hence the actualization of its potentiality. Those rational souls that have succumbed to the animal pleasures and failed to actualize themselves, remain

after separation yearning after the bodily faculties (that no longer exist) needed for this actualization. Such souls remain unfulfilled and incapable of attaining what they ultimately desire, contemplation of the celestial intelligences and God. See, Ibn Sina (Avicenna), *Fî Ithbât al-Nubuwwât (On the Proof of Prophecies)*, M. E. Marmua (ed.), Beirut 1968, pp. 55–58; English translation in R. Lerner and M. Mahdi (eds.), *Medieval Political Philosophy: A Source Book*, Cornell University Press, Ithaca, New York 1963, p. 119. See also, 'Secret of Destiny', p. 28 of Arabic Text, p. 32.

[25] *Ishârât*, p. 742.

[26] "It is not admissible that Reward and Punishment should be such as the theologians suppose: chastisement of the fornicator, for example, by putting him in chains and shackles, burning him in the fire over and over again, and setting scorpions and snakes upon him. For this is the behaviour of one who wills to slake his wrath against his enemy, through injury or pain which he inflicts on him out of hostility against him; and this is impossible in the character of God the Exalted . . . ." "Secret of Destiny", p. 33.

[27] *Ishârât*, pp. 742ff. (including al-Ṭusî's comments).

CHAPTER 6

SOME REFLECTIONS ON THE PROBLEM OF FUTURE CONTINGENCY IN ALFARABI, AVICENNA, AND AVERROES

Barry S. Kogan

1. INTRODUCTION

If truth-values can be assigned to all propositions, including those dealing with future contingent events, does it not follow that such events are not genuinely contingent? Must they not eventually occur or not occur, as the case may be, just as these propositions state, irrespective of deliberation, choice, and chance, precisely because the facts and true propositions about them must be in accord? And even if we cannot assign truth-values to propositions about future contingent events, owing to our ignorance or to some other impediment, would an omniscient being likewise be so restricted? Would he not have all the requisite knowledge of the facts prior to their occurrence so that they would be determined in advance and therefore not truly contingent? These questions, which together make up the problem of future contingents as it was known to the *falāsifa* of medieval Islam, elicited an unusual variety of responses from Alfarabi, Avicenna, and Averroes. This variety is all the more noteworthy because they all proceed from a common line of interpretation regarding Aristotle's intention in *De Interpretatione* 9, where the issue is first discussed. All three agree that the point of Aristotle's discussion is to show that we cannot assign truth-values to future contingent propositions, i.e., that some statements are not yet either true or false. But having agreed on this significant point, they nonetheless differ markedly when they address the problem in its theological dimension; these differences certainly call for clarification.

In this connection, I think, we are much indebted to Professor Marmura for his concise and illuminating discussion of Alfarabi and Avicenna on the relation of divine omniscience to the problem of future contingents. Working with admittedly difficult and cryptic materials, he has successfully identified both the general outlines of their resolution and the gaps and ambiguities that attend them. Since I am largely in agreement with his analysis, I would like to make only a few contextual comments regarding it and then go on to round out the picture by showing how the problem was handled by their successor, Averroes.

T. Rudavsky (ed.), Divine Omniscience and Omnipotence in Medieval Philosophy, 95–101.

2. DIVINE OMNISCIENCE AND FUTURE CONTINGENTS IN ALFARABI AND AVICENNA

Marmura presents Alfarabi's argument roughly as follows:

(1) Statements about future contingent events are necessarily either true or false at some time, i.e., when they are determinate.

(2) God foreknows as determinate all true statements about future contingent events, e.g., human free choices.

(3) What God knows to be true will necessarily happen.

(4) What necessarily happens, occurs either (4a) because it is necessary in itself, or (4b) because it is necessarily caused, or (4c) because it is necessary as a consequence of a true statement.

(5) Only events which are necessary in themselves or necessarily caused [(4a) and (4b)] are incompatible with contingency or freedom.

(6) Therefore, what happens as a consequence of God's knowing a true statement [(4c)] is fully compatible with contingency and freedom.

I agree with Marmura that this argument accurately expresses Alfarabi's view, and I also agree that by omitting any reference to divine causality, it treats God as a kind of cosmic spectator. But it is hard to agree that this omission lends any significant persuasiveness to Alfarabi's position. Premise 5 is stated without argument on the part of Alfarabi, and insofar as it is undefended, it seems arbitrary to claim that only events necessary in themselves (i.e., irrevocable at the time of their occurrence) or necessarily caused are incompatible with contingency and freedom. Accordingly, some analysis of contingency in general and of human freedom as a particular example of it would be in order before premise 5 can be admitted. More to the point, however, is the fact that an event necessitated by God's foreknowledge of a determinately true statement about the future is certainly not contingent with respect to that knowledge. While it may very well be true that the passage of time allows the event to become necessary in itself (i.e., irrevocable at the time of its occurrence) and that human choice makes it causally necessary, these both turn out to be at most incidental determinants compared to God's foreknowledge in making one outcome rather than another necessary in the first place. Clearly, the threat to contingency and freedom lies not in the exercise of any compulsion, but in the very determinateness of the outcome *ab initio*.

With Avicenna we encounter the opposite view. Here Marmura rightly notes that Avicenna denies, however cryptically and perhaps reluctantly, that God knows contingent particulars in the sublunar world in their particularity. This, at least, is the import of his standard formula about "God's knowing particulars in a universal way."[1] Yet Avicenna argues explicitly that God nevertheless necessitates their emergence through the act of causal knowing. In short, he is their ultimate agent. Conceivably, this act of causal knowing could establish the requisite connection between God's knowledge and particulars, so as to allow for our saying that he does know particulars in a certain sense, i.e., causally. But even though God is said to know particulars as their cause, he still knows them in only a universal way, since as Marmura points out, the identification of corruptible individuals for Avicenna must ultimately rest on direct sensory perception. But if this is the case, Avicenna has resolved the problem of divine omniscience and future contingent events conceived as particulars only by severely circumscribing divine omniscience. At most God knows all universals and those celestial particulars which are the sole instances of their species, nothing more.[2] It is not surprising therefore that if the ultimate consequences of God's knowledge are unknown to him, his comprehensive causality, particularly in the sublunar world, should be regarded as blind. Hence, Marmura's critical conclusion is entirely valid. If God is assumed not to know particulars as such, Avicenna leaves unanswered the question of why it is the case that some souls are destined to sin and suffer misery, while others are destined not to sin and thus to enjoy eternal bliss. In sum, it is hard to see how there can be divine justice for particular persons, when God's allotments of ability and propensity toward virtue or its opposite, as well as his allotments of reward and punishment, are made without knowledge of the particular recipients involved, much less their individual deeds.

Another consequence of Avicenna's account is that the standard problem of omniscience in relation to future contingents is displaced from the Deity to the celestial souls, for they *are* said to have knowledge of individual future events within their respective spheres.[3] On the assumption that the truth or falsity of statements about the future is determined before the occurrence of the events described, Avicenna maintains that all the absurdities mentioned by Aristotle in the *De Interpretatione* discussion would follow. There would be no coincidental events and no freedom of choice for men. Accordingly, once our point of focus changes to the celestial souls, it turns out that Avicenna's views bear a striking resemblance to those of Alfarabi.

3. FUTURE CONTINGENCY AND DIVINE OMNISCIENCE IN AVERROES

If we turn now to Averroes, we find that he takes up the philosophical and theological aspects of the problem in separate discussions. Thus, in his long commentary on the *De Interpretatione* he confines himself to an analysis of Aristotle's presentation without making a single reference to divine omniscience and its bearing on future contingency. The thrust of his interpretation is stated at the outset: opposing statements about past and present events are *entirely* divisible into those that are true and those that are false, "but future things which are contingent are not *entirely* divisible into the true and the false".[4] For if they were, they would be necessary and nothing would come about by chance or any indeterminate cause, just as Aristotle suggests. Having said this, however, Averroes is also concerned to show that the indeterminate truth-value of future contingent propositions does not thereby preclude all knowledge about the future. To this end, he distinguishes between three senses of possibility. The first kind of possibility is one whose realization is no more, but is also no less likely than its non-realization; either outcome may equally well occur. The second kind refers to those possibilities that are realized "for the most part"; their realization is probable, as we might say. The third kind refers to those possibilities that are realized only rarely. Given this set of distinctions, Averroes goes on to argue as follows:

> It is evident that those opposites which divide up [entirely] into the true and the false in regard to material things of all kinds, divide up into the true and the false in necessary kinds of things according to their proper determination in themselves. This is because their truth and falsehood is determinate in themselves outside the mind, although we do not possess determinate knowledge about them and are ignorant of their condition. However, in material things which are possible and contingent in regard to future things, if one is true, then the other is false, since it is necessary that one of the two contradictories come about in the future. But it is not determinate in itself, because according to their very nature they are devoid of determination, just as they likewise are for us. Therefore, knowledge of this class of things cannot be had, because the thing itself is unknown. However, in regard to things which are possible for the most part and not equally possible with respect to either alternative, it is more likely that one of the two opposites be true than the other, since the thing's existence is more likely than its non-existence. Thus, in this class of things determinate knowledge about a given future thing can be had before it come to be, namely, about some future thing whose custom it is to come about for the most part.[5]

Thus it appears that Averroes is just as prepared to include high statistical probability within the realm of scientific knowledge as his modern scientific successors. Predictions about future events constitute genuine knowledge, if they are verified for the most part.

When Averroes turns to the theological dimension of the problem in his other writings, however, it becomes clear that he is chiefly concerned with the dilemma of explaining how God can know particular changes that occur in the world without a corresponding change in his knowledge taking place. Thus he argues in the *Ḍamīma* to the *Faṣl al-Maqāl* that "either the knowledge [of God] varies in itself or the things that come into existence are not known to it".[6] By setting up the problem in this way, he is led to reject explicitly the notion of foreknowledge, which he associates with the Mutakallimun. For whenever a contingent possibility is realized in fact, one may always ask whether a change occurs in God's knowledge or not. To grant that it does implies prior ignorance of what has changed in his knowledge as well as other difficulties. But to deny that a change occurs implies that the knowledge that God has of a thing before it exists can be identical with the knowledge he has of it after it exists; Averroes regards this alternative as unacceptable because it disregards the distinction between non-existence and existence.

His proposed solution is to stress that God's eternal knowledge is radically different from our originated knowledge.[7] It is the cause of the existence of beings, whereas our originated knowledge is the effect of their existence. From this he concludes,

> Just as no change occurs in an agent when his act comes into being, i.e., no change which has not already occurred, so no change occurs in the eternal Glorious Knowledge when the object of Its knowledge results from It. Thus the difficulty is resolved and we do not have to admit that if there occurs no change, i.e., in the eternal Knowledge, He does not know beings at the time of their coming into existence just as they are.[8]

Now it appears as if the object of God's eternal knowledge is simply the changeable particular. But if we press Averroes to be more explicit about its identity, he makes the puzzling claim in the *Tahāfut* that God's knowledge is neither of particulars nor of universals, but is nevertheless more like knowledge of the individual or particular than of the universal.[9] What he seems to mean by the first part of this claim is that God's knowledge does not result from or in any way involve abstraction, whereas human intellectual knowledge of both particulars and universals does result from abstraction. Since God's knowledge cannot receive the forms of particular objects *ab extra* without changing, his knowledge, properly speaking, is therefore neither of the particular nor of the universal. The subsequent suggestion that God's knowledge is more like that of the particular than of the universal, seems to be based on two considerations. (1) In the Aristotelian noetic, knowledge of universals carries an additional dimension of potentiality *vis à vis* that of particulars. While the knower in knowing is cognitively identical with a particular form, this form which is actually known *can* be taken to characterize an indefinite number of individuals. It can be used for purposes of identification again and again within kinds, universally.[10] Thus the universal concept, insofar as it is a *capacity* to re-apply a particular act of knowing to similar cases as they arise, would be less appropriate as the object of God's active and eternal knowledge than would the particular. (2) God's causal knowledge appears to consist in cognitive identity with the paradigms of all specific natures in their best order.[11] It thus sets in motion the natural processes that generate particular individuals and states of affairs primarily as a formal and final cause and only derivatively as an efficient cause. The ultimate effects or "objects" of this knowledge will be individuals, because only individuals as opposed to universals can be meaningfully understood as moving toward an end. This is evidently why Averroes can conclude his discussion of causal knowledge in the *Tahāfut* by saying, "He who has understood this understands the divine words, 'Neither shall the weight of an atom in either heaven or the earth escape it, i.e., His knowledge'."[12] For God may know even the lowly atom, if to know it is to be its formal and final cause.

4. CONCLUDING COMMENTS

By way of evaluating Averroes' position, we may note first of all that the discussion of future contingents in the long commentary on the *De Interpretatione* bears no intrinsic relation to the discussions in the *Ḍamīma* and the *Tahāfut*. How Averroes would have explained that relation remains for the time being entirely conjectural; still it may be the case that he believed that there was no such relation to be explained. Second, if we focus upon the theological discussion, i.e., that having to do with God's knowledge, we should note that Averroes seems to assign two meanings to the word "know" in his doctrine of causal knowing and to alternate between them in developing the theory. One of these is the notion of cognitive identity with intelligible objects. This is at least consistent with the attempt to explain a recognizable doxastic attitude or epistemic state. But the second meaning, i.e., actualizing particular potentialities as a final cause, merely begs the question. For why should the process of causal knowing actualize particular potentialities which are presumably external to itself any more than a philosopher's reflections? The only capacities brought to fulfillment by such activity are presumably the thinker's own. Thus when the theory of causal knowing is recognizably epistemic, it is not causal; and when it is causal, it is not epistemic. How that difficulty can be resolved, if at all, is something that Averroes evidently leaves unanswered.

NOTES

[1] Avicenna, *al-Shifā': al-Ilāhiyyāt*, G. C. Anawati (ed.), *et al.*, Cultural Dept of the Arab League, Cairo 1960, II, 404ff. Cf. Averroes, *Tahāfut al-Tahāfut*, M. Bouyges (ed.), Imprimerie Catholique, Beirut 1930, p. 455.

[2] E. Marmura, 'Some Aspects of Avicenna's Theory of God's Knowledge of Particulars', *Journal of the American Oriented Society* **82** (1962), 292–312.

[3] Avicenna, *al-Shifā': al-Ilāhiyyāt* Book 10:1; vf. Avicenna, *Al-Najā*, M. S. Kurdi (ed.), Cultural Dept of the Arab League, Cairo 1938, 302ff. Averroes, *Tahâfut al-Tahâfut*, p. 497.

[4] Averroes, *Aristotelis De Interpretatione . . . cum Averrois Cordubensis Expositione*, Juntas 1574, fol. 81r E.

[5] *Ibid.*, fol. 82v G–I.

[6] Averroes, *Averroes on the Harmony of Religion and Philosophy*, G. F. Hourani (ed.), Luzac and Ca, London 1961, p. 73, (*Ḍamīma*, 129 ll.2–40).

[7] *Ibid.*, p. 74, (*Ḍamīma*, 130 ll.12–15). Cf. *Tahāfut al-Tahāfut*, pp. 462–463, 468.

[8] *Ibid.*, p. 74, (*Ḍamīma*, 130 ll.15–19).

[9] Averroes, *Tahāfut al-Tahāfut*, pp. 345, 462.

[10] Aristotle, *Metaphysics* 13: 1087a 15–21; Averroes, *Tahāfut al-Tahāfut*, p. 345. See also J. Owens, *The Doctrine of Being in the Aristotelian Metaphysics*, Pontifical Institute of Medieval Studies, Toronto 1963 (2nd edition), pp. 427–30 and *Aristotle: The Collected Papers of Joseph Owens*, J. R. Catan (ed.), State University of New York Press, Albany, N.Y. 1981, pp. 48–58.

[11] Averroes, *Tahāfut al-Tahāfut*, p. 339.

[12] *Qur'an* 34:3.

PART THREE

JEWISH PERSPECTIVES

CHAPTER 7

THE BINDING OF ISAAC: A TEST-CASE OF DIVINE FOREKNOWLEDGE

Seymour Feldman

1. INTRODUCTION: THE BINDING OF ISAAC AS A PARADIGM FOR PHILOSOPHICAL EXEGESIS

The commentary is a particular favorable mode of Jewish literary expression. Shortly after the last biblical book, *The Book of Daniel*, had been written, the *Commentary on the Book of Habbakuk* was composed; this work, which is perhaps the first known biblical commentary, was discovered several decades ago amongst the Dead Sea scrolls of the Qumran library.[1] Not too long afterwards the roots of biblical exegesis were firmly entrenched both in Judea and in Jewish Alexandria. In the latter community a type of exegesis emerged whose first specimen was to be the progenitor of a genre which will have a long and diverse career: the philosophical commentary. Philo of Alexandria wrote more than a score of books in the form of biblical commentaries, in which both the language and ideas of Greek philosophy were used to explain the biblical text. In Judea, however, a different mode of biblical exegesis was being developed. Instead of seeing the Bible as the source of esoteric philosophical meanings, the Rabbis used and read the biblical text for legal and homiletical instruction. Eventually a whole body of rabbinical *midrash* upon the Bible was created that has served as a paradigm for a different type of commentary.[2] In this essay I shall focus on the style of exegesis introduced by Philo, but I shall make use of several medieval examples of this philosophical mode of biblical commentary. The authors I shall study will be either philosophers who also wrote biblical commentaries or philosophers who, although not writing any specific commentary upon a biblical book, frequently comment upon biblical material in their philosophical writings; finally, I shall discuss an author who, although a homileticist and not a philosopher at all, makes use of philosophical ideas in his exegetical writings.

The proof-text for my study will be one of the more illustrious stories in the Bible, the Binding of Isaac, a theme expanded and embellished by the Talmudic rabbis and commented upon by rabbis throughout the ages both in writing and in speech. However, instead of making Abraham or Isaac the

T. Rudavsky (ed.), Divine Omniscience and Omnipotence in Medieval Philosophy, 105–133.

primary hero, which was the practice of the Rabbis, I shall place God in the forefront of my philosophical *midrash* on Genesis 22. Moreover, since God is my main concern, neither Abraham nor Isaac, most of my discussion will focus upon the first and penultimate sentences of the biblical story: "And God tested Abraham" (Genesis 22:1) and "Now I know that you are a God-fearing man" (Genesis 22:12). If we look at the two verbs in these verses, we see that the story of the Binding of Isaac can be read as a story about *God's knowledge*. For, at first it appears that since God was uncertain about Abraham's piety, he tested him; afterwards, when the test was completed, it appears that God acquired new knowledge that removed his uncertainty. Obviously, such a literal reading of the text raises serious philosophical problems which will preoccupy and vex theologians and exegetes throughout the ages. In this essay I shall illustrate how several medieval Jewish philosophers and exegetes used this biblical story to discuss the classic problem of divine omniscience and future contingents.

However, before we reach our hermeneutical domain of medieval Jewish bible exegesis, there is a preliminary way-station at which we must first pause. In the second century Rabbi Akiba enunciated a formula that in a sense constitutes one of the main ground-rules of our inquiry. In the volume of the *Mishnah* known as *Pirke Avoth* ("Sayings of the Fathers") Rabbi Akiba proclaimed: "Everything is seen, yet freedom is given".[3] It is clear from this brief statement that already in the 2nd century Jewish theology had at least recognized, if not solved, the apparent incompatibility between divine omniscience and human freedom. It has been noted by Henry Fischel that several of Rabbi Akiba's dicta, as well as those of some of his colleagues, were stimulated by Hellenistic philosophy.[4] If this were true, then Rabbi Akiba's formula could be seen as synthesizing the seemingly incompatible Stoic thesis of determinism and the Epicurean antithesis of free-will. However we interpret the philosophical provenance of Rabbi Akiba's formula, it is important to see it as a pervasive theme throughout most medieval Jewish theology. It can well serve as a measuring-rod in determining how far any of our medieval exegetes will have moved from classical Jewish theology.

2. THE BIBLICAL COMMENTARIES OF SAADIA GAON

Although Philo was the first full-fledged philosophical biblical exegete, the first such commentator to have major significance in the Jewish tradition was Saadia ben Joseph, more commonly known in Jewish literature as "Saadia Gaon" (882–942). Saadia produced a work that was to influence subsequent biblical exegetes as well as a major portion of the Jewish religious community. This was his Arabic translation of the Bible, the first such translation, which is still used by Arabic-reading Jews. Together with the Arabic commentary, which he wrote as a complement to the translation, his translation of Genesis 22:1–12 will serve to introduce our subject. For Saadia's translation is itself a small-scale commentary as well, in which are found frequent interpretations, rather than translations, of the biblical verse in question. Occasionally his exegesis expresses a philosophical motif; e.g., the frequent removal of anthropomorphic connotations from the text, a tendency that was initiated by the older Greek and Aramaic translations but not consistently adhered to. In our particular text of Genesis 22 this "philosophizing" tendency is evident and provides us with our opening theme.[5]

The usual translation of the opening verse of our chapter reads: "and after these things God *tested* (*'nisa'*) Abraham" (my emphasis). In his rendition of this verse Saadia uses for the Hebrew verb 'nisa' an Arabic equivalent that is ambiguous – 'imtaḥana'. This verb can mean: (1.1) test in the sense of *examine*; or (1.2) test in the sense of *afflict*. It is evident that in this particular verse either of these two connotations will yield a significant reading of the story. Saadia's use of the Arabic 'imtaḥana' to render the Hebrew 'nisa' throughout his translation of the Bible is fairly consistent; yet its connotation varies according to the context. I am inclined to construe 'imtaḥana' in our verse according to the second sense, *afflict*. I do so for two reasons: First, it would seem that subsequent readers of Saadia's translation understood the verb 'imtaḥana' as connoting affliction. In his discussion of this topic Maimonides, in particular, mentions those people who believe that God sends down calamities upon individuals in order to increase their divine reward even though they do not deserve such visitations. Although he does not mention Saadia specifically, Maimonides is, I believe, clearly referring to the interpretation of 'nisa' (*'imtaḥana'*) in the sense of *afflict*. As we shall see in our next section, Maimonides will *reject* this understanding of the "trial" of Abraham's binding of Isaac. Second, in his translation of Job 4:2 Saadia gives the same Arabic translation of the Hebrew 'nisa'; but here it is clear that Job is being tested in the sense of being afflicted. Accordingly, although 'nisa' meaning test makes good sense in our story, I emphasize its connotation of *afflict*.

Assuming then that God decided to afflict Abraham, let us now ask, why? One answer we can preclude *ab initio*. On philosophical-theological grounds Saadia believed firmly in divine omniscience in the strong sense, i.e., God knows everything, including future contingents. Accordingly, God did not afflict Abraham in order to see how Abraham would bear up in adverse circumstances. If he is omniscient he knows that Abraham would endure these travails quite well, indeed extraordinarily well. There must, then, be some other point to the "trial". To discover the purpose of Abraham's affliction we must turn to the end of our story, right after Abraham has lifted up his knife ready to kill Isaac and hears the divine voice ordering him to desist from this extreme act. The standard translation of the subsequent verse is: "For now I know ('yad'ati') that you are a God-fearing man". However, Saadia's Arabic translation of the verb 'yad'ati', is quite different. Instead of the expected ''araftu' ("I knew"), we have ''arraftu alnas', which means "I have made known to mankind". That is, Saadia has removed any suggestion that verse 12 is about God's knowledge at all. Since God is omniscient in the strongest possible sense, *God* didn't learn anything new when Abraham was about to kill Isaac. Rather, he made *others know* what they otherwise would never have dreamed of knowing; namely, there is at least one person who is willing to go to the limits of the love of God by sacrificing his only son. Thus, the purpose of Abraham's affliction is the education of mankind, not the education of God.[6]

Saadia's exegesis of Genesis 22:1–12 is consistent with his philosophical discussion of the problem of divine foreknowledge as developed in his treatise *The Book of Beliefs and Opinions.*[7] There Saadia attempts to solve philosophically the dilemma between God's foreknowledge and man's freedom, a problem that had been noted but not solved by Rabbi Akiba. As far as I know Saadia provided the first Jewish philosophical defense of the claim that the dilemma is spurious and that human freedom is compatible with divine foreknowledge. Saadia's dissolution of the dilemma is based upon a distinction made by the *Mut'aziliya*; these Muslim theologians distinguished between '*x* knowing *p*' *and* '*x* causing *p*'. Just because I know that tomorrow there will be a sea-battle doesn't mean that I have brought it about that there will be a sea-battle; and this is equally true for God. For the Mut'aziliya and Saadia, God's foreknowledge does not *make* the event known come about. If the event is some human act, then the real cause of the event is the man who performs the deed; he is the true agent of the act, not God. Nor is the act the outcome of the cooperative effort of two agents, man and God, as some Muslim theologians suggested. Saadia insists on ascribing agency in the domain of human action to man alone, who is for Saadia is fully free agent, whose capacity to choose is unimpaired by God's omnipotence (as many Muslim theologians believed).[8] Even though an omniscient God knows *ab initio* what each of us will do with our power to choose, we are free in our exercise of this power. In Anthony Kenny's terms, Saadia is then a reconciliationist of the indeterminist type.[9]

3. DIVINE OMNISCIENCE AND THE COMMENTARY TRADITION IN MAIMONIDES

The next chapter in our anthology naturally follows our first, since the author of our second interpretation of the Binding of Isaac was influenced in part by Saadia's reading of the story. As an Arabic-speaking Jew Moses Maimonides grew up with Saadia's translation of the Bible, and to some extent his understanding of our theme was shaped by this translation. However, we shall see that he contributed several new features to the history of this exegetical trope. Unlike Saadia, Maimonides did not write a commentary on the Bible. Nevertheless, as the reader of the Preface to Maimonides' *Guide of the Perplexed* knows, biblical exegesis was the very motive that led to the writing of the book. Throughout the *Guide* Maimonides shows his deep interest in hermeneutical problems, and he eventually devotes a special chapter to the topic of *trial* in the Bible, including our theme of the Binding of Isaac.

Treating this subject immediately after his discussion of the sufferings of Job, Maimonides begins his analysis with a critique of the previously mentioned traditional view that such suffering is an expression of divine love; the Rabbis called it, "the chastisements of love". It would seem then that Saadia's rendering of 'nisa' as 'imtaḥana' connoting *afflict* had taken root amongst Arabic-reading Jews, who interpreted Genesis 22:1 as meaning: And God afflicted Abraham, in analogy with the afflictions of Job. Thus, along with other righteous individuals, Abraham was afflicted by God out of love in order to receive greater reward. Maimonides is unhappy with this view, for it is inconsistent with the principle that God is just and perfect. After all, how could God punish someone who is innocent? Rather, one has to adhere to another Rabbinic idea, namely "there is no suffering without sin".[10] Accordingly, Maimonides rejects the interpretation proposed by Saadia and others that God afflicted Abraham. But what about the other connotation of the Arabic 'imtaḥana' previously noted: to test in the sense of examine? On this interpretation the purpose of the Binding of Isaac would be to see whether Abraham exhibits a certain quality that hitherto was not known to God. But a test in this sense usually implies some uncertainty that we try to remove by subjecting the examinee to an experiment whose outcome will yield information to the examiner. In interpreting the verb 'nisa' ('imtaḥana') in this way, however, we and Maimonides would be clearly departing from Rabbi Akiba's principle that everything is known by God! Indeed, in his discussion of the Binding of Isaac, as well as in chapters 16–20 of Part III of the *Guide*, Maimonides defends strong omniscience just as vigorously as did Saadia. Thus, we have to find some interpretation of 'nisa' besides *afflict* or *examine*.

To this purpose let us turn to the end of the story in the hope that Maimonides' interpretation of verse 12 will help us elucidate the problematic verb in verse 1. What he says with reference to the phrase "For now I know . . ." is more explicit. Following Saadia's translation/interpretation of the verb 'yad'ati' Maimonides reads verse 12 as meaning: "For now I have made known to all mankind that you have attained the limit of what it is to be a God-fearing man". Thus, Maimonides agrees with Saadia on the meaning of verse 12. However, whereas Saadia understands 'nisa' in verb 1 as connoting *afflict*, Maimonides suggests that it should be construed as connoting "making a paradigm". The root of the verb 'nisa' is, on this interpretation 'nassas', connoting *emblem, beacon,* or *model,* as in Isaiah 5:26, 11:12, and 62:10 or in Psalms 60:6. Abraham's binding of Isaac serves as an example for all of us to follow if we want to fear and love God. Thus, in the light of verse 12 we construe Maimonides' reading of verse 1 as follows: "And God decided to make Abraham the paradigm of what it is to fear and love God".[11]

Being committed to strong omniscience, Saadia and Maimonides both made the Binding of Isaac a lesson for others, certainly not for God. In this sense the "testing" of Abraham was not designed for the benefit of the examiner, as are school examinations, but for the edification of third-parties who will read about the results of the test. Some tests are given not to provide information to the examiner but to show off the examinee to others. Consider the proud parents of a three-year-old who tell the child to read a book before some dinner-guests; the parents know quite well that the child will do it, since they have prior evidence of this ability. Similarly, God tests Abraham, knowing that he will pass, just as he tests Job, confident that he too will pass. However, whereas in Job's case the person to convince is Satan, in Abraham's case, it is the reader of the story who is to be instructed. By proving himself worthy of God's confidence Abraham serves as a paradigm of what it is to fear and love God. Accordingly, we could say that instead of rendering the initial verb 'nisa' as "test", we should construe it as "put to the test" in order to show to others what "mettle" the testee is made of.[12]

Nevertheless, if God is fully omniscient so that for him there was no testing of Abraham in the sense of an examination to see how things will turn out, Maimonides, like Saadia, is still faced with the problem of explaining how Abraham was free in his binding of Isaac. Now we must consider the other part of Rabbi Akiba's dictum. Maimonides' avoidance of this horn of the dilemma differs significantly from Saadia's solution. Consistent with his general reluctance to side with the Mut'aziliya, Maimonides develops a different analysis of divine cognition that he believes is sufficient to dissolve the classic dilemma between divine foreknowledge and human freedom. Whereas the Mut'aziliya doctrine is based upon an analogy between the non-causative character of human cognition and divine cognition, Maimonides' analysis moves in the reverse direction. He denies any analogy at all between the human and divine modes of knowledge. Appealing to his general theory of divine attributes, according to which the most proper and correct descriptions of God are negations, or negative predications, he now applies the *via negativa* to the specific attribute of knowledge.[13] Maimonides argues that the term 'know' has a radically different meaning when it is applied to God from its usual connotation when predicated of man. Among the various differences between the two applications is precisely God's unique ability to foreknow some event without this knowledge making the event non-contingent. If it is asked, *how* does God's knowledge differ from man's knowledge such that foreknowledge in the former does not annual the contingency of the event, Maimonides gives two replies, one "low-brow", the other "high-brow". The low-brow answer is simply that we don't understand how God knows anything, any more than we understand his essence, since his knowledge is identical with his essence. Earlier in the *Guide* Maimonides prepared his readers for this answer, stressing both the limits of man's metaphysical knowledge and the importance of the *via negativa*.[14]

His more sophisticated answer, however, is that God's knowledge is *a priori*, whereas human knowledge is *a posteriori*. In this context this distinction amounts to the following claim: whereas man *acquires* his knowledge primarily from sensation, God simply *has* his knowledge; in this sense God's cognition is *original*, or non-acquired. For unlike man, God needs no data from which to derive or to ground his beliefs. In the case of knowing some future state-of-affairs, this distinction would mean that whereas we form beliefs about the future on the basis of present and past data, God does not. He simply knows the future! Our knowledge is always derivative; that of God is never derivative. Accordingly, when Abraham is commanded by God to sacrifice Isaac, a reader of the story may *infer on the basis of Abraham's previous trials* that he would "pass' this one too. But this judgment would be *a posteriori*. God, however, doesn't infer anything about Abraham from any antecedent data; he just "sees" that Abraham will bind Isaac. His knowledge is not then a well-grounded prediction, but a direct "intuition" of the future.[15]

4. GERSONIDES' REJECTION OF THE MAIMONIDEAN INTERPRETATION

Maimonides' attempt to preserve human freedom within the framework of his commitment to divine omniscience in the strong sense proved to be quite controversial. Especially disturbing was the direct link between this doctrine and his theory of negative divine attributes, which several of the major post-Maimonidean medieval Jewish philosophers rejected. To some of these philosophers the *via negativa* was more of a problem than a solution of a problem.[16] With the critique of the latter theory came differences of opinion concerning his theory of divine cognition and his interpretation of the Binding of Isaac.[17] This is how the situation appeared to Levi ben Gershom, or Gersonides (1288–1344), who both as a philosopher and a biblical commentator found Maimonides' reading of the Binding of Isaac and his doctrine of divine foreknowledge unacceptable.[18] The gist of Gersonides' rejection of Maimonides' (or for that matter Saadia's) interpretation of our story is that what makes the episode most interesting is virtually eliminated on that reading. For Gersonides there is here a genuine test, one whose outcome was *not known to anybody* before Abraham actually lifted up his knife. God really tested Abraham, since neither he, Abraham nor anyone else knew how far Abraham would go in his fear of God. In short, on Gersonides' reading of the Binding of Isaac, the testing of Abraham is such that contrary outcomes were genuinely possible right up until Abraham's lifting of the knife. Throughout the whole story Gersonides senses a mood of contingency and uncertainty, *even for God*.[19] But if this is so, are we required to abandon Rabbi Akiba's dictum that *everything* is foreseen? Has Gersonides' commitment to the principle of human freedom forced him to abandon the traditional dogma of divine omniscience? Before we answer this question let us see first how Gersonides glosses our story.

If for Saadia and Maimonides the climax of the story is the sentence "For now I have made known to all mankind", for Gersonides the significance of the episode lies in the opening two verses. Assuming that God really tested Abraham, Gersonides proceeds to examine closely the precise content of God's test, which almost always has been interpreted as the commandment to sacrifice Isaac. However, Gersonides claims that the verbal phrase in the second clause of verse 2 – standardly translated as "offer him there as a sacrifice" – can be given a different translation, and it is this possibility of an alternative rendering that constitutes the test. As Gersonides reads this passage, the story goes like this. Wanting to test Abraham's loyalty and faith, God gives him an *ambiguous* commandment that can be construed in two ways: either (2.1) take Isaac to a mountain and there sacrifice him; or (2.2) take Isaac and *bring him up* (v'ha'alehu) to the mountain for the purpose of teaching him what it is to offer sacrifices to God. In case someone might think that alternative (2.2) is far-fetched, Gersonides reminds us that the Hebrew allows for this interpretation, and he is right. So what we have is this: God tests Abraham by giving him a command that is *intentionally ambiguous* in order to see whether Abraham will construe it according to its normal, or usual, connotation, alternative (2.1), or according to an extended, or remote sense, alternative (2.2). God knows that in general most men would in these circumstances choose (2.2). On the other hand, God also knows that man has free-will and that someone who truly fears and loves him will understand the command according to its usual meaning, sense (2.1). The test consists then in how Abraham will interpret God's ambiguous command and how he will act.[20]

Now imagine Abraham's three-day journey to the mountain. All during this trip he is still trying to determine for himself what exactly God wants him to do. When he reaches the foot of the mountain, he tells his servants to remain there while he and Isaac ascend the mountain; but he also informs them that *both of them* will return. Even on the third day Abraham is still not sure what will happen. *Maybe* God didn't intend him to sacrifice Isaac – so he thinks. Right up to the moment when Abraham reaches the top of the mountain and sees *no* lamb, there was an element of indeterminancy, or contingency, caused by the ambiguity of God's command. This ambiguity enabled Abraham to hope that he would be extricated from his dire predicament. Down deep, however, he believed otherwise: he knew that the ordinary meaning of God's language was that he should *sacrifice Isaac*; he knew that the alternative rendering, although possible, was stretching the language to its limits.

Throughout this whole three-day journey not only was Abraham unsure of what the outcome would be, but *God too* didn't know how Abraham would act. Remember – God *tested* Abraham. According to Gersonides, a good test is one that involves indeterminancy, and indeterminate outcomes are incompatible with foreknowledge. So right up to the moment when Abraham bound Isaac and raised his knife, God *didn't* know what Abraham would do. Accordingly, for Gersonides, the testing of Abraham precluded God's foreknowledge of the result of the test. It would seem then that Gersonides, unlike Saadia or Maimonides, reads at least verse 1 literally: the story of the Binding of Isaac is about *God's* education.

But does this mean that God is not *omniscient*? This claim depends upon how we understand the concept of omniscience. In analogy with one standard medieval definition of divine omnipotence – God can do whatever is doable – [21] Gersonides defines omniscience as knowing whatever is knowable. But what, according to Gersonides, is knowable? Once we have defined the domain of knowable states-of-affairs, we shall have understood the claim that God is omniscient.

In his *Supercommentary on Averroes' Commentary on Aristotle's De Interpretatione*,[22] Gersonides interprets Aristotle's sea-battle inquiry in such a way that for him, as well as for Aristotle, statements about future contingents have no truth-value. Or, as Gersonides says elsewhere, they are "completely potential".[23] This means that such statements are not knowable; for according to Gersonides we can know only what is true. In the present case of divine knowledge, we must then say that when God has first given the command to Abraham, he does not know what Abraham will do, since the statement 'Abraham will bind Isaac' has then no truth-value. However, in not knowing this statement God is not thereby cognitively imperfect; for, since statements about future contingents have indeterminate truth-values, they are not knowable. Omniscience, we have to remember, is knowing whatever is true, or whatever is knowable. Accordingly, for Gersonides, the real indeterminancy of Abraham's binding of Isaac is *compatible* with divine omniscience, *properly interpreted.*[24]

Although the focus of Gersonides' analysis of Genesis 22:1–12 is on the testing of Abraham, he still needs to provide some account of verse 12. Since God doesn't have, on his view, foreknowledge of future contingent events, it might be thought that Gersonides could easily read the passage literally. However, as any good medieval thinker he was committed to some version of the principle of divine immutability. So the literal rendition: "For now I know . . .", with its suggestion of the acquisition of a new piece of knowledge, is unacceptable. Unfortunately Gersonides' exegesis of this passage is all too brief. However, on the basis of his general theory of divine cognition, as well as his interpretation of the test, I would suggest two alternative accounts of his understanding of this verse, one I dub "weak", the other "strong". On the weak interpretation God's knowledge in verse 12 is only the knowledge that the passing of the test is possible for someone, even though most people would fail it. Verse 12 on this account records (3.1) the fact that Abraham passed this test and (3.2) the fact that God knows *a priori* that this test is passable. Accordingly, the meaning of this passage would be as follows: "for now the test has been successfully completed; and I know that someone could become a God-fearing person". On the strong interpretation, however, God knows more than just the possibility that someone can pass the test. If we assume with Aristotle that in the long run all genuine logical possibilities are realized, then at some time someone will actually comply with the divine command to sacrifice his child.[25] Since God is omniscient insofar as he knows all true propositions, he knows that at some time someone will in fact perform the required deed. The actualization of Abraham's deed, however, doesn't affect God's knowledge, interpreted weakly or strongly; it merely shows that the propositional function 'x is a God-fearing man' is satisfied in at least one case. Prior to the actual performance of the deed, God knew therefore either that such an instantiation is possible or that this function will be instantiated by someone.

Now it might be objected that if God can know at the most only that some person will choose to comply with the divine command to sacrifice his child, such knowledge is inferior to the knowledge possessed by Abraham and Isaac who know that *Abraham* is that person. This seems to be a curious and unacceptable consequence of Gersonides' theory. Curious perhaps – but not necessarly unacceptable. For it could be said in reply that knowledge is of the universal. God knows the general facts of the universe, of which one is that *some* person can or will make the sacrifice required by God. The fact that it is Abraham who satisfies this description is not only contingent but accidental, and there is no science of the accidental.[26] Admittedly, Abraham and Isaac are aware of this accidental fact; but this recognition doesn't constitute knowledge in the strict sense. Better to use Plato's word '*doxa*' to characterize such information, for which perhaps an English neologism needs to be introduced, since the standard translations 'belief' or 'opinion' for this Greek term have been either pre-empted for other purposes or abused beyond redemption. The important point is, however, that God suffers no diminution from his omniscience if he is unaware that Abraham in particular instantiates the propositional function 'x is a man who is prepared to sacrifice his son if God commands him to do so'. When that function is instantiated, it does not constitute *knowledge for anybody*, since particular accidential facts are not *known*. Perhaps this is in part what Aristotle meant when he said that poetry is truer than history.[27]

How then would Gersonides interpret Rabbi Akiba's dictum? Seemingly his understanding of the Binding of Isaac story and his philosophical theory of divine cognition are both at odds with Rabbi Akiba's first thesis that everything is foreseen. But the "gates of interpretation are wide-open".[28] Although Gersonides does not, to my knowledge, comment upon Akiba's dictum, we could construct a commentary based upon what we know already of Gersonides' views. The crucial term in Akiba's formula is the first word. The Hebrew '*ha-kol*' is in fact ambiguous: it can connote either (a) everything or (b) all. In the former we have a distributive emphasis placed upon the universal quantifier: each and every individual event is seen by God. In the latter case we have a collective nuance: the human race as a whole is observed by God. I suspect that had Gersonides written a commentary on Rabbi Akiba's statement, he would have opted for the collective connotation of the Hebrew 'ha-kol'.

Confirmation of this hypothesis is obtained by examining Gersonides' interpretation of a biblical verse in which the universal quantifier occurs again in the context of the topic of divine cognition. The verse occurs in *Psalms* 33:15, and is usually translated as: "He (God) fashions the hearts of them all ('yaḥad') and considers all ('kol') their doings". Gersonides emphasizes the two words: 'yaḥad' and 'kol'. Accordingly, on his rendition the verse reads: "He who has created *all together* their hearts, he who observes *all* their works". This translation is then glossed by him as follows: "God has created all together (i.e., generically) the heart of men and their thoughts insofar as the latter collectively derive from the astrological patterns established by God (at creation). In this sense he knows all their deeds, i.e., all together, not in the sense that his knowledge extends to each individual as an individual. Thus, it is explained (in the Psalm) that God knows all their deeds in a general way".[29] On the basis of his interpretation of this verse we can plausibly extrapolate an interpretation of Rabbi Akiba's phrase such that for Gersonides it means: human action in general is known by God, i.e., he knows the general characteristics of human behavior but not what each individual will do in a given situation. The latter is given over to man, who freely chooses to comply or not to comply with God's commands. After all, the significance and poignancy of the Binding of Isaac is precisely Abraham's *choice* to sacrifice Isaac. For Gersonides, Abraham exercised his freedom in complying with the divine command; however, he also emphasizes the indeterminateness *in God's knowledge*.

5. CRESCAS' REINSTATEMENT OF STRONG OMNISCIENCE

Gersonides' categorical denial of divine foreknowledge of future contingencies, as well as its correlative interpretation of the Binding of Isaac, was too novel and bold to be well-received by his co-religionists. Many of his successors both in philosophy and in biblical exegesis took him to task for this theory, which one modern scholar has characterized as "a theological monstrosity".[30] This was also the attitude of the earlier philosophical critic of Aristotelian philosophy, Hasdai Crescas (d. 1410), who severely censured Gersonides' doctrine of divine knowledge and subjected it to detailed criticism. Like Maimonides, Crescas was committed to the theory of strong omniscience, a thesis that he believed was entailed by the very existence of a divinely revealed legislation, which is given to a specific man and to a particular people. Thus, for Crescas strong omniscience is a root-principle of Judaism, the denial of which undermines the entire religion. True to his method of first citing Scripture to support his thesis and then providing philosophical argumentation for it – a procedure contrary to that employed by Gersonides – , Crescas quotes several appropriate biblical passages, including the Binding of Isaac. Thus, he too sees this story as relevant to the general philosophical question of divine knowledge.

For Crescas the question of divine omniscience concerns three specific issues: (4.1) whether God knows particulars; (4.2) whether he knows the future, or non-existent states of affairs; and (4.3) whether his foreknowledge is compatible with the contingency of future events. Crescas' discussion of the Binding of Isaac is specifically introduced in connection with (4.2), although in the course of his philosophical analysis of divine cognition he will address himself to (4.3) as well. His chief difficulty with the story of Abraham is that if God has foreknowledge, how are we to interpret verse 12 of our story, especially its suggestion that something new was learned by God? His problem is aggravated by his commitment to a Rabbinic tradition that the episode of the Binding of Isaac is to be taken literally. Since what Abraham did was *real*, language of the narrative must be taken seriously. But if this is so, what do we do with verse 12? It suggests that God didn't know something about Abraham until *after* he bound Isaac! How then can we provide a *literal* reading of verse 12 without implying any change in God's knowledge?[31]

To answer this question, let us revert to the opening verse of our story, for Crescas' understanding of the episode differs significantly from the analysis of the test advocated by Saadia and Maimonides. Whereas both Saadia and Maimonides understand the testing of Abraham to be "other-directed", Crescas makes Abraham the focus of the examination. Uncharacteristically Crescas appeals to an important theorem in Aristotle's moral psychology that virtuous actions make a person virtuous. Continuous practice in giving charity results in a habit, or disposition, for charity. Or, more familiarly, "practice makes perfect". Applied to Abraham, this dictum means that the purpose of the test was to strengthen Abraham's already high level of piety and indeed even to increase it, thus enabling him to receive a greater award. Expressed in Aristotelian terminology, Abraham's test was designed to actualize his strong potential for the fear and love of God. Accordingly, the testing of Abraham had as its purpose Abraham's religious progress, not the edification of others. Indeed, who was there besides Isaac?[32]

But if the moral of the story is that Abraham moves from one level of piety to a higher level, doesn't this suggest that when verse 12 states, "For now I know that you are a God-fearing man", God has literally learned something new? It would seem that by making Abraham's religious development the purpose of the test, Crescas has made it especially difficult for himself to find an acceptable literal reading of verse 12. Herein lies the advantage of the Saadia-Maimonides interpretation. However, the difficulty is only apparent. True, before the third day of our episode Abraham had achieved a certain level r of religious development, which on the third day increased to level *z*. This was the rationale of the test. The increase from *r* to *z*, however, does not imply any change in God, since he knows on the first day that Abraham will attain level *z* on the third day, just as he knows whatever level of piety Abraham or anyone else has attained at any time. Accordingly, using the past-tense form of the verb God can literally say to Abraham after he has bound Isaac, "I *knew* ('yad'ati') that you are a God-fearing man". Being both omniscient in the strong sense and immutable God can say that his knowledge "antedates" whatever happens. What happens may of course be new and it is ever-changing; but while Abraham's piety changes God's knowledge does not. In this sense Crescas claims, the use of the past-tense verb here is quite appropriate. What Abraham's deed accomplishes for God is very slight: it merely corroborates what he himself knew prior to the act. Using Aristotelian jargon Crescas retells the story like this: Abraham moves from a potential state of maximum piety to the actual state of maximum piety. This was the telos of the act of binding Isaac. Yet God knew both that on the first day of the episode Abraham was only potentially at the maximum level and that on the third day he would really attain that level. Accordingly, Abraham literally "acts out" God's cognitive script.

As it stands, however, this script contains two rough spots: First, what does Crescas mean by saying that God literally *knew* what Abraham would do? In particular, do temporal conditions characterize God's knowledge?

Can we use such phrases as, "God already knew–" "God now knows–" or "God will know–"? Second, if Abraham was only "corroborating" or "acting out" what God had initially planned, is Abraham anything but a puppet? The poignancy and suspense in the story, even to a reader who has read it several times, lies precisely in the possibility that Abraham might not obey God's command. Crescas' interpretation of the Binding of Isaac may be successful in preserving divine omniscience, but it seems to have purchased this dogma by abandoning the traditional doctrine of free-will. After all, Rabbi Akiba also said, "freedom is given!"

Fortunately, Crescas doesn't terminate his discussion of divine cognition at this point. He proceeds to give a detailed defense of Rabbi Akiba's full formula that in intention, as well as in content, looks very much like Maimonides' general position on this question. Nevertheless, as he develops his argument it becomes clear that he is in fact expressing some new themes that ultimately constitute, I believe, a distinct doctrine of divine omniscience. This doctrine will make use of two key notions, one that bears a striking similarity to the classic solution proposed by Boethius and Aquinas, whereas the other is derived from Avicenna's cosmology.

We have already noted that for Maimonides God's knowledge is *a priori:* it is non-acquired, non-derivative. Crescas accepts this characterization but emphasizes another aspect of the *a priori* status of divine cognition, which is mentioned but not sufficiently discussed by Maimonides. For Crescas the most important feature qualifying God's knowledge is the term 'eternal'. Maimonides had already described God's knowledge ('yedi'ah') as 'qodemeth', where the adjective 'qodemeth' connotes either "eternal" or "prior".[33] However, Maimonides wasn't too informative on the full import of this thesis. As was his practice he typically characterizes God's eternal knowledge *negatively*, i.e., as not being like human knowledge. Not accepting in general Maimonides' doctrine of negative divine attributes, Crescas wasn't completely satisfied with this indirect description of divine cognition. And it is at this point that Crescas introduces an idea that is reminiscent of Boethius and Aquinas. The main thrust of this idea is that God's knowledge is eternal in the sense of being *timeless*, i.e., *atemporal*. A human being knows temporally insofar as he successively accumulates data over time and synthesizes them into a unified proposition. Both the knower and that which is known are "in time". God, however, knows timelessly: He "sees" everything as if all events or facts are "present before him in an eternal now". To God there is no past or future, no flow of time; indeed, there is no time at all for God. Accordingly, his eternal vision encompasses and locates every seemingly temporal event in a non-temporal schema. Or, if some temporal language is to be retained, we may say that God's epistemic vision is like our perception of some present event, wherein the observer is compresent with that which he perceives. Similarly, God is eternally "compresent" with *all* facts or events.[34]

Although Crescas does not employ the example used by Boethius and Aquinas of a man standing on a hill gazing down at a group of travellers on a road, he could have easily adopted it for his theory.[35] To such a person the spatial positions of ten moving people, for example, are *simultaneously* apprehended; whereas to an observer standing on ground-level these positions would be perceived *successively* Now if God is the "highest observer", i.e., he is "standing above time", he would see every position at one glance. Although the man on the hill sees more at any given moment than the man on ground-level, there is a limit to human perception: even if our human observer were to look down at the earth from a space satellite, he would still see only *some* things, even if many, simultaneously. But this limitation doesn't obtain in God's case; for, since he is "outside" time and space, his vision encompasses all facts simultaneously. This would mean, in Abraham's case, that both his binding of Isaac and his previous lower level of piety are eternally comprehended in God's timeless knowledge.[36]

Assuming that this notion of timeless cognition of temporal facts makes sense as an analysis of Rabbi Akiba's claim "Everything *is* foreseen", let us now turn to his second thesis "yet freedom is given".[37] If God knows that Abraham will bind Isaac, will Abraham be free when he in fact binds him? It is incumbent upon Crescas to explain how, notwithstanding God's omniscience, Abraham had a free choice. For, as Crescas explicity says,

> If God's knowledge necessitates that part [of the pair of contradictory alternatives] which is known to Him, surely there would be no real imperative in the commandments and warnings of the Torah; for there is no imperative to the one commanded except when it is assumed that the person is a voluntary agent, not forced nor compelled.[38]

If then Abraham's deed has any moral and religious significance, it must have been a freee act. But is it, if God knows eternally that he *would* bind Isaac?

In attempting to take the sting out of the doctrine of divine omniscience in the strong sense, Crescas now introduces a theme derived from Al-Farabi and Avicenna. The latter thinkers were concerned to show how the universe could be both eternal and yet created, necessary and still contingent. They devised an ontology that allowed them to speak of (5.1) things that were absolutely eternal, i.e., necessary *per se*; (5.2) things that were absolutely created, i.e., contingent *per se*; and finally (5.3) things that are contingent *per se* but necessary *per causam*. The last category of existents comprises items that, although contingent in essence, exist necessarily by virtue of their being the effects of an absolutely necessary being, i.e., God. For Al-Farabi and Avicenna, the heavenly bodies are instances of such beings, and since these entities define a universe, one can therefore say that the world as a whole is necessary and eternal, even though contingent in its very essence. Crescas makes use of the ontic hybrid of the contingent and necessary being not only in his cosmology,[39] but in his account of divine cognition as well. God's eternal, i.e., timeless, knowledge of Abraham's eventual binding of Isaac *implies* that Abraham will lift up his hand to do the deed. In this sense, Abraham's performance of the binding is *necessary*. But the necessity involved here is trivial and innocuous. It is trivial, since *any* instance of the epistemic function '*x* knows *p*' implies '*p*': God is no more privileged than Isaac, if he too had *known* that his father was prepared to sacrifice him. The necessity is also innocuous – and this is our main concern now; for, even though Abraham "had" to bind Isaac, since God know he would do so, he was nevertheless *free* when he did the deed. He was free because his act was contingent in itself, albeit caused, and hence necessary, insofar as God knew that he would do it. Contrary to Saadia, Crescas suggests that God's knowledge is indeed causative, since his knowing '*p*' does fix or determine the truth-status of '*p*'. However, Crescas wants to argue that this "epistemological determinism" doesn't annul the inherent contingency of the act. Under a different set of circumstances Abraham *could have* done the opposite; otherwise, there would have been no real test. Speaking logically we can say that the statement '*p*'–'Abraham will bind Isaac' is a contingent truth; however, given the truth 'God knows that Abraham will bind Isaac', the statement 'Abraham will bind Isaac' necessarily follows. For Crescas, it is enough that '*p*' itself is a contingent truth; this fact guarantees the contingency of the event and the freedom in the deed. Abraham was therefore worthy of praise and earned his reward. In theory, he could have done otherwise, although in fact he could not have done so, since God knew what he would do.[40]

Although Crescas' theory of divine cognition is Avicennian in origin and language, the notion of a foreseen deed as being both contingent and necessary corresponds to Aquinas' distinction between conditional and simple necessities. On the one hand, Aquinas contends, if God knows '*p*', where '*p*' designates a contingent event, '*p*' is necessarily true only on the condition, that God knows *p*. If God knows not-*p*, then of course p is not only not true, but necessarily false. In this context the truth of the antecedent in this conditional by itself says nothing about the *intrinsic* modal status of the consequent. The necessity here lies only in the consequence, or implication. On the other hand, a proposition is simply, or absolutely, necessary if and only if it is a logical truth, a statement that is true under all conditions. Accordingly, whether we describe Abraham's binding of Isaac as conditionally necessary or necessary by virtue of its cause insofar as it is foreknown, it is still contingent, and hence free.[41]

Equipped with this doctrine of divine cognition, let us now return to the troublesome climax of our story and try to read it according to this theory. Observe first that the Hebrew verb in verse 12 'yad'ati', although usually rendered "I know", is literally a past-tense form, signifying "I knew". Accordingly, since God's knowledge is eternal, Crescas could legitimately say that a *literal* rendition of this sentence would yield "For I knew that you are a God-fearing man". Of course, the phrase "I knew" has to be construed properly: 'I knew' is to be philosophically glossed as "I know eternally (i.e., timelessly) that you . . . ". Actually, there is an interesting fact about the way in which the Hebrew verb form 'yad'ati' is used in the Bible that is relevant to Crescas' philosophical point. Frequently this seemingly past-tense form has present-tense significance; e.g., when they make their trip to Egypt, Abraham says to Sarah: "Behold now, I know ('yad'ati') that you are a pretty woman" (Genesis 12:11). To construe the verb in this passage as in the past-tense would be to misread the whole point of Abraham's comment to Sarah.[42] Let us now give this philosophical point a philosophical twist: the expression "I knew" where the 'I' designates God signifies the timeless present, the eternal now in which God sees everythhing simultaneously. Reading verse 12 literally, Crescas could say that the phrase "God knew" means that God knows eternally, i.e., timelessly, all events, including Abraham's binding of Isaac, which, although future to Abraham and Isaac on the first and second days of the story, was "already" known by God.

But what about the temporal adverb ''ata', usually rendered as "now"? Doesn't this particle convey the impression that God has acquired a new piece of information? However, the connotations of this Hebrew word are many. If used adverbially as a temporal modifier of a verb, it acquires its meaning from the tense of its associated verb, just as 'iam' does in Latin. If the verb has reference to the past, ''ata' would signify "already". Thus, we could read verse 12 as, "For I *already knew* that you are . . ." But, as we have suggested, the verb in this passage should be understood as connoting the timeless present; hence a non-temporal connotation for the particle ''ata' is required. And indeed, Biblical Hebrew records instances of such usage, where this word signfies "indeed", "surely" (Genesis 31:42; I Samuel 24:21; I Kings 17:34). Accordingly, we can now read verse 12 as follows: "For indeed I knew eternally (i.e., timelessly) that you would attain this new level of piety which you have now exhibited, thus confirming my antecendent knowledge". Abraham was truly put to the test by God; yet no new cognitive event occurred with respect to God. Moreover, Abraham's deed was voluntary, since his binding of Isaac was not a logically necessary fact. After all, God could have commanded him to sacrifice Sarah.

6. ARAMA'S EXEGESIS OF THE BINDING OF ISAAC

The last chapter in our story is devoted to an interpreter of the Bible who in several respects can be regarded as an enemy of philosophy. Writing during the catastrophic period of Spanish Jewish history before, during and after the expulsion from Spain in 1492, Isaac Arama (d. 1494), like some of his other traditional coreligionists, blamed philosophy for the many Jewish conversions to Christianity and the subsequent divine punishments visited upon Spanish Jewry.[43] Nevertheless, Arama was a philosopher "in spite of himself". Throughout his major work consisting of a set of sermons on the weekly readings from the Pentateuch, philosophical vocabulary, ideas and citations abound; frequently the titles of the sermons indicate specifically that the topic of the sermon will be philosophical. Typical of many traditional Hebrew authors, Arama gives a title to his book that contains a word alluding to his own proper name. In this case the title is "the Binding of Isaac", which is a fitting closing theme to our own study.[44]

When he gets to the weekly Biblical reading containing the story of Abraham's trial, Arama clearly recognizes and states that the central theme of this chapter is the problem of divine knowledge of future contingents. Like Maimonides he accepts fully Rabbi Akiba's two assumptions that God does have foreknowledge of everything and that man has free-will. Accordingly, for Arama the classical dilemma is spurious: these two allegedly contradictory theses can be reconciled. Fully conversant with the traditional philosophical literature, Arama rejects both Gersonides' acceptance of the dilemma and defense of free-will and Crescas' deterministic dissolution of the dilemma. Arama accuses the former of heresy insofar as Gersonides has purchased free-will at too high a price, i.e., the abandonment of divine foreknowledge of future contingents. Crescas, on the other hand, is faulted for his determinism, with whose softness Arama refuses to be mollified. A necessary act is one that cannot be prevented or avoided, and if that is what our actions are like, then there is no point in ascribing to them any sense of contingency, which at best would be only abstract and logical. Real freedom is the power to do either *p* or not-*p* at the time we are about to perform the act; but Crescas' "reconciliation" removes from us this power since what we do has already been fixed insofar as God knows eternally what we do. Rejecting both Gersonides and Crescas, Arama thus subscribes to Maimonides' unqualified reconciliationist position. His interpretation of the Binding of Isaac story differs in several respects from that of Maimonides, however, and introduces several additional features to Maimonides' theoretical position on the question on divine cognition.

Let us begin with the opening verse of our story – "And God tested Abraham". Unlike Maimonides, Arama does not minimize the test in this episode. Although he does recognize the paradigmatic dimension of Abraham's deed, he considers it to be more a consequence or implication of Abraham's act rather than its primary intention. Like Crescas, Arama sees the test as having Abraham as its focus; yet Arama is not so much concerned with providing Abraham with an opportunity to strengthen his piety but with affording him an occasion to learn something new about religion. God tested Abraham in order to teach him that rational, or philosophical, morality is not absolutely binding, that there are situations wherein this morality has to be "suspended". Anticipating Kierkegaard, Arama asserts that rational morality would of course prohibit murder, especially of one's own child. By commanding Abraham to sacrifice his son God taught him that there is a "higher morality", determined by God's will. A few chapters earlier in Genesis Abraham argued with God about the justice of killing a *whole* nation, even though the majority of its inhabitants were guilty of heinous crimes. In that debate Abraham appealed to a rational morality that construed the standard of justice such that each person could be punished only according to *his* deed and that obligated God himself to adhere to this rule. In testing Abraham with the command to sacrifice Isaac, God wanted to teach Abraham that this standard of morality has its limits and that God's will is supreme. By passing this test Abraham learned that rational morality can be modified, restricted or temporally annulled by God in certain situations. Although God had foreknowledge of Abraham's passing the test, the test had, nevertheless, pedagogical value for Abraham, and for that matter all of us who read the story.[45]

Having thus preserved the literal sense of verse 1, Arama then turns to verse 12, with its suggestion that some new piece of knowledge was acquired by God as the result of Abraham's deed. Actually, for Arama this is the more troublesome of the two verses, and most of his discussion focuses upon it. Its apparent literal meaning cannot be made consistent with three medieval Aristotelian principles: (6.1) knowledge perfects its possessor; (6.2) God is perfect; (6.3) God cannot change. If God learned anything new as the result of Abraham's deed, then the first thesis would seem to be true of God implying that theses (6.2) and (6.3) are false. Accordingly, Avicenna simply denied that God knows particular events at all, such as Abraham's binding of Isaac.[46] And we have seen that this is Gersonides' view as well. Since Arama minimizes the Saadia-Miamonides analysis of the test, he does not subscribe to their interpretation of the word 'yad'ati' as a causative-transitive verb 'to make known to others'. Nor does he adopt the "easy way out" suggested by his friend Don Isaac Abravanel, who adhered quite closely to the literal meaning of the passage and ascribed verse 12 to the angel, claiming that since angels do *not* have foreknowledge, they can learn something new.[47] Although Arama does assign the *speaking* of verse 12 to the angel, he regards the angel merely as God's representative and messenger; moreover, for Arama angels *do have* foreknowledge. So the problem remains: if we construe verse 12 literally, some kind of information seems to be acquired by God and/or his angel that would appear to perfect its recipient. But no less than Avicenna or Gersonides, Arama is unwilling to accept this conclusion. God isn't perfected by anything nor is he subject to change. So what shall we do with verse 12?

In replying to this question Arama distinguishes between two kinds of knowledge. The first and primary kind of cognition is knowledge of necessary truths and of things that are themselves necessary and eternal beings. The second type of cognition is knowledge of contingent truths and of generated and perishable things. Now it is the first kind that is genuine and real knowledge; the possession of this type of information does "perfect" the knower. To lack this knowledge is to be deficient and imperfect. However, this is not the case with the second kind of information. As we have seen from our discussion of Gersonides, cognition of contingent particulars was not regarded as knowledge proper. On this point Arama agrees. Arama proposed that we should label the possession of information about contingent particulars not with the term 'knowing' but with the phrase 'not being ignorant of'. The latter expression, reminiscent of Maimonides' *via negativa*, conveys the idea of awareness of accidental facts; the former term signifies cognition of necessary and eternal beings and facts. Accordingly, however we ultimately interpret verse 12 one thing is clear: Abraham's deed does not constitute genuine knowledge that would perfect its possessor. To be sure, Abraham's binding of Isaac doesn't elude God's sight, but it doesn't perfect him or constitute his essence; for God's essential knowledge is only of himself. Of all contingent facts and things he is to be sure *not ignorant*; their occurrence, however, in no way makes God what he is, no more or no less than they constitute my essence. They must "happen".[48]

Nor does verse 12 imply that with Abraham's passing of the test God or his angel had suffered some change, if only in cognitive capital. Since God has "foreknowledge" of the event in the sense of his not being ignorant of it, nothing really transpires in God or his knowledge. True, on the first day of this three-day episode the sentence 'Abraham has bound Isaac' was not true, although it became true on the third day. Now it would seem that the change in truth-values of this sentence imports some change in God or his angel, if only in the trivial sense that he is conscious of the eventuation of a contingent fact of which he is already not ignorant. To remove this worry Arama appeals to Al-Ghazzali's reply to Avicenna's original query about God's knowledge of temporal facts. Al-Ghazzali claimed that God is no more affected by the eventuation of a fact that he has known than the pillar is changed by my moving to the left of it after having stood to the right of it.[49] As new facts occur, new cognitive *relations* come about; but such relations do not result in any change in God or for that matter in any other knower who was not ignorant of their eventual coming-about. After all, if I *know* that at t_1 there will be no eclipse of the moon but that at t_2 there will be an eclipse and finally that at t_3 there was an eclipse at t_2, did I change in knowing all these facts, even as they come about? A real change in God would have occurred, if a proposition '*p*' had been true at t, but God didn't know it and thereafter came to know it; or, if he hadn't known that '*p*' would be true at *t*, and then learned of its truth subsequently. However, this is not what transpired at the Binding of Isaac or at any other time. God "knew", i.e., he wasn't ignorant, when he commanded Abraham that the latter would obey. When Abraham did obey, certain changes in the world took place, e.g., Abraham's progress in piety and religious knowledge; but these changes did not affect God.[50]

After having explained the sense in which God can have foreknowlede of such temporal facts as the Binding of Isaac without such information affecting him in any real way, Arama then makes a claim that is both novel and puzzling. Novel, because I have not found such a statement in any previous Jewish author writing on his topic; puzzling, since on the surface it seems to be inconsistent with his belief that God is immutable. I shall first cite the passage and then comment upon it.

In this way [i.e., the analysis of divine foreknowledge in terms of God's non-ignorance of non-essential information] we can say that God's knowledge of one of the alternatives of a pair of future contingent events pertaining to human free action is *consequent upon* what in fact eventuates, not that their existence is consequent upon His knowing them. For, since with respect to such events God is merely non-ignorant of their eventuation, why should we not attribute the *dependency* of this non-ignorance to the existence of such actions? For what will or what has happened of them is not unknown to Him in any way.[51]

Let us first recall Saadia's attempt to distinguish sharply between knowing something to be so and causing it to be so. God's foreknowledge, Saadia insisted *doesn't cause* the event, which he foreknows, to come about. Saadia was worried by any suggestion of God's causing human deeds such that the latter would be the result of divine agency, and hence would be deprived of freedom. Arama appears to remove any such fear by going in the opposite direction and by saying that God's knowledge is in some way "dependent upon" what in fact transpires. Equally concerned to preserve human freedom, Arama too wants to remove any causative element in God's knowledge. But in fleeing from divine determinism he seems to have fallen into the trap of divine mutability, which he so carefully tried to avoid earlier.

Perhaps not, if we interpret this passage as follows. In reading the solution proposed by Saadia, someone might still think that since God has foreknowledge of what will transpire, the event itself is just a mere "after-image" of the foreknowledge, and as such is "bound" to come about, and hence no real contingency is inherent in the event.[52] After all, if God knows '*p*', then *p*; and since this is an instance of a theorem in epistemic logic, one could say that '*p*' *must* be true. Thus, we get the seeds of the classic error, noted by Boethius and Aquinas, of going from "It is necessary that if God knows '*p*', *p*" to "God knows '*p*' implies that '*p*' is necessary". Arama attempts to block this inference by proposing that we understand divine omniscience as the non-ignorance of non-essential information; i.e., if some such event occurs, God is not ignorant of it. Formulated symbolically, divine omniscience, as Arama understands it, would be expressed as $(p) \Box [(p \supset (\text{God knows } p)]$. Put in this way, divine knowledge is in a sense "consequent upon" the way things turn out. But it is clear that this "dependency" is harmless. Obviously, assuming that God is omniscient,then given some truth,we can say with certainty that he is not ignorant of it. A thing being the case or a proposition being true is in this sense a sufficient condition for God knowing it; or, God's knowing *p* "hinges upon" '*p*' being true. After all, can God know false propostions? Accordingly, Arama's claim turns out to be less troubling than it seemed at first sight.[53]

Arama's analysis of our story has so far yielded the following results: First, God put *Abraham to the test* in order to teach him something new about religious morality. The test was designed to provide information not to the examiner but to the examinee. Second, contingent temporal facts do not constitute real knowledge; being aware of them is merely not being ignorant of their facticity. Third, God has foreknowledge of these contingent temporal facts, but their occurrence in no way brings about a change in God nor does it perfect his essence or knowledge. The import of these conclusions is therefore that verse 12 does not record any new and significant cognitive insight for God or his angel, who, let us remember also has foreknowledge. But if verse 12 is not epistemological in its primary intention, what then is the angel saying? In reply Arama first backtracks into general moral theory and emphasizes the Aristotelian point that an ethical action differs from action in the arts in that the latter activities are primarily concerned with the final product. When I commission an artist to paint a portrait of my wife, I am concerned solely with the finished painting, not with the intentions of the painter or how he managed to produce the work. In moral action, however, this is not so. Here we are especially interested in the motives of the agent and whether he has the requisite moral knowledge and habits; otherwise, his action would be a mere accident[54] Now Abraham's test was concerned with his state of mind towards God's command. Once he showed his readiness to kill Isaac by binding him to the altar and lifting up the knife, he passed the test. At this point the angel intervenes and announces to Abraham that *the test is indeed* over and that he has successfully completed it. There is now no need for him to carry out the dreadful deed, since in moral action the attitude of the agent is primary, and God and his angel, but not Abraham, knew this already. Accordingly, Arama reads verse 12 as follows: "For now the test is over and you have in fact reached the desired level of piety, even though you haven't slaughtered Isaac, Moreover, I was not unaware of the level of perfection you have now achieved, just as I was not unaware of the level of piety you had or will have attained". Arama explicitly states that the angel was *not* saying that it *now* has come to know something which it didn't know earlier. Rather, according to Arama, the angel was merely "bragging" that it knew already, without the deed needing to be actually performed, that Abraham would pass the test.[55] In a sense, the angel is telling Abraham that he has for all practical purposes *sacrificed* Isaac.[56]

7. CONCLUSION

In this essay we have examined several medieval exegetical examples of a biblical-philosophical theme. All of these hermeneutical models were reconciliationist in intention, working within the framework of Rabbi Akiba's dictum; yet we have seen how differently they go about reconciling the apparently incompatible theses of divine omniscience and human freedom. These diverse philosophical schemata in turn shaped the ways in which these philosophical exegetes understood the story of Abraham's binding of Isaac. Despite their common concern to preserve divine immutability and omiscience and human freedom, they diverged in their understanding of this episode. To Gersonides, whose general doctrine of divine cognition is the most radical theory of God's knowledge in medieval Jewish thought, human freedom is so important that God's omniscience must be redefined in order to accommodate it. Accordingly, human freedom and divine omniscience are for him inversely proportional: the stronger the notion of freedom the weaker the concept of omniscience. Hence, God doesn't know what *Abraham* will do. To all our other exegetes this inverse relationship is totally unacceptable. Strong omniscience must be preserved at any cost even if we have to admit, in a stronger or weaker voice, that when Abraham bound Isaac, he "had" to do it. This "had" is of course capable of various interpretations so that its force is weakened. But for our defender of strong omniscience Abraham was nevertheless free in what he did.

Like most biblical themes and philosophical questions the Binding of Isaac and the problem of omniscience continue to be of interest. In the later Jewish exegetical and theological literature discussions on these topics persist.[57] Contemporary philosophers for the most part no longer read the Bible either for the solutions to their problems or for the problems themselves. In this respect at least they differ from their medieval predecessors. Nor do modern biblical scholars interpret the Bible philosophically; the "gates of interpretation" have been closed quite narrowly ever since the 17th century lens-maker Spinoza issued his hermeneutical rule not to read into the text of Scripture what isn't there.[58] Now we read the Bible with only philological and historical spectacles; our distorting philosophical lenses have been taken away from us. But are philology and history all-sufficient? Can we read an important religious text without assuming a philosophical perspective or responding to it with philosophical questions? Indeed, what *is* the literal meaning of any of the more interesting Biblical stories?

NOTES

[1] *Scroll of Habbakuk*, in G. Vermes (ed.), *The Dead Sea Scrolls in English*, Penguin Books, Baltimore 1962.

[2] Good examples of this kind of exegesis are *Midrash Rabbah* and *Mekhilta*. The Hebrew term 'midrash' connotes interpretation, homily.
[3] *Mishnah*, Pirke Avoth, III: 15.
[4] Fischel himself does not comment upon this particular saying. Cf. H. Fischel, *Rabbinic Literature and Greco-Roman Philosophy*, E. J. Brill, Leiden 1973.
[5] For a detailed study of Saadia's biblical hermeneutics see M. Zucker's *Al tirgum RS "G le Torah*, Philipp Feldman, Inc., New York 1959. A briefer and English discussion of this topic can be found in H. Malter's *Saadia Gaon, His Life and Works*, Hermon Press, N.Y., 1969.
[6] See Zucker's citations from Saadia's polemical works: Zucker, *idem*, pp. 136, 142. This interpretation was anticipated by the Rabbis in *Genesis Rabbah* 56:7.
[7] Saadia Gaon, *The Book of Beliefs and Opinions*, translated by S. Rosenblatt, Yale University Press, New Haven 1948.
[8] *Idem.*, Book IV, chapters 3–4. H. A. Wolfson, *The Philosophy of the Kalam*, Harvard University Press, Cambridge Mass, 1976, chapter VIII; Augustine, *On Free Choice of the Will*, Book III, transl. by A. S. Benjamin and L. H. Hackstaff, Bobbs-Merrill, Indianapolis, 1964.
[9] A. Kenney, *The God of the Philosophers*, Oxford Unversity Press, Oxford 1979, chapter 5.
[10] Maimonides, *The Guide of the Perplexed*, trans. by S. Pines, University of Chicago Press, Chicago, 1974, Part III, chapter 24; *Babylonian Talmud*, Sabbath 55a.
[11] Maimonides, *Guide*, III:24 (end). Isaac Abravanel (d. 1507) also interprets the verb 'nisa' in this manner. He also claims that despite appearances to the contrary this was the true import of Maimonides' exegesis of the Binding of Isaac. (Isaac Abravenel, *Commentary on Genesis, ad locum*).
[12] This is the translation of verse 1 in the new edition of *The Torah* published by the Jewish Publication Society of America, Philadelphia 1977.
[13] Maimonides, *Guide*, I:51–60.
[14] *Ibid.*, III:20. See also Maimonides, *Mishneh Torah*, Hilchoth Yesode HaTorah, chapter 2:10, Maimonides Publishing Co, New York, 1927.
[15] Maimonides, *Guide* III:20–21.
[16] This is especially true for Levi ben Gershom, or Gersonides, who devotes an entire chapter in his treatise on divine cognition to a refutation of Maimonides' theory of divine attributes. (Gersonides, *The Wars of the Lord*, Book III, chapter 1. This part of Gersonides' *magnum opus* has been separately translated into French and English: Levi ben Gershom, *Les Guerres du Seigneur*, Livres III et IV, trans. by C. Touati, Mouton, Paris 1968; *Gersonides: The Wars of the Lord; Treatise Three: On God's Knowledge*, trans. by N. Samuelson, University of Toronto Press, Ontario 1977.
[17] Another difficulty implicit in Maimonides' doctrine of divine cognition is the suggestion that since God's knowledge is original and creative, it is *causative*. This suggestion is explicity stated by a late medieval commentator on the *Guide*, Shem Tov ben Joseph ben Shem Tov, who characterizes God's knowledge as "active, perfecting and causative, whereas human cognition is passive, perfected and caused" (Shem Tob ben Joseph Falaquera, *Moreh ha-Moreh*, Pressburg, 1837) The problem with saying that God's cognition is causative is that He would cause, via His knowledge, Abraham to bind Isaac; Abraham's freedom would then become problematic. Aquinas too characterized God's knowledge as causative. (Aquinas, *Summa Theologiae*, Part I q. 14 a. 8.)

[18] The best and most comprehensive study of Gersonides is C. Touati's *La Pensée Philosophique et Théologique de Gersonide*, Les Editions de minuit, Paris 1973.
[19] Maimonides also stresses the suspenseful three day journey up Mt. Moriah. But for him the suspense is in or directed toward the spectator or reader. Moreover, Maimonides emphasizes the length of the journey in order to point out that Abraham's act was deliberate and thoughtful.
[20] Gersonides, *Commentary on Genesis*, Parshat Vayera, Venice 1547; (reprinted in Israel 1967 or 1968), 30d–31c. In his commentary on Genesis 22:1 Abraham ibn Ezra (1092–1167) refers to a similar interpretation.
[21] *Maimonides, Guide* III:15, Aquinas, *Summa Theologiae* I, q.25, a.3.
[22] Gersonides, *Supercommentary on Averroes' Commentary on Aristotle's On Interpretation*, chapter 9. This Hebrew text was translated into Latin and reprinted in the Venice, 1560 edition of Averroes' Commentaries on Aristotle.
[23] Gersonides, *The Wars of the Lord*, Book VI, Part I, chapter 10.
[24] *Ibid.*, Book III, chapter 4. Some recent writers have labelled the position advocated by Gersonides "weak omniscience". (J. R. Lucas, *The Freedom of the Will*, Clarendon Press, Oxford 1970, chapter 14; R. Swinburne, *The Coherence of Theism*, Clarendon Press Oxford 1977, chapter 10.
[25] Aristotle, *Metaphysics* 1047b 4–6; *On the Heavens*, 281b, 16–23; J. Hintikka, *Time and Necessity*, Clarendon Press, Oxford 1973, pp. 93–113; S. Knuuttila, 'Time and Modality in Scholastics in *Reforging the Great Chain of Being: Studies of the History of Modal Theories*, S. Knuuttila (ed.), D. Reidel, Dordrecht 1981.
[26] Aristotle, *Prior Analytics* I:31 and 33; *Metaphysics*, VI:2.
[27] Aristotle, *Poetics* 9, 1451 b 5–10. N. Samuelson, *Gersonides on God's Knowledge*, pp. 52–53; *idem.*, 'Gersonides' Account of God's Knowledge of Particulars', *The Journal of the History of Philosophy* 10 *(1972), pp. 399–416.*
[28] A useful principle and apt phrase of Maimonides; *Guide* II:25.
[29] Gersonides, *The Wars of the Lord*, Book III, chapter 6, my translation.
[30] I. Husik, *A History of Medieval Jewish Philosophy*, Jewish Publication Society of America, Philadelphia 1948, p. 346.
[31] Hasdai Crescas, *The Light of the Lord (Or Adonai)*, Book II, Principle 1, chapter 1 (beginning). On the distinction between God's dialogue with Abraham about Sodom and the Binding of Isaac see Maimonides' *Guide* II:45. According to Maimonides, Abraham's religious experience at the moment of the binding of Isaac was that of "a vision" (*bemar'eh*), which took place while he was awake. Abraham's dialogue with God about Sodom, however, was a lower level of prophecy, which Maimonides labels 'A vision of Prophecy' (*bemar'eh ha-nevuah*).
[32] Crescas, *Light*, Book II, Principle 1, chapter 1. Crescas' understanding of Abraham's test seems to derive from the exegetical tradition of his Northern Spanish predecessors the exegetes Rabbi Moses ben Nachman (d. 1270) and Nissim of Geronda (c. 1310–1375). This hermeneutical trope may have been derived from Jehudah Halevi, *Kuzari*, V: 20, transl. by H. Hirschfeld, N.Y. 1946; Hebrew transl. by J. Ibn Shemuel, Tel Aviv 1972.
[33] Maimonides, *Guide* III:21.
[34] Crescas, *Light*, Book II, Principle 5, chapter 3. Boethius, *The Consolation of Philosophy*, Book V, section 6; Aquinas, *Summa Theologiae*, Part I q. 14 a. 13.
[35] Some of Crescas' philosophical successors do use Boethius's example of the man on

the hill: Abraham Shalom, *Neve Shalom*, Venice 1574, Book XII, second question, chapter 2, 211 b; Yehudah Moscato, *Perush Qol Yehudah l'Sefer Kuzari shel Yehudah Halevi*, Book V paragraph 20, Both Shalom and Moscato knew Latin, and it is possible that they read Boethius or Aquinas.

[36] A number of contemporary philosophers have argued that Boethius' theory is subject to serious difficulties: N. Pike, *God and Timelessness*, Schocken Books, New York 1970; A. Kenny, *The God of the Philosophers*, ch. 5.

[37] Several commentators on the *Mishnah* interpret Rabbi Akiba's dictum à la Crescas and in fact attribute this interpretation to Maimonides. (See the commentaries of *Tifereth Yisrael* and *Tosephot Yom Tov* on Avoth III:15. See also Moses Almosnino, *Perush al Pirke Avoth*, Salonika 1563, *ad locum*).

[38] Crescas, *Light*, Book II, Principle 1, chapter 1. My translation.

[39] E. Fackenheim, 'The Possibility of the Universe in Al-Farabi, Ibn Sina and Maimonides', *Proceedings of the American Academy of Jewish Research* 16 (1946–47), pp. 39–70; G. F. Hourani, 'Ibn Sina on Necessary and Possible Existence', *The Philosophical Forum* 4 (1972), pp. 74–86; Crescas, *Light*, Book III, Principle 1, chapter 5; S. Feldman, 'The Theory of Eternal Creation in Hasdai Crescas and Some of his Predecessors', *Viator* 11 (1980), pp. 289–320.

[40] Crescas, *Light*, Book II, Principle 1, chapter 4. I give a critical analysis of this doctrine in my 'Crescas' Theological Determinism', *Da'at* 9 (1982), pp. 3–28.

[41] Aquinas uses the terminology of *de dicto* and *de re* necessities to formulate this distinction. (Aquinas, *Summa Theologiae* I, a. 14 a. 13 ad 3.) Leibniz uses the terms 'absolute' and 'hypothetical' necessities. (Leibniz, G. *Theodicy*, Part I, Paragraphs 36–59).

[42] S. D. Luzzatto, *Grammatica della Lingua Ebraica*, Padova 1853, p. 518, paragraph 1265.

[43] Y. F. Baer, *A History of the Jews in Christian Spain*, Jewish Publication Society of America, Philadelphia 1961, volume 2, pp. 254–258.

[44] I. Arama, *The Binding of Isaac* (*Sefer Akedat Yitzhaq*) Pressburg 1849 (reprinted Jerusalem 1961), Vol. 1 Genesis, Gate 21; S. Heller-Wilensky, *Rabbi Yitzhaq Arama v'Mishnato Ha-filosofit*, Jerusalem 1956, chapter 7; C. Pearl, *The Medieval Jewish Mind: The Religious philosophy of Isaac Arama*, Vallentine Mitchell, London 1971, chapter 5.

[45] Arama, Gate 21, page 151b.

[46] M. Marmura, 'Some Aspects of Avicenna's Theory of God's Knowledge of Particulars', *Journal of the American Oriental Society* 82 (1962), pp. 299–312.

[47] Isaac Abravanel, *Commentary on Genesis, ad locum.*

[48] Arama, 150b–151a.

[49] Al-Ghazali, *The Destruction of Philosophy* (*Tahâfut al-Falâsīfa*) trans. by S. Kamali, Pakistan Philosophical Congress, Lahore 1963, 13th Discussion. A more accurate and felicitous translation is found in S. Van den Bergh's translation of Averroes' *Tahāfut al-Tahāfut*, Oxford University Press, Oxford, 1954, vol. 1, p. 278.

[50] Aquinas, *Summa Theologiae* I, q. 14 a. 15. William of Ockham, *Predestination, God's Foreknowledge and Future Contingencies*, translated and edited by M. Adams and N. Kretzmann, Appleton-Century Crafts, New York 1969, Appendix 1, Distinction 39. For a contemporary critical discussion of this problem see N. Kretzmann, 'Omniscience and Immutability', *Journal of Philosophy* 63 (1966), pp. 409–421.

[51] Arama, 151a, my translation and italics.

[52] This was Boethius' reaction to Augustine's solution. (Boethius, *The Consolation of Philosophy* V, section 3).

[53] The Hebrew term for 'consequent upon' used by Arama is 'nimshekhet'. In the medieval Hebrew treatises on logic the standard term for the *consequent* of an implication is 'ha-nimshakh'. Thus, Arama's claim can be understood simply as the thesis that if '*p*' is true, *then* God is not ignorant of it. The term 'consequent upon' is therefore not to be construed temporally or even epistemologically but logically.

Arama's position shows some similarity to the view of Anselm of Canterbury, who makes use of the notion of "consequent necessity" to solve the problem of divine omniscience. Whereas "antecedent necessity . . . is the cause of something's being so, . . . there is also a consequent necessity, which is brought into being by a state of affairs". According to D. Henry, Anselm's "consequent necessity" is equivalent to logical necessity, which is all the necessity that, Anselm and Arama suggest, is involved in this topic. (D. P. Henry, *The Logic of Saint Anselm*, Clarendon Press, Oxford 1967, pp. 174–180).

Whether or not Arama was familiar with Anselm's Latin writings is difficult to determine. Several of his Jewish philosophical contemporaries did know Latin (e.g., Abraham Shalom, Isaac Abravanel), but whether he did is not certain.

[54] Aristotle, *Nicomachean Ethics* II:4. Arama, 152a–153a.

[55] Arama, 155a.

[56] There is a Rabbinic tradition that in fact Abraham did kill Isaac, who subsequently returned to life. (*Babylonian Talmud*, Ta'anith, 16a). Another tradition relates how Abraham drew a little of Isaac's blood before the angel intervened. (*Genesis Rabbah*, 56:7). See S. Spiegel's *The Last Trial*, Jewish Publication Society of America, New York 1969, for an excellent presentation of these and other legends.

[57] Isaac Abravanel, *Commentary on Genesis, ad locum*; S. D. Luzzatto, *Commentary on Genesis, ad locum*; M. L. Malbim, *Commentary on Genesis, ad locum*; L. Jacobs, 'Divine Foreknowledge and Human Freedom', *Conservative Judaism* 34 (1980), pp. 4–16.

[58] B. Spinoza, *The Theological-Political Treatise*, R. H. M. Elwes (transl.), Dover, N.Y., 1951, chapter 7, pp. 98ff.

CHAPTER 8

PHILOSOPHICAL EXEGESIS IN HISTORICAL PERSPECTIVE: THE CASE OF THE BINDING OF ISAAC

Jeremy Cohen

1. INTRODUCTION

As it surveys Jewish philosophers' readings of Genesis 22 from Saadya to Isaac Arama, Seymour Feldman's 'The Binding of Isaac: A Test-Case of Divine Foreknowledge' aptly demonstrates how biblical exegesis served the needs of medieval rationalists.[1] Jewish thinkers exploited the account of God's testing of Abraham as an appropriate context within which to focus on the theological dilemma of divine omniscience vs. human freedom, and they invariably interpreted the biblical story to suit their respective arguments on the issue. Professor Feldman's essay not only sheds light on Jewish formulations of the doctrine of divine foreknowledge, but also illuminates the important affinity between the medieval religious philosopher and the Bible. We have before us a valuable illustration of the omnipresent spectre of Scripture in the medieval mind and the preoccupation of even the rationalist with the sacred folk literature of his people.[2]

I would suggest, however, that in considering the link between philosophy and exegesis, especially with regard to Genesis 22, two correctives to the approach of Feldman's essay can enhance the value of the material which he scrutinizes – both for the philosopher and for the student of religious and cultural history.

2. THE MIDRASHIC ROOTS OF MEDIEVAL PHILOSOPHICAL EXEGESIS

First, Feldman's opening, sharp line of demarkation between philosophical and rabbinic modes of biblical commentary detracts from a justifiably more integrated impression of traditional Jewish cultural concerns. Certainly during the Middle Ages, the foremost of rabbinic exegetes were often themselves prominent philosophers. And one may not conclude that their commentaries on Scripture – as in the case of Saadya, Gersonides, or Isaac Arama – fail to manifest the legal and homiletical orientations of their talmudic forebears.[3] In the case of the Binding of Isaac, the thinkers addressed by Feldman did

T. Rudavsky (ed.), Divine Omniscience and Omnipotence in Medieval Philosophy, 135–142.

not conceive interpretations of Genesis 22:1 and 12 to buttress their positions, but they adjusted long-standing exegetical and midrashic traditions to meet the needs of their philosophical arguments. Each of their approaches appears in rudimentary form at least in classical rabbinic literature.

1. Saadya and Moses Maimonides, we recall, explained the testing of Abraham as a means whereby God could publicize the piety of the patriarch, displaying his compliance with God's will as a standard for all to follow.[4] The fifth-century midrashic compendium *Genesis Rabbah*, in a dictum ascribed to the late first/early second-century tannaitic sage Yosi the Galilean, precedes Maimonides in relating *nissah* (usually translated "put to the test") in Genesis 22:1 to *neis*, meaning banner or flag. "God *nissah* Abraham", then, really means, "He exalted him like a ship's pennant".[5] The same rabbinic work similarly anticipates Saadya's understanding of the angel's *ki 'attah yada'ti* in verse 12 as "now I have made known to all that you love me".[6]

2. Gersonides' reading of Genesis 22 as a genuine test of Abraham – i.e., that God did not know in advance precisely how Abraham would respond – embodies the position attributed to none other than Rabbi Akiva himself: "He tested him unequivocally".[8] Akiva is here entirely consistent with his more famous teaching, "All is observed (*safui*), but free will is given;" for despite its frequent misinterpretation, this homily does not posit divine foreknowledge. As Ephraim Urbach has argued cogently, Akiva means that God observes everything and will hold men accountable for their actions, precisely because they do have true freedom of choice.[9]

3. The assertion of Ḥasdai Crescas, that God tested Abraham precisely because he already knew how Abraham would react and thus to raise his fear of God from potentiality to actuality (thereby perfecting it), reiterates yet another classical rabbinic homily.[10] Comparing God to a variety of craftsmen, *Genesis Rabbah* records in connection with the Binding of Isaac:

> Rabbi Jonathan said: "A potter does not test defective vessels which cannot withstand being struck once without breaking. What then does he check? Sound vessels which if he strikes even repeatedly will not break. So God does not test the wicked, but the righteous . . .". Rabbi Yosi ben Ḥananiah said: "A flax-worker, when he knows his flax to be of good quality, as much as he pounds it, it improves and glistens; yet when it is of poor quality, he barely has to strike it once before it comes apart. So God does not test the wicked, but the righteous".[11]

Isaac Arama too held that God tested Abraham for the sake of instructing and edifying the patriarch.[12]

3. JUDAEO-CHRISTIAN INTERACTION REFLECTED IN EXEGESIS ON GENESIS 22

Second, a thorough appreciation of the doctrinal significance of Genesis 22 for medieval Jewish exegetes must extend beyond the confines of the Jewish intelligentsia – indeed, beyond the boundaries of the entire Jewish community. Shalom Spiegel and others have shown how rabbinic traditions concerning Abraham's trial captured many fundamental aspects of the Jewish religious experience, some of them perhaps originating even before the acceptance of monotheism in the ancient Hebrew psyche. And the Binding of Isaac was no less important for the medieval Jew. His world view perpetuated earlier ideas of "the merit of the fathers", which in the case of Isaac's willingness to die a martyr's death had facilitated the initial redemption of the Jews from Egypt and might continue to work on behalf of the dispersed and exiled Jewish community. Medieval Jewry undoubedly identified with Abraham and Isaac. Persecuted and subjugated by Gentile power, they often viewed themselves, like Isaac, as on the brink of destruction: would that their own attempt to live pious, God-fearing lives might (like Abraham's) induce God to save them. Especially because some rabbinic homilies suggested that Isaac may in fact have been sacrificed by Abraham, the Binding became the prototype for later acts of *qiddush ha-Shem*, or martyrdom in the "sanctification of God's name".[13]

This last rabbinic appreciation of the biblical story blatantly reflects upon the contribution of Christian society and culture – whether as a direct influence or as a hostile threat to be reckoned with – to the medieval Jewish world view. From the earliest generations of the Church, Christian exegetes looked to the Binding of Isaac as a prefiguration of the self-sacrifice of Jesus on the cross, with the important qualification that while Abraham ultimately sacrificed a ram in Isaac's stead, Jesus offered himself in actuality.[14] Such a popular Christian notion understandably challenged a Jewish estimation of the Mosaic Torah as needing no additional fulfillment. It motivated medieval rabbis to assert (1) the perfect consummation of the sacrifice of Isaac, and (2) the truly salvific quality of the "merit" which derived therefrom, as well as from similar acts of martyrdom on the part of contemporary Jews. Liturgical poets composed numerous penitential prayers entreating God for mercy and grace (*seliḥot*) around the theme of the Binding of Isaac. Yet the most revealing preoccupation of medieval Jewish martyrs and writers with the Binding of Isaac occurs within the context of the Crusades – a tendency not at all surprising given the Crusades' focus on the life, death, and memory of

Jesus, Christianity's martyr par excellence. Attacked in 1096 and 1146 by Christians anxious to avenge the murder of Jesus, Jews responded, as it were, in kind, by proclaiming their faith in and by emulating an earlier and (in their view) more perfect act of martyrdom. The Hebrew chronicles of the Crusade massacres and contemporary martyrologies are strewn with references to the Binding of Isaac. In a poem entitled 'The Aqedah', for instance, Efraim ben Jacob of Bonn (1133–ca. 1200) suggested not only that Isaac died a martyr's death, but that Abraham was actually prepared to sacrifice him a second time in response to the divine command! A witness to the events of the Second Crusade, Efraim deems as unsurpassable the sacrifice of Isaac, an offering reenacted repeatedly in the life of his community; his poem passionately concludes:

O righteous One, do us this grace!
  You promised our fathers mercy to Abraham.
Let then their merit stand as our witness,
  And pardon our iniquity and our sin, and take us for Thine inheritance.

Recall to our credit the many Akedahs,
  The saints, men and women, slain for Thy sake.
Remember the righteous martyrs of Judah,
  Those that were bound of Jacob.

Be Thou the shepherd of the surviving flock
  Scattered and dispersed among the nations.
Break the yoke and snap the bands
  Of the bound flock that yearns toward Thee.[15]

On the other hand, Jewish exegesis of the Binding of Isaac story was mirrored in Christian scholarship; all three rabbinic interpretations considered above appeared in the works of medieval Catholic theologians.[16] Most patristic writers and many medieval scholars – including Alcuin (d. 804), Rupert of Deutz (d. 1130), Thomas Aquinas, Nicholas of Lyra (ca. 1270–1349), and Dionysius the Carthuisan (ca. 1402–1471) – echoed the interpretation of Saadya and Maimonides. In Rupert's words, " 'God tested Abraham', not in order that He whom no knowledge escapes might come to know, but so that we [Abraham's] future descendants should not be ignorant of the greatness of our ancestor, whose faith has been demonstrated to us for our emulation".[17] Paul of Burgos (or Pablo de Santa Maria, d. 1435), although he initially defended this view against the attacks of Jewish scholars, ultimately abandoned it for an approach much akin to that of Gersonides: God in fact did test Abraham, but the Bible's language must be understood so as not to detract from the divine perfection. Paul's comments reveal not only the mutual interests of Jewish and Christian scholars, but also the relevance of the Binding of Isaac in their ongoing religious polemic.

That which is said here [Genesis 22:12] in the name of God, "Now I know", may be understood as "I have made others know", as is commonly held. But certain Jews reject this interpretation, saying that no one was here with Abraham at the time of the sacrifice, with the sole exception of Isaac – on account of whom alone it would not be said, "I have made others know". Yet this line of argument does not seem to be valid, because by this episode Abraham's obedience was made known to the angels, who previously perhaps did not recognize it to be on so great a level. Likewise for other believers, who trust in the deeds of Abraham on the authority of sacred Scripture. Still, however, this interpretation does not seem correct: For this act of sacrifice is attributed to Abraham inasmuch as he himself performed it . . . . And so by this act Abraham made others know that he feared God, and Scripture would therefore have more properly said, "Now you have made others know that you feared God". Hence it seems that this statement – "Now I know" – can properly be explained metaphorically, just like other things which are said of God by way of comparison. Thus when it is said, "God became angry", and the like, it is understood to mean, insofar as He was in a state of rage. Similarly in our own episode when it is said, "God tested Abraham", it must be understood that God, who wanted to have proof of something unknown, was with respect to Abraham in the manner of putting to the test – yet not that this [something] was unknown to God who knows everything. In the same way when it is said, "Now I know", it can be explained metaphorically; it may be understood from this that God in this event was in the manner of one who newly comes to know something. This is evident inasmuch as after the incident God promised Abraham greater things than he had promised him previously.[18]

Yet a third group of Christian exegetes, including Augustine, Gregory the Great, the authors of the *Glossa ordinaria* and Hugh of St. Cher (c. 1200–1263), shared Ḥasdai Crescas's and Isaac Arama's opinion that God sought not to gain insight for himself but to raise Abraham's piety from a latent state to an active one, thereby teaching the patriarch a profound religious lesson.[19]

4. CONCLUSION

The multi-faceted interest of medieval Jews and Christians in the Binding of Isaac accordingly demonstrates that not even the interpretations of philosophers may be properly appreciated in an historical vacuum. For the Jewish thinkers considered by Feldman, the biblical tale raised questions that touched upon key issues and themes in the classical and contemporary rabbinic mind, serving to link these philosophers with – rather than to distinguish them from – ancient traditions of rabbinic exegesis. The various interpretations of Genesis 22 also manifest the complexity of medieval Jewish-Christian relations, interactions deriving from competition and hostility but which simultaneously fostered common cultural concerns along with intellectual exchange.

NOTES

1 See above, pp. 105–133.

2 On various aspects of the pervasive concern with the Bible among medieval intellectuals, see, among numerous others, B. Smalley, *The Study of the Bible in the Middle Ages*, (2nd ed.), 1952; repr., Univ. of Notre Dame Press, Notre Dame 1964; H. A. Wolfson, *Philo: Foundations of Religious Philosophy in Judaism, Christianity, and Islam*, Harvard University Press, Cambridge Mass. 1947, pp. 439–60; S. W. Baron, *A Social and Religious History of the Jews*, (2nd ed.), Vol. 6, Columbia University Press, New York 1958, pp. 235–313, 441–86; H. de Lubac, *Exégèse médiévale: Les quatre sens de l'Ecriture*, 2 pts. (in 4 vols.), Théologie 41–42, 59, Aubier, Paris, 1959–64; and P. Riché, *Écoles et enseignement dans l'Occident chrétien de la fin du Ve siècle au milieu de XIe siècle*, A. Montaigne, Paris 1979.

3 See W. Bacher, *Die Biblelexegese der jüdischen Religionsphilosophen des Mittelalters vor Maimuni*, Karl J. Trubner, Strassburg 1892, esp. pp. 1–44; E. I. J. Rosenthal, 'Saadya Gaon: An Appreciation of His Biblical Exegesis", *Bulletin of the John Rylands Library* 27 (1942), pp. 168–78; A. S. Halkin, 'Saadia's Exegesis and Polemics', in *Rab Saadia Gaon: Studies in His Honor*, L. Finkelstein (ed.), Jewish Theological Seminary of America, New York 1944, pp. 117–41; M. Zucker, *Rav Saadya Gaon's Translation of the Torah* [Hebrew], Michael Higger Memorial Publications 3, New York 1959; E. Renan, *Les écrivains juifs français du XIVe siècle*, Imprimerie Nationale, Paris 1893, pp. 240–98; C. Touati, *La pensée philosophique et théologique de Gersonide*, Les Editions de Minuit, Paris 1973, pp. 49–82; I. Bettan, *Studies in Jewish Preaching: Middle Ages*, Hebrew Union College Press, Cincinnati 1939, pp. 130–91; and S. Heller – Wilensky, *The Philosophy of Isaac Arama in the Framework of Philonic Philosophy* [Hebrew], Jerusalem 1956, pp. 29–31.

4 Saadya ben Joseph, *Perush . . . 'al ha-Torah we-'al-Na"kh*, J. Gad (ed.), 2, London 1959, p. 16 (cf. Zucker, *Rav Saadya*, p. 264, n. 106*); Moses ben Maimon, *Guide of the Perplexed* 3.24 (see also 3.10–23).

5 *Genesis Rabbah* 55.6, J. Theodor and Ch. Albeck (eds.), (2nd ed.), 2, Jerusalem 1965, pp. 588–89 with nn.; a similar interpretation appears in 55.1, pp. 584–85 with nn.

6 *Ibid.*, 56.7, p. 603, Cf. *Midrash Tanḥuma*, Shelaḥ, §43, S. Buber (ed.), 1 1885; repr., Jerusalem 1964, p. 110; *Numbers Rabbah* 17.3; and the ms. cited by M. M. Kasher, *Torah Shelemah* [Hebrew] 3, 2, (2nd ed.), Jerusalem 1938, p. 898, no. 135.

7 Levi ben Gerson, *Perush . . . 'al ha-Torah*, 1, Venice 1547, pp. 306–316.

8 *Genesis Rabbah* 55.6, pp. 588–89 with nn.

9 Mishnah *Avot* 3.15; E. Urbach, *The Sages: Their Concepts and Beliefs,* trans. by I. Abrahams, (2 vols.), Magnes Press, Jerusalem 1975, 1:256–68, 2:802–7.

10 Ḥasdai ben Abraham Crescas, *Or Adonai* 2.1.1, 1860; repr., Tel Aviv 1963, 28a–b.

11 *Genesis Rabbah* 55.2, pp. 585–86 with nn. A similar interpretation is espoused by Judah ha-Levi, *Kuzari* 5.20.

12 Isaac Arama, *Sefer Aqedat Yitṣhaq*, J. Falk (ed.), 1 Pressburg 1849, 151b–152a, declares that Abraham's trial was of the sort undertaken "in order that the one tested might actualize his perfection, and his intellect and understanding might be enhanced". Arama explains this understanding both in terms of Abraham's peculiar situation of realizing he must sacrifice Isaac despite God's previous promises to him, and as encompassing the more general "obligation to follow the divine counsel and commandment, over the dictates of human reason, out of love and fear". The idea that God tests his righteous followers even when normally sacrosanct principles of ethics and justice come to be undermined naturally brings to mind the story of Job, echoing the Babylonian Talmud's own analogy (*Sanhedrin* 89b) between the latter and the Binding of Isaac: "Satan said before the Holy One, blessed be He: 'Lord of the universe, you have endowed this old man [Abraham] with offspring at the age of one hundred; yet of the entire feast which he made [upon Isaac's being weaned] he did not have one dove or pigeon to offer you'. He [God] said to him [Satan], 'He has done nothing but for his son's sake. If I said to him, "Sacrifice your son to me, he would sacrifice him at once". And immediately 'God put Abraham to the test [. . .] and he said, "Take your son."' "

13 See S. Spiegel, 'The Legend of Isaac's Slaying and Resurrection' [Hebrew], in *Alexander Marx Jubilee Volume*, S. Lieberman (ed.), Jewish Theological Seminary of America, New York 1950, Heb. pp. 471–547, subsequently *The Last Trial*, trans. by J. Goldin, Jewish Publication Society of America, New York 1969; Urbach, *The Sages*, 1:483–511 (esp. 501–5), 2:799–916; G. Vermes, *Scripture and Tradition in Judaism: Haggadic Studies*, Studia post-biblica 4, E. J. Brill, Leiden 1961, pp. 193–218; D. Noy, 'Ha-Aqedah ke-Av-Ṭippus shel Qiddush ha-Shem', *Maḥanayim* 60 (1962), pp. 40–47; and G. Vajda, *L'amour de Dieu dans la théologie juive du Moyen Age*, Etudes de philosophie médiévale 46, Paris 1957, s. vv. Abraham, Isaac. Cf. also below, n. 15.

14 The relationship between Jewish and Christian doctrines and traditions concerning the Binding of Isaac has been discussed and debated by several generations of scholars. Recent summaries of the opposing theories, including citations of the pertinent source material and scholarly literature, appear in R. J. Daly, 'The Soteriological Significance of the Sacrifice of Isaac', *Catholic Biblical Quarterly* 39 (1977), pp. 45–75; and in P. R. Davies and B. D. Chilton, 'The Aqedah: A revised Tradition History', *ibid.*, **40** (1978), pp. 514–46. On Christian comparisons of the Binding of Isaac with Jesus' crucifixion, see also Spiegel, *Last Trial*, pp. 81 ff. with nn., and the valuable survey of D. Lerch, *Isaaks Opferung christlich gedeutet: Eine auslegungsgeschichtliche Untersuchung*, Beiträge zur historischen Theologie 12, Tübingen 1950.

15 See the works cited in n. 13 above, and G. Dreifuss, 'Isaac, the Sacrificial Lamb: A Study of Some Jewish Legends', *Journal of Analytical Psychology* **16** (1971), pp. 69–78; and I. Elbogen, *Der jüdische Gottesdienst in seiner geschichtlichen Entwicklung* [Hebrew], 3rd edition, trans. by J. Amir, J. Heinemann *et al.*, (eds.), Tel Aviv 1972, pp. 171, 218. Illustrative passages in the Crusade chronicles are found in A. M. Habermann (ed.), *Sefer Gezeirot Ashkenaz we-Ṣarefat*, Jerusalem 1945, pp. 32, 43, 50, 52, 75, 81, 123, trans. in *The Jews and the Crusaders: The Hebrew Chronicles of the First and Second Crusades*, S. Eidelberg (ed.), University of Wisconsin Press, Madison 1977, pp. 32, 33, 49, 58, 60, 83, 92, 132. Efraim's "The Aqedeh" has been published by Spiegel, 'The Legend', pp. 538–47 (= *Last Trial*, pp. 143–52); see also *Last Trial*, pp. 17–27, 129–38 with nn.

16 On mutual influences between Jewish and Christian thinkers, see, among others, R.

Loewe, 'The Jewish Midrashim and Patristic and Scholastic Exegesis of the Bible', *Studia patristica* 1 (1957), pp. 492–514; Smalley, *Study*, esp. chs. 3–4; A. Grabois, 'The *Hebraica Veritas* and Jewish-Christian Intellectual Relations in the Twelfth Century', *Speculum* 50 (1975), pp. 613–34; and the somewhat different perspective of S. Pines, 'Scholasticism after Thomas Aquinas and the Teachings of Hasdai Crescas and His Predecessors', *Proceedings of the Israel Academy of Sciences and Humanities* 1: 10 (1967), esp. (on Christian influences on Gersonides' theory of divine cognition) pp. 5–9, and 90–101, and 'Saint Thomas et la pensée juive médiévale: Quelques notations', in *Aquinas and Problems of His Time*, G. Verbeke and D. Verhelst (eds.), Mediaevalia lovanensia 1,5,Louvain 1976, pp. 118 ff.

[17] Lerch, *Isaaks Opferung*, pp. 97 ff. (on patristic authors); Augustine, *De Civitate Dei* 16.32; Alcuin, *Interrogationes et Responsiones in Genesim* §§ 201, 207, PL 100:544, 545 (accepting the ms. variant of "cognoscatur" in § 207, without which Alcuin is inconsistent); Rupert of Deutz, *In Genesim* 6.28, Corpus Christianorum, Continuatio Mediaevalis, 21:405; Thomas Aquinas, *Summa theologiae* 1.114.2; Nicholas of Lyra, in *Biblia sacra cum glossis, interlineari et ordinaria, Nicholai Lyrani Postilla et moralitatibus, Burgensis additionibus, et Thoringi replicis*, 1, Lyons 1545, 78C; Dionysius the Carthusian, *Opera omnia* 1, Montreuil 1896, p. 290.

[18] *Biblia sacra*, 1:78H. (Cf. also Lerch, *Isaaks Opferung*, p. 98 and n. 1.) Paul's argument is cited and refuted by Dionysius the Carthusian, loc. cit., (n. 17). Both the Jewish objection to the *communis opinio* described by Paul as well as an earlier version of Paul's own argument appear in the comments of Abraham ibn Ezra (1092–1167) on Gen. 22:1.

[19] Augustine, *Quaestiones super Genesim* §§ 57–58, CCSL 33:22, *De Trinitate* 1.12, CCSL 50:61; Gregory the Great, *Moralia in Iob*, 28.4.13, PL 76:454; *Biblia sacra* 1:77r, 78r; Hugh of St. Cher, *Opera omnia*, 1, Lyons 1669, 294 Cf. also Aquinas, *Summa* 1–2.112.5.

CHAPTER 9

PROVIDENCE, DIVINE OMNISCIENCE AND POSSIBILITY: THE CASE OF MAIMONIDES

Alfred L. Ivry

1. MAIMONIDES' EXOTERIC POSITION STATED

As in practically every area of Maimonides' discourse, his position on the issue of providence, divine omniscience, and possibility is not obvious on a first reading of the material. Or rather, it is too obvious, obvious twice over, the difficulty being that on the face of it Maimonides contradicts himself on these issues, as he does on many others. Here too it would seem that he has both an exoteric and esoteric position. Taking the *Guide of the Perplexed* as the main source for our study, it is the esoteric position mostly which I should like to attempt to describe. My thesis is that this is Maimonides' true position, as shown by the philosophical coherence it possesses.

We may begin with Maimonides' statement in *Guide* 3:20, which offers what I see as his exoteric position.

To sum up the notion that I have stated in résumé: Just as we do not apprehend the true reality of His essence, but know withal that His existence is the most perfect of existences and not commingled in any way with any deficiency or change or being acted upon, so although we do not know the true reality of His knowledge because it is His essence, we do know that He does not apprehend at certain times while being ignorant at others. I mean to say that no new knowledge comes to Him in any way; that His knowledge is neither multiple nor finite; that nothing among all the beings is hidden from Him; and that His knowledge of them does not abolish their natures, for the possible remains as it was with the nature of possibility. All the contradictions that may appear in the union of these assertions are due to their being considered in relation to our knowledge, which has only its name in common with His knowledge. Similarly the word "purpose" is used equivocally when applied to what is purposed by us and to what is said to be His purpose, may He be exalted. Similarly the word "providence" is used equivocally when applied to what we are provident about and to that of which it is said that He, may He be exalted, is provident with regard to it. It is accordingly true that the meaning of knowledge, the meaning of purpose, and the meaning of providence, when ascribed to us, are different from the meanings of these terms when ascribed to Him. When, therefore, the two providences or knowledges or purposes are taken to have one and the same meaning, the above-mentioned difficulties and doubts arise. When, on the other hand, it is known that everything that is ascribed to us is different from everything that is ascribed to Him, truth becomes manifest. The differences between the things ascribed to Him and those

T. Rudavsky (ed.), Divine Omniscience and Omnipotence in Medieval Philosophy, 143–159.

ascribed to us have been explicitly stated, as have been mentioned above, in its dictum *Neither are your ways My ways.*[1]

With this quotation from Isaiah we could well draw our discussion to a pious and mercifully brief close, taking refuge in the equivocal nature of language about God, which ostensibly permits us to make assertions of a traditional sort, even though we do not understand the meaning of what we say. As Maimonides has said, "When . . . it is known that everything that is ascribed to us is different from everything ascribed to Him, truth becomes manifest".

Maimonides, however, has not said that everything ascribed to us is *totally* different from everything ascribed to God, just that everything is different. He would probably have liked to make the stronger claim, as he has elsewhere (I:56), but his very discussion of the issues belies that. There are a necessary similarity and a univocal core of meaning in the concepts mentioned which serve as a base for discussion and comparison, even if that comparison leads to tremendous disparities. Maimonides clearly believes in the essential difference between God and man, but that does not necessarily imply a total difference, as we shall see, his protestations to the contrary notwithstanding.

Maimonides himself, in the passage just quoted, initially makes some definitive and presumably comprehensible statements about God's existence and knowledge, to which the Divine purpose and providence are related; and he surrounds this chapter with further intelligible discussion, analysis actually, of these themes. It is not, therefore, unwarranted to follow "the master" in examining these concepts critically, beginning, as Maimonides does here, with God's essence and existence.

2. THE CREATOR AND HIS CREATION: THE NATURE OF GOD, MATTER AND FORM

The concepts of essence and existence are identical in God, both for Maimonides as well as for Avicenna, whom Maimonides joins in describing God as the Necessary Existent, *wājib al-wujūd*, he whose essence is existence *simpliciter*. As such, God's existence is uncaused, having no reason or reality other than itself, its essence absolutely self-contained and pure being.[2] All the customary Divine attributes – life, power and knowledge, for example – must necessarily be identified with this simple essence, as Maimonides makes clear in I:57; for to introduce distinctions in God's being would entail multiplicity and require explanation. It was felt that this would deprive the Necessary Existent of its singular status as pure being.

The Necessary Existent is, however, for Maimonides even more than for Avicenna, also regarded as solely responsible ultimately for the being of the world, that is, for the many and diverse beings in the world.[3] The uncaused One is thus the cause (in whatever sense we use the term) of the many, and the Necessary Existent, supposedly without losing its essential unity and absolute autonomy of being, functions as though it indeed is the source of those properties of life, power and knowledge which, among others, exist in the world.

Though Maimonides insists upon the identification of the multiplicity of Divine attributes with the single Divine essence, the basic problem of the simple One being the source of the many and thus putatively multiple itself is a conundrum he cannot resolve. It is a mystery of being for Maimonides similar to that whereby the One is said to know all, i.e., the many, in a single way.[4] Lacking other necessary independent principles of being besides the Necessary Existent, Maimonides has no principle of multiplicity which can account for its initial appearance. It is not for nothing that the world is created from nothing, for Maimonides, and neither is it negligent on his part that matter, the requisite principle, never receives the full status it enjoys in Aristotle's thought, where it may be seen as the eternal live-in partner of form.[5]

Far from regarding it as a spouse or partner of form, however, Maimonides calls matter a "harlot", likening it to Satan, darkness, and evil.[6] Its fatal flaw, for Maimonides, is its inherent transiency, its impermanent and corruptible nature. Originating in the absence of all beings, created from nothing, matter remains impressed in Maimonides' consciousness as related to privation, to the absence of forms associated with specific beings. Such forms are potentially present in the matter, but it itself is void of all but the disposition to receive them. Matter comes as close as one can get to non-being, where being is identified with permanent substance.

Of course, Maimonides makes it clear in numerous places, and particularly in his discussion of Aristotle's description of the nature of the universe, with which he explicitly concurs,[7] that he realizes that matter plays a necessary role in the physical world: it both provides a substratum for forms and individual existence, and serves as a principle of change and potentiality. As part of the way things are, with matter always specifically informed, Maimonides is even prepared to acknowledge that the world in its entirety, matter included, exhibits the wisdom and goodness of its Creator.[8]

This more generous and accepting attitude of Maimonides to matter does not, however, disguise his deeply felt aversion to material and corporeal things. For him, matter is basically a necessary evil, necessary as the condition for the realization of form in the world, evil because of its incipient insubstantiality. At the same time, however, matter is not viewed as essentially insubstantial, for it is created as a genuine substance, however elusive its origins or nature.

The non-being (or privation, *al-'adam*) which precedes the creation of the world is not for Maimonides a real substance: it is not Nothing. Similarly, the matter which serves as the substratum for form is not regarded as an independent principle of (non-) being, an autonomous counter-force to form. Matter so regarded could provide the rationale for viewing physical existence as a *real* "veil" (Maimonides' imagery, *Guide* 3:9), a veritable kingdom of evil to be overcome.

This would more than justify Maimonides' negative attitude to matter and matters physical, as well as provide a rational explanation for creation from nothing. Maimonides, however, does not avail himself of this option, which would have been familiar to him from both philosophical and mystical sources.[9] He prefers his creation to be purely "from nothing",[10] and he remains irrationally set against matter. He is irrational, since the same Aristotelian reading of form and matter which precludes his accepting a basically dualistic world view, should have prepared him to accept with greater equanimity the necessary – and hence desirable – role of matter in being. Thus, what must be said here is that Maimonides accepts the Aristotelian definition of substance as including matter, but places it within a Neoplatonized value scheme in which the substantiality of matter is markedly inferior to that of form. It is form which is preeminently substance for Maimonides, form which is derived from the "form of forms", form with which the *donatur formarum* (*wāhib al-ṣuwar*) is necessarily and permanently involved.[11] Matter, unlike form, is neither with God from all eternity, nor close to him after its creation. It serves as a showcase and/or trial for form, but has little intrinsic worth. The best thing Maimonides can say of it is that it is good, in spite of being "a concomitant of privation entailing death and all evils", because of the "perpetuity of generation and the permanence of being through succession" in which it participates.[12] At every stage of this succession, however, it is form which dominates matter, even as it is form which is dominant in Maimonides' thinking.

The form which the Divine mostly takes, for Maimonides as well as for most medieval (and classical) philosophers, is of course Intelligence.[13] He *is*

Intelligence itself, the source of order, proportion and (proper) form. As Intelligence, or Intellect, God's being is a knowing, not just of itself as Aristotle would have it, but of all that is intelligible, the entire intelligible universe. He is the cause of this universe in all but the material mode of causation.[14] According to Maimonides, God's knowledge thus has to be "over all" in existence, that is over all that may be known, since his knowledge is an expression – our expression – of his creative activity in the world.

This action is, moreover, regarded as an expression of God's goodness; it is, indeed, identical with his goodness. For God is the "Pure Good" as well as the Intelligence and Form of the world (as well as its Necessary Existent), and all these terms are identical with his essence. Maimonides says in the opening of 3:19 of the *Guide*, that "it is a primary notion that all good things must exist in God", and that he has no deficencies. Maimonides takes this to mean that God cannot be ignorant of anything, since "ignorance with regard to anything is a deficiency". That which God brings into existence and/or knows is therefore good. As he is the first cause or principle of all that exists, all in the universe must be good, a necessary consequence of his omniscience and omnipotence.

This summary of Maimonides' position is both right and wrong. He believes it to be the case, but only after offering serious, though discrete, qualification. For to accept this view literally would make the Deity already responsible for the evil in the world, which Maimonides acknowledges, however reluctantly, to be real.[15] The incorporeal nature of the Divine as well as his unity are also threatened by the literal view of omniscience, since the objects of God's knowledge, which knowledge is his essence, are and become that which exists in the world. The physical universe would then be the direct result of God's action, which is another term for his essence, so that the created world, with all its warts, would equal the Creator.

3. THE PROCESS OF EMANATION (AL-FAYḌ)

To avoid this pantheistic and materialist consequence, Maimonides adopts the originally Neoplatonic scheme of emanation, which is meant to provide just the mechanism desired to both bridge and maintain the gap between the One and the many, as well as between the spiritual and physical spheres of being.[16] Maimonides, we should note, utilizes the emanative idea for the first purpose only, his notion of creation from nothing offering an alternative description, if not explanation, for the origin of matter.

If matter does not emanate from the One, though, in Maimonides' scheme of things, the forms of this world do; and this emanation must include, paradoxically, the form of matter. It is known to God as an intelligible concept, an object of his intelligence, as everything else is known to him and exists with him. How God turns this intellection of matter into a physical reality is, Maimonides believes, totally beyond our comprehension.[17] It is no more comprehensible, however, than his mode of knowledge itself, which comprehends the identity of the One and the many.

Yet there is an important difference between the mystery of creation and the mystery of God's knowledge, as Maimonides treats them. He is very eager to establish the possibility of creation from nothing, but completely opposed to speculating about its nature; whereas he is not reticent in discussing God's omniscience, however problematic a topic it is. We are, therefore, on surer ground in describing the particular form his belief in this concept takes.

I do not wish to give the impression that Maimonides is really enlightening on the notion of emanation (*al-fayḍ*), the mechanism of providence in general. The term is used frequently, together with appropriate and conventional imagery, but without any of the actual ontic structures that normally accompany it and which render it comprehensible.[18] The Maimonidean world upon which the Divine One casts its light, "unfolding" its being, beauty and goodness, is in its structure more of an Aristotelian place than anything else, a world divided into supra- and sub-lunar spheres, each with its hylomorphic constitution. It is not a world of universal substances, neither the World Mind and Soul, as in classic Neoplatonic thought, nor any other completely separately existing universal being.

The forms of the world which are one in God are, accordingly, many in the world itself, via emanation, though without a gradual unfolding of the many from the One. The world is not, and then suddenly it is, in its entirety, for Maimonides. Yet here he is very clear: there is no creation from nothing of these forms in the world, there is no hiatus in their being; they derive from God, in whom they are necessarily eternal, being "part" of his eternal essence.

God is present in the world, then, for Maimonides, through the forms of everything that exists. This presence is not equally found in all members of a given species, since the forms of individual bodies may not be well realized, of which we will soon have more to say. The Divine presence is found, rather, in the species itself, as the definitive form of that species, though Maimonides is quite explicit that species don't really exist independently of their constituent individual members.[19]

The forms of things do exist separately from matter, we have seen, in the mind of God, and have done so eternally. Though the mode of existence of these forms "there", as God, is beyond our comprehension, it is clear to Maimonides that it is just this eternal existence of theirs which gives us assurance of the stable, even permanent, nature of our universe. While the world as we know it, with its combination of material and formal elements, is created, the essential nature of beings, their ideal forms, are eternal.[20]

These ideal forms, the pure forms, are, then, the objects of God's knowledge, and constitute his being and that of the essential being of the universe. The two beings are one and the same in God, though not in the universe, through the mystery of emanation. The isolated sparks of the Divine in the world (to use a later image) are further removed from the totality of God's being by their association with matter, the very antithesis of form and permanence. Though created by God, matter is intelligible to him only and necessarily in its intelligible mode, as form. God therefore knows the principle of matter, which in good part is that matter itself – to the degree that it exists by itself – is free of God's knowledge.

Of course, since matter never exists "by itself", for Maimonides, it is never not known to God, to some degree. Yet, while matter does not exist by itself, it has a self of its own, which self is a real substance.[21] It is this irreducible physical core of an object, the material cause itself, which is beyond direct Divine knowledge and ministration. God has willed this to be so, for Maimonides: he has chosen to create a substance over which he has no immediate control, the concrete, individual instances of which he is ignorant.

4. MAIMONIDES' THEORY OF PROVIDENCE

To say that Maimonides considers God's knowledge to be confined to the forms of things, and to the forms in general, as representative of the species, seems to contradict his frequent assertions to the contrary. God is not ignorant of anything, Maimonides says in a number of places, asserting that divine omniscience extends to all individual existents. Nor is God's knowledge limited to currently existing individuals, but he is said also to know everything that will occur in the future too.[22]

Maimonides explicitly qualifies this position, however, as soon as he develops his theory of providence.

> For I for one believe that in this lowly world – I mean that which is beneath the sphere of the moon – divine providence watches only over the individuals belonging to the human species and that in this species alone all the circumstances of the individuals and

the good and evil that befall them are consequent upon the deserts, just as it says: *For all His ways are judgment* (Deut. 32:4). But regarding all the other animals and, all the more, the plants and other things, my opinion is that of Aristotle. For I do not by any means believe that this particular leaf has fallen because of a providence watching over it; nor that this spider has devoured this fly because God has now decreed and willed something concerning individuals; nor that the spittle spat by Zayd has moved till it came down in one particular place upon a gnat and killed it by a divine decree and judgment; nor that when this fish snatched this worm from the face of the water, this happened in virtue of a divine volition concerning individuals. For all this is in my opinion due to pure chance, just as Aristotle holds.[23]

The restriction of individual providence to human beings is not for Maimonides just a matter of Scriptural fiat, though he is quick to cite chapter and verse in support of his position that, in regard to "animals other than man", the Biblical texts "refer to providence watching over the species and not to individual providence".[24] It is logic, however, and not authority which dictates Maimonides' position, for as he says quite candidly in the continuation of the previously quoted citation:

According to me, as I consider the matter, divine providence is consequent upon the divine overflow; and the species with which this intellectual overflow is united, so that it became endowed with intellect and so that everything that is disclosed to a being endowed with the intellect was disclosed to it, is the one accompanied by divine providence, which appraises all its actions from the point of view of reward and punishment.[23]

For Maimonides, then, providence is entailed by emanation: it "is consequent upon the divine overflow" (*al-ʿināyah al-ilāhīyah . . . tābiʿah lil-fayḍ al-ilāhī*) which is immediately called an "intellectual" overflow (*al-fayḍ al-ʿaqlī*). "Providence" is the term primarily given to this intellectual overflow as it reaches the only species which has a faculty capable of receiving it directly, or "purely". Man's rational faculty alone is believed to be "conjoined" (*ittaṣala*) to this divine intellect, and in consequence of this unique natural endowment (though willed by God to be man's nature), shared by all members of the species, man alone is individually, and necessarily, the object of divine providence. As Maimonides says elsewhere, "this consideration follows necessarily (*lāzim*) from the point of view of speculation, provided that, as we have mentioned, providence is consequent upon the intellect".[25]

Maimonides then continues with the following significant remark:

It would not be proper for us to say that providence watches over the species and not the individuals, as is the well-known opinion of some philosophic schools. For outside the mind nothing exists except the individuals; it is to these individuals that the divine intellect is united. Consequently providence watches only over these individuals.[25]

This last statement is puzzling, given the above quoted view of providence watching over the species of species other than ours. Maimonides could not mean to say here that just our species is non-existent; that is rather a categorical statement negating the ontological reality of all species. They all have a nominal reality only, for Maimonides, given identity by the common form which their individual members possess. The divine intellect relates to this specific form, being, in Maimonides' view, responsible for it.[26]

This form, together with all others, exists separately only in God's mind, though in a manner, Maimonides says, beyond our comprehension, so that we should not say even that "it" exists there either. From God, however, the entire formal aspect of the universe emanates in an order of his own devising. This order becomes the nature of the world,[27] understood through categorization into genera and species. The divine intellect or providence may, accordingly, be said to "watch over" the species,[28] i.e., over the specific form present in individual members of the species, and to do so for every species in nature.

Homo Sapiens may be said to receive individual treatment primarily in the sense that he alone is *aware* of the divine intellect, and only he is able to benefit from this awareness by modifying his behaviour in accordance with it. The rational faculty which is man's *proprium*, given to him by God, enables man to respond consciously and individually to the knowledge he acquires, and thus to become responsible for his own destiny in a way other creatures are not.

The emphasis on man's ability to control his destiny distinguishes for Maimonides his view of providence from that of Aristotle. Maimonides stresses the role chance (*ittifāq*) plays in Aristotle's scheme, in contrast to its absence, for the sage, in his own theory. The two men are not really far apart, as Maimonides tells it, on the issue of individual versus species providence, as a close inspection of Maimonides' presentation of Aristotle's view would reveal.[29] It is, accordingly, in the total control which the true philosopher can supposedly exercise over his environment that Maimonides feels providence is most fully expressed.

If, as he (Aristotle) states, the foundering of a ship and the drowning of those who were in it and the falling-down of a roof upon those who were in the house, are due to pure chance, the fact that the people in the ship went on board and that the people in the house were sitting in it is, according to our opinion, not due to chance, but to divine will in accordance with the deserts of those people as determined in His judgments, the rule of which cannot be attained by our intellects.[30]

Though the unsuspecting reader may well think passages of this sort affirm providence to be an action taken by God *ad personam*, willed specifically (for or) against a particular individual, this is not the case. The individual who acts on the basis of correct or incorrect knowledge is responsible for what happens to him in all circumstances, Maimonides is saying, and this is the will of God. It is a will which functions "in accordance with that which is deserved" (*bi-ḥasb al-istiḥqāq*), i.e., deserved for such a person, whoever he is. The divine judgments in these matters, Maimonides concludes, are beyond our understanding. We do know, however, that these are "judgments" (*aḥkām*), general determinations of the permanent, unchanging wisdom (*ḥikmah*) of God, and need not be taken personally, in the usual sense of that term.

It is we who appraise God's actions from the point of view of reward and punishment, we who personalize the actions of the divine overflow, which become individualized in the varied responses we – and all corporeal being – bring to it. This understanding of providence agrees with Maimonides' general theory of divine attributes, which restricts the legitimate predication of attributes to God to those of a negative or relational kind. The latter category considers events in this world as effects of God's actions, and consciously interprets his inscrutable being in terms of behavior familiar to us.[31]

We could say therefore that the divine intellect is essentially impersonal and functions of necessity, but for the element of will which Maimonides, as is customary in medieval philosophy, regards as essential to the divine being. What happens in the world is regarded as a necessary consequence, directly or indirectly, of God's will. He wills, ultimately, without any external constraint, to be himself, a Necessary Existent, all the actions of which are perfect and good, necessarily. God freely wills, likewise, to emanate "part" of his being onto the world; an emanation, like creation, which follows necessarily from his nature, being part of his eternal, unchanging plan. The will of God is thus synonymous with his wisdom, as Maimonides says often,[32] and his freedom, we may add, synonymous with necessity. The divine will is perhaps most successful a term when taken as representing the outwardly oriented and purposive nature of the divine being, a purpose which, for Maimonides, should be said to extend to individuals, though not intended in the personal way we like to believe.

Maimonides is actually quite open about God's knowledge being of a general sort, dealing with universal concepts and species. This follows necessarily from his nature, i.e., from his wisdom and will combined, which is to say, from his very being. Statements of a more personal and traditional kind are also to be found throughout the *Guide*, but on close analysis they yield readings consistent with the philosophical position I have outlined.[33] The social and political problems Maimonides would have faced in presenting his views unadorned, unreconciled to traditional Jewish belief in a personal God and providence, are obvious. Fortunately for him, both the political theory he embraced and his view of prophecy – topics beyond our present discussion – complemented his metaphysical theory and encouraged him to believe in the legitimacy of traditional formulations of these issues. As he says at one point, the opinion of some thinkers and necessarily that of those who adhere to a religious law (*kullu muttasharri'in*) is that "(God's) knowledge has for its object the species, but in a certain sense (*bi-ma'nī mā*) (it) extends to all the individuals of the species".[34] For socio-political reasons Maimonides often dwells on the individual aspect of providence, but he does not reduce it to that. Nor could he, given that God's providence follows his essence, and that is fixed, necessary and essentially universal.

5. DIVINE OMNISCIENCE AND POSSIBILITY

The necessity that encompasses the divine intellect reflects upon the world, for Maimonides, and is a reflection of it. Not only are certain things, viz., logically contradictory things, impossible even for God to affect; but also, and equally, only certain things are possible for him, viz., those which agree with his essence, being derived from it. As God is the ultimate principle of being, his essential will is to let things be, to bring into being whatever may exist, the limits of possible existence being dictated by his wisdom. That wisdom in turn is characterized by goodness, which "indubitably", Maimonides says, (to which we would add "preeminently"), includes existence.[35] It thus follows necessarily from God's nature that there be an existent world and that it include all that may possibly exist; for to exclude eternally a real possibility would be to deprive the world of a good being, an act inconsistent with the nature of the "Pure Good".

A real possibility for Maimonides thus turns out to be identical, after creation, with actual possibilities (mostly) familiar to us, and potentially existing in material beings. The purely logical possibility of something existing merely by not running afoul of the law of contradiction – the notion of possibility which appealed to the Islamic theologians [36] – is not for Maimonides a sufficient criterion of possibility. The truly possible for him is also that which God has eternally determined to be so, willing that which his wisdom dictates. As Maimonides says, "He wills only what is possible, and not everything that is possible, but only that which is required by His wisdom to be such".[37] (Lest one think this statement implies after all that Maimonides does accept the notion of an ontological category of purely theoretically existing possibilities, think of what this would entail: the existence of ideal entities neither willed nor necessitated by God! Nor does it help to image that these possibilities could actually exist and be necessary in another world, for Maimonides is referring here to a category of possibilities that never actually exists, a category that in his thought is self-contradictory, given the necessity of God's goodness and perfection).

That which exists, then, is, for Maimonides, a necessary consequent of God's necessary existence, and is as such good. In his initial discussion of the presumed evil of mortality, Maimonides puts it this way:

> Everything that is capable of being generated from any matter whatever, is generated in the most perfect way in which it is possible to be generated out of that specific matter; the deficiency attaining the individuals of the species corresponds to the deficiency of the particular matter of the individual. Now the ultimate term and the most perfect thing that may be generated out of blood and sperm is the human species with its well-known nature consisting in man's being a living, rational, and mortal being. Thus this species of evils must necessarily exist.[38]

In this passage Maimonides succinctly puts the paradoxical nature of God's omniscience. It encompasses deficiencies and evils of a sort, real enough and even necessary, but not ultimately or essentially significant. Ultimately, in fact, they are witnesses to God's perfection and goodness. This goodness is available to anyone willing to participate in it, both through actions which correctly nurture and sustain life, and even more so, through intellectual efforts to reunite with the divine overflow. Since the overflow is constant, this conjunction is possible for man; the overflow sustains all the forms of the world, including that of man, in their permanent order.

On the other hand, the constancy of God's emanation, the continuous unfolding of ideas or forms from his eternal being, allows Maimonides to say with conviction that God knows all things, both now and in the future. God knows all of them through the formal principles with which he endows them; and he knows the future, as the present, since for God there is neither past, future or present, just an eternal now.[39] The permanent forms of nature which come from God are of course related always to particular matters in particular times and places; but these are the accidents of existence, concomitants of matter, itself known only in the broadest of terms. Time and place, as matter, are known to God in principle only, the principle being that forms require them. For God it is sufficient to know that although his forms will always have a "certain" concrete and temporal identification, a particular material manifestation of one sort or another, nevertheless they will necessarily exhibit, whatever the occasion, certain eternal properties. It is these forms which interest God, or as we should say, these which are intelligible to him.

Maimonides points a number of times to the difficulty of believing that the one divine being should know the species of many things, and yet he finds it necessary to assert this.[40] It would have been relatively easy for him to go further and posit the existence of individual souls prior to their birth, i.e., of particular forms eternally known to God. He is reluctant to do this, however, for reasons which he makes rather clear: such knowledge would deprive man of his freedom and God of his justice, two principles which Maimonides recognized as tenets of Judaism. This kind of omniscience would remove the contingent nature of the possible, that aspect of a material body which for Maimonides contains its various potential states of being, all equally real. In interpreting the actions of all bodies as strictly determined, this kind of omniscience would in effect deprive matter of its freedom, and with that its relative distance and residual autonomy from God. Matter would then be harnessed as completely to God's will as is form now, and this in turn would make God necessarily and totally responsible for all the evil and deficiencies with which matter is now associated. Divine foreknowledge of this kind threaten's God's goodness, on the one hand, and the reality of the world as our senses and intuitions reveal it, on the other.

It is, accordingly, perfectly consistent of Maimonides to say that God's knowledge "that a certain possible thing (*mumkin mā*, literally, "something possible") will come into existence, does not in any way make that possible thing quit the nature of the possible",[41] and other statements to that effect. They may be read in a way that seems to indicate God knows specifically which possibilities will be realized, and Maimonides does this deliberately. Yet he is actually making the point that God knows the possibilities – all the possibilities, including that which is realized – inherent in everything.

6. DIVINE PROVIDENCE AS THE EXPERIENCING OF ULTIMATE FELICITY

That God allows man (and other animals) to be free is part, then, of the necessary order of being which he has created. It is a sign of his providential regard for man, and of his loving-kindness, judgment and righteousness.[42] These attributes, which man is to emulate, are most in evidence, for Maimonides, in the providence which God bestowed on the patriarchs and Moses, traditional symbols in the Jewish tradition of righteous and deserving men. Yet the providence which Maimonides describes in regard to these figures, as in general, is not the traditional kind. It is a providence which disdains not only material possessions and wealth, but even physical life itself.[43] That the patriarchs and Moses succeeded materially and politically is a consequence of the providence they enjoyed, an unusual byproduct, usually unnecessary if not counterproductive to providence. For the true providence and perfection of man, as Maimonides states in a number of places and particularly towards the end of the *Guide*, is an intellectual (or intellectual *cum* psychic) experience which elevates the individual into the presence of the divine, offering him a rapturous participation in the eternal beauty and love of God.[44] This ultimate perfection has nothing to do with physical or social concerns; indeed Maimonides depicts man as able to free himself from such concerns entirely in the felicitous moment of conjunction.[45] In so doing, Maimonides says, man frees himself from evil, indeed, from evil "of any kind". Here the perfect man has achieved full control of his environment, for he has transcended it entirely. In connecting his intellect fully with that of the divine intellect, man assumes a new identity, at least for as long as he can maintain the conjunction. He is now like the angels: pure form, part of eternal being, savoring a taste of eternity. The natural evils which can befall all men cannot touch him, for he is no longer mortal – at least, not essentially so.[46] Should anything happen to his physical body while in this state, it will not affect his mind, his true being, which is with God.

The evil of this world, connected to its matter, thus has, in Maimonides' opinion, a lesser degree of substantial being than does the good, which is connected to form. If the latter may be compared to essential being, then the former comes close to being a kind of accidental being, albeit a necessary accident. Maimonides is too much the Aristotelian to relegate matter to the status of non-being and illusion, or to break the hylomorphic knot of Aristotelian physics. However, in his understanding of providence and the many issues connected with it (though not, interestingly, as regards the issue of freedom and determinism), Maimonides comes perilously close to abandoning his Aristotelian anchors and setting off on a Neoplatonic sea.

NOTES

[1] Following the translation of S. Pines, *Moses Maimonides: The Guide of the Perplexed*,

University of Chicago Press, Chicago and London 1963, III: 20 (43a), p. 483. All translations except when otherwise noted will be taken by permission from this work. References in parentheses are to the page numbers of the Judaeo-Arabic edition, *Dalâlah al-Ḥa'irîn*, S. Munk (ed.), Jerusalem 1929.

2 See *Guide* I:57, 63 (82a), p. 154; II:1 (8a), p. 247. Avicenna's remarks on the Necessary Existent have been assembled, in translation, by G. Hourani, 'Ibn Sina on Necessary and Possible Existence', *The Philosophical Forum* IV. 1 (1972), pp. 74–86. Cf. too A. Altmann, 'Essence and Existence in Maimonides', in *Studies in Religious Philosophy and Mysticism*, Cornell University Press, Ithaca 1969, pp. 108–120.

3 Maimonides' Necessary Existent acts more "unilaterally" than does Avicenna's, since the Muslim philosopher explicitly recognizes the necessity to posit eternal supernal beings in addition to the Necessary Existent, accomplished through the mechanism of emanation. Cf. Ibn Sina, *Al-Shifâ': Al-Ilâhiyyât*, I. Madkhour, *et al.* (ed.), Cultural Dept. of the Arab League, Cairo 1960, 9:4, p. 402 ff., and see L. Gardet's discussion of these matters, *La Pensée Religieuse d'Avicenne*, J. Vrin, Paris 1951, pp. 48 ff. For Maimonides' view, cf. *Guide* I:69 (89a), p. 167 f.; I:70 (91b), p. 172; II:12 (26a), p. 279 f.

4 See *Guide* III:20 (42a), p. 482, and see too I:60 (76a), p. 144f.

5 See *Metaphysics* VIII 1 ff,; XII 2 ff.

6 Maimonides' view of matter, and its relation to evil and privation has much in common with Avicenna's thought, the ideational roots of both being traceable to Plotinus. Cf. Avicenna's *Al-Shifâ'*; *al-Ilâhiyyāt, op. cit.*, 4:2, pp. 171 ff., found in the Latin edition of S. Van Riet, *Avicenna Latinus: Liber De Philosophia Prima sive Scientia Divina I–IV*, Louvain-Leiden 1977, pp. 200 ff.; and *al-Ilâhiyyât* 9:6, pp. 416 ff., now translated by S. Inati, *An Examination of Ibn Sîna's Solution for the Problem of Evil* (Ph. D. Dissertation, University of Buffalo, 1979), pp. 222–238. For Plotinus, cf. *Enneads* I 8.3, 7, transl. by S. McKenna, Pantheon Books, New York, 1953; II 4.4 ff., 16; II 5, and see J. Rist, 'Plotinus on Matter and Evil', *Phronesis* 6 (1981), pp. 154–166.

7 *Guide*, Introduction to the Second Part (4b), p. 239.

8 *Ibid.*, III:8 (12a), p. 431; 10 (17a), p. 440.

9 Such sources could be found in the diverse philosophical and theosophical literature present in the Egypt of Maimonides' day, particularly that of a Neoplatonic and gnostic bent. Possible sources are among those discussed by S. Pines in his introduction to the *Guide*, particularly pp. lix f., 1xxv f., xciii ff., and cxxiii. See too Pines' article, 'Shi'ite Terms and Conceptions in Judah Halevi's *Kuzari*', *Jerusalem Studies in Arabic and Islam* II (1980), p. 196, 240 ff.

10 See my article, 'Maimonides on Possibility', *Mystics, Philosophers, and Politicians: Essays in Jewish Intellectual History in Honor of Alexander Altmann*, J. Reinharz *et al.* (ed.), University of North Carolina Press, Durham 1982, p. 77 f.

11 Cf. particularly *Guide* I:69, p. 166 f.

12 *Ibid.*, III:10 (17a), p. 440.

13 *Ibid.*, I:2 (13b), p. 24; III:19 (40b), p. 479 *et passim*.

14 *Ibid.*, I:69 (89a), p. 167.

15 *Ibid.*, III:16 (30b), p. 463.

16 See the Fifth and Sixth *Enneads* of Plotinus, a good portion of which was available to Maimonides in various Arabic abridgements, particularly that known as 'The Theology of Aristotle'. The Arabic Plotinian material has been translated by G. Lewis and may be

found set against its probable Greek source in the edition of P. Henry and H. R. Schwyzer, *Plotini Opera* II, Desclée de Brower, Paris, 1959, and cf. particularly pp. 263 ff., 291ff., 353, 393 f., 439ff., 474 ff.

17 Cf. *Guide* II:17, pp. 294 ff., and see above, note 10.

18 Cf. *Guide* I:58 (71a), p. 136; 69 (90a), p. 169; II:12 (25b), p. 279; III:9 (15b), p. 437.

19 *Ibid.*, III:18, p. 474 f.

20 *Ibid.*, III:19, 20.

21 *Ibid.*, II: Introduction, Premisses 21–25, pp. 238, 239; III:10 (17a), p. 440.

22 *Ibid.*, III:16 (31a), p. 463; 20 (42b), p. 482; 21, p. 484 f.

23 *Ibid.*, III:17 (35b, 36a), p. 471.

24 *Ibid.*, 37a, p. 473.

25 *Ibid.*, III:18 (39a), p. 476.

26 Cf. A. Altmann, *op. cit.*, p. 111 f.

27 *Guide* III:10 (40b), p. 479.

28 "Watching over" is the expression Pines uses to convey that which in the Arabic is given more neutrally, usually as a Providence which is simply "over" ('alâ) its objects. Cf. *Guide* III: 51 (127a), p. 624 f.

29 *Ibid.*, III:17, pp. 464–466, and see too III:51, p. 625.

30 *Ibid.*, III:17 (36a), p. 472. An alternative translation of the last part of this passage could well be, ". . . but to divine will, in accordance with that which is deserved in His judgments, the canon of which our intellects cannot comprehend".

31 Cf. *Guide* I:51 ff., 58.

32 See *Guide* II:22 (40b), p. 319; 25 (55b), p. 329; III:13 (24a), p. 452 f., p. 456, end of chapter.

33 See *Guide* III:17 (36a), p. 471; 20 (41b), p. 480 f.; 21 (44a), p. 485. These and other passages are presented in detail in my paper on 'Neoplatonic Currents in Maimonides' Philosophy', part of the Proceedings of a symposium on 'Maimonides in Egypt', held at Tel Aviv University, 1982, edited by J. Kraemer.

34 *Guide* III:20 (41b), p 481.

35 *Ibid.*, III:25 (56b), p. 506.

36 *Ibid.*, I:73, Tenth Premise, p. 206; see too my article, "Maimonides on Possibility', *op cit.*, p. 68 ff.

37 Cf. *Guide*, III:25 (56a), p. 505, and compare Maimonides' earlier remark (55b) in this chapter, "the entire purpose (of creation – A. I.) consists in bringing into existence the way you see it everything whose existence is possible; for His wisdom did not require in any way that it should be otherwise; for this is impossible, since matters take their course in accordance with what His wisdom requires".

38 Ibid., III:12 (19b), p. 444.

39 *Ibid.*, III:20 (41b), p. 480 f., and see too I:57 (69b), p. 133.

40 *Ibid.*, III:30 (41b), p. 481, and cf. I:60 (76a), p. 144.

41 *Ibid.*, III:20 (42b), p. 482.

42 *Ibid.*, III:53, 54, pp. 630 ff. These traits are, of course, not necessarily related to free choice, which some scholars believe Maimonides could not accept, on their interpretation of his view of strict causality. Cf. S. Pines, 'Studies in Abul-Barakāt al-Baghdādī's Poetics and Metaphysics', *Studies in Philosophy, Scripta Hierosolymitana* 6 (1960), pp. 195–198; A. Altmann, 'The Religion of the Thinkers: Free will and Predestination in

Saadia, Bahya, and Maimonides', *Religion in a Religious Age*, S. D. Goitein (ed.), Association for Jewish Studies, Cambridge Mass. 1974, pp. 41–45.

[43] Cf. *Guide* III:24 (53a), p. 500 f., and 51 (126b), p. 624.

[44] *Ibid.*, III:51 (125a), p. 621.

[45] *Ibid.*, 128a, p. 625.

[46] *Ibid.*, 129a, p. 628.

CHAPTER 10

DIVINE OMNISCIENCE, CONTINGENCY AND PROPHECY IN GERSONIDES

Tamar Rudavsky

1. INTRODUCTION

Gersonides, writing in fourteenth-century France, offers an interesting and provocative analysis of the problems inherent in prophecy and its relation to divine omniscience.[1] This cluster of problems can be summarized as follows. Many scriptural prophecies concern contingent events. Hence the existence of prophetic statements about future contingent events suggests that these events can be foreknown. If they are foreknown how can they be contingent? And yet if they are not foreknown, how can the events in question be prophesied? In short, what sense can we make of prophetic statements which purport to relate information about future contingent events?[2]

Emphasizing the connection between prophecy and divine omniscience, Gersonides presents a theory of prophetic statements that is meant to complement his position with respect to divine foreknowledge. Gersonides is an indeterminist in the sense that according to his theory, God does not have foreknowledge of future contingent events. Yet, God is able to transmit to the prophet true statements about such events. In an attempt to reconcile the apparent conflict between God's lack of knowledge and the transmission of prophecies about future contingents, Gersonides construes these statements as disguised universal conditionals.

In this paper I wish to examine Gersonides' theory of prophecy in light of his theologically indeterminist position. The fullest exposition of this position is found in his work *Milḥamot Adonai*.[3] This work is a compilation of a number of issues having to do with immortality, prophecy, God's foreknowledge and providence. Treatise III deals specifically with the problems associated with God's omniscience, while treatises II and IV discuss the ramifications of the problem with respect to prophecy and providence.

My contention is that ultimately Gersonides' analysis is seriously flawed. More specifically, I shall claim that his solution fails to account for prophecies regarding future contingent events. However, his solution fails for interesting reasons and raises important questions about the logical status of prophetic

T. Rudavsky (ed.), Divine Omniscience and Omnipotence in Medieval Philosophy, 161–181.

statements. My analysis will proceed as follows. In parts 2 and 3 the main points of Gersonides' indeterminist solution to the problem of divine omniscience will be discussed briefly. In parts 4 and 5 this solution will be applied to the problem of prophecy, with particular emphasis upon the conditional nature of prophetic statements. And in part 6 this analysis will be considered critically.

2. CONTINGENCY, CHANCE AND HUMAN CHOICE

Gersonides is one of a minority of Jewish philosophers to uphold a theory of astrological determinism, according to which states of affairs are determined by the heavenly bodies. Within this deterministic scheme, however, Gersonides recognizes a domain of contingency which comprises chance events, possibilities and human choices. Each of these represents an area which is not subject to the absolute necessity of the stars. We shall see that Gersonides does not ever explain how contingency can ultimately coexist with astral determinism; he is committed, however, to introducing contingency into a largely deterministic scheme.

Gersonides defines contingent events as those which are "devoid of determining causes",[4] as opposed to events which come to pass as a result of their own determinate causes. He goes on to say, however, that contingent events are nevertheless structured:

> We assert that it is already clear that contingent events (*b'mikreh v'htzdamen*) have a certain structure, inasmuch as there are already many individuals to whom many good things happen, all of them occurring by chance and it is these who are called fortunate . . . This necessarily entails that contingent events (*b'mikreh*) will have a mode of determination and structure. As to what that mode is, I wish I knew![5]

Gersonides' point in this passage is that inasmuch as the determination of contingent events occurs on the astral level, they are ordered. However, their causes are incomplete. For as we shall see below, Gersonides will argue that the causes of human volition are not subject to the stars.

Contingent events are reflected most clearly in the domain of human agency. Following Aristotle, Gersonides argues that absolute necessity contravenes human deliberation and will:

> There is little doubt that according to this assumption [determinism] all voluntary affairs connected to will (*ratẓon*) are necessary and there would be no free choice. And this is the lie from which Aristotle fled in the *De Interpretatione*. In truth there will be no choice since when what is chosen is necessary, the choice is not called a choice, since 'choice' refers to (a situation in which) two parts of a contradictory are possible.[6]

A similar point is made in Gersonides' supercommentary on *De Interpretatione*. Arguing that arguments in favor of fatalism destroy the nature of the possible, Gersonides goes on to state that from fatalism many absurdities result, including the pointlessness of human deliberation. But, he claims, "we need no teacher from whom to learn that deliberation itself and the will is a cause from which many things arise". And furthermore, "this sort of possibility appears in the agent . . . becasue the agent has free choice and (the power of) decision, so that he can actualize each opposite".[7]

Gersonides goes on to distinguish two levels of human agency. From the astrological perspective, that is, viewed from the perspective of the heavenly bodies, human events are determinate and structured, and by implication necessary. The active intellect, which is the efficient cause of the order found in all events, knows this order by knowing the determinate essences of things. Viewed from the perspective of their possibility, however, these events are indeterminate and contingent, and by implication not necessary.[8]

It should be noted that these distinctions are ontologically rooted in events and are not epistemically motivated. Gersonides is not suggesting that humans, acting out of ignorance of the determining causes of their behavior, believe (falsely) that their actions are based on human volition. Rather, he is claiming that human beings, by virtue of their intellect and will, can overcome the determining influences of their astrological signs. Granted, according to Gersonides, this ability is rare, and real instances of volition are uncommon: "despite the fact that deliberate human choice made out of rational consideration has the power to disrupt this determination, such an eventuality will occur very rarely."[9] Intellect and will, however, can move humans to do something other than what has been determined from the standpoint of the heavenly bodies. For God has placed within humans purposive reason "so as to move (humans) toward something other than that which has been determined from the aspect of the heavenly bodies, insofar as this is possible to make straight that which chance has convoluted."[10]

Clearly, astrological determinism and human freedom are contradictory states of affairs; however, aside from baldly stating that in some cases human freedom is preserved in the face of determinism, Gersonides does not explain how these two contradictory states can be reconciled. Little hint is given in *Milḥamot* to suggest that Gersonides is even aware of the tension between the two. Instead of philosophical explanation, the most we have is Gersonides' repeated phrase "Would that I knew!" in the face of perplexity. Gersonides might be suggesting that human volition is independent of material causation and hence is not subject to the influence of the stars.[11] This point is not developed in detail, however.

Gersonides claims as well that some states of affairs occur by chance (*b'mikreh*). Speaking in treatise IV of *Milḥamot* of the origin of evil, Gersonides distinguishes between evils which arise from human choice and those which arise from chance:

> Of those misfortunes which arise externally and not from temperament and choice, such as the overturning of a country, earthquakes or lightning, and the like, it is clear that they cause evil only by chance (*b'mikreh*). For example, a fire may accidentally fall upon a man and kill him, or the earth may envelop its inhabitants who found themselves there by chance.[12]

In these examples chance events occur without regard to human intention. However, not all chance events occur independently of human agency. In *Milḥamot* II Gersonides gives the following characterization of a chance event. In describing chance events which are viewed under the mode of indetermination, Gersonides says that characterizations of such events are

> analogous to the claim that were we to dig a hole so deep as to make a pit, we would find a treasure – for this is infrequent, i.e., if we were to find a treasure each time that we dug so deeply as to form a pit.[13]

This example is amplified further in the following passage:

> A thing is said to be by chance because it is the result of an incomplete cause – e.g., when someone digs a ditch and finds a treasure. For this is classified as that which comes about by chance because he does not dig a ditch of that sort for the sake of that end, and it is not necessary that a man who digs a ditch should find a treasure. And so we say that finding a treasure while he is digging that ditch is by chance.[14]

3. DIVINE OMNISCIENCE AND POSSIBILITY

Gersonides has not demonstrated how contingency and determinism can coexist. However, it is clear that in order to safeguard human freedom, Gersonides wants to postulate the existence of contingency within the sphere of astrological determinism. He must therefore address the issue of whether God's knowledge is limited to necessary states of affairs, or extends to the domain of contingency as well. Gersonides addresses the issue by dealing with two subsidiary problems: whether God's knowledge extends to particulars, and whether his knowledge extends to future contingents, which form a subset of particulars.

In answer to the first problem, Gersonides argues that in a certain sense

God does know particulars. In an apparent attempt to mediate between the view of Aristotle, who claimed that God does not know particulars, and that of Maimonides, who claimed that he does, Gersonides adopts what he considers to be a compromise position, claiming that

> there remains no alternative but that in one way He knows them (particulars) and in another respect He does not. The respect in which God knows contingents is the respect in which they are ordered – that is, God knows their essences.[15]

This passage is problematic, to say the least. Gersonides' point is that God does not know particulars insofar as they are not ordered, that is, in their particularity. By 'ordered', Gersonides seems to be suggesting that God knows the essences or universal natures of particulars without knowing them *qua* particulars:

> God . . . knows those things which exist in this world insofar as they possess a universal nature, i.e., essences. (But he does) not (know) them insofar as they are particulars, i.e., possibles. In this way there is no plurality in his essence.[16]

Gersonides' point is that all God knows is that certain states of affairs are parrticular, but he does not know in what their particularity consists. That is, God's knowledge extends only to the domain of genera and species. God knows individual persons, for example, only through knowing the species man. In effect Gersonides is claiming that God knows only universals. In an attempt not to deny explicitly God's knowledge of particulars, Gersonides suggests that God's knowledge pertains only indirectly to particulars. What God knows are the constitutive properties of concepts; these properties are then applied to the domain of particulars. I shall return to a critique of this position shortly.

Gersonides' second point concerns God's knowledge of future contingents. In contradistinction to Maimonides who claimed that God's knowledge does not render the objects of his knowledge necessary, Gersonides maintains that divine knowledge precludes contingency. However, we have seen that Gersonides does assert the existence of contingency in the universe. In order to retain the domain of contingency, Gersonides adopts the one option open to him, namely that God does not have prior knowledge of future contingents. According to Gersonides, God knows that certain states of affairs may or may not be actualized. But insofar as they are contingent states, he does not know which of the two alternatives will in fact be actualized. For according to Gersonides, if God did know future contingents prior to their actualization, there could be no contingency in the world.[17]

Gersonides claims that God's inability to foreknow future contingents is not a defect in his knowledge:

His lack of knowledge . . . of which of two possible alternatives *qua* possible will be actualized is not a deficiency in him. This is because perfect knowledge consists in knowing the nature of the thing. Were the thing to be conceived to be other than it is, this would be error and not knowledge.[18]

In this fashion, Gersonides concludes, the problem of divine omniscience is resolved in favor of indeterminism. With respect to future contingents, God knows their ordered nature or essence, and he knows that they are contingent, but he does not know which of two alternatives will become actualized. According to Gersonides, then, future contingency has been retained with no apparent sacrifice of omniscience.

It should be noted, however, that despite his contention, Gersonides has not, in fact, successfully retained both contingency and omniscience. In a recent paper I have argued that ultimately Gersonides' analysis of divine omniscience is inadequate to account for knowledge of particulars. Without entering into the details of my critique here, let me simply suggest that Gersonides' analysis does not allow for God's knowledge of particulars. In other words, it can be argued that on Gersonides' account, the one thing that God does not know is the existential status of a particular, and unless God knows that, he does not know whether a universal species is vacuous.[19] However, inasmuch as Gersonides is the only Jewish philosopher to uphold indeterminism as a solution to the problem of divine omniscience, it will be instrumental to examine the implications of his view with respect to theological issues.

4. INDETERMINISM AND PROPHECY

The logical implications of indeterminism affect prophecy in the following way. The indeterminist claims in effect that propositions about the future have no present truth-value. Gersonides, for example, states in his supercommentary on Aristotle's *De Interpretatione* that positing a truth value for future contingents leads to absurdity:

If every affirmation and negation were to divide the true from the false, it would have to be the case that as regards future things one of the propositions would be determinately true before the occurrence of the actual thing. And so the greatest absurdity would follow.[20]

According to Gersonides, therefore, future contingent statements "do not divide the true from the false completely when the statements are uttered".[21] That is, such statements are neither true nor false.

But if statements about future contingent events have no determinate truth value when uttered, how do we account for the truth value of prophetic statements? Prophecies comprise a subclass of future contingent statements. If they are not true when uttered, they would seem to have no assertive value for their recipients. And yet if they are true when uttered, they suggest that the events prophesied are inevitable. Gersonides does not wish to eliminate the force of prophetic statements altogether. He is therefore hard-pressed to explain not only how prophecies are possible in a system which denies the possibility of foreknowledge of future contingents, but also how to construe their logical form. In order to extricate himself from possible theological embarrassment, Gersonides must demonstrate that his theory of divine omniscience does not preclude the possibility of prophetic statements.

Gersonides' theory of prophecy, developed in treatise II of *Milḥamot* is anticipated in his earlier supercommentary on Averroes' *Epitome of Parva Naturalia.*[22] In the *Epitome* Averroes had argued that since foreknowledge cannot occur with respect to contingent events, prophecy was limited to causally determinate events.[23] Gersonides, however, rejects Averroes' solution. He distinguishes between the prophet and philosopher as follows: the role of the prophet is to foretell human happiness or beatitude, whereas that of the philosopher is to foretell natural occurrences. Unlike the philosopher, who is a good natural scientist projecting causally determinate events, the prophet is concerned with future contingent events. Hence the difference between them lies in the content of their knowledge and not merely in their respective methods.

This distinction is maintained in *Milḥamot* as well. Prophecy, Gersonides claims, is not the result of chance or guesswork but rather represents knowledge on the part of the prophet. Inasmuch as prophecy concerns contingent human choices, Gersonides asks, how "(is it) possible that this communication received by us be concerned with future contingent events?"[24] According to Gersonides, two dilemmas arise from admitting that the prophet can foretell future contingents. The first is that if prophetic statements about future contingent events are true when uttered, then since the option prophesied has already been determined and structured, contingency will be abolished. That is, according to Gersonides, "all those matters are then 'by necessity' and deliberate choice (in human affairs) would be nullified . . . all things would exist by necessity and voluntary choice would be futile".[25] And since, according to Gersonides, contingency occurs only with respect to events involving human beings, once contingency is removed from the human sphere, it follows that all things would exist by necessity.[26]

Related to the first, the second problem concerns the epistemological level of prophetic events. According to Gersonides, in order for something to be known, it must be ordered: that is, it must contain prior causes which determine its essence. Genuine knowledge is construed by Gersonides as the comprehension of a thing through the causes of its existence. But by definition, contingent events are devoid of determining causes; hence future contingents cannot be foreknown. As Gersonides states the problem, "if we assume that the contingent event which befalls human beings would be completely devoid of determination and structure, we would then be unable to give a causal account of the communication to which they are conformed prior to their actual occurrence".[27] If these events cannot be foreknown, however, how can statements about future contingent events be transmitted to a prophet?

Gersonides' theory must therefore answer two general questions:

(1.1) inasmuch as God does not know particulars *qua* particular, how is the prophet able to receive prophecies about particular human beings and events?

(1.2) if contingent events cannot be foreknown, how can the prophet prophesy about future contingent events?

5. THE TRANSMISSION OF PROPHETIC STATEMENTS

(1.1) is stated by Gersonides as follows: "How is it possible for the (active) intellect to inform us about the particular thing *qua* particular, as is the case with this communication, since it can transmit only knowledge of what resembles itself, viz the general structure?"[28] This question not only reflects the problem raised by Gersonides' own theory of divine omniscience, but echoes similar concerns of Averroes. In his *Epitome*, Averroes developed a theory of prophecy according to which the active intellect is devoid of matter and can comprehend only universal natures. Averroes claimed that "it is not in (its) nature to comprehend the particular".[29] So how does the prophet receive from the active intellect the knowledge of particular events? According to Averroes, the active intellect transmits messages of a general nature which are picked up by the imaginative faculty of the prophet as pertaining to particulars:

(The active intellect) endows the imaginative soul with the universal nature that the individual that comes into being possesses, that is to say, a comprehension of its causes, and the imaginative soul will receive it as a particular by virtue of the fact that it is in matter.[30]

In other words, according to Averroes, the active intellect disperses general knowledge and the imaginative faculty receives this knowledge in the mode of particularity. Averroes does not explain how the information is transformed from the general to the particular mode; nor does he explain why the active intellect disperses messages at all.

In his commentary on Averroes' *Epitome*, Gersonides did not take issue with this analysis. However, in *Milḥamot* he disagrees with Averroes, arguing that knowledge of a particular is transmitted by the active intellect not *qua* particular but rather "insofar as this individual is a contemporary of other human beings who were born in his zone; when the heavenly bodies were in the same position that they had when he was born".[31] That is, all those born under the same astrological sign have a similar general nature. The prophet then receives this general information and, with the aid of the hylic intellect which supplies him with "all those accidents through which he is individuated inasmuch as he is a particular human being of that description",[32] the prophet's imaginative faculty then interprets the prophecy. The crucial difference between Averroes and Gersonides is that in Gersonides' analysis the prophet does not receive particular knowledge. At the point of origin the emanation in question is general: the prophet, with the aid of the hylic intellect, then enters into the process and instantiates the message. Particularity is effected by what Gersonides calls the "available phantasms which constitute the instrumentalities for the production of that particularity".[33] In other words, the prophet, who receives an emanation of a general nature, specifies it in terms of his own phantasms.

The transmission of prophetic messages according to Gersonides can be summarized as follows: The active intellect, which functions as the intermediary between God and the sublunar world, grasps certain essences of particulars. These essences, which for the most part are determined by the heavenly bodies, are transmitted in the form of universal statements to the prophet who then instantiates them with particular details. These messages are not transmitted to any particular prophet, since the active intellect has no awareness of individual prophets. Rather, according to Gersonides, prophets are persons predisposed to receive prophetic messages; because they have been thinking about those very messages being transmitted by the active intellect, their intellects are attuned to receive the general messages broadcast at random by the active intellect.[34]

Gersonides has explained the particularity of prophetic statements by emphasizing that particular details are supplied not by the active intellect but by the prophet. But do these details include contingent events as well? In order to account for the contingency of prophetic statements, Gersonides develops a theory of the conditional nature of prophetic statements. He maintains that although not all prophetic statements found in scripture are in conditional form, nevertheless they all contain implicit antecedent premises which must be satisfied prior to the actualization of the prophecy in question. These conditionals account for both the particularity and the contingency of the events prophesied.

Samuelson has offered an illuminating analysis of what Gersonides might have had in mind with an example of Jeremiah who prophesies to Zedekiah that if Zedekiah leads Judah to battle with Babylon, Judah will be destroyed.[35] The active intellect has transmitted a general conditional statement based on the nature of warfare in general. This statement is broadcast at large, as it were, and can be received by any person predisposed for such messages. According to Samuelson, the general conditional resulting from this knowledge is of the form

(2.1) The nature of war is such that if any nation F of which x is true should go to war with any nation G of which y is true, then F will be destroyed by G.

Recognizing that Judah is that nation of which x is true, and that Babylon is the nation of which y is true, Jeremiah is able to instantiate Judah for F and Babylon for G. His prophetic statement is of the form

(2.2) If Judah goes to war with Babylon, Judah will be destroyed by Babylon.

According to this analysis, both particularity and contingency have been preserved within the context of prophetic statements. God knows certain universal conditions which are transmitted via the active intellect to the prophet. These are then instantiated by the prophet. In the case of (2.2), whether or not Babylon destroys Judah depends upon whether or not Judah engages in war with Babylon, and that is dependent upon Zedekiah's free choice.

A number of other examples are adduced by Gersonides as well. Thus in Genesis 41: 4–48, Joseph prophesied to Pharaoh that a famine would occur and last seven years. Although the prophecy is presented in the form of an indicative statement, Gersonides suggests that the suppressed conditional implied by this prophecy is of the form

(2.3) If Pharaoh does/does not do such and such, a famine will occur for seven years.[36]

Since it is up to Pharaoh either to realize the antecedent or not, the occurrence of the famine ultimately depends upon the satisfaction or nonsatisfaction of the antecedent.

6. THE LOGICAL STATUS OF PROPHETIC STATEMENTS

We have thus seen that according to Gersonides, the prophet instantiates prophetic statements which have been transmitted to him in the form of universal conditionals. But what is the logical force of these conditionals? That is, what connection obtains between the antecedent and consequent of these conditional statements? Gersonides addresses this issue while attempting to formulate criteria for distinguishing between true and false prophecy. We have already seen that human volition is able to contravene astrological determinism in that humans are able to avoid the negative destiny ordained by the heavens. Hence prophetic statements pertaining to future contingent situations are such that on the one hand the prophesied event will occur, and yet on the other hand the event prophesied can fail to occur.

One implication of this situation is that true prophets cannot be distinguished from false prophets on the basis of the fulfillment or non-fulfillment of their prophecies alone. Assume, for example, that both a true and a false prophet predict a contingent event c. In both cases, c can either occur or fail to occur, but for different reasons. In the former case, human volition can bring about $-c$ even though the (true) prophet prophesied the occurrence of c, and in the latter case, since the false prophecy may or may not have any correlation with reality *per se*, either c or $-c$ can occur. Inasmuch as it is not possible to ascertain prior to the occurrence of c whether the prophet is a valid predictor, we are tempted to question the ultimate utility of prophetic statements.

In light of this difficulty Gersonides suggests that the best criterion for recognizing a true prophet is the valid prediction of a miracle, since this is something that only a true prophet could foreknow. Unfortunately, however, miracles are in short supply, and most prophets cannot be tested against this criterion. In the absence of miracles, Gersonides then suggests that the second best criterion consists in *all* of a person's prophecies *always* coming true. That is, the greater the success-frequency, the greater the chance of a person's being a true prophet. [37] The main problem with this criterion is its applicability only over a long time period.

Gersonides does offer one final criterion, based on a distinction between malevolent and benevolent prophecies. Genuine malevolent prophecies may or may not occur: they serve as warnings of what negative events might ensue if certain conditions are not met. Genuine benevolent prophecies, on the other hand, must come to pass, since according to Gersonides, both human intellect and will work for the good.[38] Based on this distinction, Gersonides formulates the following criterion for testing a prophet: if a benevolent event is prophesied, and it does not occur, the person is not a prophet, for only malevolent prophecies can be contravened by human volition.[39] This criterion suggests the following set of conditions.

(3.1) If a malevolent prophecy comes true, the person may or may not be a prophet.

(3.2) If a benevolent prophecy comes true, the person may or may not be a prophet.

(3.3) If a malevolent prophecy fails to come true, the person may or may not be a prophet.

(3.4) If a benevolent prophecy fails to come true, the person is a false prophet.

(3.1), (3.2) and (3.3), taken separately, represent necessary but not sufficient conditions for recognizing a true prophet. Only (3.4) states a condition sufficient for recognizing a false prophet. But if the prophet must always be tested against the non-occurrence of benevolent prophecies, does this not suggest that all genuinely prophesied benevolent events are necessary?

In order to safeguard the contingency of benevolent events, Gersonides introduces a distinction between conditional and unconditional benevolent prophecies. Unconditional prophecies are those "whose improbability of non-occurrence we have asserted in the good which is ordained by the heavenly bodies".[40] Conditional prophecies, on the other hand, reflect the good ordained by particular providence: a benevolent conditional prophecy "contains within its predicted occurrence a condition and for this reason it does not occur by necessity".[41] In order for such a prophecy to be fulfilled, certain prior antecedent conditions must be satisfied.

The following prophecies are used by Gersonides to illustrate benevolent conditionals. In Leviticus 26:14, the statement is made that the Israelites will acquire many benefits by walking in the ways of scripture.[42] This prediction can be understood in terms of the following conditional:

(4.1) If you walk in the ways of scripture, I (God) will benefit you in many ways.

Although not explicitly stated in the text,this prediction implies that these benefits will not be acquired by the Israelites if they abandon the ways of God. That is (4.1) suggests

(4.2) If you do not walk in the ways of scripture, these benefits will be removed.

(4.2) suggests that the benevolent conditional prophecy is rescinded in just those cases in which the prior antecedent conditions are not met; it therefore supports the contention that not all benevolent prophecies are necessary.

Gersonides' next example is slightly more complex. In Exodus 32:10 God says to Moses

(5.1) "Therefore let me alone, that my wrath may wax hot against them, and that I may consume them; and I will make of thee a great nation".

Interpreting this prediction in light of Gersonides' previous analysis, we see that the consequent expresses a benevolent situation which seems to depend upon a malevolent antecedent. For (5.1) can be construed in several ways. It might be read as an implied threat of the form

(5.2) If you let me alone so that my wrath waxes hot, then I will consume them and make of thee a great nation.[43]

But (5.2) is unacceptable for Gersonides, for it suggests that God does not want Moses to commit an intrinsically good action. That is, (5.2) seems to imply both

(5.3) If you let me alone (i.e., do not pray for the good of another), I will ultimately reward you (make of you a great nation).

(5.4) If you do not let me alone (i.e., do pray for the good of another), I will punish you (not make of you a great nation).

Both (5.3) and (5.4), according to Gersonides, are unworthy of a benevolent God who supports the good behavior of his subjects. In order to avoid the untoward implications of (5.3) and (5.4), Gersonides interprets (5.1) as follows:

the intent of this verse is to be taken as saying that even if Moses does not employ himself to save them, he should not be fearful that God will destroy Israel, because from Moses there will issue forth a great people. And thus, there was not removed from him the benevolent promise despite his praying for Israel.[44]

That is, Gersonides interprets (5.1) as

(5.5) Even if you do not let me alone, I will consume them and make of thee a great nation.

In other words, Moses will be benefited, and the benevolent conditional will be actualized regardless of his (Moses') actions.

But doesn't (5.5) suggest that in some cases, at least, the antecedent and consequent are independent of one another? For (5.5) seems to suggest that God will reward Israel regardless of what Moses does. If that is so, what is the logical value of the conditional? In order to resolve this problem, Charles Touati has suggested that Gersonides' example marks a simple temporal succession from antecedent to consequent.[45] But Touati's solution is inadequate, for by Gersonides' own account, prophecies aim to accomplish more than simply to state a temporal succession of events. Gersonides has wanted to claim that some benevolent conditionals at least reflect a non-accidental connection between antecedent and consequent, but he has not explained how they differ from unconditional benevolent conditionals. What Gersonides has suggested is that not all benevolent conditionals state a connection between antecedent and consequent. But without any connection at all, the conditional in question no longer satisfies its original function, namely to capture the connection between antecedent and consequent.

In Gersonides' final example this problem becomes even more apparent. In I Samuel 10:3–5, Samuel prophesies to Saul that Saul will encounter three men on the road; these men will give him two loaves of bread which he will then accept.[46] Recasting this prophecy as a conditional, we have

(6.1) If Saul walks down the road, he will encounter three men who will offer him two loaves of bread which he will accept.

But what is the force of (6.1)? The whole point of such conditionals is that they do not follow laws, but rather reflect the free choices of a free agent. But if an event is truly contingent in Gersonides' sense, how can it function as the referent of a consequent in a universal conditional? It is difficult to see what information could be contained in the antecedent. For if the antecedent represents a necessary state of affairs, then the conditional is either trivial or false. And if it represents a contingent state of affairs, the conditional has not transmitted any information of a relevant nature.

In short, Gersonides' analysis has not accounted for the conditional nature of prophetic statements.

7. PROPHETIC STATEMENTS RECAST AS SUBJECTIVE CONDITIONALS

One way to salvage Gersonides' account of prophetic statements may be to recast his conditional prophecies as subjunctive conditionals. Two kinds of examples have been expressed in the conditional prophecies used by Gersonides: those in which the consequent expresses God's antecedent will, and those in which the consequent expresses human choices. Most of the conditional prophecies discussed by Gersonides fall into the former class; that is, they express prophecies in which God's future consequent will follows upon certain antecedent human choices. In these cases, the prophet receives the information of what God will do in certain situations; (4.1) is an example of such a prophecy. Unfortunately, how God becomes aware of these situations, and how he knows the relevant antecedent human choices in question, are problems Gersonides does not address.

In addition, however, Gersonides has provided examples of prophecies in which the consequent describes human and not divine actions. According to Gersonides, because these prophecies reflect laws of nature, they can be stated as universally quantified material conditionals; (2.2) is an example of such a prophecy. As described above, these universal conditionals are transmitted by the active intellect to the prophet. As such, these prophecies are subject to a problem which plagues all law-like statements, namely how to distinguish between accidental connections between antecedent and consequent. As recent philosophers have pointed out, such conditionals seem to presuppose a metaphysically suspicious sort of non-logical necessity.[47]

In order to account for this necessity, philosophers such as John Pollock have suggested that these law-like statements be construed not as material implications but rather as subjunctive conditionals of the form

(7.1) "If it were true that p, then it would be true that q".

Pollock has distinguished at least two such subjunctive conditionals: necessitarian conditionals and even-if conditionals. In Pollock's analysis, necessitarian conditionals employ the term 'since'. In these conditionals the truth of the antecedent guarantees the truth of the consequent; that is, the antecedent necessitates the consequent (although such relations are not always causal). Pollock's example of a necessitation conditional is

(7.2) "If a match were struck, it would light since it was struck".

These conditionals are of the general form

(7.3) "If it were true that *p*, then it would be true that *q since* it was true that *p*".

Even-if conditionals differ from necessitation conditionals in that they do not posit a connection between antecedent and consequent. That is, the consequent is already true regardless of the truth of the antecedent. In Pollock's example,

(7.4) "*Even if* the witch doctor were to do a rain dance, it would not rain",

whether it rains is in no way dependent upon the actions of the witch doctor.[48]

Applying Pollock's distinction to Gersonides' conditional prophecies, the following points can be made. (2.2) is a necessitation conditional which expresses certain necessary (but not necessarily causal) connections between the antecedent and consequent. This conditional can be transmitted by a natural scientist or philosopher simply by ascertaining the underlying law-like situations which bring about the prophesied event. (5.1) ostensibly describes God's reactions to Moses. When (5.1) is recast in terms of (5.5), it expresses an even-if conditional, in that there is no connection between antecedent and consequent. What (5.5) says is that God will act in certain ways regardless of the actions of Moses. According to Moses, God is able to transmit this prophetic statement, for surely he knows how he will act in any situation in which the antecedent events do not in any way determine his actions.

Can we apply Pollock's analysis to (6.1) as well? (6.1) differs from both (2.2) and (5.5) in that it is concerned neither with necessary connections nor with God's actions, but with a truly contingent state of affairs. It is reminiscent of another contingent prophecy found in I Samuel 23:12. In this passage, David is surrounded by Saul and asks God whether Saul will capture him and his men; David is told by God that if he remains in Keilah, his men will be surrounded and captured by Saul. This prophecy became a paradigm in later scholastic sources and can be rendered as follows:

(8.1) If David remains in Keilah, he and his men will be surrounded and captured by Saul.[49]

Although (8.1) is not mentioned explicitly in Gersonides' writings, it has not passed unnoticed by Jewish philosophers. Ibn Daud, for example, in commenting upon I Samuel 23:12, presents the following characterization of that passage:

An example (of contingent statements) would be that of David, peace be unto him, "Your servant has indeed heard that Saul seeks to come to Keilah to destroy the city. Will they deliver me up?" He repeats the question and says, "Will the citizens of Keilah deliver up me and my men to Saul?" And the Lord said, "They will deliver you up". The meaning of "they will deliver up" in the response of God is that it is possible (*efshar*) that they will do this . . . . If their capture were not contingent to God, may he be exalted, David would not have escaped from it.[50]

It is clear from his interpretation of the phrase "it is possible that they will do it" that according to Ibn Daud, whether or not David will be captured remains an indeterminate event.

Ibn Daud's interpretation of (8.1) is similar to what Pollock has termed 'might-be' conditionals. These conditionals are of the form

(8.2) If p were true, q might be true.

Alternatively, (8.2) can be read as

(8.3) It is not the case that q would be false if p were true.[51]

Applying this reading of might-be subjunctives to our two prophetic examples, we can recast (8.1) as

(8.4) If David were to remain in Keilah, he and his men might be surrounded and captured by Saul.

Similarly, we can recast (6.1) in terms of

(8.5) If Saul were to walk down the road, he might encounter three men who would offer him two loaves of bread which he might accept.

(8.4) and (8.5) both retain the contingency of the consequent, a characteristic important for both Ibn Daud and Gersonides. However, (8.4) and (8.5) tell us no more than the fact that given a situation p, q may or may not occur. The occurence of the antecedent in no way sheds light upon the future occurence of the consequent. In these cases, the prophet knows no more than the casual observer. But if that is so, then Gersonides has not explained the important status of the prophet, for the prophet has not transmitted information of a relevant nature about the future. Once again, the logical status of prophetic statements remains deficient.

7. CONCLUSION

In summary, the following points have emerged. Like his philosophical contemporaries, Gersonides attempted to explain how God can know future contingents without this knowledge affecting the contingency of the objects known. In contradistinction to his peers, however, who attempted to retain both foreknowledge and contingency, Gersonides argued that foreknowledge coupled with infallibility precluded the contingency of the objects of God's knowledge. Unable to adopt a compatibilist solution, Gersonides therefore upheld a form of incompatibilism in an attempt to preserve the existence of contingency in the world. Claiming that only a very small class of actions are truly contingent, Gersonides argued that God's knowledge pertains to those actions only insofar as they are ordered and not *qua* contingent. That is, according to Gersonides, God knows particulars only as universals and not in their particularity. This knowledge is then transmitted to the prophet in the form of universal conditional statements. The prophet instantiates these statements and is able to apply them to future contingent events.

I have tried to argue that this analysis does not adequately account for the conditional nature of prophecies. My criticisms have been two-fold. My first critique, developed more fully elsewhere, has been that on Gersonides' account, God does not truly have knowledge of particulars. Because God cannot know human affairs, Gersonides' discussion of prophecy must account for how the prophet has access to knowledge unavailable to God.

My second critique was aimed at the underlying logic of conditional statements. We have seen that Gersonides employs two kinds of conditional prophecies: those in which the consequent expresses God's will, and those in which the consequent expresses human choices. Read in light of Gersonides' indeterminism, the first class of statements raises problems of its own, for it is not clear how God knows the particular events to which he is reacting. The second class of prophetic events seems to resemble law-like statements and is subject to the ambiguity inherent in all such statements. It would appear on this reading that the prophet is a good natural scientist. Two problems arise with this interpretation, however. The first is that it does not accord with Gersonides' own conception of prophecy. For as we have seen, Gersonides wishes to distinguish the natural scientist from the prophet. Secondly, this analysis does not account for those prophecies, like (6.1), in which the consequent expresses a truly contingent event. Such events cannot be foretold by either a scientist or a prophet.

The question arises whether, according to Gersonides, prophetic events can be foreknown by anybody? It would appear not. The most anybody can know (God included) is that certain events might occur in light of certain antecedent conditions. But surely we don't need a prophet to tell us that!

Ultimately Gersonides' system leaves little room for a theory of prophecy in which future contingent events are determinately prophesied. The most a prophet can tell us is *that* certain events are contingent; he cannot tell us *which* contingent possibility will be actualized. This inability on the part of the prophet to transmit the content of future contingent events is a severe limitation on the content of prophetic knowledge. Ultimately Gersonides has not successfully reconciled contingency and prophecy in his philosophical theology.

NOTES

[1] The philosophical questions raised by Gersonides (Levi ben Gerson, 1288–1344), are contained in his major work *Sefer Milḥamot Adonai (Wars of the Lord)*, Leipzig 1866. A recent English translation of book three of this work can be found in *Gersonides: The Wars of the Lord; Treatise Three: On God's Knowledge*, translated by N. Samuelson, University of Toronto Press, Toronto 1977. In this paper references will be made both to the Hebrew edition (*Milḥamot*), as well as to Samuelson's translation (*Wars*). In both cases reference will be made to treatise, chapter, and page number. For an extensive bibliography of scholarly works on Levi ben Gerson, cf. M. Kellner, 'R. Levi ben Gerson: A Bibliographical Essay', *Studies in Bibliography and Booklore* **12** (1979), pp. 13–23. References to specific articles will be made in the present essay when relevant; however, the following works should be noted for their treatment of Gersonides' theory of divine omniscience: N. Samuelson, 'Gersonides' Account of God's Knowledge of Particulars', *Journal of the History of Philosophy* **10** (1972), pp. 399–416; T. M. Rudavsky, 'Divine Omniscience and Future Contingents in Gersonides', *Journal of the History of Philosophy* **21** (1983), pp. 513–536; C. Sirat, *Les théories des visions surnaturelles dans la pensée juive du' moyen-âge*, E. J. Brill, Leiden 1969; C. Toutai, *La Pensée Philosophique et Théologique de Gersonides*, Les Editions de Minuit, Paris 1973; Gersonides, *Les Guerres du Seigneur*, Livres III, et IV, translated by C. Touati, Mouton, Paris 1969.

[2] Gersonides presents a modified version of the problem of prophecy in *Milḥamot* II.1.

[3] Allusions to the problem of divine omniscience occur in other contexts as well, most notably when Gersonides is discussing issues connected with prophecy and divine providence. For these discussions, cf. Gersonides' commentary on Job, in A. L. Lassen, *The Commentary of Levi ben Gershon on the Book of Job*, Bloch Publishing Co., New York 1946; and in A. Altmann, 'Gersonides' Commentary on Averroes' Epitome of *Parva Naturalia* II.3', *PAAJR* 66–67 (1979–1980), pp. 1–31 (henceforth referred to as *Altmann*).

[4] *Milḥamot* II.2, p. 94.

[5] *Milḥamot* II.2, p. 95.

6 Altmann, *op. cit.*, pp. 17–18.
7 Gersonides, *Supercommentary on Averroes' Commentary on Aristotle's De Interpretatione*, Chapter 9 (found in the 1562 edition of *Aristotelis omnia quas extant opera . . . Averrois Cordubensis in ea opera omnes qui ad haec usque tempora pervenere commentarii . . . cum Levi Gersonidis in libros logicos annotationibus . . . a Iacob Mantino in Latinum conversi* . . . Venetiis, apud Iunctas, MDLXII (vol. I, ff. 82^{vb}K – 83^{rb}F). An English translation of this portion of Averroes' commentary and Gersonides' supercommentary has been prepared by Professor N. Kretzmann. The quoted passage is found in 83rb D 46ff.
8 This distinction will allow Gersonides to maintain that the objects of prophetic knowledge are determined and structured from one standpoint, and undetermined and unstructured from another standpoint: "The aspect from which they are determined and structured is that of the heavenly bodies . . . the aspect in which they are contingents, i.e., indeterminate and unstructured, is that of our intellect and will". Cf. *Milḥamot* II.2, pp. 96ff.
9 *Milḥamot* II.2, p. 97.
10 *Milḥamot* II.2, p. 96.
11 A similar point is made by Thomas Aquinas. In his *Summa Contra Gentiles* Bk III, ch. 41, Thomas maintains that only man's body is subject to the stars; his intellect is subject to intellectual substances, while man's will is subject to God's influence. Cf. also *Ibid.* Bk. III ch. 84; D. W. Silverman, *The Problem of Prophecy in Gersonides*, PhD dissertation, Columbia University, 1975, p. 103.
12 *Milḥamot* IV.3, pp. 160–161.
13 *Milḥamot* II.2, p. 96.
14 Cf. Gersonides' *Supercommentary on Averroes' Commentary on Aristotle's De Interpretatione*, Chapter 9, 83 ^{ra}A 11. 5–10.
15 *Wars* III.4, p. 232.
16 *Wars* III.1, pp. 99–100.
17 *Wars* III.4, pp. 233–234.
18 *Wars* III.4, pp. 235–236. Abraham Ibn Daud, in his work *Sefer-ha-Emunah ha-Ramah (The Exalted Faith)*, edited by S. Weil, Frankfurt 1852, (II, vi, 2, p. 96), develops a similar view according to which God's lack of knowledge of future contingents is not a deficiency in him. For a discussion of the historical importance of Ibn Daud's position, cf. S. Pines, 'Scholasticism after Thomas Aquinas and the Teachings of Hasdai Crescas and his Predecessors', *Proceedings of the Israel Academy of Sciences and Humanities*, vol. 1, no. 10, (1967), pp. 90ff.
19 For an elaboration of this critique, see my paper 'Divine Omniscience and Future Contingents in Gersonides', *op. cit*.
20 Gersonides' *Supercommentary on Averroes' Commentary on Aristotle's De Interpretatione*, Chapter 9, 82^{vb}K 34–36.
21 *Ibid.* 82^{vb}L 15.
22 Averroes' position is stated in his *Qissur Sefer Ha-Ḥush We-Ha-Muḥash Le-Ibn Rushd*, H. Blumberg (ed.), Medieval Academy of America, Cambridge 1954. Blumberg's English translation of this work – henceforth called *Blumberg* – is found in his *Averroes' Epitome of Parva Naturalia*, Cambridge, Medieval Academy of America, 1961.
23 Gersonides summarized and rejected Averroes' position in *Milḥamot* II.2, p. 95.
24 *Milḥamot* II.2, p. 95.

[25] *Milḥamot* II.2, p. 94.
[26] *Ibid.*
[27] *Milḥamot* II.2, pp. 94–95.
[28] *Milḥamot* II.6, p. 104.
[29] *Blumberg, op. cit.*, p. 43.
[30] *Blumberg, op. cit.*, p. 46.
[31] *Milḥamot* II.6, p. 106.
[32] *Ibid.*
[33] *Milḥamot* II.6, pp. 105–106.
[34] In elucidating the process of prophecy, Samuelson employs the analogy of a radio station which transmits messages from a great distance. These messages can be received by anybody who satisfies the requisite criteria, ie has a strong enough receiver, has no local competing stations, etc. See Samuelson, *op. cit.* pp. 285–6.
[35] Samuelson discusses Gersonides' example in his introductory comments to *Wars*. Cf. *Wars*, pp. 50, 238.
[36] *Wars* III.5, p. 286.
[37] *Milḥamot* VI, Pt. 2, ch. 13, p. 460.
[38] *Milḥamot* VI, Pt. 2, ch. 13, p. 461.
[39] *Ibid.* "It is likely that a prophet may be tested completely if (the predicted event) does not occur. Then it can be truly seen that he is not a prophet; for if the good was ordained from the aspect of the heavenly bodies, it is unlikely that it would not occur. However, if the (predicted) good does occur, this is not sufficient to show that he is a prophet, for it is possible that it be conveyed in divination or in a dream".
[40] *Milḥamot* VI, Pt. 2, ch. 13, p. 461.
[41] *Ibid.*
[42] *Ibid.*
[43] Gersonides discusses this example in *Milḥamot* VI, Pt. 2, ch. 13, pp. 461–462. An analogous discussion occurs in his *Commentary on the Pentateuch*, Exodus 32:10, Venice 1547.
[44] *Ibid.*
[45] Touati, *op. cit.*, p. 463.
[46] *Milḥamot* II.2, p. 94.
[47] For recent discussions of the status of conditionals, cf. the collection of articles edited by E. Sosa, *Causation and Conditionals*, Oxford University Press, Oxford 1975.
[48] Cf. J. Pollock, *Subjunctive Reasoning*, D. Reidel, Dordrecht 1976, pp. 25–44 for these and other examples.
[49] For recent discussion of this prophecy in late scholastic sources, cf. R. M. Adams, 'Middle Knowledge and the Problem of Evil', *American Philosophical Quarterly* 14 (1977), pp. 109–117. In this paper, Adams is concerned primarily with the formulations of Suarez and Molina.
[50] Cf. Abraham Ibn Daud, *Sefer-ha-Emunah ha-Ramah*, ed. by S. Weil, Frankfurt A. M., 1852, II vi, 2 p. 97. In this work, Ibn Daud develops a view of divine omniscience similar to that of Gersonides; although he does not fully expand the implications of his theory with respect to prophecy, it is interesting to note this one implication. Pines has suggested a possible influence between Ibn Daud and Gersonides; cf S. Pines, *op. cit.*, pp. 91ff.
[51] Pollock, *op. cit.*, pp. 31ff.

PART FOUR

CHRISTIAN PERSPECTIVES

CHAPTER 11

DIVINE OMNIPOTENCE IN THE EARLY *SENTENCES*

Ivan Boh

1. INTRODUCTION

The influx of the New Logic[1] during the twelfth century made itself felt not only in the purely logical and linguistic discussions of the period but in the theological controversies as well. This is especially true for the theological schools of Paris in the mid-century. However, the new art was not always welcome. Thus, Walter of Saint-Victor, a conservative theologian, speaks very harshly about "the four Labyrinths of France", i.e., about Peter Abelard, Peter of Poitiers, Peter Lombard, and Gilbert of Porrée, criticizing them for having introduced dialectic into theology.[2] He considered this logicizing of the theological domain not only fruitless but pernicious.

In spite of this strong logical influence upon the early *Sentence* literature, most modern philosophical discussions of topics such as divine omnipotence, omniscience, benevolence, and the like, have avoided detailed analyses of the positions taken on these matters in the twelfth century by the Christian "rationalist" theologians, drawing instead upon more philosophical medieval authors, such as St. Thomas, Duns Scotus, William Ockham and others.[3] Presumably this is so because the discussions found in the *Sentence* literature are comparatively short and the argumentation sketchy. Yet even a casual reading through the crucial passages exhibits the genuine philosophical concern and logical acumen of authors who knew well their Bible and the *auctoritates* and who, at the same time, were impressed with dialectic as a powerful tool of rational discussion and rational persuasion. The *Sentence* literature was crystallized into a special genre; the positions of these scholastic philosophers on problems such as divine omnipotence, omniscience, and benevolence must usually be sought in the commentaries on one of these early "Prototypes", i.e., on the *Sentences* of Peter Lombard. Although the strictly philosophical content of the early *Sentences* is at times deficient, the subsequent historical importance of the genre should not be underestimated.[4]

In this chapter I have selected for discussion one concept, that of omnipotence. However, I do not pretend to discuss it in a purely analytic, a-historical

T. Rudavsky (ed.), Divine Omniscience and Omnipotence in Medieval Philosophy, 185–211.

manner, but rather precisely as it was presented in the formative years of scholastic method and scholastic philosophy and theology. Out of the many sources which I could have taken as representative of this period, I chose the following three: (1) The *Sententiae* of Roland Bandinelli[5] who served as pope from 1159–1181 under the name of Alexander III and who wrote his work independently of Peter Lombard before 1150; (2) The *Sententiae* of Peter Lombard himself[6] (written between 1145 and 1152) on which at least 1406 commentaries were written[7] – the last important one seems to have been that by William Estius (d. 1613);[8] and (3) The *Sententiarum libri quinque* of Peter of Poitiers,[9] which was written only two decades after the *Sentences* of Lombard, with some dependence on this latter writer, and which seems to have helped enormously in the success of Lombard's work.[10] My purpose is to clarify what was and what might have been meant by the term omnipotence in this early *Sententiae* literature.

2. DIVINE OMNIPOTENCE IN ROLAND BANDINELLI'S *SENTENTIAE*

Roland's *Sententiae* was one of three important eleventh century theology treatises inspired by the thought of Abelard, in particular by his *Introduction to Theology*[11] which contained several heretical theses which led to Abelard's condemnation at the council of Sens in 1141. Roland's views were seen to be sufficiently orthodox, so that his intellectual heritage and affinity with Abelard's thought did not interfere with his rise in the hierarchy. He was an independent intellectual who held in respect the authorities of Augustine, Ambrose, Jerome, and Gregory and did not hesitate to refer to Abelard by name, but ultimately decided on questions at hand by appeal to rational evidence.[12]

Roland is, of course, aware that Abelard came into personal difficulties because he did not conform to the position of the Church; there is no doubt as to whom 'some' (*quidam*) refers in the following statement: "Some who are deviating from the position of the Church say that God could not make more things than he makes or is going to make, nor omit any of those things which he makes or is going to make";[13] Roland will argue that this view is philosophically false on the ground that the argument leading to it has been misconstrued and its premises wrongly understood. When Roland discusses God's disposing of things he refers to Abelard by name: "Master Peter said that he could not have arranged more things than he did arrange", and again argues for the contrary position. He will likewise reject the following views:

that God could not have predestined more individuals than he has predestined,[14] that not more things could have pleased God than in fact pleased him[15], and that God could not have permitted more things than he had permitted.[16] Again, with respect to God's knowledge, Roland rejects Abelard's claim that God could not know more things than he knows insofar as one understands here by 'knowledge' the kind of knowledge which the tradition will refer to as knowledge by vision[17]; and it is in this last sense that Roland understands knowledge.

In view of such radical disagreements with Abelard it is perhaps difficult to see what Denifle, Gietl, Luscombe, and others have in mind when they link Roland with Abelard.[18] Whatever the contents of Roland's teachings in Bologna[19] prior to the establishment of the University, it seems that his written work is "Abelardian" more in spirit and in form than in content: an investigative attitude of mind, the *quaestio* method, a careful examination of the recognized authorities, employment of logical tools for analysis, and some Abelardian terminology (*omnisapientia, omnibenignitas, omnibonitas*).

In his *Sententiae*, Roland does not start with a definition or description of 'omnipotence', nor is he calling for a definition; in fact the title of the pertinent section is 'On divine power'. In the course of the discussion, the words 'omnipotence' and 'omnipotent' are used as terms which already have a certain more or less recognizable meaning which Roland should like to make explicit by attempting to answer certain questions about God. He states three relevant questions:

(1a) Whether God could make more things than he makes;[20]

(1b) Whether whatever he can do from eternity, he can do now, and whatever he can do now he always, from eternity, was able to do and always should be able to do;[21] and

(1c) Whether whatever he will be able to do in the future he can do now, and whatever he can do now, he will be able to do in the future and always should be able to do.[22]

He first produces an argument for a negative reply to (1a), i.e., for the conclusion that God cannot make more things than he makes. In the background of Roland's discussion is of course the position of Abelard who accepted this conclusion as true and well founded.[23] A phrase used by Solomon, viz., 'the lord God omnipotent who can do whatever he will', provides a clue for Roland's argument: If it is in his power to do something only when he wills it, it follows that if he does not will something, then it is not in his power to do it. Thus, only what he wills can he do. If then he can only do what he wills to do, it follows that he does (*operatur*) only the things he wills. So he could not make more things than he does make.[24]

Reflecting on the formal features of this argument, we might first observe that the most suggestive interpretation of the claim made about God, viz., 'God can do everything', or 'there is nothing that God could not do', is not even mentioned, presumably on the ground that the claim is too strong. Using 'M*' for 'can' or 'is able', 'β' for 'bring about' – directly or indirectly; 'Ox' for 'x is omnipotent'; 'Wxy' for 'x wills y', we can formalize Roland's argument[25] as follows. First of all,

O_1: 'Oa' means '$(\forall x)\mathrm{M}^*\beta ax$'

and

O_1': 'Oa' means '$\sim(\exists x)\sim \mathrm{M}^*\beta ax)$'

are both unacceptable. The argument continues through several valid steps, but turns out to be invalid as it stands in its final step or else the whole argument begs the question. Roland (or his opponent) starts with

O_2: '$(\forall x)(\mathrm{M}^*\beta ax \supset \mathrm{W}ax)$'

and infers from it

O_3: $(\forall x)(\sim \mathrm{W}ax \supset \sim \mathrm{M}^*\beta ax)$

and then infers – by reiteration – O_2 (only what he wills is God able to do).

The second part of the argument tacitly assumes at least two intuitively acceptable logical principles, one from alethic modal logic, the other from the general theory of consequences, principles which Roland could have gotten from Abelard's *Dialectica* or from Garlandus' *Dialectica.*[26] Given O_2 $(\forall x)(\mathrm{M}^*\beta ax \supset \mathrm{W}ax)$ ('God can do x only if he wills x') he infers 'God does (*operatur*) x only if he wills x', i.e.,

O_4: $(\forall x)(\beta ax \supset \mathrm{W}ax)$.

This indeed follows if we assume the modal principle *ad esse ad posse*

$$p \supset \Diamond p$$

(and further link in a suitable way the ideas represented by '$\Diamond$' and 'M*') and also adopt the principle corresponding to the standard rule of consequence: *Quidquid antecedit ad antecedens antecedit ad consequens*, i.e.,

$$(q \supset r) \supset [(p \supset q) \supset (p \supset r)],$$

with substitutions $\beta ax/p$, $\mathrm{M}^*\beta ax/q$, $\mathrm{W}ax/r$.

The final conclusion of this chain argument, viz., 'God could not make more things than he does make', however, is ambiguous. One can understand it in a weak sense as

O_5: $\sim\Diamond(\exists x)(\beta ax \;\&\; \sim Wax)$

or in a strong sense as

O_5': $\sim\Diamond(\exists x)[(\beta ax \;\&\; \sim Wax) \vee (Wax \;\&\; \sim\beta ax)]$.

While O_5 does follow from O_4, O_5' does not follow either from O_4 or from O_2. It would only follow from another interpretation of 'God can only do what he wills to do', that is, from reading it not as O_2 $(\forall x)(M^*\beta ax \supset Wax)$, but as

O_2': $(\forall x)(M^*\beta ax \equiv Wax)$.

But on that reading one would beg the question.

St. Augustine, too, had stressed that "God is not said to be omnipotent because he can do all things, but because whatever he wills, he can do; that is, whatever he wills he does."[27] Thus, he explicitly rejects O_1 and endorses

O_6: 'Oa' means '$(\forall x)(Wax \supset M^*\beta ax)$

or, perhaps

O_6': 'Oa' means '$(\forall x)(Wax \equiv M^*\beta ax)$'

The additional interpretive remark, 'that is, whatever he wills he does', suggests that what Augustine has in mind is

O_7: 'Oa' means '$(\forall x)(Wax \supset \beta ax)$'

or, perhaps

O_7': 'Oa' means $(\forall x)(Wax \equiv \beta ax)$.

As Roland understands selected passages from Augustine, the latter also claims that for God to will and to be able are the same, and he draws the conclusion: 'therefore whatever he wills he is able to do and whatever he is able to do he wills'.[28] From which Roland concludes further that if whatever God is able to do he does do, then he cannot make more things than he does. The moves here are as follows:

O_8: $(\forall x)(Wax \equiv M^*\beta ax)$
O_9: $(\forall x)[(Wax \supset M^*\beta ax) \;\&\; (M^*\beta ax \supset Wax)]$
O_{10}: $(\forall x)[(M^*\beta ax \supset \beta ax) \supset \sim\Diamond(\exists x)(M^*\beta ax \;\&\; \sim\beta ax)]$.

The antecedent of O_{10} is readily available from O_9 and O_7 by hypothetical syllogism and so Roland gets from Augustine's statements by perfectly logical moves the Abelardian conclusion.[29]

$$O_{11}: \quad \sim\Diamond(\exists x)(M^*\beta ax \,\&\, \sim\beta ax).$$

There are moral considerations as well which seem to put on God certain constraints. Thus, Roland (ostensibly relying on certain statements of Augustine) points out the following dilemma: "If God wanted to create all things best, but could not do it, he would be impotent; but if he could, and would not, he would be jealous". It appears that God must create the best of the possible worlds categorically and not merely hypothetically: that is, he must create rather than not create and whatever he creates must be such that he could not have created it better or in a better way. This axiological or moral constraint is perhaps the most potent underlying motive for Abelard's acceptance of the Principle of Plenitude of Being.[30] And whoever accepts the Principle of Plenitude must also reject unactualized possibilities. Those philosophers who held that God creates all and only those things which he in fact creates are simply complying with this all-encompassing ontological Principle.[31]

It is agreed in all quarters that there are some things which God cannot do; that, e.g., he cannot sin or run, and the like. Roland argues that the reason for this is either because it does not befit him to do it or because it is unjust for him to do it. For example, the reason why God cannot move a stone from its place is because it does not befit him to do so. That this is not a befitting thing for God is made clear by the fact that he omits doing it (*quod exinde apparet, quod dimittit*). "For if it were fitting for him to move it, he would move it."[32] Going through various examples, Roland infers the general epistemological principle: We know what is not befitting for God to do by observing what he does not and never will do. For if it were befitting for him to do it, he would (at some time or other) do it. Applying Roland's principle is problematic, however, for it is difficult to observe what God will never do. Do we recognize such cases because we already have all the natural kinds in question exemplified? Or do we think that God will not do something because it would be self-contradictory for him to do it?

There is one interesting case mentioned which seems to open a way for total voluntarism with respect to creation. Let there be two things, A and B. These are either two good things, or two bad things or else two things one of which is good and the other bad. Let us assume that A and B are both bad; then God could not make either. If one of them be good and the other bad, then the one which God does not do is the bad one and the one that he does make is good. For God cannot make the bad one and omit the good one. Let both A and B be good; then they are two equal or two unequal goods. If they are unequal, then the one which God omits doing is a lesser good, and the one he does make is the greater good. "But if the two goods be said to be equal, then there will be no reason why God makes what he does make, and why he omits making what he in fact omits and so whatever God makes, he makes indiscriminately and without any reason".[33]

However, Roland soon closes the door to voluntarism. His view seems to be the following: If God did not as a matter of fact make either of the two equal goods, this was so because from eternity he did not will to make them, and he could not possibly do what he does not want to do; nor can he make anything against his (eternal and unchangeable) disposition.[34] Roland again comes to the comprehensive formula for whose parts he had argued above (on behalf of the "Abelardians"), i.e.,

$$O_{12}: \quad (\forall x)(M^*\beta ax \equiv Wax \equiv \beta ax).$$

It should be noted here that although Roland has conflated possibility with actuality, he does not deal with other modal concepts, i.e., necessity and impossibility, as such. In particular, he has not tried to argue that whatever is is necessary, and that whatever is not is impossible. His only concern has been to rule out unactualized possibles. We have hinted, of course, at the axiological principle at work which leads to a theological determinism to the effect that God must choose the best; Roland could have stopped short, however, and accepted a simple theological voluntarism on behalf of the "Abelardians", thus saving them from having to accept the fallacious view expressed by '$p \supset \Box p$' which seems to be entailed by their position.

Next we find Roland arguing on the basis of authority and reason for the contrary view, i.e., that God could make and do more things than he in fact makes and does. Christ "could have asked" (*potuit rogare*) his Father to send him more than twelve legions of angels, but he did not ask (*non rogavit*); i.e., "thus he could have done something which he did not do" (*potuit ergo quod non fecit*). Again, "God can give rain today, but he is not going to give it. So God can do something which he is not going to do".[35] Thus, it is a biblico-historical truth that

$$O_{13}: \quad (\exists x)(M^*\beta ax \,\&\, {\sim}\beta ax)$$

from which it follows that in general

$$O_{14}: \quad \Diamond(\exists x)(M^*\beta ax \,\&\, {\sim}\beta ax).$$

The realm of unactualized possibles is thus open.

The main line of defense of the unactualized *possibilia* view is an indirect kind of argument to the effect that if that view were correct, it would follow that whatever God or anyone else does, he does of necessity. "If God could not do what he does not do nor omit doing what he does do, then it follows that whatever he does, he does so with necessity, and whatever he omits doing he omits by necessity". Which, presumably, is unacceptable. Again, "If God could not make more things than he does make, it follows that a limit is imposed upon the divine power in virtue of which divine power is placed under a determinate number".[36]

Is it possible to deal effectively with the counter-examples which were brought against the view that God cannot make more things than he in fact makes, e.g., that Christ "could have asked for, etc".? One could argue that what is meant is that "he could have asked for, etc., *if he wanted to*", but since he did not want to ask, he could not have asked. A still more interesting example is the following: "He who raised Lazarus in body could have raised Judas in mind" could be understood as claiming that God could have raised Judas if he wanted to; or as claiming that it was not inconsistent with the nature of Judas that he be raised. Roland offers here an interesting simile: "It is not repugnant to the nature of a stone lying on the bottom of the sea, that it could be seen by me, and yet I cannot see that stone: just so it was not repugnant to the nature of Judas that he could be saved by God, and yet God was not able to save him".[37] Unlike the previous example and the first of the two explications of "could have raised Judas" which reverted to the equivalence "$M^*\beta ax \equiv Wax$', the second explication seems to open the possibility of a different understanding of possibility, either as a primitive notion or a notion definable in terms of the idea of logical consistency.

Abelard, however, had given a more subtle analysis of the case:

> When we say that he [Judas] could be saved by God, we reduce possibility to the facility of human nature, as if, that is, we said that it is not repugnant to the nature of man to be saved, since he is in himself changeable in such a way as to allow both his salvation as well as his damnation and he presents himself to God as treatable either in this or in that manner. But when we say that God could save him who is definitely not to be saved, we reduce the possibility to the divine nature itself, namely, that it is not repugnant to the nature of man that God save him: and this is completely false. Certainly it is repugnant to the divine nature to make Judas something, i.e., saved which is offending his dignity and the doing of which is not befitting to his nature at all.[38]

Roland's own position, of course, is that God can do more things than he does and at this point sees it as his task to take care of authorities and arguments for the opposing position.[39] Starting with Solomon's phrase, "the lord God, who has it in his power, if he wills", Roland sees it as compatible with his own position. For although it does suggest that God can do something if he wills it, it does not say that he cannot if he does not will it. This can be seen in a simile: It is in the power of a rich person to give money to some poor person, if he wills; but it does not follow from this that it is not in his power if he does not will. However, "God is not said to be omnipotent because he can do all things;" that is, says Roland, "he is not said to be omnipotent under the aspect of being able to do all things, but because whatever he wants, he is able to do *ex se*."[40] Roland is thus clearly dissociating himself from O_1 $(\forall x)(M^*\beta ax)$ in favor of O_6 $(\forall x)(Wax \supset M^*\beta ax)$. He is also rejecting O_6' $(\forall x)(Wax \equiv M^*\beta ax)$, interpreting the claim "it is the same for God to will and to be able" (*idem est Deo velle et posse*) as a metaphysical claim that God is a simple agent and that the distinctions between his attributes are not real (God-willing and God-able are materially one and the same), rather than as a statement of necessary and sufficient conditions for what God can do.

Concerning the axiologically grounded contention that "if he God could create all things the best (*valde bona*) and did not want to do so, he would be jealous", Roland says that this would be true if he omitted creating the best out of malice. But he does not speculate on the question what could it mean for God to create things out of malice. He also brings up the question of two goods A (–to create) and B (–not to create). He agrees that they are both goods and also that they are equal goods. "But yet it is not without reason that he [God] does one and omits the other".[41] There is a "secret justice" according to which he does one and omits the other (just as there is a "secret justice" as to why one individual is reprobated through justice and another elected by grace).

The logical distinction equivalent to the composite and divided sense of the later tradition is employed several times by Roland, although he uses different terminology. When it is said that God "could not make any of those things which he omitted," this is true *coniunctim*, but *divisim* it is false; that is, it cannot be that he could make what he omits, when he omits it; or that he could omit making what he makes when he makes it. But yet, what he omits he could make at some time, and what he does make he could omit.

3. THE NOTION OF OMNIPOTENCE AMPLIFIED IN THE *SENTENCES* OF PETER LOMBARD

I now pass over to the *Sentences*[42] of Peter Lombard, a work which Luscombe describes as "the least read of the world's great books".[43] It was perhaps for reasons of unquestionable theological orthodoxy amidst the lively controversies over topics of great interest as well as its appealing style that Peter Lombard's *Sentences* rather than some other similar work captured the attention of heads and teachers of various schools and eventually of the whole theological educational system. The tradition of revisions of Lombard's original version of the *Sentences* was established very early; just as early the tradition of commentaries on these *Sentences* arose. The actual history of the commentary practice by individuals such as Peter of Poitiers which eventually came to be institutionalized in the newly established universities is still awaiting the efforts of cultural historians. The development of these ideas raised by Peter Lombard have, of course, been studied at least from the perspective of structural history insofar as most great medieval philosophers and theologians left a commentary on the *Sentences* under that name or under whatever other names the commentaries happened to become known (e.g., Duns Scotus' *Reportatio Parisiensis* and *Opus Oxoniense*).[44]

Lombard's discussion of omnipotence is found in Book I, distinctions 42, 43, and 44 of his *Sentences*. While Lombard, like Roland, is obviously arguing against the (heretical) Abelardian position, his examination of the topic is at the same time more comprehensive and also more cursory. He, too, wants to render God's omnipotence (and omniscience) consistent with God's other attributes, i.e., his immutability and his goodness. At the same time he wants to preserve both unactualized possibles and even more so divine and human freedom.

He begins with the question: Is God omnipotent because he can do all things, or only because he can do all things that he wills to do (*an quia omnia possit, an tantum, quia ea possit quae vult*).[45] Immediately he turns to authorities who support at least the claim that God can do all things. First he quotes St. Augustine: "God can do anything, but does not do anything except what is consistent with truth and justice".[46]

There follow counter-examples from Abelard and Hugh of St. Victor, although Lombard does not refer to Abelard by name. It is noted that we can do things which God cannot, so how can he be said to be omnipotent? For example, he cannot walk, talk, and the like, activities which are alien to God's incorporeal and simple nature. But although God cannot do these kinds of things, not having a body, he does have power to bring them about in others; that is, he can and does create individual bodily substances who can and do perform these activities directly.

Other actions which God can in no way do are sinning, lying, etc.

Lombard, however, characterizes these kinds of actions as infirmities; they are not to be credited to a power, but to lack of power or to impotence. No being could be omnipotent if it exhibits any such infirmity. As St. Augustine had said, "It is God's great power not to be able to lie".[47] A similar way of explaining is used when cases such as God's inability to die, to fall, to be conquered, etc., are mentioned. The upshot of such considerations is that if we are to say that "God can do all things", we should be prepared to specify what cannot count as a significant part of the claim and to explain why it cannot.

The omnipotence of God will show itself in two ways: (i) God can do all things he wills to do (*omnia facit quae vult*) and (ii) There is no passive potency in God (*nihil omnino patitur*).[48] The acts in question, of course, must be such that God's performing them would not be inconsistent with his dignity. Several important authorities (e.g., Augustine and John Chrysostome) are adduced to support the following view of divine omnipotence: "God is said to be omnipotent only because he can do all things that he wills to do, not because he can do all things".[49]

However, things are not so simple and Lombard shows himself to be a first rate analytic thinker. He "meditates" in the paragraphs that follow along these lines: Suppose we hear Augustine saying: "He is not said to be omnipotent, because he could do all things". Perhaps Augustine said this because he is using "all things" so broadly that under that term bad things were subsumed also, that is, things which God neither wills nor could do. He is therefore not necessarily denying that God could do all things which it would be fitting for him to do. Again, when Augustine says: "For no other reason is he truly said to be omnipotent except for the reason that if he wills to do anything whatever, he can do it", he is not denying that he could also do things which he does not will to do. He put his opinion the way he did specifically against those opponents who claimed that God wills many things which he is not able to do.

Again, Lombard warns, beware how you understand the statement "He can whatever he wills". Do you mean (2a) whatever he wills himself to be able to (*quidquid vult se posse*)? or (2b) whatever he wills to make (*quidquid vult facere*)? or (2c) whatever he wills to happen (*quidquid vult fieri*)? If you are prepared to call God omnipotent in the first sense, then Peter, too, or any of the saints, could be said to be omnipotent; for he is able to do whatever he wills himself to be able to do, and further he can make whatever he wills to make. For he does not will to make except what he does make, nor to be able to do except what he can do. However, it is not in his power to make happen whatever he wills to happen. Peter wills, for example, that persons worthy of salvation be saved; nevertheless he is not strong enough to save them. God, on the other hand, can also make happen whatever he wills to make. For if he wills something to happen *per se* (directly, through himself) he can make that thing *per se* and does make it *per se*; as he made the heaven and earth *per se*, because he willed so. But if he wills something to come about through a creature, then he operates through it also, as when he makes houses and similar artifacts through men. Furthermore, God is able to do things of himself (*ex se*) and through himself (*per se*); but a man or an angel, no matter how blessed he may be, is not able to bring about things either through himself or of himself.

The preceding paragraph is a close paraphrase of Peter's perspicuous discussion (itself based on Hugh of St. Victor, *Summa Sent*. 1, c. 14) of the distinctions to be made in our explication of authorities in the light of reason and logic. The fact that such analyses of the phrase "whatever he wills" make sense and that not every kind of willing or wanting would serve as a suitable interpretant for '*Wxy*' in such claims as O_6 and O_6' gives Peter Lombard a further refinement of that notion of omnipotence which is based on the connection between the possibility of action and acts of will.[50]

4. LOMBARD'S REJECTION OF THE ABELARDIAN NOTION OF OMNIPOTENCE

Lombard spends five pages against those who say that God can do nothing but what he wills and does. His main targets are, of course, Abelard and his spiritual disciples (e.g., Master Hermann, Master Omnebene, et al.).[51] The *motivation* of Abelard and the Abelardians for holding such a view was of course quite understandable to Lombard and in fact shared by him. What Abelard tried to do was to exclude mutability from God's power; his denial that God could do or know more than he does was seen by him as part of this effort. Lombard disagreed on this latter score and argued against the position which seemed to limit divine omnipotence.[52]

The central thesis of the Abelardians under consideration was this: "God cannot make anything other than he does, nor make in a better way that which he makes, nor fail to make something which he does make".[53] The reason why God can do only what he does is that

> he can only do what is good and just to be brought about; but it is not good and just to be brought about by him except what he does bring about. For if there is some other thing which is good and just for him to make than the things which he does

the part of Lombard "curious", but does not offer any explanation why he considers it to be such. It seems to me no more curious than the arguments for the Abelardian position. Both require the employment of ordinary language and ordinary ways of understanding examples in a discussion of the problem which *ex hypothesi* applies to eternal and intangible things such as God, the Principle of the Good, the Principle of Plenitude of Being and the universal principles of logic. What I do find "curious" about Lombard's thinking is the move he makes immediately after refuting the Abelardians. He uses, *in support of his own contention* a comment made by St. Augustine in *Super Genesim*[63]: "God could have created man such that he could not sin, nor even wish to sin; and if he created him such, who doubts that he would have been better?"[64] Now if Lombard is speaking about a particular individual and about his accidental characteristics, the example would perhaps support his view: just as an artisan can make a better particular knife (a knife which can cut better – if that is the essential function of a knife), so could God create a better individual human being (one who can achieve his end *qua* human being in a better, more direct, smooth, and sure way). But if what Augustine meant was that God could have created another grade of being, would it still make sense to talk about God creating a better *man*?

Is it in God's power not only to make things better than he makes, but also to make them in a different or better manner than the one he actually employs? Again, Lombard starts with a distinction: "If one is referring to the wisdom of the maker, then the manner could be neither different nor better". The reason is that God's wisdom is identical with God's eternal being and thus immutable; and so God could not make anything with a different wisdom. However, "if 'manner' (in the above sentence) refers to the thing itself which God makes, then we say that the manner could be different and better".[65]

Lombard concludes the subject with a paraphrase from the thirteenth book of Augustine's *On the Trinity*: "Hence Augustine says that another mode of our salvation was possible to God who can do all things; but that there was no more appropriate mode of healing our misery".[66] Here "appropriate" suggests "*the best* under the circumstances", i.e., no other way would be logically or metaphysically possible for healing. But since he may be using here 'possible' in such a way as to be consistent with 'necessary', he may be merely saying in the first clause that God *chose* the best possible way for our salvation, although he *could* have chosen a worse one. But is it appropriate to say that God may act in a less perfect way than otherwise available? Lombard does not hesitate to speak in precisely such terms, since he goes on in the same paragraph: "Thus, if we consider the things which he makes, God could make them in some different and better manner, or in some different and equally good manner, or even *in a less good manner* than he in fact makes them of course, relating the manner to the quality of the work of creatures, not to the wisdom of the Creator".[67]

5. DIVINE OMNIPOTENCE IN PETER OF POITIERS' *SENTENCES*

Let us now take a look at the discussion of omnipotence in the five books of *Sentences* by Peter of Poitiers (or Peter Pictavian). There are two chapters in Pictavian's first book of *Sentences* that deal directly with the subjects of divine power and omnipotence. These are Chapters 7 – "In what sense is God said to be omnipotent?" and 8 – "Whether God can do whatever he was able to do?" Much of Chapter 7 covers material already traversed by Roland and Lombard. Yet, as one reads along, there are novel cases and examples, and further-on there is quite a bit of novel argumentative material. The Abelardian problem of whether God can do more than he does, etc., is covered, but it is resolved in favor of the view that

O_6: $(\forall x)(\mathrm{W}ax \supset \mathrm{M}^*\beta ax)$

is to be accepted, but

O_6': $(\forall x)(\mathrm{M}ax \equiv \mathrm{M}^*\beta ax)$

is to be rejected.[68]

The prevalent method of resolving the problem is by making distinctions. This method is applied by him much more systematically and thoroughly than by either Roland or Lombard. The brevity achieved is often remarkable. For example, take the claim: "God can only do what is good to come about from him".[69] Pictavian distinguishes between two senses: Sense (a) – *per compositionem*: "God can only do what would be good if it were brought about by him"; Sense (b) – *per divisionem*: "God can only do what is good, i.e., he cannot do anything which is not now good". If the original is understood in the composite sense, it is true; if in the divided sense, it is false and rejectable.

Pictavian is just as thorough and effective with his analysis and rejection of other Abelardian theses, such as "God can only do what his justice requires", "God is governed by an eternal rule within himself", etc.

In other cases, Pictavian calls attention to elementary logical fallacies. For example:

God cannot do only what he does not will (Augustine).
Therefore, God can do only what he wills (Fallacious conclusion)

Counter-example:

Only that is not an animal which is not a man (Supposition)
Therefore, nothing is an animal which is not a man (Fallacious conclusion)

Another example:

It is impossible that God makes whatever he can make.
Therefore God cannot make whatever he can make.

Counter-example:

It is impossible that something white be black (composite sense)
Therefore something white can be black (divided sense – Fallacious conclusion)[70]

Pictavian, unlike Roland and Lombard, mentions Jerome's statement to the effect that God could not restore a virgin after she has been violated. The case is mentioned as an example of what God could not do and presumably in support of the conclusion that God is not omnipotent. He explains that some have interpreted Jerome as claiming that God "cannot make the status of married people and continent people comparable to the status of a virgin, i.e., equally suitable and ready for God's service";[71] and further that although God could elevate the status of the former and make it higher than the status of virgins; yet, with respect to a certain suitability and pleasing character, God could not make that status comparable to that of virgins. Pictavian does not find this interpretation appropriate; he himself thinks that Jerome was speaking hyperbolically, talking about the worth of the virginity of Paula and Eustochius. This is not uncommon in sacred writings. The venerable Bede, for example, also uses locutions which should not be taken literally: "God *cannot* give to his faithful that clarity on earth as he reserved for them in heaven". Pictavian remarks that here 'cannot' does not mean that he does not have the power to do so but rather 'that he *does not want*' or 'can't' *out of a moral sense of justice.*[72]

Pictavian goes through many other kinds of cases which seem to suggest difficulties for God's omnipotence. Can God create something that is both a man and a donkey? Can God change a stick into a serpent? Can God enable a virgin to give birth? And so on. After making many acute observations concerning such puzzling questions, Pictavian offers a classification of God's work into three generically different kinds:

There are three genera of works which are from God. Some of these come about by the authority of God, by mediation of a seminal cause, as for example, that trees bloom, bear fruit, and the like; and these are called natural works (*opera naturalia*); there are other works which are brought about by men – but that they take place is nevertheless from God – , and such are all the artifacts, (*artificialia*) thrones, temples, and the like; and there are other works which he performs through his authority, without mediation by anything, in order to show his grace to us; for example, that a virgin gives birth, that a stick is changed into a serpent, that a woman is turned into a statue of salt; and all these are miraculous works (*opera miraculosa*).[73]

According to Pictavian, any created nature is such that God could make anything out of it, whatever he wills; but, he adds, it is not "in his nature to make, if he does make, but only through his will". Further,

that this substance is a serpent is not so in virtue of some mediating inferior cause but exclusively through God's will effecting it; nevertheless it is no less a serpent on that account. Just as Adam was made from the mud, he did not become one by mediation of some inferior nature, but only through God's will . . .[74]

Could God make one and the same thing to be man and donkey? Yes, he could. That two contradictory opposites both be true? Yes, provided one be taken according to the superior nature;

it is true for example that a virgin gives birth according to a superior nature, and it is true that a virgin does not give birth according to the inferior nature. But it is not possible for God to effect that both be true according to the superior nature, for in that case his excellence would be diminished, because he would be author of contrariety and discordance. Nor could God make it so that both be true according to the inferior nature . . . .[75]

Pictavian explains: Since, according to theology, man and God are the same (that is, in Christ), man and God are not opposed; so, if man and donkey were the same, the predicables *man* and *donkey* would not be opposed. So when they say that it is impossible for God to make it so that man be a donkey without man being a donkey, this must be denied; "it is indeed possible that this be true; 'God makes a man a donkey', without this being true: 'man' is 'donkey' " (*immo possible est hoc esse verum: Deus facit homines asinum, hoc existente non vero: homo est asinus*).[76] Pictavian admits, of course, that this would be false according to man's inferior nature, but true according to his superior one. He insists on a precise way of formulating statements, and hence many claims which were seen as placing a limit on God's power are no longer seen as a threat.

6. OMNIPOTENCE AND TEMPORALITY

One final major concern shown by these three authors should be at least mentioned. This is the concern about the relationship of God's power to the temporal placement of events. Roland puts the question in these terms: "Whether whatever God can do now he always was able and always will be able to do; and whether whatever he was able to do from eternity he can do now and should always be able to do; and whether whatever he will be able to do in the future, he was able to do from eternity and can do now?"[77] The counter-examples seem obvious. Thus, from eternity God was able to create a world out of nothing but now he cannot.[78] Roland's defense of the immutability of divine power is not simply the claim that God's essence is immutable, but is the implied contention that a power is distinct from its exercise. Thus, in relation to the power to create the world out of nothing he remarks: "we say that he has the same power which he had from eternity to create the world out of nothing such that if the world today did not exist, he could create it out of nothing".[79]

Lombard considers the following counterexample: God was able to be incarnated, to die and to rise again, and the like, but he apparently cannot do so now; it thus appears that his power has been diminished.[80] His first move towards a solution of this problem is to compare divine power with knowledge and will.

> Just as he always knows whatever he ever knew, and always wills whatever he ever willed; he does not ever lose any knowledge or ever change his will, which he ever had; so also is he always able to to whatever he ever was able to do; he is not deprived of any of his power. For he is not deprived of the power to be incarnated or to rise again, even though he could not now be incarnated or rise. For just as he once had the power to be incarnated, so he has the power now to be incarnated . . .[81]

The second way of dealing with the difficulty has a linguistic twist of sorts, reminiscent of what Knuuttila labeled as the 12th century *nominales* movement.[82] Lombard wants to hold that what one knows in the following two cases is exactly the same: God once knew that he would rise again, and he now knows himself to have arisen: "the knowledge to have known that at some time in the past (*olim scivisse*) and to know that now is not different but is completely the same".[83] Lombard again carries the analogy through the case of will to the case of power:

> God always has the power to do whatever he ever was able to do, that is, he has all that power which he once had and of the whole of that thing over which he once had the

power; but he cannot always do all that which he once was able to do; rather he is *either able to do or else to have done* what he once was able to do.[84]

Peter of Poitiers, too, spends almost eight pages on the subject. While he does not say anything essentially different from the solutions given by his two predecessors, he goes into a greater variety of examples and is at his best deploying his grammatical and logical skills.

7. A CONCLUDING REMARK

The three early *Sentences* provide in rough outline all the essential ingredients for a discussion of the meaning of the concept of omnipotence and its interrelationship with the cluster of concepts making up analytic natural theology. When we consider the intense intellectual activity, both theological and philosophical, which took place during the next four centuries and which was so often directly stimulated by the *Sentences* of Peter Lombard, we can look upon the incursion of the New Dialectic into theological discussion – regretted as it was by Walter of Saint-Victor and others in the twelfth century – as a very healthy and fruitful move.

NOTES

1 The New Logic (*logica nova*) is a collective name for Aristotle's two *Analytics*, the *Topics*, and the *Sophistical Refutations*, recovered in the Latin West early in the twelfth century; to be distinguished from the Old Logic (*logica vetus*) which consisted basically of Aristotle's *Categories* and *On Interpretation* in *The Organon*, Porphyry's *Isagoge*, and Boethius's logical writings.

2 L. M. De Rijk, *Logica Modernorum*, vol. I, van Gorcum and Co., Assen 1962, pp. 163 f. For selective critique of Peter of Poitiers, see Walter of Saint-Victor, *Contra quatuor Labyrinthos Franciae*, crit. ed. by P. Glorieux, in *Archives d'histoire doctrinale et littéraire du Moyen Age* 19 (1952), pp. 187–335.

3 There is a considerable body of literature found in contemporary Anglo-American philosophical and theological journals on each of these topics. A very useful anthology of articles on omnipotence is L. Urban and D. N. Walton, *The Power of God: Readings on Omnipotence and Evil*, Oxford University Press, Oxford 1978, which contains both historical and contemporary materials. A monograph by A. Kenny, *The God of the Philosophers*, Oxford University Press, Oxford 1978, covers both topics. A lengthy discussion of omnipotence is found in J. F. Ross, *Philosophical Theology*, Bobbs-Merrill, Indianapolis 1979. Many analytic studies of concepts connected with the discussions of God's properties, such as N. Kretzmann, 'Omniscience and Immutability,' *Journal of*

Philosophy **63** (1966), 409–421; E. Stump and N. Kretzmann, 'Eternity', *Journal of Philosophy* **78** (1981), 429–458, and others in the same family provide models for dealing with difficult concepts of philosophical theology. Finally, articles such as F. Alluntis and A. B. Wolter, 'Duns Scotus on the Omnipotence of God', *Studies in Philosophy and the History of Philosophy*, J. K. Ryan (ed.), 5 (1970), pp. 178–222; W. J. Courtenay's 'John of Mirecourt and Gregory of Rimini on Whether God Can Undo the Past', *Recherches de Théologie ancienne et médiévale*, 39 (1972), 224–256 and 40 (1973), 147–174; J. Wippel, 'The Reality of Non-existing Possibles,' *Review of Metaphysics* **34** (1981), 729–758; and the like, provide models for concept analysis closely tied to historical figures.

[4] See, for example, M. Grabmann, *Die Geschichte der scholastischen Methode*, reprinted Darmstadt 1956, vol. II, for development of *Sentenzliteratur*.

[5] *Die Sentenzen Rolands, Nachmals Papstes Alexander III* (Hrsg. Fr. Ambrosius M. Gietl, O. P.), Freiburg im Bresgau 1891. Reprinted Amsterdam 1969.

[6] *Sententiae in IV Libris Distinctae*, crit. ed. by A. Haysse, Grottaferrata, 1971.

[7] Cf. F. Stegmüller, *Repertorium Commentariorum in Sententias Petri Lombardi* (2 vols.), Würzburg 1947.

[8] Cf. P. S. Moore and M. Dulong (eds.), *Sententiae Petri Pictaviensis*, University of Notre Dame Press, Notre Dame 1943, p. xv. The authors are referring to M. Grabmann, *Die Geschichte der scholastischen Methode* II, p. 406.

[9] All references to Peter of Poitiers will be made to the edition of Moore-Dulong mentioned in *n*. 8.

[10] Cf. Moore-Dulong, 'Introduction'.

[11] Peter Abelard, *Introductio ad theologiam*, V. Cousin (ed.) in *Petri Abaelardi Opera II*, Paris 1859. Also in J. P. Migne, *Patrologia Latina*, Paris, 1844, (henceforth cited as *PL*) 178, cols 979–1114.

[12] This does not mean, of course, that he also agreed with the views of Abelard but only that he considered them to be important philosophical views on the subject on which one needs to take some intellectual stand. As Gietl remarks: "Wohl theilt Roland manche Anschauungen Abälards . . . , in vielen und wichtingen Punkten aber tritt er mit Entschiedenheit den Ansichten desselben entgegen . . ." Cf. Gietl's 'Einleitung' to *Sentenzen Rolands*, p. xxviii.

It is amazing that neither Roland nor Hugh of St. Victor nor Peter Lombard cared very much for the work of Anselm.

[13] Cf. the condemned theses on Abelard in H. Denzinger, *Enchiridion Symbolorum, Definitionum et Declarationum de Rebus Fidei et Morum* (Editio 31, C. Rahner, S. J.), Herder, Barcelona 1957, nn. 368 sqq, 393 n. See esp. n. 374.7: "Quod ea solummodo possit facere vel dimittere, vel eo modo tantum vel eo tempore, quo facit et non alio".

[14] "Secundum *magistrum Petrum* non potuit plura predestinare quam predestinaverit; secundum nos vero plura potuit predestinare quam predestinavit", Gietl, p. 65.

[15] "Secundum *magistrum Petrum* non potuerunt plura beneplacuisse ei quam beneplacuerint; secundeum nos plura potuerunt ei beneplacuisse quam beneplacuerint, et plura possent tibi beneplacere quam beneplaceant", Gietl, pp. 66f.

[16] "Secundum *magistrum Petrum* non potuit plura permittere quam permiserit; sed secundum nos plura potuit permittere quam permiserit, et plura posset hodie permittere quam permittat", Gietl, p. 68.

[17] "Dicebat enim *magister Petrus*, quod Deus non potest plura scire quam scit . . . Nos

vero dicimus Deum plura posse scire quam sciat, hec taliter distinguendo: 'Deus potest plura scire quam sciat', id est, de pluribus potest habere Deus cognitionem, de quibus non habet, hoc falsum est; habet enim cognicionem, scilicet scientiam de presentibus, preteritis atque futuris . . . et de his etiam que nec erunt nec esse possunt. Si vero dicatur, 'plura potest scire', etc., hoc est, plura possunt esse subiecta eius cognicioni de ipsis rebus, hoc verum est. Licet enim omnes res cognoscat et de omnibus scientiam habet, tamen de ipsis aliqua potest scire que non scit . . . Si vero obiciatur: ergo scientia eius potest augeri, dicimus, quod non sequitur. Non enim dicitur scientia augeri vel minui gratia scitorum, sicut nec visio dicitur augeri vel minui gratia visorum. Licet enim plura videam hodie quam heri viderim, non inde tamen dicitur mea visio augmentata: ita licet Deus plura possit scire quam sciat, non tamen dicimus eius scientiam posse augmentari". Gietl, pp. 81ff.

"For a *locus classicus* on the concept of *scientia visionis*, as opposed to *scientia simplicis intelligentiae*, see Aquinas, *Summa theol.* I, q. 14, esp. a. 9 and a.12. As J. Wippel reads Aquinas, "God's knowledge of things that actually have been, are, or will be, is called his *scientia visionis*. His knowledge of possibles that neither are, were, nor will be is called his *scientia simplicis intelligentiae*". *Review of Metaphysics* **34** (1981), p. 733, n. 8.

[18] Cf. H. Denifle, 'Die Sentenzen Abaelards und die Bearbeitungen seiner Theologia', *Archiv für Literatur-und Kirchengeschichte des Mittelalters* **1** (1885), p. 621; Gietl, loc. cit; D. E. Luscombe, *The School of Peter Abelard*, Cambridge University Press, Cambridge 1969, pp. 14–60; pp. 224–281.

[19] Gietl considers the *Sentences* to be a fruit of Roland's teaching in Bologna: ". . . erweisen sich die Sentenzen Rolands als die reifste Frucht jener theologischen Schule, die Mitte des 12. Jahrhunderts vor der Constitution der Universität zu Bologna bestand. Der Einfluss, den Abälard schon auf Gratian ausgeübt, macht sich auch in ihnen geltend . . . Trotzdem ist der Einfluss Abälards kein so mächtiger wie in der Sentenzen Omnebene's, den Denifle mit Recht einen Abälardianer nennt". p. 1xi.

[20] "Utrum plura possit facere Deus quam facit". Gietl, p. 49.

[21] "Utrum quicquid potuit ab eterno, possit modo, et quicquid potest modo, semper ab eterno potuerit et semper debeat posse. "Gietl, *ibid.*

[22] "Utrum quicquid poterit in futuro, possit modo, et quicquid potest modo, semper in futuro poterit et semper debeat posse". Gietl, *ibid.*

[23] Cf. *Introductio in theologiam* III, n. 5, col. 1093 f.

[24] "Quod autem Deus plura non possit facere quam faciat, auctoritate Salemonis probatur qua dicitur: 'dominator Deus omnipotens, cui subest posse, cum vult'. Si subest ei posse tantum cum vult: ergo cum non vult, non subest ei posse. Tantum igitur que vult potest. Si tantum que vult potest: ergo tantum que vult operatur. Non ergo plura potest facere quam faciat". Gietl, pp. 49 f.

[25] This notation is an adaption of the notation of D. Walton's article 'Some Theorems of Fitch on Omnipotence', in *Power of God*, pp. 182–191, and of his 'The Omnipotence Paradox', *ibid.*, pp. 153–164.

[26] Cf. L. M. de Rijk (ed.), *Petrus Abaelardus: Dialectica*, Van Gorcum and Company Assen, 1956, p. 278, for example, for the rule analogous to $(q \rightarrow r) \rightarrow [(p \rightarrow q) \rightarrow (p \rightarrow r)]$, "Quidquid antecedit ad antecedens, antecedit ad consequens". Also, *Garlandus Compotista: Dialectica*, L. M. de Rijk (ed.), Van Gorcum and Company Assen 1959.

[27] The quote comes from Augustine's *De civitate Dei*, xxi, c. 7, n. 1, and can be found

in Rolands text: "Non enim dicitur Deus omnipotens, eo quod omnia possit, sed quia quicquic vult potest, scilicet quicquic vult operatur". Gietl, p. 50.

28 "Si idem est Deo velle et posse: ergo quicquic vult potest et quicquid potest, vult". *Ibid.*

29 Cf. Gietl, pp. 50–56 for the total context of the discussion.

30 I am alluding here to the terminology and the structural historical interpretation as found in A. Lovejoy's, *The Great Chain of Being, A Study of the History of an Idea,* Harvard University Press, Cambridge Mass. 1936. Whether Abelard would indeed accept the Principle of Plenitude of Being in just the form used by Lovejoy is certainly disputable; and as Eleanore Stump rightly pointed out in a discussion of this paper, even if he did accept the Principle, he need not do so in order to maintain his position on omnipotence. Nor were Abelard's adversaries successful in their refutations of Abelard's position as they may have thought. Professor Stump pointed out in a discussion that they should first face the problem of divine simplicity. After all, the concept of omnipotence is intertwined with related concepts such as immutability, goodness, and perhaps most important, with simplicity. As long as Roland, Peter Lombard, and Peter of Poitiers used simplicity in a noncritical way and at the same time endorsed the idea of immutable divine will (with the positive connotation of free choice), they were able to escape Abelardian necessitarianism, i.e., the position that whatever God does flows with necessity from his (simple) nature. But a fully-worked out concept of divine simplicity may make such an escape more difficult. Of course, one should also remember that neither Abelard nor his opponents could claim to be able to talk "literally" about such a being.

31 Cf. A. Lovejoy, *op. cit.*, pp. 67–98; J. Hintikka, "Gaps in the Great Chain of Being', in *Proceedings of the APA* 49 (1975/76), 22–38; and S. Knuuttila, *Reforging the Great Chain of Being*, D. Reidel, Dordrecht 1980, pp. 163–257.

32 "Si enim omnia valde bona vellet creare et non posset, foret impotens; si posset et nollet, foret invidus. Idem quoque ratione probatur. Aliquid est quod Deus non potest facere. Illud erit aut peccare aut currere vel huiusmodi. Aliqua est ratio, quare id non potest facere. Hec erit, aut quia non convenit eum facere, aut quia iniustum est eum id facere. Si ideo non potest currere vel peccare, quia non convenit eum facere: ergo eadem ratione lapidem aliquem de loco suo non potest movere, quia non convenit, ut moveat, quod exinde apparet, quod dimittit. Si enim conveniret, ut moveret, et moveret. Idem alia ratione. Impossibile est, Deum aliquid facere, quod non sit iustum eum facere; sed non est iustum cum facere, quod nec fecit nec faciet: ergo non potest facere, quod non facit nec faciet. Quod non sit iustum eum facere, quod non facit nec faciet, exinde apparet, quia non facit. Si enim iustum esset, ut faceret, procul dubio illud faceret". Gietl, p. 51.

33 "Si vero duo equalia bona esse dicantur, nulla erit ratio, quare quod facit faciat, et quod dimittit dimittat, et sic quicquid Deus facit, indiscrete et absque ratione facit". Gietl, p. 52.

34 "Item, voluntas eius inmutabilis et invariabilis est. Ab eterno autem noluit facere quod dimittit; non potest autem facere aliquid nolens: ergo non potest facere eorum aliquid que dimittit, quia non potest facere ea que non vult facere. Item, non potest Deus facere contra suam dispositionem; ab eterno autem disposuit, se non facturum quod dimittit: ergo non potest illud facere, aut si potest facere, et contra suam dispositionem facere". Gietl, p. 52.

35 "Contra probatur auctoritate Domini dicentis: 'possum rogare Patrem meum, et exhibebit michi plus quam xii legiones angelorum'. Potuit rogare, non autem rogavit: potuit ergo quod non fecit . . . Idem . . . Potest Deus dare pluviam hodie, non autem dabit: ergo potest facere quod non est facurus". Gietl, pp. 52f.

36 "Item, si Deus non potest facere quod non facit neque dimittere quod facit: ergo quicquic facit necessitate facit, et quicquic dimittit necessitate dimittit. Item, si Deus non potest plura facere quam faciat: ergo terminus interponitur potencie Dei, quare sub certo et determinato numero Dei cadit potencia". Gietl, pp. 53f.

37 "Natura lapidis, qui est in fundo maris, non repugnat, quin lapis ille possit videri a me, et tamen ego non possum videre lapidem illum: ita natura Jude non repugnabat, quin Judas posset a Deo salvari, et tamen Deus non poterat eum salvare". Gietl, p. 55

38 *Introductio in theologiam* III, in *PL* 178, n.4, col. 1099.

39 "Nobis autem asserentibus Deum plura posse facere quam faciat, obviare quodammodo videntur predicte auctoritates et rationes . . ." Gietl, p. 56.

40 "Item, 'non dicitur Deus omnipotens, quod omina possit', id est, non ea ratione dicitur omnipotens, quia potest omnia, sed quia quicque vult, potest ex se". Gietl, p. 57.

41 "Quidam dicunt, quod creare est maius bonum. Nos vero dicimus, quod quantum in se est creare, et non creare quantum in se est, equalia, et tamen non sine ratione hec facit et illud dimittit". Gietl, p. 57.

42 All references to Lombard's sentences are to Book I of the Hayesse critical edition. See n. 6 above.

43 Cf. D. E. Luscombe, *The School of Peter Abelard* Cambridge University Press, Cambridge 1969, p. 262.

44 As A. Kenny and J. Pinborg remark, "In writers such as Scotus and Ockham commentaries on the *Sentences* of Lombard follow the form of a *Quaestio disputata*". Cf. *Cambridge History of Later Medieval Philosophy*, N. Kretzmann *et al.* (eds.) Cambridge University Press, Cambridge 1982, p. 26.

45 Lombard, *Sent.* I, d. 42, c. 1 (1984), p. 294.

46 "Ait enim Augustinus in libro *Quaestionum veteris et novae Legis:* 'Omnia quidem potest Deus, sed non facit nisi quod convenit veritati eius iustitiae!" *Ibid.*

47 "Unde Augustinus in xv libro *De Trinitate*: 'Magna, inquit Dei potentia est, non posse mentiri'." *Ibid.*, d. 42, c. 2 (185), p. 295.

48 *Sent.* I, d. 42, c. 3 (186), p. 295. Lombard probably got this characterization of omnipotence from Hugh of St. Victor, *De Sacram.* I, 2, 22.

49 "His auctoritatibus videtur ostendi quod Deus ex eo tantum dicatur omnipotens, quod omnia potest quae vult, non quia omnia possit". Sent. I, d. 42, c. 3 (186), 2, p. 296.

50 Centuries later, John Eckius, lecturing at Ingolstadt around 1542 and writing his "annotatiunculae" on the first book of Lombard's *Sentences*, read into Lombard's text elements of the famous distinction between the absolute and the ordained power of God which would soon be employed by Aquinas and which in a more radical form played such an extensive role in the fourteenth century philosophy. Writing on Distinction 42 Eckius comments: "God's ordained power is one through which he is himself cooperating with creatures according to the common law which he had implanted into them. St. Augustine says about this power: 'God so governs the things which he created that he allows them to make their own proper motions'. Furthermore, God gives the fruits

of the earth and other things, but by his ordained power. The absolute power of God is that power which does not concern the common rule which he has implanted in things but extends to all that which it would not be self-contradictory to come about. For example, when fire consumes clothing it is according to the common course and the nature of fire. But that it did not attack and consume the three boys in the furnace was due to God's absolute power. Thus, by his absolute power God could save Judas, because it would not be self-contradictory for this to happen". J. Eckius, *In primum librum Sententiarum Annotatiunculae*. W. L. Moore, jr. (ed.), E. J. Brill, Leiden 1976, pp. 122f. Cf. W. J. Courtenay, 'The Dialectic of Omnipotence in the High and Late Middle Ages', in the present volume, for a detailed discussion of the development and the role in philosophical discussions of the *de potentia absoluta/ordinata* distinction.

51 Cf. Gietl, *op. cit.*, pp. v – 1xx; also Luscombe, *op. cit.*, pp. 14–59 and pp. 224–260; and Lombard, *Sent.* I. d. 43, pp. 298–303.

52 Not only is he arguing against the position which would have limits on God's power imposed from the outside; he also expresses himself sarcastically against the persons holding such opinion when he says: " . . . quidam tamen, de suo sensu gloriantes, Dei potentiam coarctare sub mensura conati sunt". d. 43, c. unicum (187), 1; p. 298.

53 "Non potest Deus aliud facere quam facit, nec melius facere id quod facit, nec aliud praetermittere de his quae facit". *Sent.* I, d. 43 (187). 1, p. 298.

54 "Non potest Deus facere nisi quod bonum est et iustum fieri; non est autem iustum et bonum fieri ab eo nisi quod facit. Si enim aliud iustum est et bonum eum facere quam facit, non ergo facit omne quod iustum est et bonum eum facere. Sed quis hoc audeat dicere?" *Ibid.*, pp. 298f.

55 *Ibid.*, p. 299.

56 *Ibid.*, pp. 299ff.

57 A. Lovejoy, *op. cit.*, p. 70.

58 *Ibid.*, pp. 70f.

59 *Capitula Haeresum Petri Abelardi: in St. Bernardi Opera* in *PL* **182**, col. 1052; quoted by Lovejoy, *op. cit.*, p. 73, n. 9.

60 *Scil.*, *De div. quaest.* 83, p. 50 (*PL* **40**, 31s).

61 "Deus quem genuit, quoniam melioriem se generare non potuit; nihil enim Deo melius, debuit aequalem. Si enim voluit et non potuit, infirmus est; si potuit et noluit, invidus. Ex quo conficitur aequalem genuisse Filium". *Sent.* I. d. 44, c. 1 (188), p. 304.

62 Cf. *Sent.* I, d. 44, c. 1 (188).

63 Cf. *De Genesi ad litt.*, XI, c. 7, n. 9 (*PL* **34**, 433).

64 "Talem potuit Deus hominem fecisse, qui nec peccare posset nec vellet; et si talem fecisset, quis dubitat eum meliorem fuisse?" Lombard adds: "Ex praedictis constat quod potest Deus et alia facere quam facit, et quae facit meliora ea facere quam facit". *Sent.* I, d. 44, c. 1 (188), p. 304.

An interesting contemporary discussion of the problem at hand is that by J. Hick, 'Can God Create a World in Which All Men Always Freely Choose the Good?' found in *The Power of God*, Urban and Walton (eds.), pp. 217–222. Cf. also J. Hick's *Evil and the God of Love*, Macmillan, New York 1966.

65 "Si modus operationis ad sapientiam opificis referatur, nec alius, nec melior esse potest . . . Si vero referatur modus ad rem ipsam quam facit Deus, dicimus quia et alius et melior potest esse modus". *Loc. cit.*, pp. 304f.

66 "Unde Augustinus in xii libro *De Trinitate* dicit quod fuit et alius modus nostrae

liberationis possibilis Deo, qui omnia potest; sed nullus alius nostrae miseriae sanandae fuit convenientior". *Loc. cit.*, p. 305.

[67] "Potest igitur Deus eorum quae facit quaedam alio modo meliori, quaedam alio modo aeque bono, quaedam etiam minus bono facere quam facit; ut tamen modus referatur ad qualitatem operis, id est creaturae, non ad sapientiam Creatoris". *Loc. cit.*, p. 305.

[68] Cf. Moore-Dulong (eds.), *Sent.* I, c. 7, p. 49.

[69] *Ibid.*, p. 52.

[70] Cf. *Ibid.*, pp. 57f.

[71] *Ibid.*, p. 59.

[72] "Deus in terra claritatem illam non potest dare fidelibus suis, quam eius reservat in celis. Sed accipiendum est 'non potest', id est non vult, vel 'non poest' de institia". Bede: *In Marc. evang. exposit.* III, 8 (*PL* 92, 218A). Quoted in Moore-Dulong, p. 60.

[73] "Notandum igitur est tria esse genera operum que a Deo sunt quorum alia fiunt auctoritate Dei, mediante seminali causa, ut quod arbores florent, fructificant, et alia huiusmodi, et ea dicuntur opera naturalia; sunt alia que fiunt ab hominibus – quod tamen fiunt, a Deo est – qualia sunt artificialia omnia, scamma, templa, et huiusmodi; sunt alia que operatur auctoritate sua, nullo mediante, ad gratiam suam nobis ostendendam, ut quod virgo peperit, quod virga in serpentem mutata est, mulier in statuam salis versa, et hec omnia sunt opera miraculosa". Moore-Dulong, p. 66.

[74] "Est igitur in uniuscuiusque natura ut Deus possit de ea facere quod voluerit, non est tamen in natura eius ut faciat, si facit, quia non agit opus miraculosum mediante natura, sed sola sua voluntate. Unde quod hec substantia est serpens non est aliqua inferiori causa mediante, sed sola Dei voluntate id efficiente; non tamen ideo minus est verus serpens. Sicut et quod Adam de limo terre factus est homo, non fuit mediante inferiori natura, sed sola Dei voluntate". *Ibid.*, pp. 66f.

[75] "... ut verum est virginem peperisse secundum superiorem naturam, verum est non virginem peperisse secundum inferiorem naturam. Sed quod ambo sint vera secundum superiorem naturam, id non posset Deus efficere, cum in hoc eius excellentia minueretur, quia auctor esset contrarietatis et discordie. Nec etiam potest Deus facere ut ambo sint vera secundum inferiorem naturam". *Ibid.*, p. 67.

[76] *Ibid.*

[77] "Utrum quidquid Deus potest modo, semper potuit et semper debeat posse, et utrum quicquic ab eterno potuit, possit modo et semper debeat posse, et utrum quicquic poterit in futuro, ab eterno potuit et possit modo". Gietl, p. 58.

[78] *Ibid.*, p. 59.

[79] "Quod dicitur: 'ad eterno potuit mundum de nichilo creare' etc., dicimus, quoniam et illud hodie potest et habet illam eandem potenciam, quam ab eterno habuit mundum de nichilo creare, ut si mundus hodie non esset, et ipsum de nichilo creare posset". *Ibid.*, p. 60.

[80] "Praeterea quaeri solet utrum Deus semper possit omne quod olim potuit. Quod quibusdam non videtur, dicentibus: Potuit Deus incarnari, potuit mori et resurgere, et alia huiusmodi, quae modo non potest. Potuit ergo quae modo non potest, et ita habuit potentiam quam modo non habet: unde videtur eius potentia imminuta". Lombard, *Sent.* I, d. 44, c. 2 (180), p. 305.

[81] "Quia sicut omnia semper scit quae aliquando scivit, et semper vult quae aliquando voluit, nec unquam aliquam scientam amittit vel voluntatem mutat quam habuit, ita

omnia semper potest quae aliquando potuit, nec unquam aliqua potentia sua privatur. Non est ergo privatus potentia incarnandi vel resurgendi, licet non possit modo incarnari vel resurgere. Sicut enim potuit olim incarnari, ita et potest modo esse incarnatus". *Ibid*.

82 S. Knuuttila, *op. cit*., pp. 195–98.

83 "Ut enim olim scivit se resurrecturum, et modo scit se resurrexisse; nec est alia scientia illud olim scivisse, et hoc modo scire, sed eadem omnino. Et sicut voluit olim resurgere, et modo resurrexisse; in quo unius rei voluntas exprimitur. Ita potuit olim nasci et resurgere, et modo potest natus fuisse et resurrexisse; et est eiusdem rei potentia". Lombard, *Ibid*., pp. 305f.

84 "Fateamur igitur Deum semper posse et quidquid semel potuit, id est habere omnem illam potentiam quam semel habuit, et illius omnis rei potentiam cuius semel habuit; sed non semper posse facere omne illud quod aliquando potuit facere: potest quidem facere aut fecisse quod aliquando potuit". *Ibid*., p. 306.

CHAPTER 12

DIVINE KNOWLEDGE, DIVINE POWER AND HUMAN FREEDOM IN THOMAS AQUINAS AND HENRY OF GHENT

John F. Wippel

1. INTRODUCTION

In this chapter I shall limit myself to two thinkers from the thirteenth century, Thomas Aquinas and Henry of Ghent. Since Thomas devoted considerably more attention to this topic than did Henry, and since Aquinas's position was to become the focal point for centuries of subsequent controversy, the greater part of my remarks will be devoted to him. In discussing Thomas's position I shall try to cover the points suggested in my title by reducing them to two major concerns: (1) Thomas's explanation of God's knowledge of future contingents; (2) his views concerning the causal character of God's knowledge and God's will. In each case I shall attempt to show how Thomas reconciles his explanation with man's freedom. Henry lectured as Master in theology at the University of Paris from 1276 until ca. 1292, and on the present topic may serve as an interesting link between Aquinas and Duns Scotus (though Scotus's position will not be examined here).[1] Henry had developed a radically different kind of metaphysics from that of Aquinas.[2] Of greatest interest to us will be Henry's explanation of God's knowledge of future contingents.

2. GOD'S KNOWLEDGE OF FUTURE CONTINGENTS IN AQUINAS'S *DE VERITATE*

As is well known, Thomas Aquinas always maintained that God knows individuals and individual events, including future contingents. For instance, to take a representative text from the mid-1250's, in qu. 2, art. 12 of his *De veritate* he explicitly addresses himself to this issue.[3] He begins his reply by criticizing two unsatisfactory solutions. According to one position, which errs by likening God's knowledge to that of man, God does not know future contingents. Aquinas immediately rejects this view because it would imply that God's providence does not extend to human affairs. According to another extreme position, God does know future contingents, but only because they happen out of necessity, in other words, because they are not

T. Rudavsky (ed.), Divine Omniscience and Omnipotence in Medieval Philosophy, 213–241.

really contingent. Thomas rejects this view because it would result in a denial of man's freedom. He concludes by defending the more difficult middle position. God does know future events, but this does not prevent some of them from being contingent.[4]

In developing his defense of this position in the same context, Thomas begins by noting that even in man some of his cognitive powers and habits do not admit of falsity. He cites sensation, science, and our intuition of first principles. Then Thomas contrasts the necessary with the contingent. As he understands the necessary here, it refers to that which cannot be prevented from occurring even before it exists. This is so because its causes are unchangeably ordered to its production. Given this, such necessary things or events, even when they are future, can be known by habits and powers such as those he has just mentioned.[5] By the contingent Thomas here means that which can be impeded before it is actually brought into being. Once such a contingent thing has actually been produced, however, it cannot be prevented from having actually existed. Hence, even the contingent can be grasped by one or other of those powers or habits which do not admit of falsity. For instance, when Socrates is actually sitting, my sense perception of him as sitting is correct.[6]

Thomas is attempting to make the point that even something contingent can be truly or correctly grasped once it has been realized in actuality. At the same time, he also acknowledges that insofar as something contingent is future, certain knowledge cannot be had of it. Since falsity cannot be admitted of God's knowledge, Thomas remarks that not even God can know future contingents, if this he taken to imply that he would know them *as* future.[7] For something to be known as future there must be some passing of time between one's knowing it and the actual realization of that thing in itself. Such, however, cannot be admitted of God's knowledge of the contingent or, for that matter, of anything else. God's knowledge is always ordered to that which he knows as that which is present (his knowledge) to that which is present (the object known). In order to illustrate this point Thomas offers the example of someone who observes many people passing along a road in succession. Within a given period of time our observer will have seen every individual passing by that road during a particular part of that time. During the total period of time, therefore, he will have seen each one who passed by as present to him; but he will not have seen them all as simultaneously present to him. Now if his vision of all these passersby could be simultaneous, then he would view them all as simultaneously present to him, though they would not be simultaneous with one another.[8]

Ultimately inspired here by Boethius, Thomas goes on to apply this to the case at hand. Since God's 'vision' is measured only by eternity, which itself is *tota simul* and includes the whole of time, whatever takes place in the course of time is not viewed by God as future to himself but as present. Nonetheless, Thomas also insists that what is seen by God as present to him may still be future with respect to other things which come before it in time. Because God's vision is not in time but outside time, any such event is not future to God but present. Because we are measured by time, any such event is future for us.[9]

From this Thomas concludes that just as our power of sight is not deceived when it sees an actual contingent object as present to it, so too God infallibly knows all contingents as present to him. And if our knowledge of an actually present contingent does not rob that event of its contingency, neither does God's knowledge of anything that is contingent.[10]

Thomas comments that it is difficult for us to understand this. This is because we cannot signify divine knowledge except by thinking of knowledge as we find it in ourselves, and then by also cosignifying certain differences.[11] It should be recalled that in the immediately preceding article of the *De veritate* Thomas had argued that *scientia* cannot be predicated of God and creatures either univocally or purely equivocally, but only analogically. It is true that his defense there of analogy of proportionality as the only kind to be used in such cases is something of an anomaly, and is at odds both with his earlier discussions of this in his Commentary on the *Sentences* and especially with all his later major treatments after the *De veritate*. Nonetheless, throughout his career he consistently rejects both univocity and equivocation when it comes to naming God and creatures, and defends some kind of analogy.[12]

Granted the difficulty of our adequately understanding knowledge as this is realized in God, Thomas comments that it would be better for us to say that God knows that a given contingent *is* than to say God knows that it *will be*. Or to use the language of Boethius in Bk V of his *Consolation of Philosophy*, Thomas suggests that God's knowledge of the future is more properly called *providentia* than *praevidentia* (providence rather than foreknowledge). Still, adds Thomas, in another sense divine knowledge can be styled *praevidentia* on account of the order which something known by God may have to other things to which it is future. Presupposed by all of this, of course, is the distinction between divine eternity, on the one hand, and human existence in time, on the other.[13]

As one might expect, a number of objections having to do with free future contingents were raised at this disputation. For instance, according to objection 1, only that which is true can be known. But according to Aristotle's *De interpretatione*, individual future contingents enjoy no determined truth. Therefore, God cannot have certain knowledge of them. In replying to this objection Thomas concedes that any such contingent is not determined so long as it is future. Once it is actually realized, however, it does have determined truth. And it is in this way that it is known by God. In other words, he is again applying the Boethian view that such events are not future for God but eternally present to him. Hence, in the divine and eternal present they are not unrealized but realized, not undetermined but determined.[14]

In replying to the fourth objection, Thomas appeals to the distinction between that which is necessary *de dicto* and that which is necessary *de re*. Here he is considering the statement that whatever is known by God is necessary. Taken *de dicto* the statement is composite and therefore true, since it simply means this: whatever is known by God is necessary in the sense that it is not possible for God to know that something is and for that thing not to be. But if this statement is understood *de re*, it is taken in divided fashion and is false. It would then mean this: that which is known by God is a necessary being. Thomas reminds us once more that the mere fact that things are known by God does not of itself impose necessity upon them.[15] In replying to the fifth objection Thomas makes basically the same point. If such a proposition were understood *de re*, the necessity would apply to the very thing that is known by God. In other words, the thing itself would exist necessarily. But when any such statement is taken *de dicto*, the necessity in question does not apply to the thing itself but only to the relationship between God's science, on the one hand, and the thing known, on the other.[16]

Thomas devotes considerable attention to the seventh objection and, I should add, discusses it in detail on a number of other occasions as well. The objection runs this way. In every true conditional, if the antecedent is absolutely necessary, the consequent is also absolutely necessary. But this conditional proposition is true: If something was known by God, it will be. Since the antecedent ('This was known by God') is absolutely necessary, the consequent ('It will be') is also absolutely necessary. Hence, it follows that whatever was known by God will necessarily be, and with absolute necessity. To strengthen the argument the objector reasons that the antecedent ('This was known by God') is a statement concerning the past. Statements concerning the past, if true, are necessary, since what was cannot not have been.[17]

In replying to this objection Thomas first proposes and rejects three inadequate responses.[18] Rather than delay here over these, I shall turn immediately to his personal solution. In such a proposition, he concedes, the antecedent is necessary without qualification (*simpliciter*). But the consequent is absolutely necessary only insofar as it follows from the antecedent. Thomas distinguishes between characteristics which are attributed to something insofar as it exists in itself, and others which apply to it only insofar as it is known. Those which are attributed to the thing as it is in itself apply to it according to its proper mode of being; but those which are attributed to it or follow from it insofar as it is known apply to it only according to the mode of the power that knows it, not according to the mode of being of the object that is known.[19]

In other words, Thomas here employs the Scholastic axiom that whatever is known is known according to the modality of the knower. To illustrate he proposes this statement: 'If I understand something, it is immaterial'. From this one need not conclude that the thing in question is in fact an immaterial being in itself, but only that it is immaterial insofar as it is present in my knowing power. So too, when I state, 'If God knows something, it will be', the consequent is not to be interpreted as applying to the thing according to its own mode of being, but according to the mode of its knower – in this case God himself. Granted that such a thing is future in terms of its own and temporal mode of being; according to the mode of its eternal divine knower it is present, and eternally present, to God. Given this, Thomas again comments that it would be more exact for us to say: 'If God knows something, it is', than to say 'If God knows something, it will be'.

Thomas also notes that the necessity in such statements is like that which applies to the following: 'If I see that Socrates is running, he is running'[20]. In each case we can say that the thing in question necessarily is when it is. In neither case need we conclude that the thing in question enjoys a necessary mode of being in itself, or that it is a necessary being. Or to put this another way, granted that in such propositions the consequent follows necessarily from the antecedent, this does not imply that the consequent enjoys a necessary mode of being. To state this in still another way, Thomas is here distinguishing between logical necessity, on the one hand, or that which applies to propositions, and ontological necessity, on the other. To say that such a proposition is logically necessary is to say that if its antecedent is given, its consequent necessarily follows. But this is to tell us nothing about the ontological structure or mode of being of the referent of that consequent in itself.[21]

Since Thomas evidently regards this as a serious objection, two features should be recalled from his reply. First of all, he has distinguished between that which applies to a thing in terms of its own mode of being, on the one hand, and that which applies to it only insofar as it is present to a knowing power, on the other. Secondly, equally crucial to his reply is the distinction between divine duration or eternity, on the one hand, and creaturely duration or time, on the other. Given these two points, he can insist that while all things are eternally present to God insofar as they are known by him in accord with his eternal mode of being, they also unfold in time in accord with their own modes of being. Failure to take both of these points seriously may account, at least in part, for some recent criticisms of Thomas's reply to this seventh objection.[22]

Before moving to the next major part of my paper, I should mention that the general thinking found in this article from the *De veritate* is closely paralleled by an even earlier discussion in Thomas's Commentary on I *Sentences* (d. 38, qu. 1, art. 5). The similarity applies in large measure even to the major objections and replies we have just examined in the *De veritate*.[23] Moreover, one finds essentially the same general solution with many of the same objections and replies in major later treatments, such as SCG I, cc. 66–67 (ca. 1259–1261, for Bk I);[24] *Summa theologiae* I, qu. 14, art. 13 (ca. 1266–1268);[25] *De malo*, qu. 16, a. 7 (after Nov., 1267, and inserted into this set of Disputed Questions at a later date);[26] and *Compendium theologiae* I, ch. 133 (ca. 1269–1273).[27]

3. FUTURE CONTINGENTS AND HUMAN FREEDOM IN THOMAS'S COMMENTARY ON THE *DE INTERPRETATIONE*

In addition to these, Thomas's Commentary on ch. 9 of the *De interpretatione* merits special attention. This Commentary seems to date from ca. 1270–1271. It has been shown that while writing it Thomas made considerable use of earlier commentaries by Boethius and by Ammonius.[28] In commenting on ch. 9 Thomas devotes three *lectiones* to the question of future contingents. In brief, in *Lectio* 13 he asks, following Aristotle, whether individual propositions concerning the future are either determinately true or determinately false. He agrees with Aristotle that individual propositions concerning the past or present are either determinately true or determinately false (see n. 167).[29] He notes that individual propositions concerning that which is necessary are either determinately true or determinately false when they deal with the future, just as they are when they have to do with the past or present (see n. 168). But what of individual propositions concerning future contingents? Here he also agrees with Aristotle that such are neither true nor false in determined fashion.[30] He will not conclude from this, however, that they are entirely devoid of truth value.

As Thomas interprets Aristotle, the Stagirite reaches this conclusion by showing that to defend the opposite, that is, to hold that individual propositions concerning future contingents are determinately true or determinately false, will lead to unacceptable consequences – that is, to some kind of fatalism or determinism. If it is necessary to hold that every affirmation or negation concerning individual future events is determinately true or false, it is also necessary to maintain that he who affirms or denies them determinately speaks truly or falsely. From this it will follow that every such event will be controlled by necessity (*ex necessitate*).[31] Such a conclusion would exclude three kinds of contingents: (1) those that happen by chance or fortune; (2) those that are equally open to opposites and which result from choice; (3) those which happen in the majority of cases.[32] Because Aristotle finds such exclusion of contingency completely unacceptable, comments Thomas, he must reject the position which leads to such absurdity.[33] On the other hand, Thomas also warns that one should not conclude from this that in individual contingent propositions concerning the future neither opposite is true. If such were the case, we could then only say of such a contingent that it neither will be nor will it not be.[34]

If we may bypass *Lectio* 14 for a moment, in *Lectio* 15 Thomas continues his commentary on Aristotle's text and finds him eventually reversing his earlier procedure in this same ch. 9. Instead of reasoning from propositions about future contingents to things themselves and arriving at an impasse, Aristotle now reasons from the way in which truth and necessity apply to things and then only back to the status of propositions concerning them. In brief, Thomas finds Aristotle distinguishing between absolute necessity and necessity *ex suppositione*. It is one thing to say that a thing necessarily is (and thus to assign absolute necessity to it). It is another to say that a thing necessarily is when it is. This is to assign necessity *ex suppositione* to it.[35] So too, that which is not absolutely necessary in itself becomes necessary under the supposition that its opposite is negated (*per disiunctionem oppositi*). This follows because it is necessary of each and everything either that it is or that it is not; and again, that it will be or that it will not be. These statements are true when they are taken disjunctively.[36] As regards statements concerning future contingents, therefore, one cannot say determinately that there will be a sea battle tomorrow, or determinately that there will not be. But one can say that the following statement is true when taken disjunctively: it is necessarily the case either that there will be a sea battle tomorrow or that there will not be.[37]

Of greater interest for my immediate purpose, however, is the section from *Lectio* 14 where Thomas goes far beyond Aristotle's text in order to meet objections against human freedom. Thomas directs considerable attention to two such objections. One is based on God's knowledge and the other on God's volition. According to the first, since God's knowledge is infallible, whatever he knows must take place. According to the second, since the divine will cannot be without effect, all that God wills must happen necessarily.[38] Before replying to each of these in turn, Thomas remarks that each objection mistakenly assumes that God's knowledge or God's willing is like our own. In other words, each objection is guilty of anthropomorphism. Against this Thomas counters that divine knowledge and divine willing are very different from our own (*cum tamen multo dissimiliter se habeant*).[39]

Thomas's reply to the objection against freedom based on divine knowledge is very similar to that which we have already examined from other sources. Again he contrasts the temporal character of human knowledge with the eternity of divine knowledge. Because our knowledge is subject to temporal succession, we cannot know future things as they are in themselves but only through their causes. If they are totally determined so as to follow necessarily from their causes, we can have certain knowledge of them. If they are not so determined to follow from their causes, we cannot know them; for something is not knowable insofar as it is in potency but only insofar as it is in act (n. 194).[40] In contrast, God's knowledge is eternal and therefore *tota simul*. All that unfolds in time is eternally grasped by God through one single act of intuition. By this single intuition he sees all that takes place over the course of time, and he sees each particular thing as it exists in itself. He does not, therefore, merely see or understand things as they exist in their causes.[41]

In replying to the objection against human freedom based on the divine will, Thomas continues to stress the difference between God's way of willing and ours. The divine will exists outside the order of created beings as a cause that produces every other being and every difference within created being. But the possible and the necessary are differences within the realm of being. Therefore, both necessity and contingency arise from the divine will. The divine will disposes necessary causes to produce those effects which it wills to be necessary. And it orders causes which act contingently to produce effects which it wills to be contingent. Even though all effects depend upon the divine will as upon their first cause, effects are said to be necessary or contingent by reason of the nature of their proximate causes. The first cause itself transcends the order of necessity and contingency. Such cannot be said, however, of the human will or of any creaturely cause. Every such cause falls under the order of necessity or contingency. Hence every such cause either can fail to produce its effect (which effect is therefore contingent), or else it cannot fail to produce its effect. Such an effect will therefore be necessary. The divine will, on the other hand, cannot fail. Nonetheless, not all of its effects are necessary; some are contingent.[42]

Thomas's reply to this objection may serve as a point of transition to the next section of this chapter.

4. THE CAUSAL CHARACTER OF GOD'S KNOWLEDGE AND GOD'S WILL

In the preceding parts of this chapter I have concentrated on Thomas's attempt to reconcile divine knowledge with the freedom of future contingents. Central to Thomas's proposed solution is his view that in the strict sense nothing is future for God. Because of God's eternal mode of being, every creature and every creaturely activity is eternally present to him. This holds whether that creature or its activity is past or present or future from our perspective. In a word, Thomas seems to have reduced the problem of divine knowledge of free future contingents to the problem of God's knowledge of free present contingents.

Still, even if accepted, this procedure seems to leave a major metaphysical problem unexamined. According to Aquinas, God's knowledge and God's providence are in some way causal in character. To the extent that divine knowledge causes creatures and, more important for our purposes, the actions of creatures, the problem of safeguarding a place for free creaturely activity becomes more complex. It is this aspect of the problem that one does not find examined in Boethius's *Consolation of Philosophy*. And it is to this that we must now turn.

In his earliest works and continuing throughout his career, Thomas steadfastly maintains the causal character of God's knowledge.[43] For instance, in his Commentary on I *Sentences* (dist. 38, qu. 1, art. 1), Thomas observes that science taken simply as science does not necessarily cause objects. Otherwise, all science would be causal. But insofar as the science is that of an artist who is making something, science may be said to be causal with respect to that which is produced by means of the art of that artist. Thomas develops this analogy in order to clarify the causal character of divine science.

In the case of a human artist, the artist's knowledge presents an end that is to be attained. The artist's will intends the end, and finally commands that the appropriate act or acts be performed to produce the artifact. In sum, while science enters into the production of the artifact by manifesting the end, the will does so by directing the artist's productive activity.[44] In developing his position in a parallel passage from the *De veritate* (qu. 2, art. 14), Thomas comments that one should either maintain that science causes that which is known, or else that the thing known causes science, or else that both are caused by something else. He notes that one cannot hold that the things known by God are the causes of his knowledge; they are temporal and God's knowledge is eternal. Nor can one say that both God's knowledge and the objects known by him are caused by any other single cause; for nothing in God can be caused. Therefore, God's science is the cause of things.[45]

In this same context Thomas again remarks that science *qua* science is not in itself an efficient cause, just as form *qua* form is not. Form rather exercises its causality by perfecting that in which it resides. But action, and therefore efficient causal activity, involves the production of something that flows forth from an agent. Given this, a form can serve as a principle of such productive activity only by means of some power. Hence nothing will be efficiently caused by the science of a knower except by means of that knower's will. Will of its very nature implies some kind of influx with respect to the thing willed. To this Thomas adds a second point. While God is the first cause of everything else, effects also proceed from God by means of second causes. Therefore, between God's science which is the first cause of things and those things themselves there may be two intermediaries: one from the side of God – the divine will; and another from the side of creatures – those second causes which enter into the production of so many effects.[46] As Thomas succinctly sums up the first point in *Summa theologiae* I, qu. 14, art. 8, God's science causes things insofar as his science is conjoined with his will to produce them. Thomas must make this precision, of course, in order to distinguish between God's knowledge of pure possibles, on the one hand, and God's knowledge of actual existents (whether past, present, or future), on the other.[47] One may still wonder, however, whether the causal character of God's science when it is conjoined with the divine will leaves any place for free creaturely activity.

In discussing God's knowledge of future contingents in his Commentary on I *Sentences* (d. 38, qu. 1, art. 5), Thomas had noted that one might think that contingents do not fall under divine knowledge for either of two reasons:

either because God's knowledge is an unchanging cause of things, or because God's knowledge must be certain. Thomas's answer to the second difficulty – that based on the certitude of God's knowledge and which Thomas himself here seems to regard as the more serious – is essentially the same as that we have already examined in the first part of this study.[48] His answer to the first difficulty – that based on the causal character of divine knowledge – is much like his later reply in his Commentary on the *De interpretatione*, ch. 9.[49] In brief, he reasons that when various causes are ordered (*ordinatae*) to one another so as to produce a given effect, that effect is not to be regarded as contingent or as necessary by reason of its first cause but by reason of its proximate cause. This is so because the power of a first cause is received in a second cause in accord with the mode of the latter. Thus God's science is the unchanging cause of all other things. But effects are often produced by God through the activities of second causes. Therefore, by means of necessarily acting second causes God produces necessary effects. And by means of contingently acting second causes God produces contingent effects. Presumably, Thomas would have us conclude that by means by freely acting second causes God produces free effects.[50]

In order to appreciate more fully Thomas's thinking on this, it may be helpful for us to recall the broader context of his views concerning the relationship that obtains between God as first cause and the activities performed by any created or second cause. Thomas has worked this out in considerable detail in qu. 3, art. 7 of the *De potentia* (1265–1267), and his discussion there is more or less paralleled by that found in his slightly later *Summa theologiae* I, qq. 104–105 (1266–1268). While much of Thomas's discussion in the text from the *De potentia* is especially concerned with the ways in which God intervenes in the operations of nature, his remarks also apply to God's role in free activities performed by created wills.[51] Thomas begins by reporting and then refuting two different forms of occasionalism, one of which he attributes to the *loquentes in lege Maurorum* on the authority of Moses Maimonides, and the other to Avicebron.[52]

Thomas next distinguishes four different ways in which God may be said to cause the actions performed by creatures: (1) by giving to the created agent the power by means of which it acts or, in other words, by creating the creature's active power; (2) by continuously sustaining or conserving in being this created power; (3) by moving or applying the creaturely operative power to its activity; (4) by serving as principal cause with respect to that of which the created agent is an instrumental cause. Near the end of the corpus of this same article Thomas expresses the fourth way in slightly different terms, explaining that it is by God's power that every other power acts.[53] Thomas comments that if we join to all of this the fact that God is identical with his power (*virtus*) and that he is present to every creature by keeping it in being, we may conclude that God himself operates immediately in the activities performed by creatures, including their acts of volition.[54]

In the parallel discussion in the *Summa theologiae* Thomas follows a somewhat different procedure. In qu. 104, aa. 1–2 he discusses God's conservation of creatures. In qu. 105, a. 5, while defending the fact that God intervenes in the activities performed by created agents, Thomas notes that three of the four causes can in some way be regarded as principles of action. Accordingly, God works in the causal activities exercised by other agents (1) by serving as their final cause (insofar as every other operation is for the sake of some real or apparent good, and nothing can serve as such a good except insofar as it participates in some likeness of the Supreme Good, God himself); (2) by serving as an efficient cause insofar as second causes act by reason of the first cause, which moves them to act; (3) insofar as God gives to creatures the forms which serve as their principles of operation and keeps these forms in being. (An interesting difference between this treatment and that in the *De potentia* is the fact that here Thomas correlates created agents and God as second causes and first cause respectively rather than as instrumental causes and principal cause. To correlate them as second causes and first cause seems less likely to run the risk of robbing creaturely causes of their proper causal activity, something Thomas would never permit one to do.)[55]

For our immediate purposes we may combine the third and fourth ways in which, according to the *De potentia*, God works in the actions performed by creatures. God moves the creaturely power to act (or applies it to action), and he serves as first cause with respect to those effects of which creatures are, properly speaking, second causes, according to the terminology from the *Summa*.[56] In other words, in moving any created power to act, God does so in such fashion that he is the first cause of that creature's action, while the created cause is itself a proper but second cause of that same action. Thomas would not have us take this to mean that God causes one part of the action or the effect, and the creature another part, as for instance, an elephant and a horse might combine to pull the same wagon. At times Thomas makes this point by insisting that any such action is to be attributed entirely to God as its first cause, and entirely to the created agent as its second cause.[57]

If this is Thomas's general view concerning God's role in causal activities exercised by creaturely or second causes, does he apply the same to freely acting creatures and hence to human volition? Indeed he does. Not only does God cause the free volitions of the human will insofar as he creates and sustains in being both man and his will; God causes man's acts of volition. In fact, in art. 4 of qu. 105 of the *Summa theologiae*, Thomas argues that God can move the human will by serving as its object (and hence as its final cause) in that God alone is the universal good capable of moving man's will both sufficiently and efficaciously. But in addition to this, Thomas also holds that God moves the will efficiently, by inclining it from within. Thomas assigns special priority to this interior divine causing of the will's action in that same passage,[58] and strongly defends God's efficient causation of human volition in other contexts. For instance, in the key passage from *De potentia*, qu. 3, a. 7, Thomas has stated that God immediately works in every created agent, including the activity of the will.[59]

In the *Summa contra gentiles*, Bk I, ch. 68, Thomas maintains that God knows the inner motions of the will. By knowing his essence God knows all that to which his causality extends. But his causality extends to the operations of both the intellect and the will. In other words, God causes, as first cause to be sure, the acts of the human will. Near the end of this same chapter, Thomas argues that God's causation of our acts of willing does not destroy the fact that the will has dominion over its own acts. If the will were by its nature determined only to one thing, or if it were subject to violence from an external agent, its capacity to will or not will would be destroyed. But such is not destroyed by the influence of a higher cause which gives it both its being and its operation. Hence God is the first cause of the motions of the will.[60]

In SGG III, ch. 88, Thomas comments that the only kind of agent that can cause the motion of the will without doing violence to it is that which causes the intrinsic principle of this same motion, that is to say, the very power of the will itself. This is God, since he alone creates the soul. Because of this, he alone can move the will as an agent. Or as Thomas puts it in ch. 89, not only is the power of the will caused by God; so is its very act of willing. Here Thomas appeals to his broader metaphysical claim that no agent can act by its own power unless it also acts by the power of God (see SCG III, cc. 67, 70). But that by whose power an agent acts not only causes that agent's power, but the acts performed by that power as well. Hence God causes the created will's acts of volition.[61]

Thomas is aware of objections which might be raised against human freedom because of this position. For instance, in replying to some of these in *De potentia*, qu. 3, art. 7, he counters that the fact that the human will has dominion over its action does not exclude the causal influence of the first cause. It rather means that the first cause does not so act on the will as to determine it of necessity to one thing rather than another (ad 13).[62] Again he reasons, not every cause excludes freedom in that which it causes but only one that is compelling (*cogens*). It is not in this way that God is the cause of our volitions (ad 14).[63] Or as he puts it in ST I, qu. 19, a. 8, not only do those things happen which God wills to happen; they happen in the way he wills them to happen. He wills some things to happen necessarily, and others to happen contingently. Here Thomas adds an interesting precision. It is not because proximate causes are contingent that certain effects which are willed by God happen contingently. It is rather that because God wills them to happen contingently, he has prepared contingent causes for them.[64] Even so, it does not follow from this that all that is willed by God is absolutely necessary. Such things have the kind of necessity God wills them to have, which may be either absolute or only conditional (ad 3).

In ST I, qu. 83, a. 1, Thomas replies to the following objection. Whatever is moved by something else is not free. But God moves the will. Therefore, man is not free. In replying Thomas notes that the will is a cause of its own motion, since by means of free will man moves himself to act. Still, adds Thomas, the presence of freedom does not require that a free agent be the first cause of its own motion. Thus, for something to be regarded as the cause of something else, it need not be a first cause; it can be a second cause. So too, God, as first cause, moves both natural agents and voluntary agents. Just as his moving natural causes does not destroy the fact that they are causes, neither does his moving voluntary agents destroy the fact that they are still voluntary causes. Rather, he moves each in accord with its nature.[65]

This seems to be Thomas's final philosophical word on this point. God moves every created agent to act in accord with its nature. He moves freely acting agents to act in accord with their nature, which is to say, freely. Neither the certitude of divine science nor the causal character of the divine will detracts from man's freedom. In fact, remarks Aquinas, it would be more repugnant to the divine motion if the created will were thereby moved to act necessarily rather than to act freely. Only the latter kind of divine motion is in accord with the nature of the created will.[66]

5. DIVINE SCIENCE, DIVINE WILL AND FUTURE CONTINGENTS IN HENRY OF GHENT

In the final part of this chapter I shall concentrate on Henry's account of

God's knowledge of future events, including future contingents. Since medieval times and continuing onward into the twentieth century there has been disagreement about a particular feature of Aquinas's position. Mention of this will serve to set the stage for our consideration of Henry. In brief, the problem reduces to this. In order to account for the fact that God knows future contingents, does Aquinas appeal to God's eternal mode of being and hence to the eternal presence of future contingents to God's knowledge? Or does Thomas rather appeal to the eternal and determining decrees of the divine will?[67] Without delaying here over this controversy among interpreters of Aquinas, we should recall that both points have appeared in texts examined above.[68] Nonetheless, if we ask Thomas how it is and why it is that God can know things that are future for us, it seems to me that Thomas appeals to their eternal presence in their divine knower. Because they are eternally present to God they can be known with certainty by him, and as they are in themselves.[69]

As we turn to Henry of Ghent's Quodlibet VII, qu. 2 of Christmas, 1284, a subtle shift seems to have occurred. In both qq. 1 and 2 of this particular Quodlibet Henry is much concerned with divine science. In qu. 1 he asks whether there are practical ideas in God.[70] Strictly speaking, he replies, practical ideas are not to be admitted in God. One can allow for practical ideas in God when they are taken in a broader sense, as an 'extension' of his speculative knowledge and ideas.[71] As far as Henry is concerned, if by practical knowledge one means that an agent must do that which he judges to be advantageous for himself, no such knowledge can be admitted of God. Henry will permit one to speak of practical knowledge in God when, as we have noted, this is taken in a broader sense and as an extension of divine speculative knowledge. By such knowledge God knows that certain things might or might not be done insofar as they are fitting or appropriate for the rest of creation. But even here, insists Henry, God remains perfectly free to choose or not to choose to act accordingly.[72]

In qu. 2 Henry wonders whether change or variation (*difformitas*) in things known by God will result in any change in God's knowledge.[73] Here Henry distinguishes between God's knowledge of creatures solely in terms of their essences or natures, and his knowledge of things insofar as they are to be made or done by him, that is to say, his practical knowledge of them in the qualified sense just mentioned. The first kind of divine knowledge is purely speculative.[74] Through the second kind of knowledge God knows that certain things will be made or done by him by knowing the determination of his own will. In this case the divine will itself is the foundation and cause of God's knowledge of such things, rather than vice versa.[75] Henry comments that this is why the philosophers, who hold that God produces things only by his intellect and of necessity, can much more readily postulate practical knowledge in God. Such is not so easy for the theologians, who must defend God's freedom in creating.[76]

Though Henry goes on to develop in considerable detail his explanation of both kinds of divine knowledge, here I shall concentrate on his understanding of the second – God's knowledge of things that are to be made or done by him. Several times Henry repeats the point that God knows such things by knowing the determination of his will, which will itself is unchanging. Henry stresses the point that God does not depend for his knowledge of such things on the reality of those things themselves but, to repeat, on the determination or decrees of his will. It is this that establishes or serves as the foundation for his knowledge of the things he is to bring to pass. By knowing the eternal and unchanging decree of his will, God knows in uniform fashion all creatures taken as individuals. He knows that they are when they in fact are, and that they are not when they are not. By one single intuition God also knows what individual he will produce at any given moment of time, again because he knows the eternal decree of his will.[77]

If one were to stop here, there could be little doubt that Henry grounds God's knowledge of future things on the determination of the divine will. But then Henry attempts to develop the point that God knows in uniform fashion things that are when they are, and things that are not when they are not. Here Henry introduces the theme of divine eternity. Granted that in its actual existence time flows with motion, still by reason of its essence time (and motion as well) stand as fixed before the science of God. God simultaneously sees all things, both in themselves and in their relations with one another, when they actually exist.[78] But he does this in his eternal now. Hence, things which flow with the course of time stand fixed simultaneously before the divine vision. Therefore, all things which pass through time are present to God's knowledge from eternity. This holds, continues Henry, not only because their divine ideas exist in the divine intellect and because of God's eternal knowledge of the determination of his will concerning such things. It also holds because God's vision bears upon all such things from eternity insofar as they are eternally present to him (*in sua praesentialitate*).[79]

At this juncture one might wonder whether Henry has now shifted his position and introduced the eternal presence of things to their divine knower as the means whereby God knows future things. But here Henry interjects a note of caution. One should not take this as implying, he warns, that such creatures actually exist in themselves from eternity. Their eternal presence to their divine knower does not of itself entail anything more than that they exist in the divine knowledge. In other words, it is one thing to say that God knows things as eternally present to him; it is another to say that such things exist from eternity. The second does not follow from the first. As Henry puts it, this eternal presentness of things to God does not imply their actual extramental existence, but only that they are present in their cause from eternity, a cause which is not only productive of them but which also knows them.[80]

Henry's reservations concerning this point may well have been occasioned by William de la Mare's *Correctorium* and his criticism therein of Thomas Aquinas's discussion in ST I, qu. 14, a. 13.[81] This seems most likely since some of Henry's language reflects not only Thomas's text but William's critique of the same. In the *Summa* Thomas had written: "Wherefore, all things which are in time are present to God from eternity not only because he has the *rationes* of these things present to himself, as some say, but because his vision is directed to all things from eternity (*ab aeterno*) as they are in their presentness".[82] Because of this, Thomas had argued, contingents are infallibly known by God even though they may still be future for us.[83]

William counters that this passage implies that all contingents and, for that matter, all created necessary things, are produced by God from eternity and in eternity (*ab aeterno in aeternitate*), even though they are also said to be created in time. In support William argues that things may be said to be present to God in only two ways: either as in their causal principle, or in terms of their actual existence. Since Thomas has stated that temporal beings are present to God and not merely in the first way, William concludes that Thomas must hold that all such things actually exist from eternity and in eternity.[84]

Without explicitly naming him, Henry repeats the key passage from Aquinas and seems to accept it as his own.[85] As we have already seen, Henry argues that this does not imply that temporal beings actually exist in themselves from eternity. He counters that their presentness to God applies to their eternal causal *rationes* in God, which *rationes* themselves account for the fact that such creatures are eternally known by God.[86]

Although Henry's explanation of this could be clearer, he seems to have introduced the theme of divine eternity and of the eternal presence of future things in God's knowledge in order to show that changes in this world or in creatures do not entail any kind of change in God's knowledge.[87] His development of the notion of God's eternal knowledge of creatures is evidently deeply indebted to Aquinas. At the same time, Henry seems to be sensitive to William's critique. Even though he refuses to admit that a proper understanding of the eternal presence of things to God's knowledge will result in defending their actual eternal existence, he is hard pressed to justify his refusal. What he seems to have done is to compromise Thomas's view that because of their eternal presence to God as their knower, God views all creatures, including those that are still future for us, as they are in themselves, not merely as they exist in God as their productive cause. This may be because Henry, like William, does not really grasp the significance of Thomas's claim that whatever is known is known according to the mode of being of its knower. In any event, Henry does not seem to have abandoned his earlier statements in this same question to this effect, that the ultimate foundation which accounts for God's knowledge of future things is his knowledge of the eternal decrees of his will.[88]

6. CONCLUSION

While both the notions of eternity and the causal character of the divine will have entered into Thomas's account of God's knowledge of contingents and into Henry's there are considerable differences between the two. According to Thomas, it is because things are eternally present to the divine mind that God can know future contingents with certainty and as they are in themselves. It is also true, of course, that for such events to be realized in actuality in the course of time, the divine will must intervene; but this is required to account for their actual existence, not for God's knowledge of them. According to Henry, it is because God knows the eternal decrees of his will that he knows with certainty the things he will produce and, therefore, things that are future for us. Even so, in order to avoid introducing any change into God's knowledge, Henry has also drawn upon the concept of eternity. Whether his account will allow for divine knowledge of such things as they are in themselves, or only as they are in God, their productive cause, might well be questioned.

NOTES

1 On Henry's life and career see R. Macken (ed.), *Henrici de Gandavo Quodlibet I* Leuven University Press, Louvain-Leiden 1979, pp. vii–xxiv. For a comparison of Thomas, Henry, and Duns Scotus on the question of divine foreknowledge of future

contingents see H. Schwamm, *Das göttliche Vorherwissen bei Duns Scotus und seinen ersten Anhängern*, Philosophie und Grenzwissenschaften V, Innsbruck 1934, especially pp. 91–108.

[2] For what continues to be the best overall account of Henry's metaphysical thought see J. Paulus, *Henri de Gand. Essai sur les tendances de sa métaphysique*, J. Vrin, Paris 1938.

[3] 'Duodecimo quaeritur utrum Deus sciat singularia futura contingentia', in *S. Thomae Aquinatis Quaestiones Disputatae. Vol. I: De veritate*, R. Spiazzi (ed.), Turin-Rome 1953, p. 52. For the same in the Leonine edition see *Sancti Thomae de Aquino opera omnia*, T. 22, vol. 1, Rome 1975, p. 81. Here I shall normally cite from the first-mentioned edition (Marietti), although all citations have been compared with the Leonine edition.

[4] Ed. cit., p. 53.

[5] *Ibid.* Thomas illustrates this with our knowledge that the sun will rise, or that an eclipse will occur.

[6] *Ibid.* Cf. *In I Sent.*, d. 38, qu. 1, art. 5 (*Sciptum super libros Sententiarum*, P. Mandonnet (ed.), T. 1 [Paris, 1929], p. 910). There Thomas distinguishes three situations. Before a thing exists it enjoys being only in its causes. But these may be causes (1) from which an effect necessarily follows in the sense that they (the causes) cannot be impeded; or (2) causes from which an effect usually follows; or (3) causes which are open to both possibilities. We can have science (certain knowledge) concerning future effects which follow from the first kind of cause, conjectural knowledge concerning the second, and no knowledge in the proper sense concerning the third. But as regards effects which follow from the third type of cause, once they have actually been realized in their own determined being, they can be known with certainty.

[7] " . . . unde cum divinae scientiae non subsit falsitas nec subesse possit, impossibile esset quod de contingentibus futuris scientiam haberet Deus, si cognosceret ea ut futura sunt" (ed. cit., p. 53). Also see ad 6 (p. 54). Cf. *In I Sent.* (p. 910): "et ideo contingentia ad utrumlibet in causis suis nullo modo cognosci possunt".

[8] Ed. cit., pp. 53–54. In *In I Sent.*, d. 38, qu. 1, a. 5, Thomas offers a slightly different illustration. Suppose that five different human observers saw five different events successively over a period of five hours. One can say that the five saw these contingent events successively as present to each of them. Now suppose that these five cognitive acts on the part of our observers could become one act of cognition. It could then be said that there was one cognition of these five successive events as present to that single knowing act (ed. cit., p. 911).

[9] *De veritate*, p. 54. For much the same see *In I Sent.*, d. 38, qu. 1, art. 5 (pp. 910–911). There Thomas explicitly makes the point that the divine intellect knows from eternity every contingent not only as it exists in its causes (and hence as potential or as capable of being brought into being), but also as it is in its determined being. Otherwise one would have to say that God's knowledge of such a thing changes when that thing passes from potential being to actual being.

[10] *De veritate*, p. 54.

[11] "Difficultas autem in hoc accidit eo quod divinam cognitionem significare non possumus nisi per modum nostrae cognitionis consignificando differentias" (*De veritate*, p. 54). According to the Leonine edition's preferred reading, it is differences in time that are cosignified ('temporum differentias', p. 84).

[12] See *De veritate*, qu. 2, art. 11. The literature on Thomas's doctrine of analogy is vast. For an excellent discussion of this in Thomas and for much of the earlier bibliography see B. Montagnes, *La doctrine de l'analogie de l'être d'après saint Thomas d'Aquin*, Publications Universitaires, Louvain 1963. For the unusual character of his defense of analogy of proportionality in the *De veritate* see especially pp. 65–93.

[13] *De veritate*, p. 54. Cf. *In I Sent.*, d. 38, qu. 1, art. 5, pp. 911–912 for much the same. In both contexts Thomas explicitly acknowledges his debt to Boethius. For this in Boethius see *The Consolation of Philosophy*, in H. F. Stewart and E. K. Rand, *Boethius. The Theological Tractates and the Consolation of Philosophy*, Harvard University Press, Cambridge, Mass. 1968, Bk V, pr. 6, pp. 398–410. On this in Boethius see E. Stump and N. Kretzmann, 'Eternity', *The Journal of Philosophy* 78 (1981), 429–458; J. Groblicki, *De scientia Dei futurorum contingentium secundum S. Thomam eiusque primos sequaces*, Krakow 1938, pp. 40–44.

[14] *De ver.*, pp. 52, 54. For the same objection and essentially the same reply see *In I Sent.*, loc. cit., p. 907 (obj. 2), and p. 912 (ad 2).

[15] *De veritate*, p. 52 (obj. 4); p. 54 (ad 4).

[16] *De veritate*, p. 52 (obj. 5); p. 54 (ad 5). For the same reply see *In I Sent.*, p. 908 (obj. 5); pp. 914–915 (ad 5).

[17] *De veritate*, p. 52 (obj. 7). Cf. *In I Sent.*, pp. 907–908 (obj. 4).

[18] For these see *De veritate*, p. 55 (ad 7). Compare with the inadequate solutions discussed in *In I Sent* , d. 38, qu. 1, a. 5, ad 4, pp. 912–914.

[19] *De veritate*, p. 55. Note that this particular point is brought out much more fully here than in the parallel discussion in *In I Sent.*, where it appears only implicitly at best (p. 914). However, it is clearly implied by Boethius in an earlier part of Bk V of his *Consolation*. See pr. 4 (op. cit., p. 388: 75–77): "Omne enim quod cognoscitur non secundum sui vim sed secundum cognoscentium potius comprehenditur facultatem'.

[20] *De veritate*, p. 55. Also note Thomas's concluding remark in his reply to objection 9 (objection 8 in the Leonine ed.): ". . . sic enim non loquimur nunc de cognitione futuri, prout scilicet a Deo in suis causis videtur, sed in quantum cognoscitur in seipso; sic enim cognoscitur ut praesens".

[21] In other contexts, such as *De veritate*, qu. 24, art. 1, ad 13, Thomas identifies absolute necessity with *necessitas consequentis*, and contrasts this with conditioned necessity (*necessitas consequentiae*). See ed. cit., p. 436: "Ad decimumtertium dicendum, quod ex praescientia Dei non potest concludi quod actus nostri sint necessarii necessitate absoluta, quae dicitur necessitas consequentis; sed necessitate conditionata, quae dicitur necessitas consequentiae, ut patet per Boëtium in fine *de Consol. philosophiae*". Also see SCG I, ch. 67. For a fuller discussion of the difference between 'logical' necessity or contingency, on the one hand, and 'ontological' necessity or contingency, on the other, see H. J. McSorley, *Luther: Right or Wrong*, New York, N.Y. and Minneapolis 1969, pp. 150–153. McSorley concedes that this precise terminology is not that of Aquinas.

[22] See A. Kenny, 'Divine Foreknowledge and Human Freedom,' in *Aquinas. A Collection of Critical Essays*, A. Kenny, (ed.), Doubleday, Garden City, N.Y. 1969, pp. 262–264. Kenny finds the notion of 'timeless eternity' rather hopeless. As regards the first point, he does not clearly connect Thomas's distinction between *necessitas consequentis* and *necessitas consequentiae* with the distinction between that which applies to a thing in terms of its own mode of being and that which applies to it only insofar as it is present to a knowing power. For another writer who has difficulty with Thomas's and

Boethius's views concerning the eternal character of divine knowledge see P. Streveler, 'The Problem of Future Contingents: A Medieval Discussion,' *The New Scholasticism* **47** (1973), pp. 238–240, 246. He seems to regard as more fruitful Kenny's suggestion that doubt should be cast "upon our belief that the past is somehow necessary in a way that the future is not" (p. 241). Without pausing here to discuss this point at length, it seems to me that Aquinas would assign to a past event the same kind of necessity that he assigns to a present event, that is, conditioned necessity (*necessitas consequentiae*) or necessity *ex suppositione*. See *De veritate*, qu. 2, art. 12, ad 7: "Quamvis autem res in seipsa, sit futura, tamen secundum modum cognoscentis est praesens; et ideo magis esset dicendum: Si Deus scit aliquid, illud est; quam: Hoc erit; unde idem est iudicium de ista: Si Deus scit aliquid, hoc erit; et de hac: Si ego video Socratem currere, Socrates currit: quorum utrumque est necessarium dum est". (p. 55). Granted that here Thomas explicitly refers to God's knowing something rather than to his having known it, Thomas has already explained that for God there is no past. Since any event that is temporally past in itself is eternally present to God, it enjoys the same kind of necessity as any present event that is perceived by us. Under the supposition that it is happening (or has happened), it is happening (or has happened). This does not imply that it is absolutely or ontologically necessary in itself. For a critical reaction to Kenny's critique see W. Mulligan, 'Divine Foreknowledge and Freedom: A Note on a Problem of Language', *The Thomist* **36** (1972), 293–299.

[23] A number of these parallels have already been pointed out in preceding notes. Unlike the discussion in the *De veritate*, however, Thomas begins his response in *In I Sent.* by distinguishing two major kinds of reasons which might be offered against the possibility of reconciling God's knowledge with future contingents. A first approach would reject this possibility because of the relationship that obtains between a cause and its effect. Because God's science is the cause of things, and because a necessary effect seems to result from a necessary and unchangeable cause, the possibility of any kind of contingent effect would seem to be eliminated. A second approach would be based on the relationship between science and its object. Because science is certain knowledge, it seems to require certitude and determination in that which is known. We shall defer consideration of Thomas's discussion and refutation of the first approach for the next sections of this study. It is in addressing himself to the second kind of objection, which he here regards as the more difficult, that Thomas proposes the solution we have already examined from the *De veritate*. See *In I Sent.*, pp. 909ff. Also see M. Benz, 'Das göttliche Vorherwissen des freien Willensakte des Geschöpfe bei Thomas von Aquin. *In I Sent.*, d. 38. q. 1 a. 5, '*Divus Thomas* (Freib.) **14** (1936), 255–273; **15** (1937), 415–432.

[24] In ch. 66 Thomas is attempting to account for the fact that God can know non-existent entities. Here again he stresses the point that because of his eternity God's knowledge is not subject to any kind of successive duration. Divine eternity is present to all parts or instants of time, even as the center of a circle, being outside its circumference, bears an equal relationship to all points on that circumference. Consequently: "Quicquid igitur in quacumque parte temporis est, coexistit aeterno quasi praesens eidem: etsi respectu alterius partis temporis sit praeteritum vel futurum" (Leonine manual edition, Rome, 1934, p. 61). As regards things which are not yet but will be, God knows them by his *scientia visionis* not only in knowing his own power and in knowing their proper causes, but also in knowing them in themselves. In ch. 67 Thomas

explicitly appeals again to the distinction between divine eternity and the temporal duration of creatures to account for God's knowledge of free future contingents. Once more he applies the distinction between *necessitas consequentiae* and *necessitas consequentis* (or between conditional and absolute necessity).

25 In this well known discussion Thomas notes that something contingent can be considered in itself as it now exists in actuality, or only as it exists in its cause and hence as future. Considered in the first way it can be an object of certain knowledge, even on the level of sense perception. Considered in the second way, it is not yet determined *ad unum*, and hence cannot be known with certainty by any knower. But God knows all contingents not only in the second way, but also in the first, once again, argues Thomas, because God's knowledge is measured by eternity, just as is his *esse*. See in particular objection 2 and the reply which is essentially the same as his reply to objection 7 in the *De veritate*, qu. 2, art. 12. See his reply to objection 3 for more on the difference between God's eternity and the temporal duration of creatures and for appeal to the difference between the necessary *de dicto* and *de re*. Also cf. ST I, qu. 86, art. 4.

26 On the date of this question in the *De malo* see J. Weisheipl, *Friar Thomas d'Aquino*, Doubleday, Garden City, N.Y. 1974, pp. 363, 366. I have also followed Weisheipl for the datings of Thomas's other works. Art. 7 is directed to the question whether demons can know the future. In replying Thomas again distinguishes between knowing future things in themselves, and in their causes. Only God can know future things in themselves, something that is impossible for knowledge that is subject to the order of time. God knows all things as present to him, since his knowledge is above the temporal order. Also see the reply to obj. 15.

27 See ch. 132 for a series of objections against God's providence concerning particulars, two of which apply to our immediate concern: ('adhuc') there can be no certain knowledge of individual contingents; ('praeterea') not all particulars are simultaneous. For this see *S. Thomae Aquinatis Opuscula Theologica*, Vol. 1, R. Vernardo, (ed.), Turin-Rome 1954, p. 63; and T. 42 (Opuscula III) of the Leonine edition, p. 131. See ch. 133 for Thomas's replies to these objections, replies to which the distinction between divine eternity and temporal duration as realized in creatures is again crucial. In ch. 134 Thomas makes the point that only God can know individual future contingents in themselves ('prout sunt actu in suo esse'), although in some cases creatures can know things that are future insofar as they necessarily follow from their causes, or insofar as it is likely that they will do so. For a fuller discussion of most of the texts cited in the last few notes see J. Groblicki, *De scientia Dei futurorum* . . . , pp. 15–39. Groblicki also considers Thomas's *In de Interpretatione*, ch. 9, for which see below.

28 See Weisheipl, *Friar Thomas d'Aquino*, pp. 374–375. As Weisheipl points out, Thomas commented on the Greek-Latin version of Aristotle accompanied by Ammonius's commentary on the same, the translation of which was completed by William of Moerbeke in September, 1268. For a critical edition of the commentary by Ammonius see G. Verbeke (ed.), *Ammonius. Commentaire sur le Peri Hermeneias d'Aristote. Traduction de Guillaume de Moerbeke*, Publications Universitaires de Louvain, Louvain-Paris 1961. On Thomas's usage of Ammonius in preparing his own commentary see pp. XI–XXXV. Verbeke suggests that Thomas's commentary may have remained unfinished because during the time he was preparing it he did not yet have in his hands the complete translation of Ammonius's commentary (see pp. XXXIII, XXXV). On Thomas's usage of this commentary as well as of that by Boethius see J. Isaac, *Le Peri*

hermeneias en occident de Boèce à Saint Thomas, J. Vrin, Paris 1953, pp. 100–105. As far as Boethius's commentaries are concerned, it seems that Thomas used only the second of these in preparing his own commentary.

[29] See the Leonine edition, R. Spiazzi, (ed.), *In Aristotelis libros Peri Hermeneias et Posteriorum Analyticorum Expositio*, Turin 1964, pp. 64ff. Often in citing it I shall simply list the paragraph numbers in my text or in the notes. For the present point see n. 167: "Unde Philosophus dicit, ex praemissis concludens, quod *in his quae sunt*, idest in propositionibus de praesenti, et *in his quae facta sunt*, idest in enunciationibus de praeterito, necesse est quod affirmatio vel negatio determinate sit vera vel falsa".

[30] *Ibid.*, n. 169. "Sed in singularibus et futuris est quaedam dissimilitudo. Nam in praeteritis et praesentibus necesse est quod altera oppositarum determinate sit vera et altera falsa in quacumque materia; sed in singularibus quae sunt de futuro hoc non est necesse, quod una determinate sit vera et altera falsa. Et hoc quidem dicitur quantum ad materiam contingentem: nam quantum ad materiam necessariam et impossibilem similis ratio est in futuris singularibus, sicut in praesentibus et praeteritis".

[31] N. 171.

[32] Nn. 171–172.

[33] See n. 173, near end.

[34] N. 175.

[35] Nn. 200–201. See in particular: "Et ideo manifeste verum est quod omne quod est necesse est esse quando est; et omne quod non est necesse est non esse pro illo tempore quando non est: et haec est necessitas non absoluta sed ex suppositione. Unde non potest simpliciter et absolute dici quod omne quod est, necesse est esse, et omne quod non est, necesse est non esse: quia non idem significant quod omne ens, quando est, sit ex necessitate, et quod omne ens simpliciter sit ex necessitate; nam primum significat necessitatem ex suppositione, secundum autem necessitatem absolutam" (n. 201).

[36] See n. 201, near end; and n. 202.

[37] See n. 202. Note in particular: " . . . sed necesse est quod vel sit futurum cras vel non sit futurum: hoc enim pertinet ad necessitatem quae est sub disiunctione".

[38] N. 192.

[39] N. 193.

[40] In this same context (n. 194) Thomas notes that we can have conjectural knowledge of the kind of thing that is not so determined to follow from its causes that it cannot be impeded from doing so.

[41] See n. 195. Note in particular: "et ideo uno intuitu videt omnia quae aguntur secundum temporis decursum, et unumquodque secundum quod est in seipso existens, non quasi sibi futurum quantum ad eius intuitum prout est in solo ordine suarum causarum (quamvis et ipsum ordinem causarum videat), sed omnino aeternaliter sic videt unumquodque eorum quae sunt in quocumque tempore . . . ."

[42] See n. 197. Also see Ch. Boyer, 'Providence et liberté dans un texte de saint Thomas (In Perihermeneias, Lib. 1, 2. lect. 13, 14),' *Gregorianum* 19 (1938), pp. 194–209. For much the same, but much more briefly stated, see *De malo*, qu. 16, art. 7, ad 15.

[43] In his Commentary on I *Sentences* Thomas begins to discuss divine science in dist. 35, and continues this through dist. 36. Only after all of this, in dist. 38, qu. 1, art. 1, does he explicitly ask whether God's science is the cause of things (p. 897). After giving an affirmative answer to this, it is in article 5 of that same question that Thomas addresses himself to God's knowledge of future contingents (p. 907). Thomas follows roughly

the same procedure in the much later first Part of the *Summa theologiae*. In qu. 14, art. 1, he discusses the fact that there is divine knowledge. In art. 8 he asks whether God's knowledge causes things and only thereafter, in art. 13, does he consider God's knowledge of future contingents. On the other hand, in qu. 2, art. 1 of the *De veritate* Thomas discusses the fact that science is to be said of God. In a series of subsequent articles he develops his account of divine science. In qu. 2, art. 12, as we have already seen, Thomas discusses God's knowledge of future contingents. But only after all of this, in art. 14, does he finally address himself to the fact that God's knowledge causes things. Unlike the *De veritate*, therefore, in *In I Sent*. and in ST I he had discussed the causal character of God's knowledge before taking up divine knowledge of future contingents.

[44] Ed. cit., p. 899.

[45] Ed. cit., p. 59.

[46] Ed. cit., p. 59.

[47] "Unde necesse est quod sua scientia sit causa rerum, secundum quod habet voluntatem coniunctam" (Leonine edition, prepared by P. Caramello and published by Marietti, Turin-Rome 1950, p. 82). On God's knowledge of pure possibles see, for instance, *De ver*., qu. 2, art. 8 (where Thomas refers to God's knowledge of pure possibles as speculative, and to his knowledge of possibles that were, are, or will be realized in actuality as 'quasi-practical'); ST I, qu. 14, a. 9 (where Thomas refers to God's knowledge of things that were, are, or will be, as his *scientia visionis*, and to his knowledge of pure possibles as his *scientia intelligentiae*). Also see ST I, qu. 15, art. 3, and ad 2 (where Thomas discusses divine ideas insofar as they may be called divine *rationes* – principles whereby God knows creatures; and divine exemplars – principles for God's production of creatures). For more on Thomas's theory of the divine ideas see L. Geiger, 'Les idées divines dans l'oeuvre de s. Thomas', in *St. Thomas Aquinas 1274–1974. Commemorative Studies*, A. Maurer (ed.), Toronto 1974, Vol. 1, pp. 175–209.

[48] See the text cited above in our note 23.

[49] See above in our text pp. 220–221.

[50] Ed. cit., pp. 909–910. Cf. ad 1 (p. 912).

[51] "Respondeo. Dicendum, quod simpliciter concedendum est Deum operari in natura et voluntate operantibus". See *Quaestiones disputatae*. Vol. 2, P. Bazzi (ed.), *et al*., Turin-Rome 1953, p. 56. For a discussion of this text and its parallels see C. Fabro, *Participation et causalité selon S. Thomas d'Aquin*, Publications Universitaires de Louvain, Louvain-Paris 1961, pp. 397–409.

[52] Ed. cit., pp. 56–57.

[53] Ed. cit., pp. 57–58. Note near the end of the corpus: "Sic ergo Deus est causa actionis cuiuslibet in quantum dat virtutem agendi, et in quantum conservat eam, et in quantum applicat actioni, et in quantum eius virtute omnis alia virtus agit" (p. 58).

[54] "Et cum coniunxerimus his, quod Deus sit sua virtus, et quod sit intra rem quamlibet non sicut pars essentiae, sed sicut tenens rem in esse, sequetur quod ipse in quolibet operante immediate operetur, non exclusa operatione voluntatis et naturae" (p. 58).

[55] For parallels see SCG III, ch. 67. For texts from the *De potentia*, SCG, and ST see J. de Finance, *Être et agir dans la Philosophie de Saint Thomas*, Librairie éditrice de l'Université Gregorienne, Rome 1960, pp. 232–233. It is not my intention here to enter into a discussion of the appropriateness of the expression 'physical premotion' to describe God's moving influence upon created causes in their activity. For some references and for a brief discussion see de Finance, pp. 230–231, n. 51. Also see F. X. Meehan,

Efficient Causality in Aristotle and St. Thomas, Catholic University of America Press, Washington, D. C. 1940, pp. 299ff; R. Moore, 'Motion divine chez Saint Thomas d'Aquin', *Studia Montis Regii* 1 (1958), pp. 93–137; H. Degl'Innocenti, 'De actione Dei in causas secundas liberas iuxta S. Thomam,' *Aquinas* 4 (1961), pp. 28–56. On the text from ST I, qu. 105, art. 5, see Fabro, op. cit., pp. 499–501. See n. 163 on the change in terminology from the *De potentia* and SCG, on the one hand, to ST, on the other. But, as Fabro notes, the language of 'instrumental' cause to signify second causes reappears in the *Compendium theologiae*, cc. 3, 135. For both usages and for an important distinction between two ways in which creatures may be described as 'instrumental' causes see *De veritate*, qu. 24, art. 1, ad 3; ad 4; ad 5 (ed. cit., p. 435).

56 At the same time Thomas may have in mind by the fourth way (according to the *De potentia*) in which God causes the causal activities performed by creatures an additional point – his view that God alone is the proper and principal cause of *esse*, and that creatures can cause *esse* only insofar as they act as 'instruments' of God. For this see Fabro, pp. 401–402, 468–488; Meehan, pp. 298–302. This could lead to the interesting question whether Aquinas admits that creatures can cause *esse*, a point which cannot be pursued here.

57 See SCG III, ch. 70. Note in particular: "Sicut igitur non est inconveniens quod una actio producatur ex aliquo agente et eius virtute, ita non est inconveniens quod producatur idem effectus ab inferiori agente et Deo: ab utroque immediate, licet alio et alio modo . . . . Patet etiam quod non sic idem effectus causae naturali et divinae virtuti attributitur quasi partim a Deo, et partim a naturali agente fiat, sed totus ab utroque secundum alium modum: sicut idem effectus totus attribuitur instrumento, et principali agenti etiam totus" (ed. cit., p. 306).

58 ST I, qu. 105, art. 4. Note in particular: "Potest autem voluntas moveri sicut ab obiecto, a quocumque bono; non tamen sufficienter et efficaciter nisi a Deo . . . . Similiter autem et virtus volendi a solo Deo causatur. Velle enim nihil aliud est quam inclinatio quaedam in obiectum voluntatis, quod est bonum universale. Inclinare autem in bonum universale est primi moventis, cui proportionatur ultimus finis . . . Unde utroque modo proprium est Dei movere voluntatem: sed maxime secundo modo, interius eam inclinando" (ed. cit., p. 498).

59 See n. 54 above.

60 Ed. cit., p. 64.

61 See in ch. 88: 'Solus igitur Deus potest movere voluntatem, per modum agentis, absque violentia' (p. 331). Ch. 89 is entitled: 'Quod motus voluntatis causatur a Deo, et non solum potentia voluntatis'. Note in particular: "Deus non solum dat rebus virtutes, sed etiam nulla res potest propria virtute agere nisi agat in virtute ipsius, ut supra ostensum est. Ergo homo non potest virtute voluntatis sibi data uti nisi inquantum agit in virtute Dei. Illud autem in cuius virtute agens agit, est causa non solum virtutis, sed etiam actus . . . Deus igitur est causa nobis non solum voluntatis, sed etiam volendi" (pp. 331–332). Cf SCG III, ch. 67, p. 300.

62 "Ad decimumtertium dicendum, quod voluntas dicitur habere dominium sui actus non per exclusionem causae primae, sed quia causa prima non ita agit in voluntate ut eam de necessitate ad unum determinet sicut determinat naturam; et ideo determinatio actus relinquitur in potestate rationis et voluntatis" (ed. cit., p. 59).

63 "Ad decimumquartum dicendum, quod non quaelibet causa excludit libertatem, sed solum causa cogens: sic autem Deus non est causa operationis nostrae" (*ibid*).

64 Note in particular: "Non igitur propterea effectus voliti a Deo, eveniunt contingenter, quia causae proximae sunt contingentes; sed propterea quia Deus voluit eos contingenter evenire, contingentes causas ad eos praeparavit" (ed. cit., p. 114). This statement should not be taken as contradicting Thomas's view that effects are said to be necessary or contingent by reason of the nature of their proximate cause (see citations given in notes 42 and 50 above). In those passages Thomas was indicating that if we wonder whether an effect is necessary or contingent, we should look to the nature of the proximate cause. Here he is rather making the point that, viewed from the standpoint of divine final causality, God has prepared contingent causes for given effects because he wills these effects to be contingent.

65 Compare this with ST I-IIae, qu. 10, art. 4: "Quia igitur voluntas est activum principium non determinatum ad unum, sed indifferenter se habens ad multa, sic Deus ipsam movet, quod non ex necessitate ad unum determinat, sed remanet motus eius contingens et non necessarius, nisi in his ad quae naturaliter movetur" (ed. cit., p. 60). For a discussion of this passage see Degl'Innocenti, pp. 39–43. Also see ST I-IIae, qu. 9, art. 6, and ad 3. For a discussion see Degl'Innocenti, pp. 44–52.

66 See ST I-IIae, qu. 10, art. 4, ad 1: "Et ideo magis repugnaret divinae motioni, si voluntas ex necessitate moveretur, quod suae naturae non competit; quam si moveretur libere, prout competit suae naturae" (ed. cit., p. 60).

67 For a brief sketch of differences among contemporary interpreters of Aquinas on this see Groblicki, op. cit., pp. 7–10. Much of his study is devoted to an examination of the interpretations proposed by Thomas's earliest critics and followers concerning this point. For an effort to trace this theme through the great classical commentators on Aquinas see F. Schmitt, *Die Lehre des hl. Thomas von Aquin vom göttlichen Wissen des zukünftig Kontingenten bei seinen grossen Kommentatoren*, Nijmegen 1950. See in particular his concluding remarks, pp. 196–202.

68 Thomas's dependency upon his understanding of divine eternity in order to account for God's knowledge of future contingents is evident from the first part of our study (see Section 2 – 'God's Knowledge of Future Contingents'). That God's science (when conjoined with his will) also serves as the first cause of all creaturely activities, including those that are free, has been developed in Sections 3 and 4 of this study. As I have observed near the end of that discussion (p. 225), in SCG I, ch. 68, Thomas notes that God by knowing his essence knows all of that to which his causality extends. This includes operations of the intellect and will. Is this not for Thomas to appeal to God's knowledge of himself as cause of the will's activity in order to account for divine knowledge of free human activity? Not necessarily, it seems to me, since Thomas's purpose in this chapter is not to indicate how God knows free human activity, but only to marshall evidence to show that God does know the motions of the will since he knows himself as cause of the same. When Thomas wants to explain how this can be so he introduces the theme of divine eternity and the eternal presence of all such things to God. It is because of this that Thomas can also hold that God does not merely know them by knowing himself as their cause, but as they are in themselves. Cf. SCG I, ch. 66.

69 In addition to the many passages cited in the first pages of this study, see the strong endorsement of this view by H. Schwamm, in his *Das göttliche Vorherwissen bei Duns Scotus und seinen ersten Anhängern*, Innsbruck 1934, pp. 91–99. See p. 99: "Den einzigen Grund für die unfehlbare Sicherheit des Vorherwissens sieht der hl. Thomas darin, dass das kontingent Zukünftige in seiner eindeutig bestimmten aktuellen Wirklichkeit

von Ewigkeit her dem göttlichen Erkennen gegenwärtig vorliegt." For a more cautious reply see Groblicki, op. cit., pp. 37–39. He comments that Thomas replies to the question how God knows future contingents in two different ways, that is, by appealing to God's knowledge of them as eternally present to him, and by appealing to God's causation of them. Groblicki proposes the following as a probable solution. When Thomas wants to show that God knows future contingents in terms of their real being, he does not merely appeal to their intentional presence in his ideas or in their causal principles but to their eternal presence to him. But when Thomas wants to account for the fact that such things are indeed real, he then appeals to the fact that they are caused by the divine will (see pp. 38–39).

70 *Quodlibeta* (Paris, 1518; repr. Louvain, 1961; in 2 vols. with continuous pagination), fol. 299v. 'Utrum in Deo sint ideae practicae'. Henry accepts the classical notion that a divine idea is nothing but the divine essence insofar as it is viewed as imitable in a given way by creatures (f. 300r). At the same time, he has an unusual view concerning the status of nonexistent possibles, or objects of divine ideas before they are realized in actuality. To them he assigns a special kind of being, *esse essentiae*, and this from all eternity. Actual existence is given to them only in time, due to the added intervention of the divine will. This does not result in real distinction between essence (*esse essentiae*) and existence (*esse existentiae*) in actually existing creatures, however, but only in something called by Henry an 'intentional distinction'. This distinction is greater than a purely logical distinction (distinction of reason), but less than a real distinction. For more discussion and for references to this see my 'The Reality of Nonexisting Possibles According to Thomas Aquinas, Henry of Ghent, and Godfrey of Fontaines', *Review of Metaphysics* 34 (1981), 740–751, and especially the references in n. 23 (p. 741).

71 Henry notes that God knows other things according to his ideas (*rationes ideales*) in two different ways: (1) insofar as they are certain essences or existences in themselves, and this by purely speculative knowledge; (2) insofar as they are *quaedam operabilia a deo*. According to some, God would know things in this second way by practical ideas and by practical knowledge. Henry comments that practical and speculative knowledge are to be distinguished not by reason of diversity in the objects that are known, but by reason of diversity in end. The mere fact that knowledge has to do with *operabilia* is not enough to make it practical. The end must be action or operation. Thus the intellect may have speculative knowledge of some *operabile*, e.g., by asking what is virtue or what is vice. But when dealing with such matter the speculative intellect can become practical by a certain extension to an end that is practical. In other words, if one who is speculating about an *operabile* extends his goal so as to know in order for his will to act accordingly, his knowledge thereby will become practical. But when it deals with purely speculative matter the speculative intellect never becomes practical in this way – by extension (ff. 300r–v).

72 Here Henry distinguishes two ways of understanding practical knowledge: (1) when the intellect considers what should or should not be done for the sake of that which is fitting for things; (2) when the intellect considers what should or should not be done in order for the agent to gain some advantage. This second type, which Henry regards as practical knowledge in the proper sense, is found only in creatures. Such is not present in God. Henry will admit of divine practical knowledge in the first sense, subject to the qualifications already mentioned. See f. 300v.

73 "Utrum difformitas scibilium circa creaturas arguat aliquam difformitatem in scientia dei" (f. 229v).

[74] Fol. 301r.

[75] "Secundo autem modo scit res sciendo determinationem voluntatis. Quia enim et quae determinat voluntas dei facienda, et hoc modo quo ea determinat, scit intellectus eius ea esse facienda et sic facienda et non e converso, ut in hoc voluntas potius sit ratio et causa scientiae et intellectus dei quam e converso" *(ibid)*.

[76] *Ibid.*

[77] For Henry's discussion of divine speculative knowledge, see ff. 301r–v. On God's knowledge of things insofar as they are *operabilia ab ipso* see f. 301v: " . . . sciendum est . . . quod quia intellectus divinus scit operanda inquantum operanda sciendo determinationem suae voluntatis quae omnino est invariabilis, non autem per ipsas res quae variantur extra influendo in esse diversimode, secundum determinationem simplicem et invariabilem divinae voluntatis, qua simul ab aeterno omnia determinavit . . ." See ff. 301v–302v for an exposition and critique of Avicenna's account of divine knowing. Henry is especially critical both of Avicenna's view that the universe is necessarily produced by God, and of his apparent denial that God knows singulars as singulars. "Sentiendum est quod ideo uniformiter scit ea esse cum sunt et non esse cum non sunt quia scit determinationem suae voluntatis . . . in cognoscendo se esse causam illius (i.e., of the Antichrist) per suam substantiam secundum actum, sive in producendo, sive in conservando, cognoscit illam rem esse . . . sic et ex parte scientiae, quia scit omnia talia sciendo invariabilem essentiam et invariabilem voluntatis determinationem" (f. 302v). On all of this see Schwamm, *op. cit.*, pp. 101–104. As Schwamm points out, Henry is not restricting himself to or especially concentrating on God's knowledge of future contingents in this discussion. He is rather accounting for God's knowledge of any existent, whether past or present or future, by appealing to the determination of the divine will (pp. 103–104). However, what Henry says certainly applies in his eyes to future contingents.

[78] See f. 303r.

[79] *Ibid.* Note in particular: " . . . et sic simul cum quolibet instanti temporis respicit singula secundum modum quo sunt se habitura, sive secundum esse, sive secundum non esse, in suo nunc aeternitatis. Et quae fluunt extra in tempore stant simul fixa in eius cognitione . . . Et sic omnia quae fluunt in tempore sibi sunt ab aeterno praesentia; et hoc non solum ea ratione quia habet rationes rerum ideales ex parte intellectus, et determinationes earum ad esse ex parte voluntatis ut principia productiva earum . . . sed quia eius intuitus fertur super omnia ab aeterno prout sunt in sua praesentialitate; ut non solum dicamus deum scire omnia tam contingentia ad utrumlibet quam alia quia cognoscit ea in seipso ut in sua causa productiva, etiam secundum rationem esse particularis et individualis . . . sed dicamus deum scire omnia tam contingentia ad utrumlibet quam alia quia praesentialitate essentiae ipsius creaturae secundum praedictum modum subduntur suo conspectui". For close parallels between this and Thomas's ST I, qu. 14, a. 13, see Schwamm, *op. cit.*, pp. 105–106.

[80] See f. 303v. Note in particular: "Et sic est illa praesentialitas rerum in Deo non in rerum existentia, sed in earum causa, non solum productiva sed formali cognitiva, ut dictum est".

[81] I would like to express my thanks to Stephen Brown for having first suggested to me that William's critique might account, at least in part, for Henry's reservations. My subsequent comparison of the texts of the two has convinced me that Henry's knowledge of William's critique can hardly be denied.

82 "Unde omnia quae sunt in tempore, sunt Deo ab aeterno praesentia, non solum ea ratione qua habet rationes rerum apud se praesentes, ut quidam dicunt: sed quia eius intuitus fertur ab aeterno super omnia, prout sunt in sua praesentialitate" (ed. cit., pp. 86–87). My rendering of *ab aeterno* as 'from eternity' could, perhaps be misleading, as could the Latin expression itself. As it is clear from our discussion in the first part of this paper, Thomas does not wish to suggest thereby that there is any kind of successive duration in God's eternity, or in the eternal presence of things in God's knowledge.

83 "Unde manifestum est quod contingentia et infallibiliter a Deo cognoscuntur, inquantum subduntur divino conspectui secundum suam praesentialitatem: et tamen sunt futura contingentia, suis causis comparata" *(ibid)*.

84 For William's text see *Les premières polémiques thomistes: I. – Le Correctorium Corruptorii 'Quare'*, P. Glorieux (ed.), Le Saulchoir, Kain, Belgium 1927, p. 18. Note in particular: "Hoc enim est simpliciter falsum et erroneum; quia hoc est ponere omnia contingentia, et multo fortius necessaria ab aeterno in aeternitate, licet in tempore sint producta de non esse in esse".

85 "Non enim sequitur omnia quae sunt in tempore sunt deo ab aeterno praesentia non solum ea ratione quia habet rationes rerum apud se praesentes secundum modum iam expositum, sed quia eius intuitus fertur super omnia ab aeterno prout sunt in sua, scilicet ipsius dei praesentialitate; ergo sunt in aeternitate; sicut non sequitur, ergo sunt in tempore, vel ergo sunt in seipsis extra intellectum" (f. 303v). Compare with Thomas's text as cited in n. 82. Note also that Henry here assigns the 'presentness' directly to God rather than to creatures.

86 See f. 303v, and the passage cited above in n. 80. For practically verbatim citation of William see Henry, lines 12–14; William, as cited above in n. 84. Also note: "Et sic quae non sunt in sua natura propria, sunt praesentia aeternitati, non solum pro tanto quia rationes ideales ut sunt causales ad producendum ea in effectu, tempus, et omnia temporalia, sint praesentes aeternitati et Deo ab aeterno et per hoc ipsa aeternitas praesens istis rationibus, sed etiam pro tanto quia istae rationes ut sunt cognitivae ad causandum cognitionem rerum in divina sapientia sunt praesentes aeternitati et Deo ab aeterno; et similiter ipsae rerum essentiae praesentes sunt aeternitati et Deo ab aeterno, sicut obiecta cognita per illas rationes in divina essentia fundatas . . . (f. 303v)".

87 See ff. 303v (near bottom)–304r (top).

88 Thus he returns to the theme of the divine will in the closing part of his discussion. See f. 304r: "Similiter quantum est ex parte sua quoad eius scientiam quasi practicam qua novit operanda determinata per eius voluntatem. Idem enim est iudicium quoad hoc de scire particularia et universalia, plura vel pauciora, quia scientia Dei secundum praedicta etsi non determinat facienda vel non facienda, perfecte tamen perscrutatur determinationem suae voluntatis quoad facienda et non facienda." Though Henry clearly defends divine knowledge of particulars, he does not multiply divine ideas in accord with individuals within species. See his Quodlibet VII, qq. 1–2, ff. 255r–257r. For discussion see my *The Metaphysical Thought of Godfrey of Fontaines. A Study in Late Thirteenth–Century Philosophy*, Catholic University of America Press, Washington, D. C. 1981, pp. 125 (and n. 71 for references), 129–130.

CHAPTER 13

THE DIALECTIC OF OMNIPOTENCE IN THE HIGH AND LATE MIDDLE AGES*

William J. Courtenay

1. THE ABSOLUTE AND ORDAINED POWER OF GOD

One of the great contributions of thirteenth-century scholastics both to the problem of divine omnipotence and the contingency of events was the development of an analytical tool commonly, though perhaps misleadingly, known as the distinction between the absolute and ordained power of God. The fundamental perception on which it was based, namely that what God created or established did not exhaust divine capacity or the potentialities open to God, was articulated by Peter Damian in the third quarter of the eleventh century, generally accepted by the middle of the twelfth century, embodied in the formula of *de potentia absoluta/ordinata* by the early thirteenth, and had become commonplace scholastic terminology by mid-century. But what was generally acknowledged to be a useful distinction expressing an accepted theological truth supposedly became, in the fourteenth century, a destructive vehicle upsetting the certainties of the natural and supernatural orders and dissolving both scientific empiricism and natural theology before the terrifying possibility of arbitrary divine intervention. The twin spectres of skepticism and fideism, so repeatedly encountered in the literature on late medieval thought a generation ago, were grounded in no small measure on the assumption that the scholastic distinction between absolute and ordained power was misunderstood or misapplied in the fourteenth and fifteenth centuries.

Within the last generation considerable strides have been made in our understanding of this distinction. We now have a far clearer picture of its origins and early development than that constructed by Grzondziel and Borchert earlier in this century.[1] We are certain of the principal and standard meaning and application of the distinction. We are aware that in the development and use of the terminology Roman law and canon law played a part alongside theology.[2] And, on the assumption that the distinction was well understood and appropriately applied in the late thirteenth century, we have what appears to be careless usage or misapplication in the late medieval period. Whether that is in fact the case is the topic of the present chapter,

T. Rudavsky (ed.), Divine Omniscience and Omnipotence in Medieval Philosophy, 243–269.

which requires a re-examination of the high as well as late medieval understanding of the distinction.

2. GLOSSING DIVINE *IMPOTENTIA*, 1050–1150

In 1067, almost a decade before Anselm wrote his first work, Peter Damian composed a treatise in the form of a letter, the product of his reflections on a memorable dinner conversation at Monte Cassino with abbot Desiderius.[3] The treatise concerned two interrelated problems that remained major issues throughout the rest of the Middle Ages: divine omnipotence and the contingency of temporal events. Yet those issues were the ones at which Damian arrived only in the course of his analysis; they were not his beginning point. In fact, Desiderius and Damian were addressing a different, more exegetical issue. In light of the firm belief and almost daily affirmation of divine omnipotence in the opening line of the creed, how is a Christian theologian to understand or interpret authoritative statements that speak of things that God *cannot* do?

That question, which occupied the attention of theologians for the next two generations, was solved by Desiderius and Damian in different ways. Desiderius, paraphrasing a line from Augustine's *Enchiridion*, defined omnipotence as the power to do what one wills.[4] Correspondingly, statements implying divine inability should be interpreted to mean non-volition. Damian found that answer insufficient. The problem with that approach was not that it placed no limits whatever on what God could will and therefore do, but that the Augustinian and Desiderian phrase, particularly as used by dialecticians contemporary with Damian, limited divine power to the boundaries of the divine will, which in turn conformed to the divine nature. God cannot do whatever he wills; he can *only* do what he wills.[5]

Damian adopted a different approach. God *can* do more than he actually *wills* to do; divine capacity exceeds divine volition. Despite the fact that Damian did not explore the internal or external conditions that govern the way God acts, he does suggest that the realm of possibility open to God is not exhausted by or limited to what God has chosen to do.[6]

These alternative approaches, each having much to recommend it, formed the foundation for later discussion. Many theologians shared Desiderius' suspicion that it was a false problem and that statements about divine inability were either meaningless or conveyed some meaning other than the words suggested. St. Anselm initially favored that approach.[7] His definition of God as that being, a greater than which cannot be conceived, also applied to the attributes of God. Since God was the highest wisdom, goodness, truth, and justice, discussions of what God cannot do, such as lie, deceive, be corrupted, or change the past are meaningless by definition. They are based on the poverty or peculiarities of our language in which statements seeming to imply ability, such as "I can lie", really imply a liability and thus cannot be applied to God.[8] Abelard a generation later also adopted this approach and made the boundaries of divine power coterminous with the nature of God.[9]

Damian's approach was not without its supporters. It expressed a deeply felt religious belief that our created world, its relationships and events, are not contingent simply because they derive from and are dependent upon God, but because they were *chosen* by God. If divine power and freedom mean anything, they mean freedom of choice, not just freedom to implement one's will. St. Anselm eventually arrived at this position, not by analyzing the nature of God but by attempting to understand and explain the Incarnation in his *Cur Deus homo.*[10] If Christ was fully human he had to have the ability to sin, the ability to lie, deceive, or do any of the culpable acts within our power, even if the ability was never and could never be actualized. And since the properties of Christ's human nature must be, through the doctrine of *communicatio idiomatum*, predicated of the divine nature, one must acknowledge God's ability to do things he does not do. Yet even here the linguistic interests of Anselm provided a check, lest the divine nature appear too volitional. Through his distinction between *posse* and *velle* Anselm attributed to Christ the ability to sin but not the ability to will to sin, which made all undesirable actions an empty capacity that could never be realized, nor could Christ have ever wished or contemplated doing so.[11] In one remarkable passage, however, Anselm laid the foundation for the subsequent *absoluta/ordinata* distinction. God does not act by any external, compelling necessity but by an internal, self-imposed necessity, freely willed.[12] This concept of a self-binding God, with the companion concept of contingent, relative necessity as opposed to absolute necessity, had a major impact on the idea of divine omnipotence, particuarly on what came to be conceived as ordained power over against power conceived in the abstract, absolute sense.

Other late eleventh-century theologians shared Anselm's eventual perception that God acts by choice rather than by necessity, even if that choice is limited by the divine nature. Thus the school of Anselm of Laon, compiling the standard gloss on scripture, interpreted phrases implying divine inability as self-imposed limitations based on the nature or will of God. "God could, but he did not want to". "God could according to his power, but not according to his justice".[13] By the early twelfth century this approach to statements of divine inability had received wide acceptance, and theologians generally acknowledged a sphere of potentiality open to God by reason of his power but not realized, indeed unrealizable, by reason of his nature – a sphere of potentiality larger than those things God has in fact chosen to do. Desiderius' formulation, *non potuit = noluit*, had been replaced by *potuit, sed noluit*.

Abelard did not subscribe to that consensus. Influenced by his reading of Augustine, Anselm and Plato's *Timaeus*, Abelard rejected any discussions of what God might have done or could do according to his power.[14] Since God's actions always conform to the divine nature and are expressions of it, God could not have acted in any way other than he did. This view, first expressed in his *Theologia christiana* in 1124 and expanded in his *Introductio ad theologiam* in or shortly after 1136, was vigorously attacked by Hugh of St. Victor, Odo of Ourscamp, William of St. Thierry, Bernard of Clairvaux, the anonymous author of the *Summa sententiarum*, and, finally, by Peter Lombard who, in his treatment of divine omnipotence in distinctions 42 and 43 of the first book of his *Liber sententiarum*, made the approach of the school of Laon, the Victorines, and the Cistercians practically dogma.[15]

3. ABSOLUTELY SPEAKING: THE DEVELOPMENT OF THE FORMULA, 1150–1250

The concept that lies behind the *potentia absoluta/ordinata* distinction was well-established in the early twelfth century and epitomized by Lombard through the Augustinian expression "potuit, sed noluit".[16] It was a half-century, however, before the concept came to be expressed by the formula *potentia absoluta/ordinata* and even longer before that formula received wide acceptance. The crucial period for the development of the terminology was the end of the twelfth, the beginning of the thirteenth century. In an anonymous commentary on the Pauline Epistles written around 1200 the author argues that we can speak of divine power in two ways, either according to what God has chosen to do or according to divine power considered in itself, without regard for what God has decreed. To this second approach the author applies the adverb *absolute*.[17] Godfrey of Poitiers, writing around 1210, further refined the language. Godfrey is the first writer, to my knowledge, who uses the term *absoluta* as an adjective modifying the divine power and who phrases the distinction in the way that was to become standard. Godfrey states that there are things that God has the capacity to do, *de potentia absoluta*, that he does not do and, indeed, cannot do, *de potentia conditionali.*[18] Other theologians developed their own terminology. William of Auxerre, around 1220, acknowledged God's power to have acted otherwise, ***de potentia pure considerata***, which added special meaning to the natural and moral orders God actually chose to establish, *de potestate determinata.*[19]

In the period from 1220 to 1245 the terms *potentia absoluta* and *potentia ordinata* gradually came into common use. For example, in William of Auvergne's *De trinitate*, written about 1225, one sees that the term *absoluta* is becoming the normal way to describe the capacity of divine power without regard for what God has in fact done.[20] Hugh of St. Cher, who commented on the *Sentences* between 1230 and 1238, argues that God is able to do some things *de potentia absoluta* that he is unable to do *de potentia ordinata.*[21] The same terms, used in the same way, can be found in the *Sentences* commentaries of Guerric of St. Quentin (c. 1240) and Albertus Magnus (c. 1244) and the *Summa Halensis* (before 1245).[22]

By 1245, then, the formula had achieved its classic shape and was being applied in a consistent manner. None of these authors speaks of two powers in God, but rather of two ways of speaking about divine power. One way of speaking is to discuss power in the abstract, without regard for God's will and actions as revealed in the present order. The other way is to view divine power in terms of what God has in fact chosen to do. Thus certain things that are theoretically possible to God, *de potentia absoluta*, are impossible to God in light of the chosen order, *de potentia ordinata*. God never acts and can never act in an "absolute" way, since the discussion of power, viewed absolutely, leaves aside the entire question of divine volition and action. (see Figure 1).

Beyond the standardization of terminology, the function or purpose of the distinction was altered in the first half of the thirteenth century. No longer were theologians attempting to gloss or reinterpret authoritative statements about divine inability. Instead the distinction came to embody a positive statement about God's relationship with the world, a relationship based on covenant and self-commitment. The distinction affirmed that what God does, including what he has done, is doing, and will do, is not done by necessity or external compulsion but by internal, voluntary choice. The order that God has established, therefore, is not necessary in any absolute sense but is only relatively or contingently necessary inasmuch as it has been established by God out of free choice. God is not bound, save in the sense that he has bound himself. We should, as good medieval christians, look at the world around us not as a world of necessary things and relationships, as

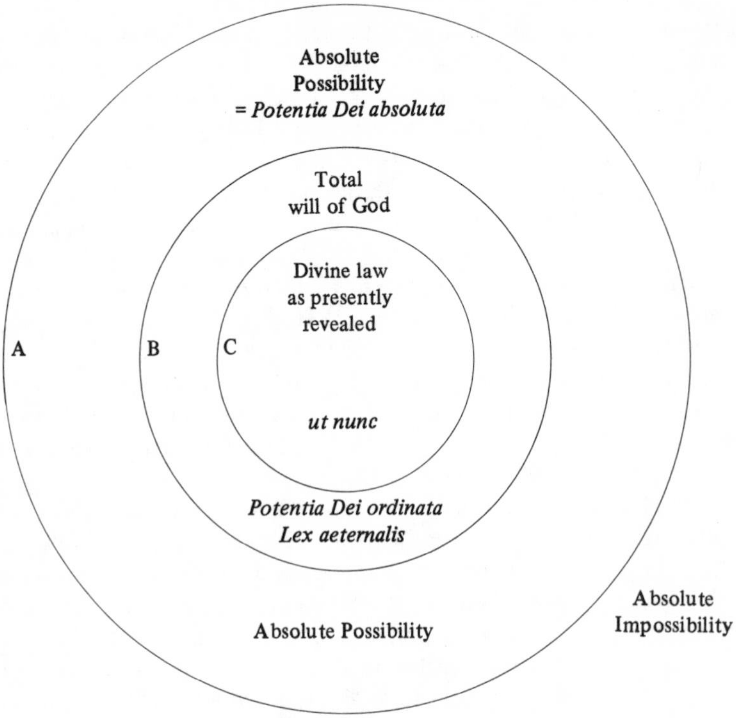

Fig. 1. The Theological Meaning.

did the uninformed Greeks and some of their Arab commentators, but as a contingent world, freely chosen and created by God.

Defined and applied in this way, the distinction sufficiently met the perceived needs of affirming the freedom of God and yet protecting the appropriateness and reliability of the established order of things. It was principally applied to theological issues (creation, incarnation, justification, and the sacraments) and stressed that what God has done (*de potentia ordinata*) was chosen from (i.e., lies within) the sphere of total possiblity (*de potentia absoluta*). If one viewed God's actions from the standpoint of time, however, there was a secondary implication that the realm of *potentia ordinata* was what God has done (reality) and the realm of *potentia absoluta* what God has not done (counterfactuals). But whichever aspect one chose to stress, at the moment of its general acceptance the distinction began to create almost as many problems as it solved.

4. DIVINE TEMPORALITY AND HUMAN SOVEREIGNTY, 1250–1300

Two groups of problems lay hidden within the *potentia absoluta/ordinata* distinction. The first group concern the difficulty of talking about the temporal acts of an eternal God. The procedure entails two hypothetical suppositions which, while false, seemed useful for theoretical analysis. One supposition places God in a temporal framework, albeit only for purposes of discussion. It hypothesizes a time before God acted, even before he willed, a time when God was faced with total possibility, limited only by the impossibility of making contradictories simultaneously true or by denying his own nature. Moreover, the freedom of an eternal God is eternal and should be expressed by the present tense, no matter how uncomfortable that makes us. As Hugh of St. Cher expressed it, "God could and still can". Yet the divine *posse*, when viewed from the standpoint of our temporal order, translates as *potuit*, not *potest*, as Damian noted.[23] Since God has obliged himself to work in particular ways and, being omniscient and consistent, will not deviate from the divine plan for creation, the choices initially open to God are no longer real possibilities once the divine plan is established. *Potentia Dei*, concludes the *Summa Halensis* at one point, *respicit res supra tempus*.[24] The second supposition ascribes to God a rational process of deliberation, of choosing a course of action out of a wider area of possibility. A God with freedom of choice is a deliberating God, even if only for an instant.

The second group of problems were not inherent in the concept but stemmed from a failure to refine the concept further or achieve an adequate consensus behind attempted refinements. As long as theologians used the distinction as a simple formula to attack divine necessity, as a rewording of the sentiment *potuit, sed noluit*, problems did not arise. But the fragile and ambiguous nature of the distinction gradually became apparent as more complex issues were assigned it. The major problem was that miracles and changes in God's laws were never fully integrated into the theory. They did not belong with the *potentia absoluta*, since power considered absolutely had nothing to do with action, and no Christian theologian seriously wanted to entertain the notion of God changing his mind and acting in a way that he did not foreknow and foreordain. And yet most discussions of *potentia ordinata* in the early thirteenth century illustrated ordained power by reference to natural and spiritual laws or ordinances now in effect, which God has at times miraculously suspended and which in the sacrament of the Eucharist he always suspends. What was needed and what was attempted but never fully developed in the thirteenth and fourteenth centuries was a subdistinction within *potentia ordinata* between the total ordained will of God (*lex aeternalis* or general providence, an equivalent concept to the *voluntas beneplaciti consequencs*) and *potentia ordinata* as it is expressed in specific laws (*lex ut nunc*) which have been altered or suspended from time to time, thus creating a home within *potentia ordinata* for the foreordained but miraculous activity of God.[25]

In the third quarter of the thirteenth century the predominant tendency among theologians was to equate the ordinated power of God with the total preordained, providential will. Beyond that there was little agreement. Albertus Magnus, Bonaventure, and Richard Rufus of Cornwall tended to identify God's wisdom, goodness, and justice with the present order of things, so that the hypothesis of a different order became an empty, theoretical construct.[26] Albert still found the distinction useful as a defense against the Avicennian and Averroistic idea of the absolute necessity of created things. Bonaventure and Rufus, on the other hand, rejected the distinction since, if the divine wisdom was identical with the present order, it seemed to imply that God had the capacity to act in an unorderly, irrational, sinful way.

Thomas Aquinas took a different approach. In his *Sentences* commentary he curiously ignored the language of *potentia absoluta/ordinata* in his treatment of the power of God, although he used it frequently in Book III.[27] Thus by 1256 he adopted the distinction and employed it subsequently in his disputed questions *De veritate, De potentia Dei, De malo*, in his *Summa theologiae*, and in his *Quodlibet* IV.[28] As with most of his period, he principally identified the ordained power of God with the total divine plan, but he did not identify divine wisdom with the present order of things. God's wisdom, goodness, and justice could have found expression in some other preordained system. The present order is therefore a product of the divine will; it is not the necessary and only product of divine wisdom.

Peter of Tarantasia was one of the few mid-century theologians to attempt a distinction between God's total ordained will and the ordained laws presently in effect.[29] If one considers things from the standpoint of *ordo simpliciter*, then God only acts *de potentia ordinata*. If one considers things from the standpoint of *ordo ut nunc*, then God can do things *de potentia absoluta* that he does not do *de potentia ordinata*. Peter was obviously sensitive to the problem and wished to affirm that God never acts without order, even in his miracles. Yet his formulation left the impression that actions in contradiction of the present order would be actions *de potentia absoluta*. That misinterpretation – the hypothesis of arbitrary, extra-legal divine action that Bonaventure and Richard Rufus found so disturbing – was reinforced by other factors in the thirteenth century.

One factor was the terminology eventually adopted. By substituting *potentia absoluta* for such phrases as *potentia pure considerata, potentia accipi absolute*, the gain in brevity was more than offset by a loss in clarity.[30] The earlier phrases unambiguously referred to power viewed in the abstract; the later phrase misleadingly suggested a type of power. A second factor was the analogy drawn between divine power and human experience.

One analogy was inherent in the theological concept from the beginning: God's freedom to choose from a larger sphere of possibility open to him is analogous to our sense of freedom, our sense of a capacity far larger than our actual choices. But instead of defining that as a distinction between ability and volition, as did Anselm, some theologians, such as Thomas, defined it as the difference between ability and legitimate action.[31] Thomas did not mean to imply that since we have the freedom to act illegally or immorally, so does God; but the parallel could leave that impression.

A second, more troublesome, analogy – one between divine power and forms of human sovereignty – entered theological discussion toward the end of the thirteenth century. Canon lawyers in the early thirteenth century sought a formula that would express the relation of papal power to ecclesiastical law.[32] On the one hand, the pope was obliged to obey and uphold the fundamental laws of the church (the *status ecclesiae*), which he could in no way alter. On the other hand, through the papal *plenitudo potestatis*, lesser, particular laws could be suspended through dispensations or privileges for the greater good of the church (the *ratio ecclesiae*). Here the theological distinction of absolute and ordained power proved useful. Without altering the concept in any way, it could be used to express the idea that the pope conforms to the law by an internal, self-imposed obligation, not by external compulsion or necessity. The underlying Roman law principle that the prince is bound by the law out of benevolence, not out of necessity, (the *lex digna* of Emperor Theodosius) provided further support.[33] Although the pope, *de potentia absoluta*, is not bound by the law, he has bound himself, *de potentia ordinata*, to act according to the law. Moreover, in order to preserve and fulfil the greater good, the total plan of God for his church, it might on occasion be necessary to alter or suspend particular laws. Just as alterations in the *ordo ut nunc* do not contradict but rather implement the *lex aeternalis*, so papal dispensations and privileges are for the general good and implement God's higher will. One might even consider the pope the means through which God alters present law to bring it into conformity with his general law.

Perhaps the earliest application of the theological distinction to papal power is mentioned in Hostiensis' *Lectura in quinque decretalium* in 1270. The context is particularly interesting, since it carries us back to the origin of the theological distinction. Hostiensis was attempting to gloss an authoritative statement implying papal inability to suspend or deviate from the law. Moreover, the case under consideration entailed a possibly inherent contradiction: whether the pope could release a monk from his vows of chastity and poverty and yet allow him to remain a monk, i.e., the degree to which those vows were part of the very definition of "monkness".

Hostiensis revealed a number of solutions that had been developed by earlier or contemporary canonists.[34] Some had adapted Jerome's approach to God's inability to restore virginity: such an act would not be congruent with papal power. Others argued the pope could so dispense, but the monk would no longer be a monk; or that the pope could not do so except by divine dispensation; or that he could if he wished (i.e., the case falls within his capacity), but he does not by custom do this. The most interesting solution in this context is the argument that although the monastic vows were part of the nature of the monastic state, the pope could, through his *plenitudo potestatis*, change the nature of the thing, *non de potestate ordinata, sed de absoluta*. As the subsequent discussion in Hostiensis suggests, he grants the right of the pope to suspend the vow for the greater good, the *ratio status ecclesiae*. Here as elsewhere Hostiensis recognized the ability of the pope, through his *plenitudo potestatis*, to act outside the law in an emergency situation. Such extraordinary action comes to be described in Hostiensis as the ability to act *de potestate absoluta*.

The analogy between divine power and human sovereignty, particularly the identification of *potentia absoluta* with *plenitudo potestatis*, introduced a disturbing element into the dialectic of divine power inasmuch as it assumed a different model . (See Figure 2.) The realm of *potentia absoluta* was not conceived as simple capacity or total possibility but as a course of action, albeit occasional. Even if such action was ideally for the common good, the papal *plenitudo potestatis* did not reflect a preordained plan in the mind of the pope, nor was it in practice devoid of self-interest. Rulers are counseled and influenced. They have also been known to change their minds. The potential arbitrariness in the exercise of human sovereignty contained serious dangers if applied to the concept of divine power.

The canonistic interpretation of absolute and ordained power was already in circulation when the famous list of 219 articles were condemned in 1277 at Paris and Oxford. 1277 marked a victory for the concept of divine

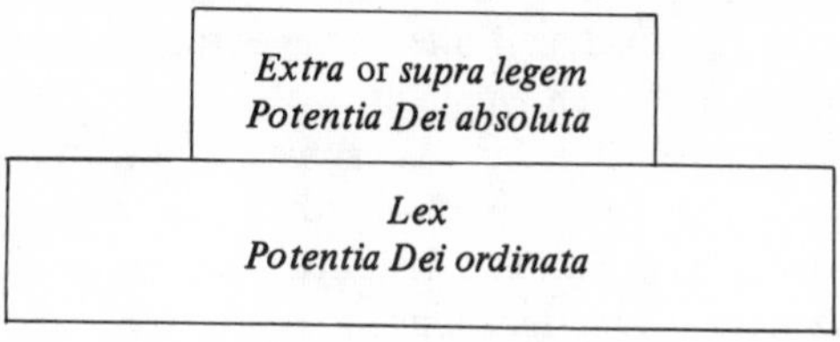

Fig. 2. The Juridical/Constitutional Meaning.

omnipotence, since many of the condemned articles restricted the freedom of God and affirmed the necessity of the world and the laws of nature. And yet that victory had little or nothing to do with the distinction of absolute and ordained power. Thomas Aquinas, part of whose thought was censured in 1277, accepted the distinction, while Henry of Ghent, viewed as a promoter of the condemnation, refused to apply the distinction to God because for him it implied the freedom to sin.[35] On the other hand, Henry was quite willing to apply the distinction to papal power and to equate *plenitudo potestatis* with *potentia absoluta*, even as he hoped a sense of propriety might restrain the pope's use of these extraordinary powers.[36]

The tendency toward the legal definition of absolute and ordained power met with a swift and strong response from some contemporary theologians. Petrus de Trabibus reaffirmed *potentia ordinata* as eternal foreordination and *potentia absoluta* as initial capacity or potentiality without regard to action.[37] God is *able* to do other things than those he has preordained, "yet it could never happen that he would act otherwise".[38]

Despite Trabibus' reaffirmation of the traditional, theological understanding of the distinction, the tendency to interpret *potentia absoluta* as a type of action rather than a neutral sphere of unconditioned possibility was unwittingly aided by Duns Scotus' treatment of the distinction.[39] In his desire to emphasize the unbound nature of God and the contingency of the orders of nature and grace, Scotus used the distinction of absolute and ordained power more than any previous scholastic. It formed the backbone of his theory of justification (*acceptatio divina*), of his view of sacramental causality, and his ethical system.[40] Scotus invariably equated *potentia ordinata* with the present order of things, *pro statu isto*, which God is obliged to follow only insofar as he chooses. God could have acted and still could act otherwise (*potest aliter agere*).[41] But Scotus acknowledged that any other action would result in another order (and thus God can never act *inordinate*) not so much because of the consistency of the divine nature but because whatever system God institutes becomes right and just on the grounds that God has chosen it.[42] The emphasis Scotus placed on law-changing and on God's ability to act outside and against his established law allowed *potentia absoluta* to appear as a form of extraordinary divine action, *supra legem.* With Scotus the legal, constitutional definition entered theological discussion. The *absoluta/ordinata* distinction applied to any free agent, not just God. Extending a line of argument in Thomas and not heeding the warnings of Henry of Ghent or Petrus de Trabibus, Scotus incorporated the analogy developed by the canon lawyers: *potentia ordinata* means acting according to the law, *de jure; potentia absoluta* is the ability to act apart from the law, *de facto*.[43] Thus the phrases *de potentia ordinata* and *de potentia absoluta* no longer simply characterized two different senses of *posse*; they now affirmed two different forms of action, one in conformity with law and one outside and against the law.

5. DOCTORS OF THE ABSOLUTE: THE FOURTEENTH CENTURY

It is well known that the *potentia absoluta/ordinata* distinction received far greater use in the fourteenth and fifteenth centuries than it had in the earlier period. Because of that it has been linked with late medieval thought and sometimes seen as a major component of nominalist theology and philosophy. But the meaning and function of the distinction in the late Middle Ages has as much to do with the conflicting interpretations of the late thirteenth century as it does with the new problems to which it was applied. This is amply illustrated by the discussion and use of the distinction in William of Ockham.

Ockham's understanding of absolute and ordained power derives from the *Summa Halensis*, Thomas Aquinas, Olivi, Trabibus, and Duns Scotus.[44] But despite the parallel uses of the distinction in Scotus and Ockham and the occasional parallels in language, Ockham's repeated and lengthy insistence on the proper meaning of the distinction was directed as much at Scotus' juridical formulation as at John XXII's misunderstanding and rejection of the distinction.[45] Ockham was adamant that these terms do not refer to two powers in God (*potentiae Dei*) but to two ways of considering the one power of God. *Absoluta* considers power alone, without regard to divine action or will. *Ordinata* considers God's power from the standpoint of his decrees, his revealed will. As did the *Summa Halensis*, Olivi, and Trabibus, Ockham locates much of the confusion on this issue in the ambiguous nature of the verb "can". *Potentia absoluta* is simply the realm of total possibility, and to state that God or anyone could *act* absolutely involves a contradiction. It is in this context, not in the context of hypothetical new orders (as with Scotus), that Ockham declares that God *only* acts in an ordained manner.[46] The persuasiveness of Ockham's definition of the distinction as well as the continuing threat of misunderstanding are underscored by Ockham's approach being repeated by Gregory of Rimini, Pierre d'Ailly, and Gabriel Biel.[47]

As had already become the pattern by the middle of the thirteenth century, Ockham used the distinction to point up the contingent, non-necessary character of our world and its relationships. His goal was always to prove non-necessity, not actual possibility. Most of Ockham's labors in this matter were, if you will, on the outer frontier between impossibility and possibility (Figure 1, circle A) in order to establish the necessary or contingent status of the opposite proposition within the case at hand. For example, if the statements "two bodies can exist in the same place at the same time" or "one can receive eternal life without the habit of grace" are absolutely impossible, then the opposite negative propositions become absolutely necessary. If, however, the former propositions are not absolute impossibilities, then the latter propositions are not absolutely necessary. In other words, in order to establish contingency versus necessity one must establish possibility versus impossibility, which is not done at the point of real possibility (Figure 1, circle B) but at the point of absolute or logical possibility (Figure 1, circle A). The ultimate goal is to determine the necessity or contingency of the case at hand, for which the *absoluta* speculation on possibility and impossibility is simply the means.

Ockham never confuses *potentia absoluta* speculation with the possibility of divine intervention, which he considered a separate issue. The miraculous biblical examples Ockham frequently cites in the context of *potentia absoluta* argumentation are not used to prove that God acts absolutely. They are divinely ordained acts, albeit special as opposed to normal, which prove that the case under consideration, which appears to involve a contradiction, is not contradictory and therefore falls within the area of possibility viewed abstractly. The miraculous example (*ordinata specialis*) proves the case (*absoluta*); the case does not make the example *absoluta*.

Ockham's use of the human analogue is similar. As did Thomas and Scotus before him, he found the freedom of the human will, the sense that one can do far more than one chooses to do or than one can legally do, a helpful analogy in distinguishing divine capacity from divine activity. At most, the papal example in Ockham serves to underscore the belief that papal conformity to law results from a self-imposed obligation, not from necessity. Ockham, far more than Thomas or Scotus, was disturbed by the idea of a pope acting contrary to Scripture and Tradition. The whole problem of contemporary church government, as Ockham saw it, was exactly the attempt of John XXII and his successors to contradict the accepted teaching of Scripture and Church. Ockham would never have applied the distinction to the papacy if he thought it would encourage absolutist behavior.

But what of developments after Ockham? Not only was there more frequent and extensive use made of the distinction in the late Middle Ages; it was particularly employed as a tool for analyzing the necessity or non-necessity of causal relationships (both physical and spiritual) or of states of affairs in the world around us.[48] The language of the agent, namely God, was still used, but the analysis was not of the actor but of that which is acted upon. Secondly, although the distinction still functioned as an expression of anti-necessitarianism, *potentia ordinata* increasingly became the realm of the realized, and *potentia absoluta* the realm of the unrealized possibiliites, counterfactuals, hypothetical arguments, *secundum imaginationem*. Thirdly, the distinction was increasingly applied to propositions in logic and physics. First in England, then at Paris and elsewhere on the Continent, theologians became fascinated with the interplay between divine decrees and moments of time, while devoting little attention to the distinction between specific decrees and the eternal, preordained plan of God (Figure 1, circle C). They were interested not so much in those regular suspensions of the natural order, such as transubstantiation, which engaged their attention in other ways, but in those temporary suspensions or changes across time which could make what was once false, true, and what was once true false.[49] In the contemplation of such moments one was instantaneously transported from one part of God's foreordained plan to another, from one type of order – familiar, reassuring, known as the present state of things or the common course of nature and grace – to another type of order in which the old rules did not apply. For a brief time as the Israelites were leaving Egypt theft and extortion were part of the ordained plan of God. For those days in which Abraham and Isaac journeyed to the appointed place of sacrifice, it was part of the revealed plan of God for a father to kill his only son. And for thousands of years circumcision had been the gateway to salvation by divine ordination, while for our authors, for over thirteen centuries, baptism had been so ordained. Fictive royal examples might also be used. A king might decree that all those found in the treasury room before noon would be rewarded, and all those discovered in the afternoon would be put to death. Again the parallel between the law-giving God and the legislative power of the king. But to the degree that such examples illustrate the transcendent power of God, answerable to no one, they also suggest the image of a capricious, arbitrary lord.[50]

Similarly, fourteenth-century thinkers explored situations or states-of-affairs that had seemed to previous generations to be impossible, such as the ability of God to deceive or the ability of God to command someone to hate him. As long as attention was focused on the nature of God, as it was from the late eleventh to the late thirteenth centuries, those hypotheses were self-contradictory. But when they were looked at from the standpoint of propositions about revealed future contingents, or the ability to will one's own damnation for the love of God, some theologians felt these cases did not involve a logical contradiction and were therefore possible *de potentia absoluta*.[51]

Most theologians in the fourteenth century were careful not to allow their discussion of God's *power* considered absolutely to become a discussion of God's *acting* absolutely. As long as the concept was being applied in the traditional manner, excessive use could never undermine the present order of things or produce uncertainty and skepticism. Yet not all theologians were that careful, and we find that the vocabulary through which the distinction was expressed varied in the fourteenth century, sometimes in ways that obscured the earlier meaning. *De potentia ordinata* is sometimes interchangeable with *de potentia naturali*, placing the emphasis on nature and man rather than God.[52] The distinction is not only applied to sovereign rulers but to anyone who acts according to law or nature (thus *de potentia ordinata*) as opposed to participation in a non-natural event which, since not impossible *de potentia absoluta*, could be realized through a special, miraculous ordinance.[53] In an unpublished paper Paul Streveler has noted the use of the phrase "ex privilegio speciali", which Robert Holcot uses interchangeably with *potentia absoluta*.[54] The technical juridical language reveals that Holcot is thinking about papal dispensation and that in such an instance absolute power is a form of extra-legal action. The same is true for Marsilius of Inghen, who preferred the phrase *de lege absoluta* in place of *de potentia absoluta*.[55]

A number of factors probably influenced this shift from absolute capacity to absolute action: (1) the syntactical structure of the terms themselves, which led to ambiguity; (2) the failure of most theologians to distinguish two senses of *potentia ordinata*; (3) the fact that any hypothetical case, *if* it were ever realized, would occur as a special miracle or a new ordinance; (4) human conceptual weakness, much as the idea of eternity is often misconceived as perpetuity or perduration; and finally, (5) the influence of the human analogy, particularly the analogy with the sovereignty of the ruler. Popes and kings did on occasion act outside, above, or contrary to the established laws of society and church. Their actions might be justified on the grounds of "reason of state" (*necessitas legem non habet*), but it was expected that they would conform to a higher good for society. Analogous to the distinction between God's general will and his specific laws, one might idealistically view royal or papal absolutism as the implementation of a general, beneficent plan from which those very laws, now suspended, were derived. In fact, however, human sovereigns, even medieval ones, have little foreknowledge or effective preordination; they *do* change their minds. Law making and law suspending are new responses to unforeseen conditions. And as a social group university scholars – the very writers of our arguments – were among the principal recipients of papal privilege and dispensation in the late Middle Ages.

Thus it was with a new but by then not uncommon meaning that Henry VIII in 1528 employed the distinction of absolute and ordained power in his appeal for a dispensation from his first marriage. "A thing that the pope perhaps cannot do in accordance with the divine and human laws already written, using his ordinary power", he might possibly be able to do "of his mere and absolute power, as a thing in which he may dispense above the law".[56] After all, if an all-knowing, foreordaining, unchanging God can be moved by prayer, how much easier to influence Christ's vicar to implement a possibility that lay within his power, considered absolutely.

NOTES

* The first two sections of this paper have drawn upon research done in 1970–72, partly as fellow of the Institute for Research in the Humanities at the University of Wisconsin.

1 H. Grzondziel, *Die Entwicklung der Unterscheidung zwischen der potentia Dei absoluta und der potentia Dei ordinata von Augustin bis Alexander von Hales*, Inaugural-Dissertation, Breslau 1926; M. Grabmann, *Die Geschichte der katholischen Theologie seit dem Ausgang der Väterzeit*, Freiburg i. B. 1933; E. Borchert, 'Der Einfluss des Nominalismus auf die Christologie der Spätscholastik', Beiträge zur Geschichte der Philosophie und Theologie des Mittelalters, **35**, *4/5*, Münster i. W. 1940, pp. 46–74. On the meaning of the term in high and late scholasticism see: P. Vignaux, 'Nominalisme', in *Dictionnaire de théologie catholique*, XI, Paris 1930, pp. 769–775; *Justification et prédestination au XIVe siècle*, J. Vrin, Paris 1934, pp. 97–140, 177–189; *Luther Commentateur des Sentences Livre I, Dist. XVI*, J. Vrin, Paris 1935, pp. 71–86; *Nominalisme au XIVe siècle*, J. Vrin, Montreal and Paris 1948, pp. 22–28; H. A. Oberman, *The Harvest of Medieval Theology: Gabriel Biel and Late Medieval Nominalism*, Harvard University Press, Cambridge, Mass. 1963, pp. 30–56; R. P. Desharnais, *The History of the Distinction between God's Absolute and Ordained Power and Its Influence on Martin Luther* (Unpublished doctoral dissertation, Catholic University of America), Washington 1966;

M. A. Pernoud, 'Innovation in William of Ockham's References to the *Potentia Dei*', *Antonianum* **45** (1970), pp. 66–97; 'The Theory of the *Potentia Dei* According to Aquinas, Scotus and Ockham', *Antonianum* **47** (1972), 69–95; W. J. Courtenay, 'Covenant and Causality in Pierre d'Ailly', *Speculum* **46** (1971), 94–119; 'Nominalism and Late Medieval Religion', in *The Pursuit of Holiness in Late Medieval and Renaissance Religion*, C. Trinkaus and H. Oberman (eds.), J. Brill, Leiden 1974, pp. 37–43; G. Gál, 'Petrus de Trabibus on the Absolute and Ordained Power of God', in *Studies Honoring Ignatius Charles Brady, Friar Minor*, R. S. Almagno and C. L. Harkins (eds), Franciscan Institute Publications, Theol. ser. 6, St. Bonaventure, N.Y. 1976, pp. 283–292; B. Hamm, *Promissio, Pactum, Ordinatio: Freiheit und Selbstbindung Gottes in der scholastischen Gnadenlehre*, Mohr, Tübingen 1977.

[2] F. Oakley, 'Jacobean Political Theology: The Absolute and Ordinary Powers of the King', *Journal of the History of Ideas* **29** (1968), 323–346; 'The 'Hidden' and 'Revealed' Wills of James I: More Political Theology', *Studia Gratiana* **15** (1972), 365–375.

[3] Peter Damian, *De divina omnipotentia in reparatione corruptae, et factis infectis reddendis* (Epist. 2, 17), in J. P. Migne, *Patrologiae cursus completus . . . series latina*, Paris 1844 ff. (henceforth cited as *PL*), Vol. 145, col. 596: "Nam dum aliquando, ut meminisse potes, uterque discumberemus ad mensam, illudque beati Hieronymi sermocinantibus deveniret in medium . . ." For a thorough examination of Damian's treatise see *Lettre sur la toute-puissance divine*, ed. & transl. with introduction by A. Cantin, Sources chrétiennes, CXCI, Paris 1972. For the later influence of one dimension of Damian's thesis see my 'John of Mirecourt and Gregory of Rimini on Whether God Can Undo the Past', *Recherches de Théologie ancienne et médiévale* **39** (1972), 224–256; **40** (1973), 147–174.

[4] *PL* **145**, 597: "Deum non ob aliud hoc non posse, nisi quia non vult". Desiderius' wording is similar to the statement of Augustine, *Enchiridion*, c. 96 (*PL* **40**, 276): "Non ob aliud veraciter vocatur omnipotens, nisi quoniam quidquid vult, potest".

[5] *PL* **145**, 597: "Si nihil, inquam, potest Deus eorum, quae non vult: nihil autem, nisi quod vult, facit; ergo nihil omnino potest eorum facere, quae non facit. Consequens est itaque, ut libere fateamur, Deum hodie idcirco non pluere, quia non potest; idcirco languidos non erigere, quia non potest; ideo non occidere injustos; ideo non ex eorum oppressionibus liberare sanctos. Haec, et alia multa idcirco Deus non facit, quia non vult, et quia non vult, non potest; sequitur ergo, ut quidquid Deus non facit, facere omnino non possit. Quod profecto tam videtur absurdum, tamque ridiculum, ut non modo omnipotenti Deo nequeat assertio ista congruere, sed ne fragili quidem homini valeat convenire. Multa siquidem sunt quae nos non facimus, et tamen facere possumus . . . Si quid igitur tale divinis paginis reperitur insertum, non mox passim procaci ac praesumptiva vulgari debet audacia, sed sub modesta sobrii sermonis proferendum est disciplina; quia si hoc diffunditur in vulgus, ut Deus in aliquo, quod dici nefas est, impotens asseratur, illico plebs indocta confunditur, et Christiana fides non sine magno animarum discrimine perturbatur". (Cf. *PL* **145**, 601).

[6] *PL* **145**, 600–601; 618–619.

[7] Anselm, *Proslogium*, ch. 7 (*Opera Omnia*, F. S. Schmitt (ed.), Thomas Nelson and Sons, Edinburgh 1946, Vol. I, p. 105).

[8] *Ibid.*, 105. "Sed et omnipotens quomodo es, si omnia non potes? Aut si non potes corrumpi nec mentiri nec facere verum esse falsum, ut quod factum est non esse factum, et plura similiter: quomodo potes omnia? An haec posse non est potentia, sed impotentia? Nam qui haec potest, quod sibi non expedit et quod non debet potest. Quae quanto magis

potest, tanto magis adversitas et perversitas possunt in illum, et ipse minus contra illas. Qui ergo sic potest, non potentia potest, sed impotentia. Non enim ideo dicitur posse, quia ipse possit, sed quia sua impotentia facit aliud in se posse; sive aliquo alio genere loquendi, sicut multa improprie dicuntur. Ut cum ponimus 'esse' pro 'non esse', et 'facere' pro eo quod est 'non facere', aut pro 'nihil facere'." Cf. *De casu diaboli*, 12 (*Opera Omnia*, I, 253). For an extensive examination of Anselm's position see my 'Necessity and Freedom in Anselm's Conception of God', *Analecta Anselmiana* **4.2** (1975), pp. 39–64.

9 Abelard, *Theologia christiana*, V (*PL* **178**, 1321–1330); *Introductio ad theologiam*, III, 4–5 (*PL* **178**, 1091–1102).

10 Anselm, *Cur Deus homo*, II, 5 (*Opera Omnia*, II, 100); II, 10 (*Opera Omnia*, II, 107); II, 17 (*Opera Omnia*, II, 122–126); 'Necessity and Freedom', pp. 53–60.

11 *Cur Deus homo*, II. 10 (*Opera Omnia*, II, 107): "Omnis potestas sequitur voluntatem. Cum enim dico quia possum loqui vel ambulare, subauditur: si volo. . . . Possumus itaque dicere de Christo quia potuit mentiri, si subauditur: si vellet. Et quoniam mentiri non potuit nolens nec potuit velle mentiri, non minus dici potest nequivisse mentiri. Sic itaque potuit et non potuit mentiri". Cf. also chs. 16 (II, 120–121) and 17 (II, 122–126).

12 *Cur Deus homo*, II, 5 (*Opera Omnia*, II, 100): "Non enim haec est dicenda necessitas, sed gratia, quia nullo cogente illam suscepit aut servat, sed gratis. Nam si quod hodie sponte promittis cras te daturum, eadem cras voluntate das, quamvis necesse sit te cras reddere promissum, si potest, aut mentiri: non tamen minus tibi debet ille pro impenso beneficio cui das, quam si non promisisses, quoniam te debitorem ante tempus dationis illi facere non es cunctatus". "Quare multo magis, si deus facit bonum homini quod incepit, licet non deceat eum a bono incepto deficere, totum gratiae debemus imputare, quia hoc propter nos, non propter se nullius egens incepit. Non enim illum latuit quid homo facturus erat, cum illum fecit, et tamen bonitate sua illum creando sponte se ut perficeret inceptum bonum quasi obligavit. Denique deus nihil facit necessitate, quia nullo modo cogitur aut prohibetur facere aliquid".

13 *Glossa ordinaria* on Gen. 19: "poterat de potentia, non poterat de iustitia".

14 *Introductio ad theologiam*, III, 4 (*PL* **178**, 1092): "Posse itaque Deus omnia dicitur, non quod omnes suscipere possit actiones, sed quod in omnibus quae fieri velit, nihil eius voluntati resistere queat". (*PL* **178**, 1094): "Hinc est illa Platonis verissima ratio, qua scilicet probat Deum nullatenus mundum meliorem potuisse facere quam fecerit; sic quippe in *Timaeo* suo ait: 'Dicendum', inquit, 'cur conditor fabricatorque geniturae omne hoc instituendum putaverit. Optimus erat. Ab optimo porro invidia longe relagata est, itaque consequenter sui similia cuncta, prout cujusque natura capax beatitudinis esse potuerit, effici voluit'." (*PL* **178**, 1095): "Patet itaque quidquid Deus faciat ac dimittat, justam ac rationabilem causam subesse, ut sola faciat aut dimittat; quae fieri vel dimitti oporteat atque ipsum deceat. Quod si quidquid facit eum facere oportet, justum est ubique ut faciat quidquid facit, ac sine dubio quidquid facit facere debet. Omne quippe quod justum est fieri, injustum est dimitti, et quisquis non facit id quod ratio exigit, aeque delinquit, ac si id faciat quod rationi minime concordat". (*PL* **178**, 1096): "Hac itaque ratione id solum posse facere videtur Deus quod facit, vel illud solum dimittere posse quod dimittit. . . . Ex his itaque tam de ratione quam de scripto collatis, constat id solum posse facere Deum quod aliquando facit".

15 Bernard of Clairvaux, *Epistle* 190 (*PL* **182**, 1053–1072). William of St. Thierry, *Disputatio* (*PL* **180**, 270); Odo of Ourscamp, *Quaestiones Magistri Odonis Suessionensis*,

II, 298, in *Analecta novissima Spicilegii Solesmensis* II, I. B. Card (ed.), Pitra, Tusculum, 1888, p. 113; Hugh of St Victor, *De sacramentis*, I, 2, 22 (*PL* **176**, 214–216); *Summa Sententiarum*, I. 14 (*PL* **176**, 68–70); Peter Lombard, *Sententiae in IV libris distinctae*, L. I, dist. 42–44 ('Spicilegium Bonaventurianum', IV; Grottaferrata, 1971), 294–306. Cf. Peter Comestor on Matthew 19, *Historia Scholastica* (*PL* **198**, 1588): "Potest enim Deus facere, ut camelus transeat per foramen acus, nullo obstante. Avarum vero, qui hic nomine divitis intelligitur, ponere in gloria, si potest de potentia, de justitia non potest".

16 Augustine, *De natura et gratia*, c. 7, n. 8 (*PL* **44**, 250; *Corpus Scriptorum Ecclesiasticorum Lationorum* **60**, 237); Lombard, *Sent.* I, dist. 43 (I, 303).

17 *Quaestiones in epistolam ad Romanos*, q. 91 (*PL* **175**, col. 457): "Quaeritur an Deus potuit facere convenientiorem modum redemptionis? Si dicatur quod non potuit, videtur quod potentia Dei terminum habeat, et non sit immensa; si dicatur quod potuit, quomodo iste convenientissimus est? Solutio: Licet in hoc terminum habeat, non tamen simpliciter concedendum, quod terminum habeat. Vel licet iste modus nostrae miseriae sit convenientissimus, non tamen est necesse, quod sit convenientissimus absolute".

18 Gaufrid of Poitiers, *Summa*, Avranches, Bibl. de la ville, Cod. lat. 121, fol. 137[r]: "Dico quod de potestate absoluta potuit ei dare. Quis enim auderet de potestate eius et immensitate disputare? Sed non potuit de potentia conditionali, scillicet manentibus decretis, quae ipse constituit". In A. Landgraf, *Dogmengeschichte der Frühscholastik*, Friedrich Pustet, Regensburg, 1954, II, 2, p. 103.

19 William of Auxerre, *Summa Aurea*, Paris 1500, fol. 27[v]: "Ad primo objectum dicimus, quod Deus de potentia pure considerata potest damnare Petrum, et habito respectu ad potentiam Dei et potentiam Petri naturalem qua potuit peccare et non peccare. Sed non sequitur: ergo, potest damnare Petrum, quia hoc verbum 'potest' in conclusione respicit merita".

20 William of Auvergne, *De Trinitate*, c. 10, *Opera omnia*, Paris 1674, p. 14.

21 Leipzig, Universitätsbibliothek, Cod. lat. 573, fol. 223[r]: "Distingui tamen debet, quod duplex est potentia Dei, absoluta et ordinata. De absoluta potentia potuit Deus et potest adhuc dare puro homini potestatem cooperationis. De potestate ordinata non potest, id est non mutato ordine rerum. Idem enim omnino est potentia absoluta Dei et ordinata. Sed potentia ordinata respicit ordinem rebus a Deo inditum". Cited from Landgraf, *Dogmengeschichte*, III, 1, p. 207.

22 For Guerric see Paris, Bibl. nat. lat. 15 603, fol. 11[r]: "Potestate absoluta potuit dare, sed non potestate ordinata, quae respicit ordinem rerum;" cited from Landgraf, *Dogmengeschichte*, III, I, p. 207. Albertus Magnus, Sent. I, dist. 42, a. 6 *Opera omnia*, A. Borgnet (ed.) Vol. XXVI, Paris, 1893, pp. 362–366; dist. 43, pp. 377–380. The *Summa theologiae*, attributed to Albert and on which Borchert relied for his interpretation of Albert, is of doubtful authenticity; see A. Hufnagel, 'Zur Echtheitsfrage der *Summa Theologiae* Alberts des Grossen', *Theologische Quartalschrift* **146** (1966), 8–39. *Summa Halensis*, Pt. I, inq. I, Tr. 4, q. 1, m. 2, c. 2, Quaracchi, 1924, I, p. 207: "Tamen comparando absolute potentiam voluntati, sic potentia in plus est quam voluntas; secundum vero quod intelligitur potentia ordinata, quae quidem ordinatio intelligitur in ratione praeordinationis, coaequantur potentia et voluntas. Distinguitur ergo potentia absoluta [a] potentia ordinata. Potentia absoluta est eorum quorum non est divina praeordinatio; potentia vero ordinata est eorum quorum est divina praeordinatio, hoc est eorum quae a Deo sunt praeordinata sive disposita". Cf. pp. 220–222, 228, 234–235.

[23] Peter Damian, *De divina omnipotentia* (*PL* **145**, 619): "... non inepte possumus dicere quia potest Deus facere, in illa invariabili et constantissima semper aeternitate sua, ut quod factum fuerat apud hoc transire nostrum, factum non sit, scilecet ut dicamus: Roma, quae antiquitus condita est, potest Deus agere ut condita non fuerit. Hoc quod dicimus: potest, praesentis videlicet temporis, congrue dicitur quantum pertinet ad immobilem Dei omnipotentis aeternitatem; sed quantum ad nos, ubi continuata mobilitas, et perpes est transitus, ut mos est, potuit convenientius diceremus ...." "Potuit secundum nos, potest secundum se".

[24] *Summa Halensis*, Pt. I, Inqu. I, Tr. 4, q. 1, m. 4 (I, 228). The *Summa Halensis* identifies *potentia ordinata* with total divine preordination, possibly influencing usage in the second half of the thirteenth century. It also establishes a trend by defining *potentia absoluta* not as the realm of total possibility out of which God chose but specifically those things that he did not choose.

[25] A number of authors distinguished two types of order or two categories within the ordained order. Thomas Aquinas and Peter Aureoli, for example, distinguished the natural order from the order of justice, while Duns Scotus distinguished general decrees from those that applied to particular persons. Thomas was well aware of the distinction between the general will of God and the present order of things. In question 19, a. 7, of the first part of his *Summa theologiae* Thomas affirmed the unchanging nature of the divine will despite the changes in divine decrees. Later, in article 6 of question 105 he cited Augustine's distinction between the common course of nature and the higher law of God (Contra Faustum, c. 26): "Deus contra solitum cursum naturae facit; sed contra summam legem nullo modo facit, quia contra seipsum non facit". For Thomas changes in God's ordinances do not represent changes in his will: "Unde cum praeter hunc ordinem agit, non mutatur". And yet Thomas did not employ this distinction in his discussion of divine power in question 25, and Peter of Tarantasia's attempt was largely unsuccessful. Pierre d'Ailly was one of the few to make this distinction in the context of his discussion of divine omnipotence. As unfortunate as it seems in retrospect, it is understandable why that distinction between normal order and special order was never fully developed in the thirteenth century. The *absoluta/ordinata* distinction was designed to establish necessity or contingency by proving impossibility or possibility. They were less concerned with the question of whether God might act in such and such a way, the question of what conditions the actions of God. But because the latter issue was handled separately and not built into or accomodated by the *absolute/ordinata* distinction, it could leave the erroneous impression that if miracles or special decrees were not in the normal order of things, they must be in the area of power considered absolutely.

[26] Albertus Magnus, I *Sent.*, dist. 42, a. 6, *Opera omnia*, A. Borgnet (ed.) Vol. XXVI; Paris, 1893, p. 366: "Ad aliud dicendum, quod potentia absolute considerata generalior est, quam est ars vel scientia practica: et ideo illa objectio non procedit, nisi de potentia exsequente, et non de potentia absolute considerata". I *Sent.*, dist. 43, arts. 1–3 (XXVI, pp. 377–380), where Albert contrasts *potentia absoluta* with *potentia conjuncta actui.* I *Sent.*, dist. 44, arts. 2–4, where Albert seems to restrict the divine wisdom to the present order of things (XXVI, pp. 391–395. Bonaventure, *Commentaria in quatuor libros Sententiarum Petri Lombardi*, I, dist. 43, dub 7 (*Opera omnia*, Vol. I; Quaracchi, Collegium S. Bonaventurae 1883), p. 778: "Aliqui distinguunt hic potentiam Dei dupliciter, dicentes, Deum posse aut de potentia absoluta, et sic potest Iudam salvare et Petrum damnare; aut de potentia ordinata, et sic non potest. Sed haec distinctio

non videtur esse conveniens, quia nihil potest Deus, quod non possit ordinate. Posse enim inordinate facere est 'non posse', sicut posse peccare et posse mentiri". Elsewhere Bonaventure seems to allow some validity to the distinction of divine capacity and volition; cf. *Breviloquium*, p. 1, c. 7; *Sent.* I, dist. 43, q. 4 (I, p. 775); *Sent.* I, dist. 43, dub. 2 (I, pp. 776–77); *Sent.* II, dist. 7, p. 1, a. 1, q. 1, ad 1. Richard Rufus, *In comm. Sent. Bonav. abbreviatio*, I, dist. 43 (Vat. lat. 12993, fol. 117rb, cited from Gál, 'Petrus de Trabibus', p. 285): "Responsio: quidam dicunt quod Deus potest de potentia absoluta et Iudam salvare et Petrum damnare, sed de potentia ordinata non potest. Sed haec distinctio potentiae non videtur conveniens, quia nihil potest Deus quod non possit ordinate. Posse enim inordinate facere est non posse, sicut posse peccare".

Henry of Ghent later repeated Bonaventure's reservations about applying this distinction to God's power. It is curious that those most responsible for perfecting the distinction in the thirteenth century were Dominicans: Hugh of St. Cher, Guerric of St. Quentin, Albertus Magnus, and Thomas Aquinas, while those most suspicious of its value have usually been associated with the Augustinian tradition: Bonaventure, Richard Rufus, and Henry of Ghent. The latter were reluctant to apply to God a distinction that to them suggested a difference between the way God normally acts and the way he occasionally acts.

Albert's position on this issue has usually (Borchert, Desharnais) been extracted from the possibly inauthentic *Summa theologiae* (see note 22 above). There *potentia absoluta* was defined as total possibility, unchecked even by the principle of non-contradiction; *potentia ordinata*, on the other hand, meant that God cannot make contradictories true at the same time. Albertus Magnus (?), *Summa theol.*, Pt. I, Tr. 19, q. 78, m. 2, solutio (*Opera omnia*, XXXI; Paris 1895), p. 832: "Ad hoc dici consuevit, quod potentia Dei potest accipi absolute, et potest accipi ut disposita et ordinata secundum rationem scientiae et voluntatis. Si accipitur absolute: tunc, ut dicit Damascenus, accipitur ut pelagus potestatis infinitae, et tunc nihil est quod non possit. Si autem accipitur ut potentia disposita et ordinata secundum providentiam et bonitatem: tunc dicitur quod potest facere ea quae potentiae sunt, et non ea quae impotentiae. Unde sic non potest facere majorem se, nec potest facere contra ordinem veritatis suae, et sic non potest facere esse et non esse simul de eodem, vel alia opposita esse simul, quia faceret contra veritatem ordinationis suae".

27 Thomas Aquinas, *Sent.* I, d. 42, q. 1, a. 1; q. 2, a. 2–3; d. 43, q. 2, a. 1–2; III, d. 1, q. 2, a. 3; q. 2, a. 4; d. 2, q. 1, a. 1; d. 12, q. 3, a. 2; d. 24, q. 1, a. 1.

28 Thomas Aquinas, *Quaestiones disputatae de potentia Dei*, q. 1, a. 5 (*Opera omnia*; Parma 1856), VIII, p. 10: "Respondeo dicendum, quod hic error, scilicet Deum non posse facere nisi quae facit, duorum fuit. Primo fuit quorumdam Philosophorum dicentium Deum agere ex necessitate naturae. Quod si esset, cum natura sit determinata ad unum, divina potentia ad alia agenda se extendere non posset quam ad ea quae facit. Secundo fuit quorumdam Theologorum considerantium ordinem divinae justitiae et sapientiae, secundum quem res fiunt a Deo, quem Deum praeterire non posse dicebant; et incidebant in hoc, ut dicerent, quod Deus non potest facere nisi quae facit". "Ex his ergo colligitur quod id quod ex necessitate natura agit, impossibile est esse principium agens, cum determinetur sibi finis ab alio. Et sic patet quod impossibile est Deum agere ex necessitate naturae; et ita radix primae positionis falsa est.

Sic autem restat investigare de secunda positione. Circa quod sciendum est, quod dupliciter dicitur aliquis non posse aliquid. Uno modo absolute; quando scilicet aliquod principiorum, quod sit necessarium actioni, ad actionem illam non se extendit; ut si pes sit confractus; posito enim opposito alicuius actionis, actio fieri non potest; non enim possum ambulare dum sedeo". "Sicut enim manifestatur divina bonitas per has res quae nunc sunt et per hunc rerum ordinem; ita potest manifestari per alias creaturas et alio modo ordinatas; et ideo divina voluntas absque praeiudicio bonitatis, iustitiae et sapientiae, potest se extendere in alia quam quae facit. Et in hoc fuerunt decepti errantes: aestimaverunt enim ordinem creaturarum esse quasi commensuratum divinae bonitatis quasi absque eo esse non posset. Patet ergo quod absolute Deus potest facere alia quam quae fecit. Sed quia ipse non potest facere quod contradictoria sint simul vera, ex suppositione potest dici, quod Deus non potest alia facere quam quae fecit: supposito enim quod ipse non velit alia facere, vel quod praesciverit se non alia facturum, non potest alia facere, ut intelligatur composite, non divisim". *Summa theologiae*, Pt. I, q. 25, a. 5, ad 1 (Ottawa 1945), I, p. 177: "... quod attribuitur potentiae secundum se consideratae, dicitur Deus posse secundum potentiam absolutam". "Quod autem attribuitur potentiae divinae secundum quod exequitur imperium voluntatis iustae, hoc dicitur Deus posse facere de potentia ordinata. Secundum hoc ergo dicendum est quod Deus potest alia facere de potentia absoluta, quam quae praescivit et praeordinavit se facturum; non tamen potest esse quod aliqua faciat, quae non praesciverit et praeordinaverit se facturum. Quia ipsum facere subiacet praescientiae et praeordinationi; non autem ipsum posse, quod est naturale". Cf. *De ver.*, q. 6, a. 4; q. 23, a. 8; *Contra err. Graec.*, q. 1, a. 16; *De pot.*, q. 1, a. 7; q. 7, a. 1; *De malo*, q. 16, a. 2; *Quodl.* IV, q. 3–4.

29 Peter of Tarantasia (Innocent V), *Sent.* I, dist. 43, q. 1, a. 4 (*In IV. Libros Sententiarum Commentaria*, Vol. I; Toulouse 1652; repr. 1964), pp. 360–61: "Respondeo: est ordo simpliciter et est ordo ut nunc. Nihil potest Deus nisi de potentia ordinata, primo modo loquendo de ordine; sed multa potest de potentia, circumscripto hoc ordine, scilicet ut nunc. Primo modo dicitur posse de potentia absoluta; secundo modo dicitur posse de potentia ordinata. Ergo multa potest primo modo quae non potest secundo modo. Ideo quaedam dicitur posse de potentia absoluta, quae non potest de ordinata, quia multa subsunt suae potentiae quae non congruit sibi ut nunc facere; posset tamen ea facere convenientia, et sic ea facere". Thomas Aquinas distinguished between present law and total divine will (*Summa theol.*, Pt. I, q. 19, a. 6–7) but not in the context of his discussion of omnipotence.

30 If an adjectival construction was to be substituted for the adverbial, *absoluta* might better have modified 'possibility' than 'power'.

31 Thomas Aquinas, *Summa theol.*, Pt. I, q. 25, q. 5, ad 1 (I, p. 176): "... in nobis ... potest esse aliquid in potentia, quod non potest esse in voluntate iusta, vel in intellectu sapiente".

32 G. Post, *Studies in Medieval Legal Thought: Public Law and the State, 1100–1322*, Princeton University Press, Princeton 1964, pp. 264–269.

33 *Corpus iuris civilis*, C. 1, 14, 4, P. Krueger, T. Mommsen, and R. Schoell (eds.), (3 vols., Berlin, 1899–1902), II, p. 68, cited in F. Oakley, 'Jacobean Political Theology', p. 330. The mid-fourteenth-century civilian and canonist, Baldus de Ubaldis, glossed the *lex digna* by using the *absoluta/ordinata* distinction to underscore the self-binding nature of human sovereignity; Oakley, p. 330. Giles of Rome used the same analogy in his *De ecclesiastica potestate*, R. Scholz (ed.), H. Böhlaus Nachf., Weimar 1929, III, 9, pp. 190–195. It should be noted that Giles does not equate *plenitudo potestatis* with *potentia absoluta* either for pope or God. Actions within the law and outside the law are both

ordained, but in different ways. In concluding a passage on the self-binding nature of papal conformity to the law (III, ch. 7, pp. 181–182) Giles states: "Verumtamen huiusmodi iurisdictio, quod sit sic casualis non est referenda ad suum posse absolutum, sed ad suum posse, ut est quibusdam regulis regulatum".

It is interesting that this analogy was not taken one step further in the constitutional structure of medieval society. One could argue that all human obedience to the law is in some sense self-imposed by way of an earlier social contract. One might view Marsilius of Padua's *legislator humanus* as a corporate personality that has voluntarily bound himself to obey the law.

34 Hostiensis, *Lectura in quinque Decretalium Gregorianarum libros*, Ad 3, 35, 6 (Venice 1581; repr. 1965), III, fol. 134r: "dixerunt quod super his non potest Papa dispensare cum monacho, quamdiu monachus est, potest tamen facere de monacho non monachum. . . . Alii dicunt, quod licet votum sit de substantia monachatus, tamen hoc potest de plenitudine potestatis, quasi dicant, non de potestate ordinata, sed de absoluta, secundum quam potest mutare substantiam rei. . . . Nec obstat, quod hic dicitur, quia quod sequitur possit exponendum est, id est, potentiae suae non congruit, sic exponitur illud Hieronymi. . . . Vel de solito cursu, quia non consuevit hoc facere, posset tamen si vellet, sic expone et hic. Vel hoc non potest Papa sine causa, sed ex magna et Deo magis placente hoc posset. . . . Alii tamen quam Papae contra iura sine causa dispensare non licet, quod si praesumpserit non valet dispensatio, vel revocatur. . . . Sed et ex causa potest Papa dispensare cum monacho, ut proprium habeat. Quid enim si tota Christianitas, vel etiam aliqua pars ipsius esset in periculo, nisi monachus fieret rex. Forte, quia non est alius qui posset vel sciret regnum regere. Nonne dices, quod monachus fiat rex in hoc casu?" Hostiensis' reference in this context to the famous passage in Jerome suggests that his analogy was derived from the theological tradition we have examined, not from the commentaries on the *Decretum*, where Jerome's text occurs in a different context.

J. Marrone, 'The Absolute and the Ordained Powers of the Pope: an Unedited Text of Henry of Ghent', *Mediaeval Studies* **36** (1974), 7–22, has called attention to another passage in Hostiensis where papal dispensation is described as *de potestate absoluta. Lectura*, Ad 5, 31, 8 (V, fol. 72v): " . . . quia Papa hoc potest facere sine concilio ecclesiarum, . . . sed episcopus hoc non potest absque laudatione clericorum suorum, et consensu ambarum ecclesiarum . . . Sed nec Papa haec, vel alios casus sibi specialiter reservatos, ut in praemissis versibus, consuevit expedire sine consilio fratrum suorum, id est Cardinalium, nec istud potest facere de potestate ordinaria, [referring to his discussion of papal dispensation in 3, 10, 4 and 3, 8, 4], licet secus sit de absoluta". See also F. Oakley, 'Jacobean Political Theology', pp. 323–346, who first called attention to the Hostiensis text.

35 Paris, Bibl. Nat. lat. 3120, fol. 139v; Marrone, 'The Absolute and Ordained Powers of the Pope', p. 17: ". . . de potentia absoluta et ordinata. Licet enim circa Deum non contingat distinguere inter potentiam absolutam et ordinatam; Deus enim, eo quod peccare non potest, nichil potest de potentia absoluta nisi illud possit de potentia ordinata. Omnis enim potentia sua quocumque modo vadit in actum ordinata [est]". As Marrone concluded, p. 18: "since Henry of Ghent identified absolute power with power used sinfully and unjustly, he thus had to deny that God possessed such absolute power". In light of the views of Henry of Ghent, there is a need to examine how the distinction was understood and used by Robert Kilwardby, John Pecham, Giles of Rome, and Godfrey of Fontaines.

[36] Although Henry of Ghent rejected the *absoluta/ordinata* distinction as it applied to God's power, he did equate papal *plenitudo potestatis* with *potestas absoluta*. Paris, Bibl. Nat. lat. 3120, fol. 140r (Marrone, p. 18): "Ecce plana distinctio inter potentiam absolutam et ordinatam circa dominum papam. Quando beatus Bernardus aliquid factitando ostendit se habere plenitudinem potestatis, quam appelo potentiam absolutam, super quo dubitat an habeat potentiam iusticie, quam appelo potentiam ordinatam".

[37] Gál, 'Petrus de Trabibus'. Trabibus' contemporary, Richard de Mediavilla, also established the boundaries of *potentia absoluta* by the principle of non-contradiction, as did Thomas; *Sent.* I, dist. 43, q. 7, as cited by E. Hocedez, *Richard de Middleton: Sa vie, ses oeuvres, sa doctrine*, E. Champion, Paris 1925, p. 245: "Respondeo, quod si dicam posse de potentia ordinata illud quod ipse facturum proposuit et rationabiliter disposuit, sic dico quod aliqua potest de potentia absoluta, quae non potest de potentia ordinata: quia absolute potest quidquid non includit contradictionem".

[38] Trabibus, as cited in Gal, p. 290: "Si loquamur de potentia ordinata, quia ille rerum ordo et numerus aeternaliter a divina sapientia et voluntate est praefixus et praeordinatus et non aliter, ideo licet alia possit facere et alia omittere, numquam tamen eveniret quod aliter fiat". For a similar discussion in Trabibus' master, Petrus Johannis Olivi, see the latter's *Quaestiones in secundum librum Sententiarum*, B. Jansen (ed.), Bibliotheca Franciscana Scholastica Medii Aevi, Vol. IV, Quaracchi 1922, pp. 63–65.

[39] John Duns Scotus, *Opera Omnia*, Vol. VI, A. Sépinski (ed.), Vatican, 1963, *Ordinatio* I, dist. 44, q. un, pp. 363–369.

[40] Among the numerous works on these aspects of Scotus' thought, see: W. Dettloff, *Die Lehre von der Acceptatio divina bei Johannes Duns Scotus* Werl 1954; A. B. Wolter, 'Native Freedom of the Will as a Key to the Ethics of Scotus', in *Deus et Homo ad mentem I. Duns Scoti*; Acta Tertii Congressus Scotistici Internationalis Vindebonae, 1970; Rome 1972, pp. 359–370.

[41] Scotus, *Ordinatio* I, pp. 364–366.

[42] *Ibid.*: "Quando autem illa lex recta – secundum quam ordinate agendum est – non est in potestate agentis, tunc potentia eius absoluta non potest excedere potentiam eius ordinatam circa obiecta aliqua, nisi circa illa agat inordinate; necessarium enim est illam legem stare – comparando ad tale agens – et tamen actionem 'non conformatam illi legi rectae' non esse rectam neque ordinatam, quia tale agens tenetur agere secundum illam regulam cui subest. Unde omnes qui subsunt legi divinae, si non agunt secundum illam, inordinate agunt.

Sed quando in potestate agentis est lex et rectitudo legis, ita quod non est recta nisi quia statuta, tunc potest aliter agens ex libertate sua ordinare quam lex illa recta dictet; et tamen cum hoc potest ordinate agere, quia potest statuere aliam legem rectam secundum quam agat ordinate. Nec tunc potentia sua absoluta simpliciter excedit potentiam ordinatam, quia esset ordinata secundum aliam legem sicut secundum priorem; tamen excedit potentiam ordinatam praecise secundum priorem legem, contra quam vel praeter quam facit. Ita posset exemplificari de principe et subditis, et lege positiva". "Ideo sicut potest aliter agere, ita potest aliam legem rectam statuere, – quae si statueretur a Deo, recta esset, quia nulla lex est recta nisi quatenus a voluntate divina acceptante est statuta; et tunc potentia eius absoluta ad aliquid, non se extendit ad aliud quam ad illud quod ordinate fieret, si fieret: non quidem fieret ordinate secundum istum ordinem, sed fieret ordinate secundum alium ordinem, quem ordinem ita posset voluntas divina statuere sicut potest agere".

43 *Ibid.*: "... potest agere praeter illam legem vel contra eam, et in hoc est potentia absoluta, excedens potentiam ordinatam. Et ideo non tantum in Deo, sed in omni agente libere – qui potest agere secundum dictamen legis rectae et praeter talem legem vel contra eam – est distinguere inter potentiam ordinatam et absolutam; ideo dicunt iuristae quod aliquis hoc potest facere de facto, hoc est de potentia sua absoluta, – vel de iure, hoc est de potentia ordinata secundum iura". The distinction to which Scotus refers appears in *Decretales Greg. IX*, 1, 3, 13 where lack of power (*impotentia*) can result from legal condition (*de iure*) or from physical impediment (*de facto*). The positive corollary, the distinction between *potentia de iure* and *potentia de facto* can be found in Hostiensis, *Lectura*, Ad 1, 3, 13 (I, fol. 14vb) and Ad 2, 28, 65 (II, fol. 200vb). The juridical flavor of Scotus' treatment of divine omnipotence has been noted by Pernoud, "The Theory of the *Potentia Dei*', pp. 84–86.

44 Ockham's discussion of the ambiguity of 'posse' was anticipated by the *Summa Halensis*, Pt. I, Inq. I, Tr. 4, q. 1, m. 4 (I, p. 228): "... sic nos loquimur de divino 'posse' duobus modis: habere potentiam vel uti potentia". Cf. Petrus Johannis Olivi, *Quaest. in secundum librum Sent.*, I, p. 64; Gal, "Petrus de Trabibus", pp. 286, 290. Ockham's reaffirmation of the traditional theological meaning of the distinction parallels that of Thomas at various points. Ockham followed the thirteenth-century practice, found both in Thomas and Scotus, of using human analogies to explain divine power; e.g., *Quodl.* VI, q. 1 (*Opera theologica*, IX, J. C. Wey (ed.), St. Bonaventure, N.Y. 1980), p. 586: "Sicut Papa aliqua non potest secundum iura statuta ab eo, quae tamen absolute potest". Ockham also followed the main lines of Scotus' ethical teaching, including the belief that God never acts *inordinate* but would, by a change of decree, establish a new order; see W. Kömel, 'Das Naturrecht bei Wilhelm von Ockham', *Franziskanische Studien* **35** (1953), pp. 39–85; David Clark, Voluntarism and Rationalism in the Ethics of Ockham', *Franciscan Studies* **31** (1971), 72–87, A. Wolter, 'Native Freedom of the Will'.

The traditional character of Ockham's teaching on this issue has been frequently noted in the last decade. See, for example, H. A. Oberman, *Harvest of Medieval Theology*, pp. 30–56; Pernoud, 'Innovation in William of Ockham's References'; 'The Theory of the *Potentia Dei*'; Courtenay, 'Nominalism and Late Medieval Religion', pp. 37–43. K. Bannach, *Die Lehre von der doppelten Macht Gottes bei Wilhelm von Ockham*, F. Steiner, Wiesbaden 1975, provides a somewhat different interpretation.

45 On John XXII's views see Ockham, *Opus nonaginta dierum*, ch. 95, Lyons 1495: "Quia iste impugnatus ut quidam istorum impugnatorum dicunt se audivisse ab ore eius, et ipse postea in sermonibus suis declaravit, negat illam distinctionem theologorum de potentia Dei ordinata et absoluta intendens multis rationibus ostendere quod quicquid potest Deus de potentia absoluta potest etiam de potentia ordinata, et quicquid non potest de potentia ordinata non potest de potentia absoluta". Ockham, *Tractatus contra Benedictum*, ch. 3; *Opera politica*, Vol. III, Manchester 1956, pp. 230–234.

46 Ockham, *Quodlibeta*, VI, q. 1 (ed. cit., pp. 585–568): "... quaedam potest Deus facere de potentia ordinata et aliqua de potentia absoluta. Haec distinctio non est sic intelligenda quod in Deo sint realiter duae potentiae quarum una sit ordinata et alia absoluta, quia unica potentia est in Deo ad extra, quae omni modo est ipse Deus. Nec sic est intelligenda quod aliqua potest Deus ordinate facere, et aliqua potest absolute et non ordinate, quia Deus nihil potest facere inordinate. Sed est sic intelligenda quod 'posse [facere] aliquid' quandoque accipitur secundum leges ordinatas et institutas a Deo, et illa dicitur Deus posse facere de potentia ordinata. Aliter accipitur 'posse' pro posse

facere omne illud quod non includit contradictionem fieri, sive Deus ordinaverit se hoc facturum sive non, quia multa potest Deus facere quae non vult facere . . ." *Summa logicae*, III–4, c. 6 (Opera philosophica, I, P. Boehner, G. Gál, and S. Brown (eds.), St. Bonaventure, N.Y. 1974), pp. 779–780: "Item, talis propositio 'Deus per suam potentiam absolutam potest aliquem acceptare sine gratia sed non per suam potentiam ordinatam' multiplex est. Unus sensus est quod Deus per unam potentiam, quae est absoluta et non ordinata, potest acceptare aliquem sine gratia, et per unam aliam potentiam, quae est ordinata et non absoluta, non potest acceptare eum, quasi essent duae potentiae in Deo per quarum unam posset hoc et non per aliam. Et iste sensus est falsus. Aliter accipitur improprie, ut ponatur ista propositio pro ista oratione: Deus potest acceptare aliquem sine gratia informante, quia hoc non includit contradictionem, et tamen ordinavit quod hoc numquam est facturus. Et iste sensus verus est". *Opus nonaginta dierum*, c. 95 (*Opera politica*, II; Manchester 1963), pp. 726–727): "Et ita dicere quod Deus potest aliqua de potentia absoluta, quae non potest de potentia ordinata, non est aliud, secundum intellectum recte intelligentium, quam dicere quod Deus aliqua potest, quae tamen minime ordinavit se facturum; quae tamen si faceret, de potentia ordinata faceret ipsa; quia si faceret ea, ordinaret se facturum ipsa. Quia igitur, ut dicunt isti, iste impugnatus nescivit videre aequivocationem huius verbi 'potest', ideo male intellexit illam distinctionem theologorum de potentia Dei absoluta et ordinata". "Rationes vero, per quas probare conatur quod praemissa distinctio de potentia Dei absoluta et ordinata non est approbanda, facile dissolvuntur. Prima enim ex falso intellectu procedit, quasi haec esset possibilis secundum sic distinguentes: 'Deus aliquid facit de potentia absoluta, quod non facit de potentia ordinata'. Haec enim de inesse secundum eos est impossibilis et contradictionem includit; quia eo ipso quod Deus aliquid faceret, ipse faceret illud de potentia ordinata". Cf. Gál, 'Petrus de Trabibus', pp. 287–288.

[47] Gregory of Rimini, *Super primum et secundum Sententiarum*, L. I, dist. 42–44, q. 1, a. 2 Venice, 1522; (repr. 1955), I. fol. 162^v – 163^r. D'Ailly, *Quaestiones super libros sententiarum cum quibusdam in fine adjunctis*, L. I, q. 13, a. 1, Strasbourg 1490; (repr. 1968), D. Gabriel Biel, *Sent.* I, dist. 17, q. 1, a. 3; Biel, *Sent.* IV, dist. 1, q. 1, a. 3, dub. 2.

[48] Fire is not necessary or contingent; the relationship of fire and combustion is necessary or contingent. It is not *charitas* that is necessary or contingent but the relationship of the habit of charity to the gift of eternal salvation that is necessary or contingent.

[49] In terminist logic there is a great deal of interest in the way in which the truth value of propositions changes with the circumstances in which it is spoken, thought, or written. This is particularly true in the fourteenth century for the time context. To give a present example, the statement "I am in Columbus" is true [at the time this paper was read], as is the statement "I was in Columbus" (at some previous time), but the statement "I was in Columbus last week" is true only if thought, spoken, or written in the week after I was in Columbus.

[50] Some of the parables of Christ pose that same time/reward problem, e.g., that of the laborers in the vineyard, or the parable of the talents. These also formed a source for fourteenth-century discussion and were so explored.

[51] Fourteenth-century discussions of certitude in light of the possibility of intuitive cognitions of non-existents provided another context for discussions of absolute and ordained power. See in particular K. H. Tachau, 'The Problem of the *Species in medio* at Oxford in the Generation after Ockham', *Mediaeval Studies* 44 (1982), 394–443.

52 Gregory of Rimini, *Super Primum et Secundum Sententiarum*, Venice 1522 (repr. 1955), I, 165 F: "... et non solum de potentia Dei, sed etiam naturali, quia in casu non ponitur Deum specialiter agere nisi quantum ad dationem praecepti". Pierre d'Ailly, *Quaestiones super Libros Sententiarum*, Strasbourg 1490; (repr. 1968), *Sent.* IV, q. 1 N: "Tercia conclusio probatur, circa quam sciendum est quod sicut dicitur quod Deus aliquid potest de potentia absoluta quod non potest de potentia ordinata, ita dico de creatura. Ideo concedo probabiliter quod licet creatura de potentia naturali seu naturaliter ordinata non possit creare vel annihilare ut dictum est. Tamen ista potest de potentia simpliciter absoluta, sive supernaturaliter seu miraculose".

53 D'Ailly, *Sent.* IV, q. 1 N.

54 Paul Streveler, 'God's Absolute and Ordained Power in the Thought of Robert Holcot'. Much of Holcot's uage is traditional, despite his fascination for time/place/decree problems of law-changing.

55 Marsilius of Inghen, *Questiones super quattuor libros Sententiarum* Strasbourg 1501; (repr. 1966), L. I, q. 20, a. 2 (fol. 84^r): "Potest uno modo intelligi de potentia Dei absoluta, scilicet agendo praeter legem quam promulgavit. Alio modo agendo secundum legem quam ordinavit et promulgavit, scilicet agendo secundum potentiam ordinatam". "Deus de lege absoluta alicui posset dare salutem nullam habenti charitatem creatam". *Sent.* III, q. 9, a. 3 (fol. 405^v): "... et ex consequente potest non velle ea conservare de lege absoluta, ergo possunt ab anima Christi tolli". By the phrase *de lege absoluta* Marsilius meant nothing other than power or possibility considered absolutely, *hypothetice* (fol. 84^r). Yet the phrase betrays the model of law-making and sovereign power, paralleling Scotus' observation that all actions of God outside the normal course of nature and grace are simply other forms of law and order: *ordo* simpliciter as opposed to *ordo ut nunc*. Marsilius in *Sent.* I. q. 43, a. 1 (fol. 183^r) distinguishes between the common course of nature and *potentia ordinata*: "... quae secundum cursum naturae possunt esse, vel etiam secundum potentia Dei ordinatam".

56 *Letters and Papers, Foreign and Domestic, of the Reign of Henry VIII*, J. Brewer *et al* (eds). (22 vols., G. E. Eyre and W. Spottiswood, London 1862–19832, IV, Pt. 2, 2158 (No. 4977); cited in Oakley, 'Jacobean Political Theology', p. 335, n. 61.

BIBLIOGRAPHY

List of Abbreviations used in Bibliography

Beiträge:	*Beiträge zur Geschichte der Philosophie des Mittelalters*, Münster.
CCSL:	*Corpus Christianorum Series Latina*, Turnhout, 1953– .
CSEL:	*Corpus Scriptorum Ecclesiasticorum Latinorum*, Vienna.
PG:	J. P. Migne, *Patrologiae cursus completus, Series Graeca*, 162 volumes, with Latin trans., Paris 1857–1866.
PL:	J. P. Migne, *Patrologiae cursus completus, Series Latina*, 221 volumes, Paris 1844–1864.

Primary Sources

'Abd al-Jabbâr: 1959–65, *al-Muġnî fî abwâb al-tawḥîd wal-'adl*, Cultural Dept. of the Arab League, Cairo.

'Abd al-Jabbâr: 1974, *Muġnī* V in *Penseurs Musulmans et religions Iraniennes*, transl. by G. Monnot, J. Vrin, Paris.

'Abd al-Jabbâr: 1971, *Muġnī* VI, in *Islamic Rationalism: The Ethics of 'Abd al-Jabbâr*, transl. by G. Hourani, Clarendon Press, Oxford.

'Abd Allâh b. Muḥammad Nâshi': 1971, *al-Kitâb al-auṣat*, in *Frühe Mu'tazilitische Häresiographie*, ed. by J. van Ess, F. Steiner, Wiesbaden.

'Abd al-Qâhir al-Baghdâdî: n.d., *al-Fraq bayn al-farq* ed. by M. 'Abd al-Hamîd, Cairo.

'Abd ar-Rahîm b. Muḥammad Khayyâṭ: 1957, *al-Intiṣâr*, ed. and transl. by A. N. Nader, Beirut.

Abraham Ibn Daud: 1852, *Sefer-ha-Emunah ha-Ramah* (*The Exalted Faith*), ed. by S. Weil, Frankfurt.

Abraham Shalom: 1574, *Neve Shalom*, Venice.

Abû l-Ḥasan 'Alî b. Ismâ'îl Ash'arî: 1929–33, *Maqâlât al-Islâmiyyîn*, ed. by H. Ritter, Istanbul.

Abû Muhammad 'Alî Ibn Hazm: 1317H, *al-Fiṣal fî l-milal wal-ahwâ' wannihal*, Vol. 1–5, Cairo.

Abû Rashîd Sa'îd b. Muhammad an-Naysâbûrî: 1979, *al-Masâ'il fî l-khilâf bayna l-Basriyyîn wal-Baghdâdiyyîn*, ed. by M. Ziyāda and R. as-Sayyid, Institut de lettres orientales de Beyrouth, Beirut.

Abû Ya 'lâ Ibn al-Farrâ': 1974, *al-Mu'tamad fî uṣûl ad-dîn*, ed. by W. Z. Haddad, Institut de lettres orientales de Beyrouth, Beirut.

Albert the Great: 1893, I *Sententiae*, in *Opera omnia*, ed. by A. Borgnet, Vol. 26, Paris.

Albert the Great: 1895, *Summa theologiae*, in *Opera omnia*, ed. by A. Borgnet, Vol. 31, Paris.

T. Rudavsky (ed.), Divine Omniscience and Omnipotence in Medieval Philosophy, 271–284.

Alcuin: *Interrogationes et Responsiones in Genesim* in *PL* **100**, 544, 545.

Al-Fārābī: 1960, *Alfarabi's Commentary on Aristotle's περὶ ἑρμηνειας* (*De Interpretatione*), ed. by W. Kutsch and S. Marrow, Imprimerie Catholique, Beirut.

Al-Ghazāli: 1963, *The Destruction of Philosophy* (*Tahāfut al-Falāsifa*), transl. by S. Kamali, Pakistan Philosophical Congress, Lahore.

Ammonius: 1961, *Commentaire sur le Peri Hermeneias d'Aristote, Traduction de Guillaume de Moerbeke*, ed. by G. Verbeke, Publications Universitaires de Louvain, Louvain.

'Amr b. Bahr Djāḥiẓ: 1938–45, *al-Ḥayawān*, ed. by 'Abd as-Salām Muhammad Hārūn, Cultural Dept. of the Arab League, Cairo.

Anselm of Canterbury: 1946, *Cur Deus homo*, in *Opera omnia* 2, ed. by F. S. Schmitt, Thomas Nelson and Sons, Edinburgh.

Anselm of Canterbury: 1946–1951, *Opera omnia*, ed. by F. S. Schmitt and T. Nelson, Thomas Nelson and Sons, Edinburgh.

Anselm of Canterbury: 1946, *Proslogium*, in *Opera omnia* 1, ed. by F. S. Schmitt, Thomas Nelson and Sons, Edinburgh.

Aristotle: 1938, *Categories*, in *Aristotle: The Organon*, transl. by H. P. Cooke, W. Heinemann, London.

Aristotle: 1955, *In Aristotelis libros Peri hermeneias et Posteriorum analyticorum expositio*, ed. by R. Spiazzi, Marietti Editori, Turin.

Aristotle: 1971, *Metaphysics*, transl. by C. Kirwan, Clarendon Press, Oxford.

Aristotle: 1947, *Nicomachean Ethics*, transl. by H. Rackham, W. Heinemann, London.

Aristotle: 1939, *On the Heavens*, transl. by W. K. C. Guthrie, W. Heinemann, London.

Aristotle: 1938, *On Interpretation*, in *Aristotle: The Organon*, transl. by H. P. Cooke, W. Heinemann, London.

Aristotle: 1961, *Poetics*, transl. by S. H. Butcher, Hill and Wang, New York.

Aristotle: 1966, *Prior Analytics*, transl. by H. Tredennick, Harvard University Press, Cambridge, Mass.

Aristotle: 1955, *Sophistical Refutations* in *Aristotle: On Sophistical Refutations, on Coming-to-be and Passing Away*, transl. by E. S. Forster, W. Heinemann, London.

Augustine: 1955, *De civitate Dei*, ed. by B. Domhart and A. Kalb in Corpus Christianorum. Series Latina, 47–48, Brepols.

Augustine: *De natura et gratia*, in *PL* **44**, 250; *CSEL* **60**, 237.

Augustine: 1968, *De Trinitate*, ed. by W. J. Mountain in *CCSL* **50**, 61, Brepols.

Augustine: *Enchiridion*, in *PL* **40**, 276.

Augustine: 1964, *On Free Choice of the Will*, transl. by A. S. Benjamin and L. H. Hackstaff, Bobbs-Merrill, Indianapolis.

Augustine: *Quaestiones super Genesim* in *CCSL* **33**, 22.

Bede: *In Marc evang. exposit* III in *PL* **92**, 218A.

Bernard of Clairveaux: *Capitula Haeresum Petri Abelardi* in *S. Bernardi Opera*, ed. by J. Leclerq and H. Rochais, in *PL* **182**, 1051.

Bernard of Clairveaux: 1530, *An Epistle of Saint Bernard*, transl. by T. Godfray, London.

Boethius: 1965, *Aristoteles Latinus II 1–2: De Interpretatione vel Periermenias*, ed. by L. Minio-Paluello, Descl'ee de Brower, Bruges.

Boethius: 1880, *Boetii Commentarii in librum Aristotelis περι ερμηνειας*, ed. by C. Meiser, Leipzig.

Boethius: 1833, *In Ciceronis Topica*, in *Ciceronis Opera*, ed. by J. C. Orelli and G. Baiterus, Zurich, Vol. 5, pt. 1.

Boethius: 1973, *The Consolation of Philosophy* in H. F. Stewart, E. K. Rand, and S. J. Tester, *Boethius, The Theological Tractates and the Consolation of Philosophy*, Harvard University Press, Cambridge, Mass.

Bonaventure: 1947, *Breviloquium*, transl. by E. E. Nemmers, B. Herder, London.

Bonaventure: 1883, *Commentarius in quatuor libros Sententiarum Petri Lombardi* in *Opera omnia* 1, Quaracchi.

Clement of Alexandria: 1951, *Les Stromates*, transl. by M. Caster, Editions du Cerf, Paris.

Comestor, P.: on Matthew 19, *Historia Scholastica* in *PL* **198**.

Die Sentenzen Rolands: 1969, *Nachmals Papstes Alexander III*, reprinted Amsterdam.

Dionysius the Carthusian: 1896, *Opera omnia*, Montreuil.

Djuwaynī: 1969, *ash-Shāmil fī uṣūl ad-dīn*, ed. by 'Alī Sāmī an-Nashshār, Alexandria.

Eckius, J.: 1976, *In primum librum Sententiarum Annotatiunculae*, ed. by W. L. Moore, Jr., E. J. Brill, Leiden.

Epicurus: 1889, *Bellerephon* in *Fragmenta Tragicorum Graecorum* ed. by A. Nauck, Leipzig.

Gabriel Biel: 1495, *Epitome et Collectorium ex Occamo Super quatuor libros Sententiarum*, Tübingen.

Garlandus Compotista: 1959, *Garlandus Compotista: Dialectica*, ed. by L. M. de Rijk, Van Gorcum & Comp., Assen.

Gaufrid of Poitier: 1954, *Summa*, Avranches, Bibl. de la ville, Cod. lat. 121, in A. Landgraf, *Dogmengeschichte der Frühscholastik*, Friedrich Pustet, Regensburg.

Genesis Rabbah: 1965, 2nd ed., ed. by J. Theodor and C. Albeck, Jerusalem.

Giles of Rome: 1929, *De ecclesiastica potestate*, ed. by R. Scholz, H. Böh Laus Nachf, Weimar.

Gregory of Rimini: 1522, repr. 1955, *Super primum et secundum Sententiarum*, Venice, Franciscan Institute Publications, St. Bonaventure, N.Y.

Gregory the Great: 1975, *Morales Sur Job* (*Moralia in Iob*), intro. and notes by R. Gillęt, Editions du Cerf, Paris.

Guerric of St. Quentin: 1954, Paris, Bibl. nat. lat. 15, 603, fol. 11^r, in A. Landgraf, *Dogmengeschichte der Frühscholastik*, Friedrich Pustet, Regensburg.

Ḥasdai Crescas: 1963, *Sefer Or Adonai* Gregg Intl., Tel Aviv.

Henry the Great: 1979, *Henrici de Gandavo Quodlibet I*, ed. by R. Macken, Leuven University Press, Louvain.

Hostiensis: 1581, repr. 1965, *Lectura in quinque Decretalium Gregorianarum libros*, Venice.

Hugh of St. Cher: 1669, *Opera omnia*, Lyons.

Hugh of Saint Victor: *De sacramentis christianae fidei* in *PL* **176**, 173–618.

Hugh of Saint Victor: *Summa Sententiarum*, in *PL* **176**, 68ff.

Isaac Arama: 1849, *Sefer Aqedat Yitzhak*, ed. by J. Falk, Pressburg.

Ibn Rushd (Averroes): 1574, *Aristotelis De Interpretatione . . . cum Averrois Cordubensis Expositione*, Venetiis apud Juntas.

Ibn Rushd (Averroes): 1961, *Averroes' Epitome of "Parva Naturalia"*, ed. and trans. by H. Blumberg, Medieval Academy of America, Cambridge, MA.

Ibn Rushd (Averroes): 1961, *Averroes on the Harmony of Religion and Philosophy*, ed. by G. F. Hourani, Luzac and Co., London.

Ibn Rushd (Averroes): 1954, *Qissūr Sefer Ha-Hūsh We-Ha-Muhash Le-Ibn Rushd*, ed. by H. Blumberg, Medieval Academy of America, Cambridge, MA.

Ibn Rushd (Averroes): 1930, *Tahāfut al-Tahāfut*, ed. by M. Bouyges, Imprimerie Catholique, Beirut.

Ibn Rushd (Averroes): 1954, *Tahāfut al-Tahāfut*, transl. by S. van den Bergh, Oxford Univ. Press, Oxford.

Ibn Sīnā (Avicenna): 1952, *Ahwāl al-Nafs*, ed. by F. Awhani, Cultural Dept. of the Arab League, Cairo.

Ibn Sīnā (Avicenna): 1958, *al-Ishārāt wa al-Tanbīhāt 3 and 4*, ed. by S. Dunya, Cultural Dept. of the Arab League, Cairo.

Ibn Sīnā (Avicenna): 1970, *al-Mantiq* (*Logic*); *al-'Ibāra* (*De Interpretatione*), ed. by M. Khudayri, revised by I. Madkour, Cultural Dept. of the Arab League, Cairo.

Ibn Sīnā (Avicenna): 1952, *al Mantiq; al-Madkhal* (*Isagoge*), edition supervised by I. Madkour, Cultural Dept. of the Arab League, Cairo.

Ibn Sīnā (Avicenna): 1938, *al-Najāt*, ed. by M. S. Kurdi, Cultural Dept. of the Arab League, Cairo.

Ibn Sīnā (Avicenna): 1960, *al-Shifā': al-Ilāhiyyāt* (*Metaphysics*), edition supervised by I. Madkour, Cultural Dept. of the Arab League, Cairo.

Ibn Sīnā (Avicenna): 1977, *Avicenna Latinus: Liber De Philosophia Prima sive Scientia Divina I–IV*, ed. by S. Van Riet, Editions Peeters Louvain-Leiden.

Ibn Sīnā (Avicenna): 1968, *Fī Ithbāt al-Nubuwwāt* (*On the Proof of Prophecies*), ed. by M. E. Marmura, Beirut.

Ibn Sīnā (Avicenna): 1966, *Risāla Fī Sirr al-Qadar* in G. Hourani, 'Ibn Sīnā's Essay on the Secret of Destiny,' *Bulletin of the School of Oriental and African Studies* **29**, 25–48.

John Buridan: 1977, *Johannes Buridanus: Sophismata*, ed. by T. K. Scott, Frommann-Holtzboog, Stuttgart-Bad Cannstatt.

John Buridan: 1509, *Quaestiones Super octo libros Physicorum Aristotelis*, Paris.

Jehudah Halevi: 1946, *Kuzari*, transl. by H. Hirschfeld, New York; Hebrew transl. by J. Ibn Shemuel, Tel Aviv, 1972.

John Duns Scotus: *Decretales Gregorianarum*, in *Opera Omnia* **9**, Vatican City Press, Rome.

John Duns Scotus: 1950, *Lectura Oxoniensis* I in *Opera Omnia* **17**, ed. by C. Balić *et al.*, Vatican Scotistic Commission, Rome.

John Duns Scotus: 1639, *Opera Omnia*, ed. by L. Wadding, Lyons.

John Duns Scotus: 1950, *Opera Omnia*, ed. by C. Balić *et al.*, Vatican Scotistic Commission, Rome.

Khalīl b. Aybak Safadī: 1931, 'Ibn Abī d-Dam,' in *al-Wāfī bil-wafayāt*, Vol. VI, ed. by H. Ritter, *et al.*, Leipzig/Wiesbaden.

Leibniz, G.: 1952, *Theodicy*, ed. by W. Stark, Yale University Press, New Haven.

Levi ben Gerson: 1547, *Commentary on Genesis*, Venice.

Levi ben Gerson: 1979–80, 'Gersonides' Commentary on Averroes' *Epitome of Parva Naturalia* II.3,' *Proceedings of the American Academy of Jewish Research* **46–47**, 1–31.

Levi ben Gerson: 1968, *Les Guerres du Seigneur*, Livres 3 et 4, transl. by C. Touati, Mouton, Paris.

Levi ben Gerson: 1866, *Sefer Milḥamot Adonai* (*Wars of the Lord*), Leipzig.

Levi ben Gerson: 1560, *Supercommentary on Averroes' Commentary on Aristotle's On Interpretation*, Chapter 9, Venice.

Levi ben Gerson: 1977, *Gersonides: The Wars of the Lord; Treatise Three: On God's Knowledge*, transl. by N. Samuelson, University of Toronto Press, Ontario.

Liber de Causis: 1882, trans. by O. Bardenhewer, *Die pseudo-aristotelische Schrift über das reine Gute, bekannt unter den Namen Liber de Causis*, Freiburg.

Luzzatto, S. D.: 1853, *Grammatica della Lingua Ebraica*, Padova.

Marsilius of Inghen: 1966, *Questiones super quattuor libros Sententiarum*, Strasburg, 1501, repr. Minerva.

Methodius: 1930, *De Autexusio*, ed. and trans. by A. Vaillant in *Patrologia Orientalis*, t. 22, fasc. 5, Paris.

Midrash Tanhuma: 1964, ed. by S. Buber, Ortsel Ltd., Jerusalem.

Molina, de L.: 1935, *De Scientia Dei*, ed. by F. Stegmüller in *Geschichte der Molinismus*, in *Beiträge zur geschichte der philosophie und theologie des mittelalters*, bd. 32.

Moses Almosnino: 1563, *Perush Al Pirke Avoth*, Salonika.

Moses Maimonides: 1929, *Dalālah al-Ha' irīn*, ed. by S. Munk, Jerusalem.

Moses Maimonides: 1963, *Mishnah Commentary*, Jerusalem.

Moses Maimonides: 1974, *The Guide of the Perplexed* 1–2, transl. by S. Pines, University of Chicago Press, London and Chicago.

Moses Maimonides: 1927, *Mishneh Torah*, Maimonides Publ. Co., New York.

Muhammad b. Shahrastânî: 1932, *'abd al-Karîm, Nihâyat al-iqdâm fî 'ilm al-Kalâm*, ed. by A. Guillaume, Oxford.

Muhammad b. Shahrastânî: 1955, *Kitab al-milal Wal-nihạl*, ed. by M. Badrân, Cairo.

Nicholas of Lyra: 1545, in *Biblia sacra cum glossis, Nicholai Lyrani Postilla et moralitatibus, Burgensis additionibus, et Thoringi replicis*, Lyons.

Odo of Ourscamp: 1888, *Quaestiones Magistri Odonis Suessionensis*, II, p. 298, in *Analecta novissima Spicilegii Solesmensis*, II, ed. by I. B. Card, Tusculum.

Origen: 1953, *Contra Celsum*, transl. by H. Chadwick, Cambridge Univ. Press, Cambridge.

Peter Abelard: 1859, *Introductio ad theologiam*, ed. by V. Cousin in *Petri Abaelardi Opera II*, Paris.

Peter Abelard: 1956, *Petri Abaelardus: Dialectica*, ed. by L. M. de Rijk, Van Gorcum, Assen.

Peter Abelard: *Theologia christiana*, 5 in *PL* **178**, 1321–1330.

Peter Aureol: 1956, *Scriptum super Primum Sententiarum*, Vol. II, ed. by E. Buytaert, Franciscan Institute, St. Bonaventure, New York.

Peter Damien: *De divina omnipotentia in reparatione corruptae, et factis infectis reddendis* (Epist. 2, 17), in *PL* **145**, 596ff.

Peter of Aliaco: 1968, repr. 1490, *Quaestiones super libros Sententiarum cum quibusdam in fine adjunctis*, Strasburg, repr. Minerva.

Peter Lombard: 1971, *Sententiae in quattuor libris distinctae*, Editiones Collegii S. Bonaventurae ad Claras Aquas, ed. by A. Haysse, Grottaferrata.

Peter of Tarantasia (Innocent V): 1652, repr. 1964, *Sent.* I, *In quattuor libros Sententiarum commentaria*, 1, Toulouse.

Peter Olivi: 1922, *Quaestiones in secundum librum Sententiarum*, ed. by B. Jansen, Bibliotheca Franciscana Scholastica Medii Avei, Vol. 4, Quaracchi.

Peter Pictavian: 1943, *Sententiae Petri Pictaviensis*, ed. by P. S. Moore and M. Dulong, University of Notre Dame, Notre Dame.

Plotinus: 1951–9, *Plotini Opera* 1–2, ed. by P. Henry and H. R. Schwyzer, Desclée de Brouwer, Paris.

Plotinus: 1953, *Enneads*, transl. by S. McKenna, Pantheon Books, New York.

Porphyry: 1975, *Isagoge*, transl. by E. W. Warren, Pontifical Institute of Medieval Studies, Toronto.

Rupert of Deutz: *In Genesim, Corpus Christianorum*, Continuatio Medievalis, **21**, 405.

Saadia Gaon: 1948, *The Book of Beliefs and Opinions*, transl. by S. Rosenblatt, Yale University Press, New Haven.

Saadia Gaon: 1959, *Perush . . . 'al ha-Torah we-'al-Na''kh*, ed. by J. Gad, London.

Shem Tob ben Joseph Falaquera: 1837, *Moreh ha-Moreh*, Pressberg.

Spinoza, B.: 1951, *The Theological-Political Treatise*, transl. by R. H. M. Elwes, Dover, New York.

Stegmüller, F.: 1947, *Reportorium Commentariorum in Sententias Petri Lombardi*, Wurzburg.

Thomas Bradwardine: 1618, repr. 1964, *Summa de causa dei contra Pelagium et de virtute causarum ad suos Mertonenses libri tres*, Lyons, repr. Minerva.

Thomas Aquinas: 1953, *De veritate*, in *Quaestiones disputatae*, ed. by R. Spiazzi, Marietti Editori, Rome.

Thomas Aquinas: 1852–73, repr. 1948–50, *Opera omnia*, ed. by P. Fiaccadori, Parma, repr. Musurgia, N.Y.

Thomas Aquinas: 1953, *Quaestiones disputatae*, ed. by R. Spiazzi, Marietti Editori, Rome.

Thomas Aquinas: 1856, *Quaestiones disputatae: De potentia Dei*, in *Opera omnia* **8**, Parma.

Thomas Aquinas: 1929, *Scripta super libros Sententiarum*, ed. by P. Mandonnet, Sumptibus P. Lethiellex, Editoris, Paris.

Thomas Aquinas: 1954, *S. Thomas Aquinatis Opuscula Theologica*, ed. by R. Vernado, Marietti Editori, Rome.

Thomas Aquinas: 1888–1904, *Summa Theologiae*, in *S. Thomas Aquinatis Opera omnia* **4–12**, Rome.

Walter of Saint-Victor: 1952, *Contra quatuor labyrinthos Franciae*, ed. by P. Glorieux, *Archives d'histoire doctrinale et littéraire du Moyen Age* **19**, 187–335.

William of Auvergne: 1674, repr. 1963, *De Trinitate*, in *Opera omnia*, Paris, repr. Minerva.

William of Auxerre: 1500, repr. 1964, *Summa aurea in quatuor libros Sententiarum*, Paris, repr. Minerva.

William Ockham: 1940 and 1963, *Opus nonaginta dierum*, in *Guillelmi de Ockham Opera Politica*, 1 and 2, ed. by J. G. Sikes *et al.*, Publications of the University of Manchester, Manchester, 1940, and H. S. Offler, Manchester, 1963.

William Ockham: 1967, *Ordinatio*, in *Opera Theologica. Scriptum in librum primum Sententiarum*, ed. by G. Gál and S. Brown, Franciscan Institute, St. Bonaventure, New York.

William Ockham: 1945, *The Tractatus de praedestinatione et de praescientia dei et de futuris contingentibus of William Ockham*, ed. by P. Boehner, Franciscan Institute Publications 2, St. Bonaventure, New York.

William Ockham: 1969, *Predestination, God's Foreknowledge and Future Contingencies*, transl. by M. Adams and N. Kretzmann, Appleton Century-Crofts, New York. Revised edition published in 1983 by William Hackett Publ., Indianapolis.

William Ockham: 1974, *Summa logicae*, ed. by P. Boehner, G. Gál, and S. Brown in *Guillelmi de Ockham Opera philosophica et theologica* I, Franciscan Institute, St. Bonaventure, New York.

William Ockham: 1980, *Quodlibeta septem*, in *Opera theologica* 9, ed. by J. C. Wey, St. Bonaventure University, St. Bonaventure, New York.

William Ockham: 1956, *Tractatus contra Benedictum*, in *Guillelmi de Ockham Opera Politica*, 3, ed. by H. S. Offler, Manchester University Press, Manchester.

William of St. Thierry: *Disputatio* in *PL* **180**, 249 ff.

Secondary Sources

Adams, M.: 1980, 'Was Ockham a Humean About Efficient Causality,' read to the New Jersey Philosophical Association.

Adams, R. M.: 1977, 'Middle Knowledge and the Problem of Evil,' *American Philosophical Quarterly* **14**, 109–117.

Alluntis, F., and A. B. Wolter: 1970, 'Duns Scotus on the Omnipotence of God,' in *Ancients and Moderns: Studies in Philosophy and the History of Philosophy* **5**, 178–222.

Altmann, A.: 1969, 'Essence and Existence in Maimonides,' in *Studies in Religious Philosophy and Mysticism*, ed. by A. Altmann, Cornell University Press, Ithaca.

Altmann, A.: 1974, 'The Religion of the Thinkers: Free Will and Predestination in Saadia, Bahya, and Maimonides,' in *Religion in a Religious Age*, ed. by S. D. Goitein, Association for Jewish Studies, Cambridge, Mass.

Bacher, W.: 1892, *Die bibelexegese der jüdischen religionsphilosophen des mittelalters vor Maimuni*, Karl J. Trübner, Strasburg.

Baer, Y. F.: 1961, *A History of the Jews in Christian Spain*, trans. by L. Schoffman, Jewish Publication Society of America, Philadelphia.

Bannach, K.: 1975, *Die Lehre von der doppelten Macht Gottes bei Wilhelm von Ockham*, F. Steiner, Wiesbaden.

Baron, S.: 1952, *A Social and Religious History of the Jews*, 2nd ed., Columbia University Press, New York.

Benz, M.: 1936, 'Das Göttliche Vorherwissen des freien Willensakte des Geschöpfe bei Thomas von Aquin. *In I Sent.*, d. 38. q. 1 a. 5,' *Divus Thomas; Jarbuch für Philosophie und Speculative Theologie* **14**, 255–273.

Bettan, I.: 1939, *Studies in Jewish Preaching: Middle Ages*, Hebrew Union College Press, Cincinnati.

Boh, I.: 1982, 'Consequences,' in *The Cambridge History of Later Medieval Philosophy*, ed. by N. Kretzmann *et al.*, Cambridge University Press, Cambridge.

Borchert, E.: 1940, 'Der Einfluss des Nominalismus auf die Christologie der Spätscholastik', *Beiträge zur Geschichte der Philosophie und Theologie des Mittelalters* **35**, 46–74.

Boyer, C.: 1938, 'Providence et liberté dans une texte de saint Thomas (In Perihermeneias, Lib. 1, 2. lect. 13, 14),' *Gregorianum* **19**, 194–209.

Brewer, J. *et al.* (eds.): 1862–1932, *Letters and Papers, Foreign and Domestic, of the Reign of Henry VIII*, G. E. Eyre & W. Spottiswoode, London.

Cantin, A.: 1972, *Lettre sur la Toute Puissance divine*, Sources chretiennes, Vol. 141, Paris.

Catan, J. R. (ed.): 1981, *Aristotle: The Collected Papers of Joseph Owens*, State University of New York Press, Albany, New York.

Chisholm, R. M.: 1966, 'Freedom and Action,' in *Freedom and Determinism*, ed. by K. Lehrer, Random House, N.Y.

Clark, D.: 1971, 'Voluntarism and Rationalism in the Ethics of Ockham,' *Franciscan Studies* **31**, 72–87.

Courtenay, W. J.: 1971, 'Convenant and Causality in Pierre d'Ailly,' *Speculum* **46**, 94–119.

Courtenay, W. J.: 1972, 'John of Mirecourt and Gregory of Rimini on Whether God Can Undo the Past,' *Recherches de Théologie ancienne et médiévale* **39**, 224–256; **40** (1973), 147–174.

Courtenay, W. J.: 1975, 'Necessity and Freedom in Anselm's Conception of God,' *Analecta Anselmiana* **4.2**, 39–64.

Courtenay, W. J.: 1974, 'Nominalism and Late Medieval Religion,' in *The Pursuit of Holiness in Late Medieval and Renaissance Religion*, ed. by C. Trinkaus with H. Oberman, E. J. Brill, Leiden.

Courtenay, W. J.: 1972, 'The King and the Leaden Coin: The Economic Background of the "Sine qua non" Causality,' *Traditio* **28**, 185–209.

Daly, R. J.: 1977, 'The Soteriological Significance of the Sacrifice of Isaac,' *Catholic Biblical Quarterly* **39**, 45–75.

Davies, P. R. and B. D. Chilton: 1978, 'The Aqedah: A Revised Tradition History,' *Catholic Biblical Quarterly* **40**, 514–46.

Degl'Innocenti, H.: 1961, 'De actione Dei in causas secundas liberas iuxta S. Thomam,' *Aquinas* **4**, 28–56.

Denifle, H.: 1885, 'Die Sentenzen Abaelards und die Bearbeitungen Seiner Theologia,' *Archiv für Literatur – und Kirchen geschichte des Mittelalters* **1**, 584–624.

Denzinger, H.: 1957, *Enchiridion Symbolorum: Definitionum et Declarationum de Rebus Fidei et Morum*, Herder, Barcelona.

De Rijk, L. M.: 1962, *Logica Modernorum*, Vol. 1, Van Gorcum & Co., Assen.

Desharnais, R. P.: 1966, *The History of the Distinction Between God's Absolute and Ordained Power and Its Influence on Martin Luther*, unpublished Ph.D. dissertation, Catholic University of America, Washington.

Dettloff, W.: 1954, *Die Lehre von der Acceptatio divina bei Johannes Duns Scotus*, Werl.

Dreifuss, G.: 1971, 'Isaac, the Sacrificial Lamb: A Study of Some Jewish Legends,' *Journal of Analytical Psychology* **16**, 69–78.

Edidin, A. and C. Normore: 1982, 'Ockham on Prophecy,' *International Journal for the Philosophy of Religion* **13**, 179–189.

Elbogen, I.: 1972, *Der judische Gottesdienst in seiner geschichtlichen Entwicklung* (Hebrew), 3rd ed., transl. by J. Amir, ed. by J. Heinemann *et al.*, Tel Aviv.

Fabro, C.: 1961, *Participation et causalité selon S. Thomas d'Aquin*, Publications Universitaires de Louvain, Louvain-Paris.

Fackenheim, E.: 1946–47, 'The Possibility of the Universe in al-Farabi, Ibn Sina and Maimonides,' *Proceedings of the American Academy of Jewish Research* **16**, 39–70.

Falk, A.: 1982, 'New Wrinkles on Old Fatalisms' (xerox).

Feldman, S.: 1982, 'Crescas' Theological Determinism,' *Da'at* **9**, 3–28.

Feldman, S.: 1980, 'The Theory of Eternal Creation in Hasdai Crescas and Some of His Predecessors,' *Viator* **11**, 289–320.

Finance de, J.: 1960, *Être et Agir dans la Philosophie de Saint Thomas*, Librairie éditrice de l'Universite Gregorienne, Rome.

Fine, G.: forthcoming, 'Truth and Necessity in *De Interpretatione* 9'.

Fischel, H.: 1973, *Rabbinic Literature and Greco-Roman Philosophy*, E. J. Brill, Leiden.

Frank, R. M.: 1978, *Beings and Their Attitudes: The Teaching of the Baṣrian School of the Mu'tazila in the Classical Period*, State University of N.Y. Press, Albany, New York.

Frank, R. M.: 1969, 'The Divine Attributes According to the Teaching of Abu l-Hudhayl al-'Allāf,' *Le Muséon* **82**, 451–506.

Frank, R. M.: 'The Neoplatonism of Ǧahm ibn Safwān,' *Le Muséon* **78**, 395–424.

Frank, R. M.: 1978, 'Reason and Revealed Law,' in *Recherches d'Islamologie, Recueil d'articles offert à Georges C. Anawati et Louis Gardet*, Bibliothèque philosophique de Louvain, **26**, ed. by S. van Riet, Leuven University Press, Louvain.

Frede, D.: 1970, *Aristoteles und die 'Seeschlacht'*, Vandenhoeck & Ruprecht, Göttingen.

Gál, G.: 1976, 'Petrus de Trabibus on the Absolute and Ordained Power of God,' *Studies Honoring Ignatius Charles Brady, Friar Minor*, ed. by R. S. Almagno and C. L. Harkins, Franciscan Institute Publications, Theol. ser. **6**, St. Bonaventure, N.Y., pp. 283–292.

Gardet, L.: 1951, *La Pensée Religieuse d'Avicenne* (*Ibn Sīnā*), J. Vrin, Paris.

Gibbard, A. and W. L. Harper: 1977, 'Counterfactuals and Two Kinds of Expected Utility,' *Foundations and Applications of Decision Theory*, Vol. 1, ed. by C. A. Hooker *et al.*, D. Reidel, Dordrecht.

Glorieux, P. (ed.): 1927, *Les premières polémiques thomistes, 1. – Le Correctorium Corruptorii 'Quare'*, Le Saulchoir, Kain, Belgium.

Grabmann, M.: 1933, *Die Geschichte der katholicshen Theologie seit dem Ausgang der Vaterzeit*, Freiburg.

Grabmann, M.: 1956, *Die Geschichte der scholastischen Methode*, reprinted Darmstadt.

Grabois, A.: 1975, 'The *Hebraica Veritas* and Jewish-Christian Intellectual Relations in the Twelfth Century,' *Speculum* **50**, 613–34.

Groblicki, J.: 1938, *De scientia Dei futurorum contingentium secundum S. Thomam eiusque primos sequaces*, Universytet Jagiellonski, Krakow.

Grzondziel, H.: 1926, *Die Entwicklung der Unterscheidung zwischen der potentia Dei absoluta und der potentia Dei ordinata von Augustin bis Alexander von Hales*, inaugural dissertation, Breslau.

Haberman, A. M.: 1977, 'Sefer Gezeirot Ashkenaz we-Sarefat,' in *The Jews and the Crusaders: The Hebrew Chronicles of the First and Second Crusades*, ed. by S. Eidelberg, University of Wisconsin Press, Madison.

Halkin, A. S.: 1944, 'Saadia's Exegesis and Polemics,' in *Rab Saadia Gaon: Studies in His Honor*, ed. by L. Finkelstein, Arno Press, New York.

Hamm, B.: 1977, *Promissio, Pactum, Ordinatio: Freiheit und Selbstbindung Gottes in der scholastischen. Gnadenlehre*, Mohr, Tübingen.

Heller-Wilensky, S.: 1956, *The Philosophy of Isaac Arama in the Framework of Philonic Philosophy* (Hebrew), Jerusalem.

Henry, D. P.: 1967, *The Logic of Saint Anselm*, Clarendon Press, Oxford.

Hick, J.: 1966, *Evil and the God of Love*, Macmillan, New York.

Hintikka, J.: 1975/76, 'Gaps in the Great Chain of Being: An Exercise in the Methodology of the History of Ideas,' *Proceedings of the American Philosophical Association* **49**, 22–38.

Hintikka, J.: 1973, *Time and Necessity: Studies in Aristotle's Theory of Modality*, Clarendon Press, Oxford.

Hocedez, E.: 1925, *Richard de Middleton: Sa vie, ses ouvres, sa doctrine*, E. Champion, Paris.

Hourani, G. F.: 1972, 'Ibn Sīnā on Necessary and Possible Existence,' *The Philosophical Forum* **4**, 74–86.

Hourani, G. F.: 1976, 'Islamic and Non-Islamic Origins of Mu'tazilite Ethical Rationalism,' *International Journal of Middle East Studies* **7**, 59–87.

Hufnagel, A.: 1966, 'Zur Echtheitsfrage der *Summa Theologiae* Alberts des Grossen,' *Theologische Quartalschrift* **146**, 8–39.

Husik, I.: 1948, *A History of Medieval Jewish Philosophy*, Jewish Publication Society of America, Philadelphia.

Inati, S.: 1979, *An Examination of Ibn Sīnā's Solution for the Problem of Evil*, unpublished Ph.D. Dissertation, University of Buffalo.

Isaac, J.: 1953, *Le Peri hermeneias en occident de Boèce à Saint Thomas*, J. Vrin, Paris.

Ivry, A.: 1982, 'Maimonides on Possibility,' *Mystics, Philosophers, and Politicians: Essays in Jewish Intellectual History in Honor of Alexander Altmann*, ed. by J. Reinharz *et al.*, University of North Carolina Press, Durham.

Ivry, A.: 1982, 'Neoplatonic Currents in Maimonides' Philosophy,' in the Proceedings of a Symposium of 'Maimonides in Egypt,' ed. by J. Kramer, Tel Aviv.

Jacobs, L.: 1980, 'Divine Foreknowledge and Human Freedom,' *Conservative Judaism* **34**, 4–16.

Kellner, M.: 1979, 'R. Levi ben Gerson: A Bibliographical Essay,' *Studies in Bibliography and Booklore* **12**, 13–23.

Kenny, A.: 1969, 'Divine Foreknowledge and Human Freedom,' *Aquinas, A Collection of Critical Essays*, ed. by A. Kenny, Doubleday, Garden City, New York.

Kenny, A.: 1979, *The God of the Philosophers*, Oxford University Press, Oxford.

Knuuttila, S. (ed.): 1980, *Reforging the Great Chain of Being: Studies of the History of Modal Theories*, D. Reidel, Dordrecht.

Knuuttila, S.: 1980, 'Time and Modality in Scholasticism,' in *Reforging the Great Chain of Being*, ed. by S. Knuuttila, D. Reidel, Dordrecht.

Komel, W.: 1953, 'Das Naturrecht bei Wilhelm von Ockham,' *Franziskanische Studien* **35**, 39–85.

Kretzmann, N. *et al* (eds.): 1982, *Cambridge History of Later Medieval Philosophy*, Cambridge University Press, Cambridge.

Kretzmann, N.: 1966, 'Omniscience and Immutability,' *Journal of Philosophy* **63**, 409–421.

Krueger, P. *et al.* (eds.): 1899–1902, *Corpus iuris civilis*, Berolini.

Langston, D.: *When Willing Becomes Knowing: The Voluntarist Analysis of God's Omniscience*, unpublished manuscript.

Lassen, A. L.: 1946, *The Commentary of Levi ben Gerson (Gersonides) on the Book of Job*, Bloch Publ. Co., New York.

Lerch, D.: 1950, *Isaaks Opferung christlich gedeutet: Eine auslegungsgeschichtliche Untersuchung*, Beiträge zur historischen Theologie **12**, Tübingen.

Lerner, R. and M. Mahdi (eds.): 1963, *Medieval Political Philosophy: A Source Book*, Cornell University Press, New York.

Lewis, D. K.: 1973, 'Causation,' *Journal of Philosophy* **70**, 556–567.

Lewis, D. K.: 1979, 'Prisoner's Dilemma Is a Newcomb Problem,' *Philosophy and Public Affairs* **8**, 235–240.

Loewe, R.: 1957, 'The Jewish Midrashim and Patristic and Scholastic Exegesis of the Bible,' *Studia patristica* **1**, 492–514.

Lossky, V.: 1957, *The Mystical Theology of the Eastern Church*, J. Clarke, London.

Lovejoy, A.: 1936, *The Great Chain of Being: A Study of the History of an Idea*, Harvard University Press, Cambridge, Mass.

Lubac, Henri de: 1959, *Exégèse médiévale: Les quatres sens de l'Écriture*, Aubier, Paris.

Lucas, J. R.: 1970, *The Freedom of the Will*, Clarendon Press, Oxford.

Luscombe, D. E.: 1969, *The School of Peter Abelard: The Influence of Abelard's Thought in the Early Scholastic Period*, Cambridge Univ. Press, Cambridge.

Madelung, W.: 1965, *Der Imam al-Qāsim ibn Ibrāhīm und die Glaubenslehre der Zaiditen*, de Gruyter, Berlin.

Malter, H.: 1969, *Saadia Gaon, His Life and Works*, Hermon Press, N.Y.

Marmura, M.: 1962, 'Some Aspects of Avicenna's Theory of God's Knowledge of Particulars,' *Journal of the American Oriental Society* **82**, 299–312.

Marrone, J.: 1974, 'The Absolute and the Ordained Powers of the Pope: An Unedited Text of Henry of Ghent,' *Mediaeval Studies* **36**, 7–22.

Maurer, A. (ed.): 1974, *St. Thomas Aquinas 1274–1974, Commemorative Studies*, Toronto.

McSorley, H. J.: 1969, *Luther: Right or Wrong*, New York.

Meehan, F. X.: 1940, *Efficient Causality in Aristotle and St. Thomas*, The Catholic Univ. of America Press, Washington, D.C.

Montagnes, B.: 1963, *La doctrine de l'analogie de l'être d'après saint Thomas d'Aquin*, Leuven University Press, Louvain.

Moore, R.: 1958, 'Motion divine chez Saint Thomas d'Aquin,' *Studia Montis Regii* **1**, 93–137.

Mulligan, R. W.: 1972, 'Divine Foreknowledge and Freedom: A Note on a Problem of Language,' *The Thomist* **36**, 293–299.

Normore, C.: 1982, 'Future Contingents,' in *The Cambridge History of Later Medieval Philosophy*, ed. by N. Kretzmann *et al.*, Cambridge Univ. Press, Cambridge.

Normore, C.: 1983, 'Instants of Time and Instants of Nature' (unpublished).

Normore, C.: forthcoming, 'The Limits of God's Power: Some Fourteenth Century Discussions,' *Paideia*.

Noy, D.: 1962, 'Ha-Aqedah ke-Av-Tippus shel Qiddush ha-Shem,' *Mahanayim* **69**, 40–47.

Nozick, R.: 1969, 'Newcomb's Problem and Two Principles of Choice,' *Essays in Honor of Carl G. Hempel*, ed. by N. Rescher *et al.*, D. Reidel, Dordrecht.

Oakley, F.: 1972, 'The "Hidden" and "Revealed" Wills of James I: More Political Theology,' *Studia Gratiana Post Octava Decreti Saeculari* **15**, 265–375.

Oakley, F.: 1968, 'Jacobean Political Theology: The Absolute and Ordinary Powers of the King,' *Journal of the History of Ideas* **29**, 323–346.

Oberman, H. A.: 1963, *The Harvest of Medieval Theology: Gabriel Biel and Late Medieval Nominalism*, Harvard University, Cambridge, Mass.

Owens, J.: 1963, *The Doctrine of Being in the Aristotelian Metaphysics: A Study in the Greek Background of Mediaeval Thought*, 2nd ed., Pontifical Institute of Medieval Studies, Toronto.

Paulus, J.: 1938, *Henri de Gand, Essai sur les tendances de sa métaphysique*, J. Vrin, Paris.

Pearl, C.: 1971, *The Medieval Jewish Mind: The Religious Philosophy of Isaac Arama*, Vallentine, Mitchell, London.

Pernoud, M. A.: 1970, 'Innovation in William of Ockham's References to the "*Potentia Dei*",' *Antonianum* **45**, 66–97.

Pernoud, M. A.: 1972, 'The Theory of the *Potentia Dei* According to Aquinas, Scotus and Ockham,' *Antonianum* **47**, 69–95.

Pike, N.: 1970, *God and Timelessness*, Schocken Books, New York.

Pines, S.: 1976, 'Saint Thomas et la pensée juive mediévale: Quelques notations,' in *Aquinas and Problems of His Time*, ed. by G. Verbeke and D. Verhelst, Leuven University Press, Louvain.

Pines, S.: 1967, 'Scholasticism after Thomas Aquinas and the Teachings of Hasdai Crescas and his Predecessors,' *Proceedings of the Israel Academy of Sciences and Humanities* **1**, 10, 1–101.

Pines, S.: 1980, 'Shi'ite Terms and Conceptions in Judah Halevi's *Kuzari*,' *Jerusalem Studies in Arabic and Islam* **2**, 196–240.

Pines, S.: 1960, 'Studies in Abul-Barakât al-Baghâdî's Poetics and Metaphysics,' Studies in Philosophy, *Scripta Hierosolymitana* **6**, 195–198.

Pollock, J. L.: 1976, *Subjunctive Reasoning*, D. Reidel, Dordrecht.

Post, G.: 1964, *Studies in Medieval Legal Thought: Public Law and the State, 1100–1322*, Princeton Univ. Press, Princeton.

Prior, A. N.: 1967, *Past, Present and Future*, Oxford Univ. Press, Oxford.

Renan, E.: 1893, *Les écrivains juifs français du XIVe siècle*, Imprimerie Nationale, Paris.

Rescher, N.: 1963, 'An Interpretation of Aristotle's Doctrine of Future Contingency and Excluded Middle,' in Rescher, N., *Studies in the History of Arabic Logic*, University of Pittsburgh Press, Pittsburgh.

Riché, P.: 1979, *Les Écoles et l'enseignement dans l'Occident Chrétien de la fin du Ve Siècle au Milieu de XIe Siècle*, A. Montaigne, Paris.

Rist, J.: 1981, 'Plotinus on Matter and Evil,' *Phronesis* **6**, 154–166.

Rosenberg, S.: 1978, 'Necessary and Possible in Medieval Logic, (Hebrew)' *Iyyun* **28**, 103–155.

Rosenthal, E.: 1942, 'Saadya Gaon: An Appreciation of His Biblical Exegesis,' *Bulletin of the John Rylands Library* **27**, 168–178.

Ross, J. F.: 1969, *Philosophical Theology*, Bobbs-Merrill, Indianapolis.

Rudavsky, T. M.: 1983, 'Divine Omniscience and Future Contingents in Gersonides,' *Journal of the History of Philosophy* **21**, 513–536.

Samuelson, N.: 1972, 'Gersonides' Account of God's Knowledge of Particulars,' *The Journal of the History of Philosophy* **10**, 399–416.

Schmitt, F.: 1950, *Die Lehre des [I] Thomas von Aquin vom göttlichen Wissen des zukünftig Kontingenten bei seinen grossen Kommentatoren*, Nijmegen.

Schwamm, H.: 1934, *Das göttliche Vorherwissen bei Duns Scotus und seinen ersten Anhängern*, Philosophie und Grenzwissenschaften V, Innsbruck.

Silverman, D. W.: 1974, 'Dreams, Divination and Prophecy: Gersonides and the Problem of Precognition,' in *The Samuel Friedland Lectures: 1967–74*, New York, pp. 99–120.

Silverman, D. W.: 1975, *The Problem of Prophecy in Gersonides*, unpublished Ph.D. dissertation, Columbia University.

Sirat, C.: 1969, *Les théories des visions surnaturelles dans la pensée juive du Moyen-âge*, E. J. Brill, Leiden.

Smalley, B.: 1964, *The Study of the Bible in the Middle Ages*, 2nd ed., Univ. of Notre Dame Press, Notre Dame.

Sorabji, R.: 1980, *Necessity, Cause, and Blame: Perspectives on Aristotle's Theory*, Cornell Univ. Press, Ithaca, N.Y.

Sosa, E.: 1975, *Causation and Conditionals*, Oxford Univ. Press, London.

Spiegel, S.: 1969, *The Last Trial*, trans. by J. Goldin, Jewish Publication Society of America, New York.

Spiegel, S.: 1950, 'The Legend of Isaac's Slaying and Resurrection (Hebrew),' in *Alexander Marx Jubilee Volume*, ed. by S. Lieberman, Jewish Theological Seminary of America, New York, pp. 471–537.

Streveler, P.: 'God's Absolute and Ordained Power in the Thought of Robert Holcot' (unpublished).

Streveler, P.: 1973, 'The Problem of Future Contingents: A Medieval Discussion,' *The New Scholasticism* **47**, 238–246.

Stump, E. and Kretzmann, N.: 1981, 'Eternity,' *Journal of Philosophy* **78**, 429–458.

Stump, E. and Kretzmann, N.: 1982, 'Topics: Their Development and Absorption into Consequences', in *The Cambridge History of Later Medieval Philosophy*, ed. by N. Kretzmann *et al.*, Cambridge Univ. Press, Cambridge.

Swinburne, R.: 1977, *The Coherence of Theism*, Clarendon, Oxford.

Synan, E. A.: 1962, 'Sixteen Sayings by Richard of Campsall on Contingency and Foreknowledge,' *Medieval Studies* **24**, 250–62.

Tachau, K. H.: 1982, 'The Problem of the *Species in medio* at Oxford in the Generation after Ockham,' *Mediaeval Studies* **44** 294–443.

Thomason, R.: 1970, 'Indeterminist Time and Truth-Value Gaps,' *Theoria* **36**, 264–281.

Touati, C.: 1973, *La Pensée Philosophique et Théologique de Gersonide*, Les Editions de Minuit, Paris.

Urbach, E. E.: 1975, *The Sages: Their Concepts and Beliefs*, transl. by Israel Abrahams, Magnes Press, Jerusalem.

Urban, L. and D. N. Walton: 1978, *The Power of God: Readings on Omnipotence and Evil*, Oxford Univ. Press, Oxford.

Vajda, G.: 1978, 'al-Khayyāt,' *Encyclopedia of Islam*, 2nd ed., Vol. 4.

Vajda, G.: 1971, 'Ibn al-Rēwandī,' *Encyclopedia of Islam*, 2nd ed., Vol. 3.

Vajda, G.: 1957, *L'amour de Dieu dans la théologie juive du Moyen Âge*, Études de philosophie médiévale **46**, Paris.

Van Ess, J.: 1978–79, 'Ibn ar-Rēwandī, or the Making of an Image,' *Al-Abhath* **27**, Beirut, pp. 5–26.

Van Ess, J.: 1978, *Theology and Science: The Case of Abū Isḥāq an-Naẓẓām*, Second Annual United Arab Emirates Lecture in Islamic Studies (19 pp.), University of Michigan Press, Ann Arbor, Michigan.

Vermes, G.: 1961, *Scripture and Tradition in Judaism: Haggadic Studies*, Studia postbiblica **4**, E. J. Brill, Leiden.

Vermes, G. (ed.): 1962, *The Dead Sea Scrolls in English*, Penguin Books, Baltimore.

Vignaux, P.: 1934, *Justification et prédestination au XIVe siècle: Duns Scot, Pierre d'Auriole, Guillaume d'Occam, Grégoire de Rimini*, J. Vrin, Paris.

Vignaux, P.: 1935, *Luther Commentateur des Sentences (Livre I, Distinction XVII)*, J. Vrin, Paris.

Vignaux, P.: 1930, 'Nominalisme,' *Dictionnaire de théologie catholique* **11**, 7177–84, Paris.

Vignaux, P.: 1948, *Nominalisme au XIVe siècle*, Montreal and Paris.

Weisheipl, J.: 1974, *Friar Thomas d'Aquino: His Life, Thought and Work*, Doubleday, Garden City, N.Y.

Wippel, J.: 1981, *The Metaphysical Thought of Godfrey of Fontaines: A Study in Late Thirteenth-Century Philosophy*, Catholic Univ. of America Press, Washington, D.C.

Wippel, J.: 1981, 'The Reality of Nonexisting Possibles According to Thomas Aquinas, Henry of Ghent, and Godfrey of Fontaines,' *Review of Metaphysics* **34**, 729–758.

Wolfson, H. A.: 1947, *Philo: Foundations of Religious Philosophy in Judaism, Christianity and Islam*, Harvard Univ. Press, Cambridge, Mass.

Wolfson, H. A.: 1976, *The Philosophy of the Kalam*, Harvard Univ. Press, Cambridge, Mass.

Wolter, A. B.: 1972, 'Native Freedom of the Will as a Key to the Ethics of Scotus,' in *Deus et Homo ad mentum I. Duns Scoti*; Acta Tertii Congressus Scotistici Internationalis Vindebonae, 1970, Rome, pp. 359–370.

Zucker, M.: 1959, *Al Tirgum RS"G le-Torah*, Philipp Feldman, Inc., New York.

NOTES ON CONTRIBUTORS

Ivan Boh, Department of Philosophy, The Ohio State University. Author of many articles on medieval logic, including 'Consequences' in *The Cambridge History of Later Medieval Philosophy* (1982).

William J. Courtenay, Department of History, University of Wisconsin-Madison. Author of numerous books and articles on fourteenth century thought, including most recently, *Adam Wodeham: An Introduction to His Life and Writings* (1978).

Jeremy Cohen, Department of History, The Ohio State University. Author of *The Fairs and the Jews: The Evolution of Medieval Anti-Judaism* (1982), as well as articles on medieval Jewish history.

Seymour Feldman, Department of Philosophy, Rutgers University. Author of many articles on medieval Jewish philosophy, including 'Crescas' Theological Determinism' (1982); and a recent translation of Gersonides' *The Wars of the Lord*, in press.

Richard Frank, Department of Semitic and Egyptian Languages and Literatures, The Catholic University of America. Author of numerous works on medieval Islamic thought, including *Being and Their Attributes. The Teaching of the Baṣrian School of the Mu'tazila in the Classical Period* (1978).

Alfred Ivry, Department of Near Eastern and Judaic Studies, Brandeis University. Author of numerous articles on medieval Jewish and Islamic philosophy, including *Al-Kīndi's Metaphysics* (1974).

Barry S. Kogan, Hebrew Union College-Jewish Institute of Religion. Author of several works dealing with medieval Jewish and Islamic thought, including 'Averroes and the Theory of Emanation' (1978), and a book-length manuscript, *Averroes' Theory of Causal Efficacy*.

Norman Kretzmann, Sage School of Philosophy, Cornell University. Author of many books and articles on medieval philosophy and logic, and co-editor of *The Cambridge History of Later Medieval Philosophy*.

Michael E. Marmura, Department of Middle East and Islamic Studies, University of Toronto. Author of numerous books and articles on Islamic philosophy, including a critical edition of Avicenna's *Fī Ithbāt al-Nubuwwāt*

T. Rudavsky (ed.), Divine Omniscience and Omnipotence in Medieval Philosophy, 285–286.

(*On the Proof of Prophecies*) (1968), and *Refutation by Alexander of Aphrodisias of Galen's Treatise on Motion*, ed. with N. Rescher (1970).

Calvin G. Normore, Department of Philosophy, University of Toronto, Author of several articles on medieval scholasticism, including 'Future Contingents in the Middle Ages', in the *Cambridge History of Later Medieval Philosophy*.

Tamar Rudavsky, Department of Philosophy, The Ohio State University. Author of several articles in medieval Jewish and scholastic philosophy, including 'Divine Omniscience and Future Contingents in Gersonides' (1983).

Josef Van Ess, Orientalisches Seminar, University of Tubingen. Author of numerous books and articles on Islamic Philosophy, including *Frühe Mu'tazilitische Häresiographie* (1971); *Ungenützte Texte zur Karrāmīya* (1980).

John F. Wippel, School of Philosophy, The Catholic University of America. Author of numerous books and articles in medieval philosophy, including 'Essence and Existence' in *The Cambridge History of Later Medieval Philosophy*, and *The Metaphysical Thought of Godfrey of Fontaines: A Study in Late Thirteenth-Century Philosophy* (1981).

INDEX

Ancient authors are cited under the names by which they are generally known. Medieval authors are cited under their first names, unless noted otherwise. Authors after 1500 are cited under their last names.

'Abd al-Jabbâr 69, 76, 77–78, 78–79
Abraham, testing of
 as climax of religious development 117–118
 as example for man 110
 God's foreknowledge of outcome 112–114, 121–123
 Job, analogy with 141
 nature of dialogue with God 131
 suspension of rational morality and 124, 128, 256
 see also Binding of Isaac
Abraham Ibn Daud 177, 181
Abravanel, Isaac, *see* Isaac Abravanel
Absolute power, *see* Power
Absolutism 254–258
Abū Bakr 54
Abūl-Hudhayl 64
Act
 artistic vs. ethical, Aristotelian view of 128
 bad, two kinds of 78–79
 Mu'tazila view of 69–70
 see also Action; Agency; Agent
Action 222
 capability of, in man 61–62
 ethical nature of, intrinsic 74, 78–79, 128
 involuntary 77
 motivation for 71–73
 see also Act; Agency, actualizing; Agent
Active Intellect 87, 93–94, 169
Ad-dawâ'î (motivation) 71
Āfa (defect), *see* Body
Agency
 actualizing 32–33
 an-Nazzam's view 69, 74–76
 Baṣrian analysis of 70–73, 75
 Boethius's view of 32–33, 47
 Gersonides' two levels of 163
 human 163
 Saadia Gaon and human 108–109
 three genera of divine, in Pictavian, 202
 see also Action; Agent
Agent
 God's effect on causal activities of 224–226
 man as true agent of his acts 108–109
 motives of 128
 state of, affecting act 71–73
 see also, Action; Agency; Agent
'Ajnâs (basic classes) 70, 78
Akiba, Rabbi 106, 108, 110–111, 112, 115–116, 119, 120, 123, 129, 132, 136
al-As'ari 74
Albertus Magnus 247, 250, 262, 263
Alcuin 138
Alexander III, *see* Roland Bandinelli
Alfarabi viii, 81, 95
 divine foreknowledge and determinism 84–86, 96
 necessity and contingency 82–84, 93, 96, 120–121
Al-fayd, see Emanation
al-Ghazzali 126
al-Ka'bi, abu l-Qasim 63, 64, 65, 75, 78
al-Khayyâṭ 55, 59, 62–63, 70
al-Murdār 54, 55

SYNTHESE HISTORICAL LIBRARY

Texts and Studies in the History of Logic and Philosophy

1. M. T. Beonio-Brocchieri Fumagalli, *The Logic of Abelard* (transl. from the Italian). 1969.
2. Gottfried Wilhelm Leibniz, *Philosophical Papers and Letters.* A selection translated and edited, with an introduction, by Leroy E. Loemker. 1969.
3. Ernst Mally, *Logische Schriften* (ed. by Karl Wolf and Paul Weingartner). 1971.
4. Lewis White Beck (ed.), *Proceedings of the Third International Kant Congress.* 1972.
5. Bernard Bolzano, *Theory of Science* (ed. by Jan Berg). 1973.
6. J. M. E. Moravcsik (ed.), *Patterns in Plato's Thought.* 1973.
7. Nabil Shehaby, *The Propositional Logic of Avicenna: A Translation from al-Shifa: al-Qiyas,* with Introduction, Commentary and Glossary. 1973.
8. Desmond Paul Henry, *Commentary on De Grammatico: The Historical-Logical Dimensions of a Dialogue of St. Anselm's.* 1974.
9. John Corcoran, *Ancient Logic and Its Modern Interpretations.* 1974.
10. E. M. Barth, *The Logic of the Articles in Traditional Philosophy.* 1974.
11. Jaakko Hintikka, *Knowledge and the Known. Historical Perspectives in Epistemology.* 1974.
12. E. J. Ashworth, *Language and Logic in the Post-Medieval Period.* 1974.
13. Aristotle, *The Nicomachean Ethics* (transl. with Commentaries and Glossary by Hypocrates G. Apostle). 1975.
14. R. M. Dancy, *Sense and Contradiction: A Study in Aristotle.* 1975.
15. Wilbur Richard Knorr, *The Evolution of the Euclidean Elements. A Study of the Theory of Incommensurable Magnitudes and Its Significance for Early Greek Geometry.* 1975.
16. Augustine, *De Dialectica* (transl. with Introduction and Notes by B. Darrell Jackson). 1975.
17. Arpád Szabó, *The Beginnings of Greek Mathematics.* 1978.
18. Rita Guerlac, *Juan Luis Vives Against the Pseudodialecticians. A Humanist Attack on Medieval Logic.* Texts, with translation, introduction and notes. 1979.
19. Paul Vincent Spade (ed.), *Peter of Ailly: Concepts and Insolubles. An Annotated Translation.* 1980.

20. Simo Knuuttila (ed.), *Reforging the Great Chain of Being.* 1981.
21. Jill Vance Buroker, *Space and Incongruence.* 1981.
22. E. P. Bos, *Marsilius of Inghen.* 1983.
23. Willem Remmelt de Jong, *The Semantics of John Stuart Mill.* 1982.
24. René Descartes, *Principles of Philosophy.* 1983.
25. Tamar Rudavsky (ed.), *Divine Omniscience and Omnipotence in Medieval Philosophy.* 1985.